Slavery and Politics

Slavery and Politics

BRAZIL AND CUBA, 1790–1850

RAFAEL MARQUESE

TÂMIS PARRON

MÁRCIA BERBEL

Translated by LEONARDO MARQUES

University of New Mexico Press — Albuquerque

Library of Congress Cataloging-in-Publication Data
Berbel, Márcia Regina.
  [Escravidão e política. English]
  Slavery and politics : Brazil and Cuba, 1790–1850 / Rafael de Bivar Marquese,
Tâmis Peixoto Parron, Márcia Regina Berbel ; translated by Leonardo Marques.
     pages cm
  Translation of: Escravidão e política : Brasil e Cuba, c. 1790–1850 / Márcia Berbel, Rafael
Marquese, Tâmis Parron.
  Includes bibliographical references and index.
  ISBN 978-0-8263-5647-5 (cloth : alk. paper) — ISBN 978-0-8263-5648-2 (pbk. : alk. paper) —
ISBN 978-0-8263-5649-9 (electronic)
  1. Slavery—Brazil—History—19th century. 2. Slavery—Cuba—History—19th century.
  3. Slavery—Government policy—Brazil. 4. Slavery—Government policy—Cuba.
  5. Brazil—Politics and government—19th century. 6. Cuba—Politics and government—
19th century. I. Marquese, Rafael de Bivar, 1972– II. Parron, Tâmis.
III. Title.
  HT1126.B4513 2016
  306.3'62098109034—dc23
                              2015016441

Funding for this translation was provided by FAPESP.
Cover illustration: Jean-Victor Frond, *Fazenda de Quissamã nas cercanias de Campos*,
lithograph.
Cover designed by Catherine Leonardo
Interior designed by Felicia Cedillos
Composed in Minion Pro 10.25/14

CONTENTS

Brazil and Cuba

A Shared History

———◦•⊹•◦———

> I hope that everything that is good for agriculture, and can incite
> imitation, will be published, which is the reason why I mention what
> the Consulado de Havana has done. . . . one [of its] greatest concerns
> has always been to stimulate agriculture, especially for what belongs
> to the less considerable establishments, because it contributes more
> safely to the increase and progress both of population and wealth. . . .
> This consideration led [it] . . . to treat coffee cultivators favorably, their
> production being one of the most precious of America.
>
> —DOMINGOS BORGES DE BARROS, "Memória sobre o café," 1813

> The wealth of the Brazilian Empire has similar foundations to those
> of Cuba and Puerto Rico, and is developed with the same means.
> Therefore, it is very important for the administration of our Antilles
> to study in detail the state of the black race in Brazil, the means used in
> agriculture and industry, and the increase or decrease experienced
> by slavery and the slave trade.
>
> —MARQUIS OF PIDAL, Spanish minister of foreign affairs, 1849

MORE THAN THREE decades separate the quotations above. The first was
written by Domingos Borges de Barros and published in *O Patriota* (the
Patriot) in August 1813. The son of an important slaveholding family from the

Bahian Recôncavo and a graduate of the University of Coimbra, Borges de Barros was part of the circle of lettered men surrounding Rodrigo de Sousa Coutinho, the Count of Linhares. The newspaper *O Patriota* had been started in Rio de Janeiro one year after the death of Coutinho with the objective of continuing his efforts to promote the diversification of exports from Portuguese America within the new context that had been created by the radical transformations of 1808. In his "Memória sobre o café," Borges de Barros considered the Real Consulado de La Habana—a corporation created by Cuban slaveholders from the western part of the island and Bourbon administrators in the 1790s—a model for the improvement of slave agriculture in Portuguese America.[1]

In 1813, the Portuguese Crown, now based in Rio de Janeiro, was witnessing the first steps of the internationalization of British abolitionism, which would become a major concern for Brazil three decades later, when the second quotation above was written. In fact, the quotation comes from a letter written in April 1849 from the Spanish minister of foreign affairs—the marquis of Pidal—to his diplomatic representative in Rio de Janeiro. The moment was delicate for Spain due to revolutionary events in France, a diplomatic break with Britain, and, especially, burgeoning plans for the United States to annex Cuba (from both the Spanish island and the US South).

Like others of his time, Pidal believed that African slavery was the key to Spanish control over Cuba, which explains his interest in the Brazilian situation. Because of this, he sent an extensive questionnaire to the Spanish consul in Rio de Janeiro, José Delaval y Rincón, about the demographics of the black population in the Brazilian Empire, their experiences with free labor in plantations, the policies to preserve slavery in the absence of the transatlantic slave trade, the size of the illegal traffic, the actions of the British Royal Navy in Brazil, the penalties for slave traders, and, finally, the political strategy of the Brazilian government in relation to the contraband slave trade.[2]

The circumstances and the authors of the two quotations above, therefore, differed sharply from each other. The immediate contexts of these documents cannot be compared, but we believe they represented different conjunctures of a single historical structure. This structure brought together the destinies of Brazil and Cuba during the nineteenth century.

This is the starting point of the present book. It explores the relationship between slavery and politics in Brazil and Cuba between the 1790s and the

1850s—from the enlightened Luso-Brazilian and Hispano-Cuban proslavery proposals of the late eighteenth century to the effective suppression of the contraband slave trade to Brazil in the mid-nineteenth century. Despite growing interest in recent years, comparative studies of Cuba and Brazil are still rare.[3] Even rarer are studies that integrate both societies into the broader context of nineteenth-century global capitalism.

Despite the differences between their political trajectories after the 1820s, Brazil and Cuba shared a common nineteenth-century history due to the centrality of slavery in both societies. This shared history started in the late eighteenth century with the enlightened projects for the economic recovery of Portugal and Spain, as well as with the responses from planter classes in Portuguese America and Cuba to the economic collapse of Saint-Domingue. After 1820, Brazil and Cuba were the only regions in the New World that continued to be supplied by a massive transatlantic traffic of enslaved Africans. For this reason, the two slave economies quickly became the leading coffee and sugar producers in the world. But the persistence of the slave trade also forced the Brazilian and Cuban slaveholding classes to deal with Great Britain and its intense diplomatic pressure.

In a world of American republics extending from north (the United States) to south (Chile), the political histories of the Empire of Brazil and the Spanish colony of Cuba were unparalleled. In the constitutional experiences leading to these political configurations (Brazil as an independent monarchy and Cuba as a province or colony of the Spanish monarchy), the proslavery platforms of Brazilian and Cuban representatives became crucial. In the Cortes of Cádiz (1810–1814), Madrid (1820–1823), and Lisbon (1821–1822), and in the Constituent Assembly of Rio de Janeiro (1823), Brazilian and Cuban deputies offered clear strategies to preserve slavery in their societies, as they would repeatedly reaffirm whenever the institution was questioned in subsequent years.

The main objective of this book is to examine the arguments and strategies in favor of slavery and the slave trade that supported the political projects of Brazilian and Cuban slaveholders in the aftermath of the Haitian Revolution, in the Iberian constitutional experiences of the 1810s and 1820s, in parliamentary experiences of the nineteenth century, and in other situations when the problem of slavery was at the center of debates. Our intention is to also discuss how these political arguments and strategies in the

Brazilian and Spanish Empires were part of the broader history of an emerging liberal order.

Our argument is based on four main points. First, Brazil and Cuba shared a common space of experience that can be traced back to their participation in the Iberian Atlantic system. This shared space of experience became much narrower after the series of events marking the conjuncture of crisis at the turn of the nineteenth century, such as the American Revolution, the rise of British abolitionism, the Saint-Domingue Revolution, the collapse of Iberian monarchies, the internationalization of British pressure against the transatlantic slave trade, and the expansion of the global market for tropical goods that accompanied the growth of industrialization. Second, as a result of this same space of experience, the planter classes of Brazil and Cuba had a similar horizon of expectation based on the idea of perpetuating slavery.[4] Third, these slaveholding classes successfully imposed their proslavery designs on the Brazilian and Spanish Empires in the early 1820s, developing political arrangements that lasted without major problems until the 1860s. As a consequence, both Cuba and Brazil experienced the crisis of slavery over the following two decades. And fourth, proslavery arguments in Cuba and Brazil can be traced back to responses to the first critiques of slavery in the late eighteenth century, but they also acquired particular characteristics in the Brazilian and Cuban environments. In any case, proslavery ideologues in both regions shared many views since at least the 1790s.

Having emerged in England, the northern United States, and France (although to a much smaller degree in the latter) in the late eighteenth century, the antislavery movement became remarkably internationalized after the 1830s. After the parliamentary victory of English abolitionists in 1833 and the appearance of Garrisonian abolitionism in 1831, a transatlantic abolitionist network involving British and US militants emerged.[5] The internationalism of the nineteenth-century antislavery movement has received a great deal of attention from historians. Less known is the internationalist proslavery response of that same period, which will be discussed in the following chapters.

The present book is also a contribution to the comparative history of slavery, a field that has been rapidly growing since the 1990s. Changing the terms of the debate started by Frank Tannenbaum in the 1940s (as will be discussed in chapter 1), historians have been comparing multiple aspects of slave societies in the Americas: the demographics of slavery and the slave trade, rural and urban slavery, patterns of manumission, slave resistance, cultural manifestations, labor arrangements, the law and legal practices, among many other topics. Many of the recent comparative studies have also adopted an Atlantic perspective, framing the experience of slaves in the New World within the broader context involving Europe and Africa.

Despite the growth of comparative and Atlantic studies, historians have generally continued to study slavery and politics in the Americas from individual imperial or national perspectives. These approaches usually isolate their objects of investigation from the broader context. This can be seen both in Atlantic studies that compare societies as isolated units (i.e., societies appear as external and without interconnections to each other) and in comparative discussions of formal aspects of Brazilian and Cuban slavery.[6]

The present study explores the history of Brazil and Cuba as part of an integrated unit, or, to use Philip McMichael's concept, a historical "whole."[7] Thus, the kind of analysis developed here moves beyond formal comparisons of the differences and similarities between the politics of slavery in Brazil and Cuba, avoiding an approach that views the two regions as static units independent from each other. The politics and ideologies of slavery in Brazil and Cuba, therefore, are examined not as essentially national phenomena but as acts linked to the broader historical and geographical contexts that were created by the problem of slavery in the nineteenth century.

The book is divided into four chapters. Chapter 1 explores the asymmetries of slavery between the sixteenth and late eighteenth centuries in the Iberian colonies and their British and French counterparts. The main argument of the first chapter is that these differences were produced by the emergence of two distinct modern historical structures. The basic characteristics of these two structures can in turn be attributed to the different moments in which they were created. With this approach, we aim to contribute to the understanding of the dynamics of slavery in Brazil and Cuba in the *longue durée* and the responses of these two regions to the tensions brought on by the Age of Revolution.

The remaining chapters explore these responses in the short term. Chapter 2 analyzes the impact of the Saint-Domingue Revolution on Portuguese America and Cuba before the collapse of the Iberian Atlantic system in 1808. It also looks at the political reconstruction of slavery in Brazil and Cuba in the context of Iberian constitutional experiences between 1810 and 1824. Chapter 3 explores the politics of slavery in the Brazilian and Spanish Empires between 1825 and 1837, from the establishment of the Brazilian Parliament and the *régimen de las facultades omnímodas* for captains general in Cuba to the ascension of the Regresso Conservador in Brazil and the exclusion of Cuban deputies from the Spanish Cortes of 1836–1837. Finally, chapter 4 discusses the period between 1837 and 1850, showing how the different Brazilian and Hispano-Cuban political responses to British antislavery pressure led to the abolition of the transatlantic slave trade to Brazil in 1850.

Politics is an aspect of social life that pervades the daily problems and demands of anonymous social actors. The decision to explore it in the institutional spheres of the Cortes and the Parliament was taken based on theoretical, methodological, and practical considerations. National representation became the basis not only of constitutional regimes in the nineteenth century but also of the expansion of slavery in the Americas. The actions and speeches of deputies, senators, and colonial authorities reveal the connections between slavery and liberalism: in other words, the modern nation-state as part of the process leading to the enslavement of Africans. For this reason, parliamentary records are the centerpiece of this study. We nonetheless decided to include government documents, diplomatic correspondence, and writings from Brazilian and Cuban slaveholders in order to better understand our subject. Our hope is that the research results presented here will stimulate further studies about the history of slavery and politics in the Americas and their place in the broader history of the capitalist world economy.

——•◦•——

Research for this book was developed between 2004 and 2009 within the FAPESP (Fundação de Amparo à Pesquisa do Estado de São Paulo) Thematic Project "Fundação do Estado e da Nação—Brasil, 1790–1850," supervised by the late István Jancsó. The ideas presented here were first discussed in a graduate seminar taught by two of the authors—Márcia Berbel and Rafael Marquese—and the visiting professor Matthias Röhrig Assunção (Essex University) in the Graduate Program in Social History at the University of

São Paulo (USP), Brazil, during the fall of 2004. The close relationship between the ideas discussed in the seminar and those developed by Tâmis Parron as part of his graduate research—also financed by FAPESP—soon became clear. Thus, we would like to first thank all the friends who were part of the Thematic Project, who helped create a perfect academic atmosphere, and Matthias Assunção, who participated in the discussions of the graduate seminar. After the book was published in Portuguese (*Escravidão e política: Brasil e Cuba, c. 1790–1850* [São Paulo: Editora Hucitec, 2010]), FAPESP sponsored this English translation prepared by Leonardo Marques.

Equally important for the results presented here were the debates within the research group Escravidão e História Atlântica, at the Graduate Program in Social History at USP. During our research we received support from a large number of friends and colleagues from various institutions: Izaskun Álvarez Cuartero, Manuel Barcia Paz, Manuel Chust, Ivana Frasquet, Reinaldo Funes Monzote, Luis Miguel García Mora, Flávio dos Santos Gomes, María Dolores Gonzáles-Ripoll Navarro, Keila Grinberg, Fábio Duarte Joly, Maria Elisa Mäder, Marco Pamplona, José Antonio Piqueras, Mónica Quijada, Ricardo Salles, Julio Sánchez Gómez, Christopher Schmidt-Nowara, Marco Antonio Silveira, Dale Tomich, Carlos Venegas Fornias, and Regina Xavier. Finally, we would like to thank Conselho Nacional de Pesquisas (the Brazilian Research Council, CNPq) and FAPESP for individual fellowships to Rafael Marquese and Tâmis Parron.

CHAPTER 1

Brazil, Cuba, and the First Two Atlantic Systems

———◆·◆·◆———

Slavery and Atlantic History

In the mid-1940s, two books comprehensively reshaped the field of slave studies in the Americas. Eric Williams's *Capitalism and Slavery* and Frank Tannenbaum's *Slave and Citizen*—published in 1944 and 1946, respectively—set the research agenda for multiple generations of historians and social scientists for the three decades that followed. In turn, that group of scholars explored themes as wide ranging as the institutional differences of American slave systems, the varied patterns of race relations, the links between metropolitan economies and colonial slavery, and the nature of abolitionist processes.

The political and historiographical perspectives of Williams and Tannenbaum, however, were diametrically opposed. A precursor to Marxist interpretations of American slavery, Williams attacked the classic interpretation of abolition espoused by historians of the British Empire, many of whom had emphasized the humanitarianism and idealism of metropolitan abolitionists. Clearly inspired by the broader context of pan-Africanism and Caribbean nationalism, the Trinidadian historian focused on economic forces in his two-part argument on the relationship between slavery and capitalism.[1] Tannenbaum's main concerns, on the other hand, were the inclusion of African Americans in US society after World War II, which was still marked by institutional segregation at the time, and the post-Holocaust experience in Europe. Unlike Williams, he emphasized culture as the key factor for understanding race relations in the Americas. The differences between the United States and Latin American countries could be, in his view, traced back to their slave systems, which were built on distinct legal and moral foundations. In Iberian America, the confluence of a legal tradition of the Justinian Code (recognizing slavery as contrary to natural law and reason) and common Church practices (establishing the rights of slaves to receive sacraments) allowed the incorporation of former slaves as full citizens in nonracist societies. The absence of both traditions in British America, on the other hand, allowed masters to define their captives as movable property, thus lacking moral personalities. Consequently, for Tannenbaum, slavery became racialized in English-speaking societies while manumissions were largely prohibited. As a result, the abolition of slavery in the United States became inevitably violent and had damaging consequences for the African American population in the postemancipation period.[2]

The diverging approaches of Williams and Tannenbaum inspired subsequent interpretations by other historians that became increasingly at odds with each other. Tannenbaum had, in fact, already criticized Williams in 1946 for his emphasis on economic factors when explaining the origins of racism in the Americas.[3] Leaving aside Williams's broader thesis on the relationship between slavery and capitalism, Tannenbaum had clearly written a politically informed critique marked by an anti-Marxist position that challenged growing nationalism in the Caribbean at the time. A compelling critique, however, also came from the other side. Tannenbaum's description of a supposedly benevolent Latin American slavery owed much to the work of Gilberto Freyre. At the turn of the 1960s, when Freyrean explanations of the Brazilian slave past and contemporary race relations came under attack, the work of Williams inspired new studies on the economic and social history of slavery in Brazil. Despite their thematic, theoretical, and historiographical differences, the so-called São Paulo school (in fact, an informal group of social scientists and historians connected to the University of São Paulo) completely embraced the two-part argument of Eric Williams.[4] A similar process took place with the historiography dealing with Cuba. Drawing on the work of the Trinidadian historian, historians criticized the contrast between Iberian and British slavery established by Tannenbaum.[5]

Notwithstanding these differences, both books can be considered precursors of what has been called "Atlantic history": an approach that attempts to explore the flows of people, commodities, and ideas that tied together the four continents of the Atlantic between the fifteenth and nineteenth centuries in an integrated way.[6] Ironically, many of the problems of *Capitalism and Slavery* and *Slave and Citizen* can still be found in much of the literature on Atlantic history. The former takes the Anglo-Saxon world as the historical norm and is informed by a conception of linear time in its interpretation of Atlantic slavery. Even in his broader study of the Caribbean, Williams explored Atlantic processes as part of a single historical structure, dictated by the persistence of sugar production and plantation slavery. These elements were analyzed under the light of events in the British and, to a much smaller extent, French worlds.[7] Similar problems can be found in current key interpretations of what exactly "Atlantic history" means, with many scholars defining it as a fixed space (the ocean) and time period (from 1492 to 1830; i.e., from Columbus's first voyage to the end of the first cycle of political independences). These problems also appear in the historiographical debates on the relationship between the rise of industrial capitalism and the antislavery movement, most of them dealing exclusively with the British Empire.[8]

Tannenbaum's book, in turn, is part of a long scholarly tradition that has juxtaposed Catholic Europe with its Protestant counterpart, or rather, the Iberian with the Anglo-Saxon world. This opposition was constructed around a dichotomy that presented Protestant Europe as modern and evolving, and Catholic Iberia as traditional and unchanging. The origins of this comparative perspective can be traced back to the famous *leyenda negra* of the late sixteenth century (a general depiction of a supposedly intrinsic violence of Spaniards). It entered the historiography through what Robert Kagan has referred to as "Prescott's paradigm," a form of analysis that negatively contrasted Spanish (and Portuguese) decadence with British and, especially, North American progress. According to this perspective, the Inquisition, Catholicism, absolutism, and the waste of New World riches that accompanied the lack of entrepreneurship indicated that the train of modernity had left behind the Iberian countries and their colonies overseas already in the seventeenth century. The latter represented the perfect antithesis of England and the United States.[9] In his comparative study, Tannenbaum simply inverted these terms, comparing the mild nature of race and slave relations in Iberian America to the brutality of their counterparts in the British colonies and in the United States. In doing so, the American historian refashioned some of the arguments of the *leyenda blanca* that had been created by nineteenth-century ideologues of the Spanish Empire, which stressed the benefits of Iberian imperialism in its incorporation of racially subaltern peoples in overseas territories. *Slave and Citizen* turned the depiction of an inherent backwardness of Spanish and Portuguese Americas upside down. In terms of race relations, the southern neighbors were a positive example for the United States.[10]

Scholars working with comparative studies of slavery and race relations have criticized Tannenbaum's interpretation. The main points of contention are, first, the alleged divergence between legal Iberian and Anglo-Saxon traditions, and, second, the limits to the understanding of social actions through the study of laws. Critics indicate the commonalities between different slave societies in the Americas, which invariably employed systematic violence and created racial hierarchies. David Brion Davis, for example, minimized the differences between the role of manumissions in Latin America and in the United States and argued that they "could well be more of degree than of kind."[11] Sidney Mintz in turn made a fundamental point in his critique of Stanley Elkin's book, which generally followed the interpretation of Tannenbaum. He argued that by looking at slavery in Latin America as a single social phenomenon—either precapitalist or traditional—both historians had placed it outside of historical analysis. Given the many changes brought by the sugar revolution, Cuban slavery in the nineteenth century could not be conflated with its seventeenth-century counterpart. The same could be said of Brazil. "The differentials in growth of the slave plantations in different colonies," Mintz argued, "are to be understood as resulting from different ecologies, differential maturation of metropolitan markets and industries, and different political relationships between creole governing bodies and the metropolitan authorities."[12]

Historians continue to compare Iberian and Anglo-Saxon societies, not only because of the many contrasts regarding slavery in these two worlds but also in relation to other institutions and practices. John H. Elliott, for example, compares different aspects of the British and Spanish Empires such as their modes of imperial legitimation and occupation of New World spaces; the efforts for the spiritual conversion of conquered peoples by Spaniards, a fundamental part of Spanish imperial ideology that had no counterpart in the British case; the "creolization" process of Spanish colonial elites through mixed-race marriages, a process that was also absent in British America; the economic bases of colonial exploitation and their respective commercial networks; the institutional structures of Spain—responsible for carrying the central authority of Madrid to many distant places—and the federative self-government of the British colonies in America; their distinct political cultures (the contractualist theories of the Second Scholastic versus the republican ideology of the Commonwealth); and, finally, their contrasting religious systems.[13]

The erudition and scope of Elliott's book do not eliminate the fact that it is, above all, a formal comparison between two empires. It consists of an inventory of their similarities and differences, approaching them as two independent units completely external to each other. Such a methodological procedure does not allow Elliott to conceptualize the Spanish and British Empires as belonging to distinct, albeit interconnected, historical temporalities. In other words, he faces the difficulties inherent in the comparative method, as had been the case in the works of Tannenbaum and many other historians. Still, Elliott makes a good case—as other scholars have also done in recent years—when stressing the importance of manumission in the Iberian world compared to its limited role in the British colonies.[14] How can we avoid the interpretive limitations in the various approaches outlined above?

Drawing on the pioneering suggestions of Sidney Mintz, some scholars have approached "the Atlantic" as a single geographic space that is shaped by multiple temporal rhythms.[15] This chapter has two main objectives. First, it aims to overcome some of the problems inherent in approaches that either deal with the Atlantic as part of a single historical time, or merely contrast Iberian with British slavery. We believe that the differences between slavery in the Iberian Atlantic system and in its northwestern European counterpart between the sixteenth and eighteenth centuries can be understood as part of two singular historical structures—two historical *times*—of the modern world that were defined by the different moments of their constitution. Second, it offers an interpretation of the general crisis of colonial slavery and colonialism in the New World at the turn of the nineteenth century as a moment of transition to a new structure, what historian Dale Tomich has called "Second Slavery."[16] Our goal is to frame the dynamics of Brazilian and Cuban slavery in the longue durée in order to understand how these areas reacted to the tensions of the Age of Revolution and created a space for action after 1808, when the Iberian Atlantic system collapsed.

The Iberian and Northwestern European Atlantic Systems

In the 1980s, David Meinig discussed the multiple temporalities of European overseas expansion in a book that played a central role in the delimitation of Atlantic history as a field of study. "Although news of the discoveries quickly reverberated through the maritime systems of western Europe," he argues, "not all societies were equally well prepared for American adventures." At the turn of the sixteenth century, Iberians were better prepared for the conquest and occupation of the New World than their northern neighbors (France, England, and the Netherlands). Despite their continuous presence in Atlantic waters, merchants from northwestern Europe were unable to "implant their versions of civilization firmly on American shores" before the seventeenth century. These distinct historical times reflected in the founding of Santa Fe (New Mexico), Jamestown, and Québec, all of them established between 1605 and 1608. They "were expressions of utterly different histories and phases of European expansion," that is, the end of the Spanish conquest of Mexico and the beginning of the English and French occupation of North America.[17]

Using the concept of "cultural hearth," Meinig argues that two cultural traditions pervaded Lisbon and Seville, the key centers of Iberian expansion: the accumulated experience with war (gained in the process of expelling Muslims) and maritime commerce (inherited from the old cosmopolitan centers of the Mediterranean). These two traditions had previously combined with each other, but on a much smaller scale and without the participation of Genoese capital. The "cultural heart" of northwestern Europe in turn emerged in the first half of the sixteenth century as a consequence not of the Christian Reconquista but of the Protestant Reformation (although the links between the English and French across the English Channel had been stimulated by Huguenots and by the commercial and political ties that dated back to the late medieval period). After the collapse of the Huguenot connection in the late sixteenth century, the London-Amsterdam-Baltic sea axis became a fundamental source of funds for expansion into the Atlantic. In the early seventeenth century, France, England, and the Netherlands had no experience in the conquest and peopling of overseas territories, developing new methods in the making; "the America created out of this northwest sector of Europe was necessarily more invention than extension."[18]

Meinig's argument is a good starting point to understanding the Iberian Atlantic system and its differences from its northwestern European counterpart. The overseas expansions of Portugal and Castile shared the same historical time and mutually influenced each other with political rivalries and economic links. On the one hand, the formation of both kingdoms took place in the context of struggles against both their common Muslim enemy and other Christian rivals on the Iberian Peninsula.[19] On the other hand, the Reconquista shaped their integration into the European economy at the time. In the case of Portugal, the final expulsion of the Moors in the mid-thirteenth century gave the country access to routes connecting the commercial centers of the Mediterranean to those of the Hanseatic League through Gibraltar. By the end of that century, Lisbon had become an important outpost in the north-south maritime trade routes.[20] The growth of sheep farming in Castile during the mid-thirteenth century was also related to the wool industry in Flanders and the Italian Peninsula. The main financer of these enterprises, as in Portugal, was Genoese capital.[21]

The rivalry between Portugal and Castile intensified during the crisis of the fourteenth century, reaching a critical moment during the events of 1383–1385. Despite the Portuguese victory at Aljubarrota (which was almost immediately used to justify the crowning of a new king and the ushering in of the Avis dynasty), the war against Castile continued until 1411. It did not take long before the political and economic disputes between the two rivals had spread beyond the Iberian Peninsula into the "Atlantic Mediterranean" (the Azores, the Canary Islands, Madeira, and Cape Verde). Demonstrating the intersection of dynastic interests and overseas expansion, the Treaty of Alcáçovas (signed at the end of the War of Castilian Succession, 1474–1479) recognized Portuguese sovereignty over the Azores, Madeira, and, especially, the territories south of the Canaries (although the latter remained under the control of the Spanish) in exchange for the recognition of Isabel as the queen of Castile.[22]

Two distinct but mutually influencing trajectories emerged already in the 1480s as a consequence of the Treaty of Alcáçovas. While Castile conquered and colonized the Canaries, in what many historians consider a prelude for the further conquest and colonization of the Caribbean,[23] Portugal explored the coast of Africa and other Atlantic islands. In Africa, the Portuguese used their Mediterranean experience and established a string of trading posts (the so-called *feitorias*) in a response to the insurmountable obstacles posed by environmental conditions and native peoples. Thus, the Castilian and Portuguese strategies to reach the Indies in the early 1490s (by following Columbus's plan and establishing an African route, respectively) can be considered different responses to a unified process of expansion that had in the Treaty of Tordesillas (1494) its corollary. As Luiz Felipe de Alencastro argues, the two Iberian crowns promoted the exploration, conquest, and occupation of the Mediterranean Atlantic and the coast of Africa in a sort of "preemptive expansionism." In other words, they acted according to each other's actions.[24]

The key issue here is the emergence of a slave complex in the Iberian Atlantic system, with Portuguese participation in the African slave trade beginning in the 1440s. This early access to African labor not only led to the disembarkation of enslaved Africans in the Iberian Peninsula but also proved important to the economic exploitation of the Atlantic islands in the following decades.[25] This meant that a crucial structural characteristic of the Iberian Atlantic system had already been firmly established by the end of the fifteenth century with the treaties of 1479 and 1494 that limited the Spanish access to Africa: the Portuguese controlled the slave trade and were on the verge of exporting it across the Atlantic.[26]

It is important to note, however, that the Portuguese were not acting exclusively by themselves. The Genoese played a fundamental role in the establishment of an economic system in the Atlantic islands not only by providing capital and expertise but also by acting as merchants involved in commercial operations with the Portuguese. Together in Madeira and São Tomé, they laid the foundations for the slave-sugar complex that was later transposed to the New World, a partnership that also took place in the Canaries with the Spanish.[27] Consequently, by the early fifteenth century, the Spanish and Portuguese—and their Genoese associates—had created the blueprint for a new form of exploitation of African slave labor that responded to and paralleled the demand for luxury goods in European urban centers. This was the main reason for the transplantation of the sugar complex of the Atlantic islands to the Caribbean shortly after the arrival of Columbus.

Still, the first three decades of Caribbean occupation were marked by gold extraction and the exploitation of local indigenous labor. The exhaustion of gold deposits and the demographic catastrophe of the indigenous population forced a general reorientation of economic activities on islands such as Hispaniola and Puerto Rico in the 1520s. At that point, the system of large-scale sugar production based on the exploitation of African slave labor that had been developed in the previous century in the Atlantic islands was transplanted and reestablished in a new world. The expertise for this transformation came from the Atlantic islands, with slaves coming directly from the

Portuguese and Genoese merchants who had access to the trade licenses granted by the Castilian Crown to private parties (a direct consequence of their association to the commercial houses of Seville).[28]

By 1520, there were three models available to Iberian metropolitan powers for their economic operations in the New World: the feitorias on the coast of Africa, the sugar plantations of the Atlantic islands and the Caribbean, and gold extraction in the latter. This third form went through a radical transformation after the Spanish conquest of indigenous empires in Mesoamerica and the Andes, with their extremely large deposits of gold and silver. After 1530, the second and the third models became predominant in America and continued to influence and impact each other. News of the conquest of Mexico and the discovery of Potosí, for example, resonated in Portuguese America, inspiring the development of the system of captaincies (also inspired by previous experiences in the Atlantic islands) and the establishment of a general government. Likewise, the growth of sugar production in Pernambuco and Bahia contributed to the economic collapse of Santo Domingo and Puerto Rico.[29]

The enduring characteristics of the Iberian Atlantic system crystallized during the second half of the sixteenth and early seventeenth centuries. The economic structure of the Spanish model was based on silver mining, which relied on forced (Peru and New Spain) and waged indigenous labor (New Spain), the adoption of a system based on an exclusive port in the metropolis (initially Seville and later Cádiz), a system of fleets and fortresses established in key intersecting points of the Caribbean (of which Havana was the main one), and the use of African labor, predominately in urban activities and gold mining. In contrast, the economic model adopted by the Portuguese was founded on sugar production (which was significantly larger than its preceding counterpart in the Atlantic islands in terms of both total global production and production per unit), the enslavement of indigenous populations in peripheral areas, and the fundamental role of African slavery and the transatlantic slave trade in central areas.

One could ask whether it is possible, or even desirable, to group these different elements into a single system. There are a number of factors besides shared historical time that suggest the Portuguese and Castilian experiences in the Atlantic shared common trajectories: first, in the integration of these metropolises and their overseas colonies into the broader circuits of the

European world economy; second, in the mechanisms for the reproduction of the labor power; third, in the colonial social structure; and, finally, in the imperial ideology of slavery.

One central aspect of the Iberian Atlantic system was the structural weakness of its metropolitan economies and their dependence on external sources of financing. From the beginning of colonial expansion, they depended on non-Iberian capital and trade networks to sustain their overseas colonies.[30] The key Genoese role in this process can be seen as part of what Giovanni Arrighi calls a "Genoese systemic cycle of accumulation," an interpretation that reinforces the argument that temporal asymmetries marked the emergence of modern Atlantic systems. Following the steps of Fernand Braudel, Arrighi considers "flexibility" and "eclecticism" to be the defining features of historical capitalism, a liquid and mobile capital driven by profit opportunities. In other words, the system is characterized by unending accumulation for the sake of accumulation.

Arrighi locates the emergence of the basic forms of historical capitalism in the late medieval period, describing significant transformations in the following centuries. These changes are analyzed using a concept he refers to as "systemic cycles of accumulation."[31] Since the advent of capitalism as a historical system, Arrighi argues, the world has seen four of these cycles: the Genoese (from the fifteenth to the early seventeenth century), the Dutch (from the late sixteenth to the late eighteenth century), the British (from the second half of the eighteenth to the early twentieth century), and the North American (from the late nineteenth to the present moment—in this case, 1994—of financial expansion). Each systemic cycle comprised specific patterns of capitalist organization, distinct geographic areas of production and circulation of commodities and capitals ("space-of-flows"), and conflicts between different political powers ("space-of-places"). "Historically," Arrighi argues, "capitalism as a world system of accumulation and rule has developed simultaneously in both spaces."[32]

Arrighi points to the existence of capitalist and territorialist logics of power in his explanation of the Genoese cycle of accumulation.[33] These modes of rule combined with each other in multiple ways since the emergence of the modern interstate system in medieval Italy. The tensions between Venice and Genoa over long-distance trade in the Mediterranean started as a product of the capitalist logic of power, but soon came to include the territorialist logic that opposed Portugal to Castile and both to their Muslim enemies. Excluded from the Levant by the Venetians, Genoese capitalists searched for an exit in the western Mediterranean during the fifteenth century through an association with the Iberian territorialist powers, financing the Castilian *mesta* system at times and the Portuguese expansion over the Atlantic islands and the coast of Africa at others. The Genoese economic connections (which had Antwerp at their center) played a fundamental role in the Iberian expansion of the fifteenth and sixteenth centuries and, consequently, in the creation of their Atlantic system. Thus, it is not a coincidence that while silver mining in the New World reached its peak and sugar production in Portuguese America expanded, the Genoese became key bankers during the imperial expansion carried out by Philip II, which soon incorporated Portugal and its overseas possessions.[34]

The second cornerstone of the shared Iberian history in the Atlantic was the mechanisms explaining the shifting dynamic from metropolis to colony over who controlled the slave trade. Enslaved Africans had been used in Spanish America since the early sixteenth century, initially in the Caribbean and later on the mainland. The growth of black slavery in New Spain and Peru—and, consequently, of the transatlantic slave trade—only took place by the mid-sixteenth century after the demographic collapse of indigenous populations and the economic transformations brought by the rise of mining. Enslaved Africans were not directly employed in the Andean and Mesoamerican silver mines but played an important role in staple-producing enclaves and major urban centers such as the coast of Veracruz and Lima, or in the alluvial gold mines of New Granada. Despite the important role of the Genoese in the early transatlantic slave trade, the Portuguese soon became the main carriers of African captives to these areas. Slave traders based in Lisbon quickly seized the opportunities opened by the growing demand for slaves in New Spain and Peru after the 1570s, initially through licenses granted by Madrid and later, after 1595, through exclusive contracts called asientos. These slave trade interests played a key role in the union of the Portuguese and Spanish Crowns in 1580. At the turn of the seventeenth century, the growth of the transatlantic slave trade not only led to a larger Portuguese presence in Africa—especially in Angola—but also facilitated the transition from indigenous to African slavery in the sugar mills of Portuguese America. Before the sugar boom in Cuba in the late eighteenth century, the peak of the transatlantic slave trade to the Castilian Indies took place during the first quarter of the seventeenth century, with Portuguese merchants disembarking 117,709 enslaved Africans.[35]

During this same period, the Dutch attacked Portuguese possessions around the world, marking the emergence of the Atlantic system of northwestern Europe. Before discussing this new Atlantic system, however, two demographic changes in the Iberian Americas after the mid-seventeenth century must be noted. After falling to its lowest demographic point during the colonial era, the indigenous population of Mesoamerica (and later, in the Andes) started to grow again.[36] The growth of the indigenous population and the rise of a large mixed-race population meant that the reproduction of the labor force did not depend on the metropolitan center anymore. A similar process, albeit for different reasons, took place in Portuguese America. The responsibility for defending Portuguese outposts in Africa against Dutch attacks fell squarely on the shoulders of Portuguese American settlers as a result of the incapacity of the Portuguese Crown to finance a military reaction from the metropolis. Consequently, the transatlantic slave trade came to be controlled mainly by individuals based in New World ports.[37] During the following two centuries (1650–1850), this became one of the most distinguishing features of Brazilian slavery.

Besides the control over demographic dynamics (natural growth in the Spanish case and a bilateral slave trade between Africa and Brazil in the Portuguese case), another fundamental characteristic emerged within the shared Iberian Atlantic system: that is, the social complexity caused by the growth of slave manumissions. Tannenbaum argued, as we have seen, that manumission generated distinct modes of slave relations in Iberian dominions. Despite all the criticisms levied against his perspective in the decades that followed, and the fact that present-day scholarship rejects the corollary that relatively benign race relations existed in the Iberian Americas, studies conducted after the 1970s have indicated that the rates of manumission were indeed higher in areas of Portuguese and Spanish colonization than in their British, French, and Dutch counterparts, a difference that must be understood in qualitative and not quantitative terms.[38]

The effects of manumission on the demographic structure of the Iberian Americas were evident since the sixteenth century. The past metropolitan experience with slavery in the Mediterranean ensured that the juridical framework and social practices that crossed the Atlantic would not become obstacles to manumission. In the central areas of the Castilian Indies, the rise of manumission—along with the devastating impact of the conquest on the indigenous population and the disembarkation of enslaved Africans— stimulated the racial mixture between these different ethnic groups. This miscegenation in turn stimulated the growth of manumission. Thus, free blacks and freedmen (not necessarily racially mixed) already represented an important part of the population in the great urban centers of Mesoamerica and the Andean coast.[39] Moreover, the *limpieza de sangre* led to the rapid integration of these groups into the colonial social structure in a subordinate position. Freedmen participated in institutions that were exclusive to them (such as militias and brotherhoods), and they were classified as *castas* during the seventeenth century in order to distinguish them from the "Republic of Indians," which had already been formally separated from the Spanish world.[40] The Portuguese colonial world did not see the emergence of castas, but the dynamics of manumission there were very similar to those in Spanish America. Institutions such as black and mulatto militias and brotherhoods not only became a common feature in Portuguese America but also inherited the existing divisions among groups of former slaves.[41]

The segregated integration of freedmen and free blacks was connected to the fourth characteristic of the Iberian Atlantic system, which was the ideology of slavery. Of all the forms of coerced labor established in Portuguese and Spanish America, the enslavement of Africans and their descendants was certainly the most extreme. Iberian men of letters had discussed slavery since the second half of sixteenth century but never justified the institution on a racial basis. They used a large number of sources—classics (especially Aristotle and the Stoics), sacred texts, the civil and canon law of the West, and the treaties of Church fathers (from Augustine to Aquinas)—and provided answers to the challenges brought by the Protestant Reformation and, especially, by the different overseas peoples that Iberians came into contact with.[42]

Iberian expansion into the Atlantic soon generated debates on the nature of indigenous peoples (of Africa and the Americas) and the rights of Iberian subjects over their labor, their conversion to Catholicism, and their formal incorporation into Christian monarchies. In a famous passage of *Politics*, Aristotle argued that some peoples were not capable of self-government and were naturally inclined to be slaves. This argument reverberated during the

Iberian expansion, with theologian John Mair describing the inhabitants of the Antilles as natural slaves already in 1509. Juan Ginés de Sepúlveda perfected the Aristotelian theory in his work *Democrates secundus* (1547), which justified the absolute temporal power (dominium) of the Spanish Crown over American peoples based on three reasons: the natives violated natural law, sinned against the true religion, and were naturally incapable of governing themselves. If they refused to submit to Spanish authority, they could be justly enslaved.[43]

Theologians in the main universities of Castile and Portugal reacted to the emerging definition of aboriginal nations as being predisposed to slavery by seeking to establish (through a revival of scholasticism) the theological, legal, and moral basis for the Iberian dominium over other peoples and, consequently, the exploitation of their labor. From this emerged the body of ideas that justified the institution of slavery in the Iberian empires for at least three centuries. This juridical-theological rationalization of black and Amerindian slavery was based on four arguments: in a just war the winner had total dominium over the defeated and could either kill or enslave him; when sentenced to death, a prisoner could alienate his own life in order to stay alive; to avoid death from scarcity, one could sell his own freedom; and children of slaves were already born without their freedom. Slavery had not been created by nature but was legitimized by it. The institution was part of the law of nations and could be regulated by the Crown.[44]

It is clear, therefore, that the racial enslavement of Africans in the Portuguese and Spanish possessions was not racially conceptualized. It is important to note two corollaries of this. First, "racialization" was clearly absent at the ideological level and in the social practices as demonstrated by the limpieza de sangre regulations. "Despite its religious basis, the statute of blood purity," historian Hebe Mattos argues, "undoubtedly led to a proto-racial stigmatization based on ascendency, which was used not to justify slavery but to assure the privileges and honor of a nobility made of Old Christians in a world of free men." In Spanish America, the mechanism *gracias al sacar* allowed mixed-race individuals with legitimate ascendancy to purchase a certificate from the Crown attesting that they were Spanish, thus giving them access to institutions that were otherwise closed to those without "clean blood."[45] Second, the conceptual framework of the Second Scholastic questioned only illicit forms of enslavement and not the *institution* of slavery.

This became clear in the controversy involving the friars Francisco José de Jaca and Epifanio de Morains in 1681–1682. While considering slave resistance a legitimate reaction to the unjust forms of enslavement in Africa, the two Capuchins never questioned the existence of slavery per se.[46]

If corporatist theories of the Second Scholastic were central to Iberian political culture in the metropolis and overseas until the late eighteenth century, the Atlantic system of northwestern Europe emerged from decidedly different intellectual and material foundations, a consequence of its distinct historical time. French and English merchants and sailors (based in ports of the English Channel such as Plymouth, Saint-Malo, and Le Havre) had been excluded from the main routes of European overseas expansion at the turn of the sixteenth century but soon started to challenge the long-standing Iberian monopoly in the Atlantic. They seized ships in the North Atlantic, attacked ports and cities in the Caribbean and Pacific Rim, and attempted to establish settlements during their coastal explorations of North America and Brazil. However, every French and English attempt to establish colonies in the Americas during the sixteenth century ultimately failed. The Iberians' ability to resist originated not only from military prowess but also from the inability of northwestern European governments to develop consistent programs of overseas expansion. The latter was caused by internal political problems brought on by the Reformation and by the absence of a connection to the financial capital of northern Italy.[47]

This situation began to change in the last quarter of the sixteenth century after the Dutch Revolt against the Habsburgs. Antwerp was then the main trade center of the Iberian Atlantic system, operating, on the one hand, as the main distributor of Portuguese spices and sugar and Spanish silver to northern Europe and, on the other, as a key provider of primary products and manufactured goods to the Iberian countries and their overseas colonies. The war of independence against Philip II destroyed the market of Antwerp and contributed to the rise of Amsterdam in the 1580s. The latter quickly became the key center of the European world economy by operating as the main connection between the Baltic and Atlantic trades. The economic strength of this new center became clear during the Dutch conflict against Spain and Portugal. Overseas exports such as Brazilian sugar and Peruvian and Mexican silver continued to flow into Amsterdam despite the efforts from Madrid to curb exchanges with the enemy.[48]

The United Provinces of the Netherlands attacked the Spanish and Portuguese Empires around the world, thereby extending the conflict to territories beyond Europe and paving the way for the establishment of English
and French colonies in the Americas.[49] As had been the case during the
Iberian expansion, the rise of the three northwestern European powers was
an integrated process marked by mutual tensions and influences. In the
early seventeenth century, the English and French initiated their activities
in those parts of the New World that had been ignored by the Spanish: the
Lesser Antilles, the east coast of North America, and, in South America, the
Guianas and the mouth of the Amazon. The Dutch strategy was more
aggressive. They inaugurated a new era of European imperialism with the
creation of the Dutch East India Company, a privatized expansionist effort
that targeted mainly Portuguese outposts in the Indian Ocean. It also had
an Atlantic counterpart, the Dutch West India Company, which also
attacked the weakest half of the Iberian Union.[50]

While the Dutch West India Company attempted to take over the Portuguese sugar complex in the South Atlantic between the 1620s and 1640s, the
French and the English consolidated their presence in the Lesser Antilles
(Saint Kitts, Barbados, Guadeloupe, and Martinique) and in North America
(the Saint Lawrence River, the Chesapeake Bay, and New England). During
this period, the Caribbean became a sort of informal "condominium" shared
by the Dutch, English, and French. Despite the territorial rights and exclusive
licenses of the French and English commercial companies, the region's scarce
resources and the constant Spanish threat blurred imperial boundaries in the
Caribbean. Each developed similar systems of economic exploitation in their
colonies: cultivating tropical products such as tobacco, indigo, and cotton
based on contract labor (coming from Europe) and, to a large extent, Amsterdam capital.[51]

The failure of the Dutch West India Company (WIC) in Portuguese
America marked a turning point in Caribbean history. After the Luso-
Brazilian revolt against the Dutch in Pernambuco, the latter transferred the
expertise on sugar production that had been used in the sugar mills of Portuguese America to French and English colonists while also connecting them
to the main routes of the transatlantic slave trade. A sugar revolution started
around the 1650s, profoundly shaping the English and French Caribbean in
the following two centuries. Precisely when sugar production based on slave

labor became the norm in the Antilles, France and England reacted against Dutch naval and commercial power by adopting mercantilist policies that excluded Dutch merchants—whether they were connected to the WIC or not—from their Caribbean operations. While the measures taken by Jean-Baptiste Colbert failed, those imposed by Oliver Cromwell and, after the Stuart restoration, Charles II effectively kept Dutch merchants away from British colonies in the following decades.[52] At the turn of the eighteenth century, when the French Antilles started to grow at the same speed as their English counterparts (based on the massive importation of enslaved Africans and supplies from the North American mainland), the Atlantic system of northwestern Europe was operating at full force.

A practical way to understand the characteristics of this new Atlantic system is to explore the same four aspects—integration into the circuits of the European world economy, mechanisms for the reproduction of labor power, colonial social structures, and imperial ideologies of slavery—that we discussed in the Iberian context. Still following in the steps of Giovanni Arrighi, it is possible to argue that the creation of the northwestern European Atlantic system was connected to what he calls the "Dutch cycle of accumulation." While triggering the Genoese financial expansion (CM phase of the cycle of accumulation), the Dutch war for independence initiated the process that removed the bankers of the Phillips of Spain from their central position in the capitalist world economy. From their original center in the Baltic, the Dutch created a new and larger commercial space that expanded in three different directions. First, Amsterdam became the key *entrepôt* of the European world economy, with extremely large warehouses capable of storing large quantities of nonperishable goods for long periods of time. This was related to the capacity of Dutch merchants to manage liquidity and outperform their actual or potential competitors. Second, as a direct consequence of this Amsterdam became the central market for money and capital after the creation of the first stock exchange, which was open to investors of any nationality. Third, sizable trade and shipping companies were created not only to generate great profits and dividends but also to manage state and war functions. There were similar companies in Italy during the late medieval period, but the scale of Dutch operations was unprecedented. The Amsterdam Stock Exchange stimulated the activities of the Dutch East India Company (VOC) (and the other way around).[53]

Finally, it is important to note the connections between the Dutch cycle of accumulation and the establishment of French and English colonies in the New World. Besides the obvious case of the WIC and the creation of a slave-sugar complex in the Caribbean, the key link was between Dutch commercial success and the mercantilist reaction of France and England in the second half of the seventeenth century.[54] After their exclusion from commercial operations in the Caribbean (and in the Baltic, where similar mercantilist policies were established), Dutch capitalists specialized in high finance over the following century. The strengthening national economies of France and England during this period—which included the economic exploitation of overseas colonies in the Caribbean based on sugar production and slavery—were novel elements in the European world economy. Thus, it is not a coincidence that the Caribbean became center stage for Anglo-French imperial conflicts during the Second Hundred Years' War (1689–1815). Moreover, as a result of the broad reconfiguration of the world economy and the global geopolitical milieu, the space-of-flows of the Genoese cycle of accumulation was replaced by its Dutch counterpart. In a peripheral position, the Iberian metropolises saw a large part of the wealth of their colonies flow into northwestern Europe.

What emerged on the American side of this new Atlantic system had no parallel in other areas of European colonization in the New World, even if we include the old sugar-producing zones of the Atlantic in the discussion. Like São Tomé, Pernambuco, and Bahia before them, the English and French plantation islands were, in fact, characterized by the intimate connection between sugar production and slavery. But, unlike those other cases, the English and French plantation systems had a highly capitalized agriculture, a vertically integrated production process (with individual entrepreneurs owning both the agricultural and manufacturing aspects of their businesses), and a tendency to focus on the production of a single product (consequently experiencing the scarcity of basic foodstuffs). Moreover, their social structure was marked by a deep demographic imbalance between a minority of free whites and an overwhelming majority of black slaves, the near absence of manumissions, and a high level of owner absenteeism.[55]

The Atlantic system of northwestern Europe was also distinguished by the central role of metropolitan merchants—based in ports such as Liverpool, Bristol, London, Nantes, and Bordeaux—in the reproduction of colonial labor power. In other words, they controlled the transatlantic slave trade. During the seventeenth century, English and French slave traders tried to follow the example set by the Dutch West India Company and created companies that had exclusive rights over the commerce of enslaved Africans. These companies were all dissolved at the turn of the eighteenth century, but they established the material structure—forts, factories, connections, and expertise—that was used during the period of imperial free trade that defined that century.

During this period, the English and French slave trades reached their peak, with the disembarkation of approximately 2.8 million captives in their Caribbean possessions. If metropolitan merchants always controlled the English and French slave trades (unlike their Portuguese counterparts after the seventeenth century), the concept of a "triangular trade" must be revised. The English and French slave ships that left Europe, Herbert Klein argues, "were not a significant element in the transportation of slave-produced American goods to the European market." There were two relatively specialized Atlantic routes: Europe-America-Europe (with the exchange of metropolitan products for tropical goods) and Europe-Africa-America (the transatlantic slave trade).[56] Finally, it is important to note the impact of the English and French slave trades on the Iberian Atlantic system. The growth of competition not only led to the rise in slave prices on the coast of Africa, but northwestern European merchants became the main suppliers of captives to the Castilian Indies after the independence of Portugal in 1640. This was yet another example of the structural weakness of the Spanish metropolis.[57]

The enslaved Africans who disembarked in the English and French Caribbean entered societies that were markedly different from the Iberian colonies. Slavery in the Iberian Atlantic system can be described as both an extended and refashioned version (hence, modern) of old slaving practices inherited from the Mediterranean world.[58] The genesis of this difference between the two systems can be traced back to the distinct historical moments of their creation. It is clear that Dutch, English, and French involvement with New World slavery in the early period followed in the footsteps of their Iberian counterparts, as shown in their slaving patterns, acculturation processes involving captives, and higher rates of manumission.[59] The French slave code of 1685 also owed much to the same legal sources that had been used by the Spanish and the Portuguese.[60] Something new came, however, with the dramatic rise of African slavery in the British and French Americas in the late seventeenth century. The British and French societies of the Caribbean and the North American South were exceptions and not the rule in the global history of slavery, mainly because of the obstacles to manumission that became endemic to them.[61]

The institutional basis for this new form of slavery dates back to the 1660s. According to the English tradition of representative government that granted significant autonomy to assemblies in the Caribbean and North America, colonial laws should reflect local priorities and needs. In the specific case of slave laws, this convention allowed the master classes who resided in the Americas to create a body of legal norms that reflected their concern for greater control over their captives.[62] All legislation created in the British colonies of the New World (always based on the *Barbados Act for the Better Ordering and Governing of Negroes* of September 1661) constructed strict boundaries that distinguished contract laborers, free whites, and the growing number of enslaved Africans from each other (and unmistakably associated Africans with slavery). These boundaries included the prohibition of interracial marriages, distinct punishments for each discrete group of workers (whipping a naked white servant could only take place with the authorization of a judge, while masters wielded unlimited power to punish their slaves), the permission to own personal property for white servants (forbidden to black slaves), and, crucially, the prohibition of private manumission of slaves. The governor and the colonial assembly only allowed manumission in special cases after a formal authorization had been granted. Freedmen (black or mixed race) and their descendants had no access to the civil and political rights of other free persons because of their African blood.[63]

These laws reflected the social dynamics (and were reinforced by them) that coalesced with the spread of slave plantations across the Caribbean islands and the southern colonies of British North America. Openly racist forms of ideological justification endorsed slavery in this new context. First, the Second Scholastic had no ideological influence over slavery in the Atlantic system of northwestern Europe. Despite a few commonalities between the Iberian neoscholastic constitutionalism and natural rights theories of the seventeenth century, the latter were markedly different from previous traditions. While natural law theories emphasized the artificial character of social contracts, the Second Scholastic considered them natural.[64] This distinction had important consequences for justifications of slavery. The new language of natural rights did not necessarily lead to a critique of slavery, and when it did it was the result of historical contingencies that will be discussed later. This was radically different, however, from the discourse of Iberian scholastics, who never criticized slavery as an institution.

John Locke noted the inherent difficulties of using the discourse of natural law to justify slavery. His use of the theory of just war, for example, was very different from that of Iberian neo-Thomists. It never made reference to slavery in the Americas, a topic that the eminent philosopher later addressed by writing the *Fundamental Constitutions of Carolina*, financing the Royal African Company, and working as secretary of the Council of Trade and Foreign Plantations and commissioner of the Board of Trade.[65] How could slavery be justified in an intellectual and political context marked by the new perspectives of natural law?

Locke remained silent, but many of his contemporaries provided answers to this issue. Leaving aside the arguments about the economic necessity of slave labor in New World plantations that pervaded mercantilist literature throughout the eighteenth century, the Atlantic system of northwestern Europe became defined by the use of racial theories that attempted to justify the exploitation of enslaved Africans. Montesquieu's climate theory was one of them. Equally important was pre-Adamism, a theory popularized by Isaac de la Peyère in the mid-seventeenth century based on the polygenic view that Adam was not the first human. This approach slowly replaced Greco-Roman and medieval interpretations that assumed human diversity had been a product of either surrounding factors (diet, the stars) or biblical passages (especially Noah's curse upon Canaan). The long and complex history of how this interpretation acquired racial connotations cannot be fully discussed here, but it is important to note two arguments that became central to polygenism in the following decades: first, that different human types could be hierarchically distributed according to their somatic and sociocultural characteristics, and second, that these were innate and transmissible from generation to generation. Many theologians rejected polygenism during the seventeenth century, but the belief in the existence of natural limits to human capacities progressively became the norm within European scientific circles, where the conflation of phenotypic and moral attributes was commonplace. English and French proslavery ideologues quickly took advantage of this new conceptual apparatus.[66]

Racial justifications of slavery thrived within the broader political culture of the British world and its imperial identities. From the Chesapeake Bay to Barbados, white settlers noticed the positive political benefits afforded by the institution at the turn of the eighteenth century. White communities increasingly considered the ownership of slaves a precondition for the exercise of civil liberties and local autonomy during this period. Atlantic republicanism—an ideology that can be traced back to the Italian political thought of the Renaissance that had been refashioned during the English Civil Wars—cemented this association between slavery and freedom. While republican ideals became relatively weak in England after the Glorious Revolution, they flourished on the North American mainland and in the Caribbean throughout the eighteenth century. Such an ideology, as British colonists quickly realized, was fully compatible with the social and economic organization of the colonies. According to the ideals of Atlantic republicanism, a republic depended on the existence of a body of free, independent, and property-holding citizens. In the case of slave colonies, the ownership of lands and captives to work them guaranteed the independence of rural owners and made them capable of engaging in political life. The imperial identity that emerged in the aftermath of the Acts of Union of 1707—based on the idea of freedom as the common element that united all the British—reinforced those associations by excluding Africans and their enslaved descendants from the new definitions of "Britishness."[67]

Such exclusion also took place within the religious sphere. After the failure of the sixteenth-century Protestant projects of colonial expansion developed by Richard Hakluyt and Samuel Purchas and the subsequent changes brought by the adoption of the Roman principle of res nullius (which argued that "empty things," including unoccupied lands, were the common property of all men until they were effectively used) to justify their right over the American colonies, ideologues of the British Empire abandoned their efforts to convert conquered peoples (Indians or Africans) to Protestantism.[68] Slave owners in the British colonies reinforced this exclusion by either ignoring or openly opposing efforts to Christianize their black slaves.[69]

The ideological characteristics of French colonial expansion in the seventeenth century were closer to their Iberian counterpart than the British, mainly because of an imperial ideology that defended the conversion of conquered peoples. The famous Code Noir of 1685, which made the conversion of all slaves employed in the Caribbean colonies mandatory, was a clear example of this.[70] It is nonetheless possible to see the unity of the Atlantic system of northwestern Europe here as well. In the early eighteenth century, the Christianization projects of the previous century were gradually abandoned as French officials became increasingly concerned with the maintenance of order in their Caribbean slave colonies. Measures such as restricting manumission, limiting the civil rights of freemen, and limiting the autonomous meetings of slaves—adopted first in Martinique and Guadeloupe— made the actions of missionaries in the name of slaves and free people of color extremely problematic. The establishment of these procedures by authorities and slaveholders in the early eighteenth century made slavery in the French colonies more similar to its British counterpart. Finally, one last example shows the contrast between slavery in the Iberian and northwestern European Atlantic systems. Despite the common Catholic background of Portugal, Spain, and France, the latter never witnessed the establishment of black and mulatto brotherhoods in its Caribbean colonies. The official response to the possible establishment of such an institution in Guadeloupe had no counterpart in the Iberian world: in 1753, the naval minister instructed French officials to suppress the creation of a brotherhood under the excuse that "the establishment of such a confraternity would be completely contrary to the regulations for policing slaves and to the precautions taken against them for the safety of the colonies."[71]

Many of the differences between the two Atlantic systems discussed here have been explored by Robin Blackburn in his monumental study about slavery in the New World, and by Pieter Emmer in a short but groundbreaking essay. Both authors, however, analyze these differences through the traditional/ modern duality. For example, Blackburn frames the differences in the categories of "baroque slavery" and "modern slavery" (the latter is also described as "commercial slavery" elsewhere in his book, a consequence of the "increasing commercialization of social relations in the metropolis"), suggesting that Iberian slavery had not been integrated into modernity. The same can be said of Emmer, who argues that "in the second Atlantic system [which had been created by the Dutch, English, and French in the Caribbean], the modern capitalist structure was much more dominating than in its Iberian counterpart."[72] Our argument here has been that the differences between slavery in the two Atlantic systems must be understood as part of *two distinct moments* of the combined and uneven process that marked the formation of the modern world. These two modern Atlantic systems coexisted after the mid-seventeenth century as two distinct temporal structures (although closely connected by the broader capitalist world economy) in a great example of what Reinhart Koselleck calls the "contemporaneity of the noncontemporaneous."[73] Perhaps one of the reasons historians continue to conceptualize these different tempo-ralities under the traditional/modern distinction may be the influence of past interpretations of the differences between the Iberian and North Atlantic empires, the subject of the next section.

The Crisis of the Atlantic System of Northwestern Europe and the Iberian Enlightenment

European powers naturally compared their own strategies with those of their rivals in the creation and development of their overseas empires. They constantly looked over their shoulders at each other, comparing the trajectories of their respective colonial projects. These assessments could help repeat the successes and avoid the failures experienced by rivals while justifying the conquest and occupation of colonial territories. Moreover, as in any comparison, discursive subjects were classified according to a hierarchy.

The sixteenth-century Iberian pioneers who explored New World territories established the pattern for the subsequent imperial expansions of other European powers. The English looked positively at the Spanish colonial experience in the Americas at the turn of the seventeenth century, but this view soon went through a radical transformation. Even before this shift, challenges to Spanish power in Europe were accompanied by criticisms of their actions in the Americas. The so-called leyenda negra, for example, played a central role in the ideology of the Dutch Revolt. The mercantilist literature also invited comparisons and negatively depicted the Spanish and the Portuguese (who were part of Spain between 1580 and 1640). The economic administration of the Castilian Indies and the Portuguese Empire became the negative counterexample of the exploitation of overseas resources. "A mercantilist pamphlet," Eli Heckscher argues, "would seldom let the opportunity pass of proving that Spain's economic policy was based on principles entirely contrary to those which the author considered correct."[74]

The negative depictions of the Iberian world created by Dutch, English, and French rivals had an internal counterpart in Spain at the turn of the seventeenth century with the *arbitristas*. These men of letters explained the decline of Castile by referencing the Greco-Roman conception of a cyclical time. This was the premise that all organisms—either living beings or inanimate institutions—had to inevitably endure a cycle of ascension, peak, and decline. Human action could never avoid the downfall, but it could slow down the process and prolong the life of the organism for as long as possible. Only by recovering all of its power and greatness could Spain truly delay its own decline.

The arbitristas, however, searched for solutions not in the Castilian past but rather by emulating contemporaneous European powers. Portuguese men of letters, many of them personally connected to arbitristas, shared these perspectives. Figures such as Duarte Gomes Solis and, after the 1640 restoration, Manuel Severim de Faria, Antônio Vieira, and Duarte Ribeiro de Macedo suggested that the solution to the problems of Portugal and its empire in the seventeenth century could be found in the commercial and manufacturing practices of Holland and France. The failure of the Olivares administration (one of the reasons behind the Portuguese rebellion of 1640) led to the ruin of the arbitristas, who, along with others, were blamed for the decadence of Spain. Reformist proposals were only later put into practice in Portugal, during the reign of Pedro II, but by the last decade of the seventeenth century they had already been abandoned.[75]

Notwithstanding the comparisons between, on the one hand, Portugal and Spain and, on the other, Holland, France, and England, the seventeenth century arbitristas remained attached to the idea of cyclical time and to the topos of the *Historia Magistra Vitae*: after all, the experiences of rival powers were part of a shared historical time, "a continuous space of potential experience."[76] When Bourbon and Pombaline reformers revived the arbitrista project in the eighteenth century, they significantly changed some of these conceptions. These enlightened reformers continued to employ the ideas of decadence and restoration, but giving them new meanings in light of the growing divergence between the commercial power of France and Britain and the peripheral position of Spain and Portugal in the European world economy.[77]

In fact, the gap between the economic and military power of Spain and

Portugal and the empires of northwestern Europe widened over the eighteenth century. The many historiographical debates explaining the reasons
for this divergence are beyond the scope of the present work, but it is important to note that the economic and geopolitical subordination of the Iberian
metropolises to France and Britain had already started during the creation
of the Atlantic system of northwestern Europe. The Portuguese war for independence against Spain, for example, was concurrent with the Luso-Brazilian
war against the WIC in the South Atlantic, and the two events had mutual
influences. In this context, the political recovery of the Portuguese Empire
depended on the diplomatic, military, and economic support of England.[78]
The gradual decline of the financial and military power of Spain—already set
in motion in the late sixteenth century and deepened by the Thirty Years'
War—in turn contributed to the success of the Portuguese restoration. The
weaknesses of the Spanish Empire had already become clear by the time of
the Peace of Westphalia (1648) but reached their peak at the turn of the eighteenth century during the War of the Spanish Succession, ultimately won by
French Bourbons. During the conflict, which can be considered the first
round of the Second Hundred Years' War, the Iberian monarchies were in an
inferior position: the traditional rivalry between Castile and Portugal had
become a minor part of the broader dispute between France and England.
During this process, the commercial networks of the Iberian Atlantic system
became subordinated to the Atlantic system of northwestern Europe.[79]

It was in this context that mining in Portuguese America expanded, with
two important consequences. First, the demographic patterns of the colony—determined by a combination of a transatlantic slave trade controlled
by local ports and high rates of manumission—went through a dramatic
growth after the discovery of gold mines at the turn of the eighteenth century. The prospects of rapid economic ascension attracted the metropolitan
and colonial population, stimulating the migration of large human contin-
gents to the new mining region. This influx was, according to one expert,
"the first mass migration in Brazilian demographic history."[80] The mines
stimulated large internal migrations and the arrival of an even larger number
of Portuguese immigrants (a total of four hundred thousand individuals
throughout the entire eighteenth century). The greatest migratory wave to
the region, however, came by force. The volume of the transatlantic slave
trade to Portuguese America, already the largest in the New World, doubled

during the first half of the eighteenth century. Between 1701 and 1720, approximately 335,000 enslaved Africans were disembarked in Brazilian ports, most of them destined for the gold mines. The period between 1720 and 1741, in turn, witnessed the disembarkation of an additional 365,000 captives. During the next two decades, finally, the number of disembarked slaves reached 384,000.

Second, the growth of mining led to important economic developments. On the local level, the colonial economy became more complex after the emergence of dynamic sectors such as cattle raising in Rio Grande do Sul and the São Francisco River valley, and foodstuff production in Minas Gerais, São Paulo, and Rio de Janeiro. Each of those sectors contributed to the growth of an internal market. The emergence of various urban centers in Minas Gerais and the growth of old cities like Rio de Janeiro and Salvador also stimulated the expansion of the internal economy. Moreover, tobacco production in the Bahian Recôncavo benefited from the rise of mining, since the product played a fundamental role in the exchanges for captives on the Gold Coast of Africa. The latter were especially valued in the mining zones.[81]

On the global level, however, gold mining not only disrupted the mercantilist policies of Pedro II but also deepened the Portuguese Empire's dependence on British trade networks. The treaties signed with Britain in 1703 stimulated the expansion of Portuguese external trade—in other words, trade beyond its imperial borders—during the first half of the eighteenth century. Imports, however, surpassed exports and soon led to trade deficits. For example, Portugal exported 94 percent of its wine production to England during this period. Still, despite being an important commercial partner, the country received only 10 percent of all British exports. Moreover, while Portugal exported only primary products (metropolitan wine, olive oil, colonial leather, and timber), England sent both basic supplies (fish and grains) and large quantities of manufactured goods. Portugal used mainly gold to pay for this commercial deficit, since Brazilian sugar and tobacco had been excluded from the English market since the 1660s. Finally, the commissaries of Atlantic fleets (established in seventeenth-century Portuguese America according to the Spanish model) generally operated as agents for the British commercial houses established in Portugal.[82]

A similar process took place in the Spanish Empire during the first half of the eighteenth century, with the growing economic diversification of their

American possessions and the loosening of metropolitan control over circuits connecting the colonies to the centers of the European world economy. After a general decline in the seventeenth century, silver mining in New Spain recovered, with previously peripheral areas such as the Caribbean coast of South America and the Río de la Plata becoming increasingly important.[83] In the metropolis, however, Spanish commercial power continued to decline as a consequence of the events of the previous century. After the treaties of Westphalia, Spain was forced to acknowledge the presence of northwestern European merchants based in Andalusia and their participation in the networks that connected Seville-Cádiz to the New World. In the late seventeenth century, English, French, and Dutch merchants entered the Spanish economic space by establishing illegal trade relations with Castilian subjects in the New World. The asiento contracts granted to the French (before the War of the Spanish Succession) and the English (after the treaties of Utrecht) further stimulated the growth of the contraband trade in Spanish America. Given the omnipresence of British and Dutch smugglers in the New World and the weight of French commercial houses in Cádiz (whose merchants enjoyed extraterritorial rights similar to those of English merchants in Lisbon), the economic subordination of Spain to northwestern European powers was as severe as that of Portugal.[84]

It is important to note the position of Cuba in this context. The island had been strategically important to Spain since the sixteenth century because of its intermediary position in the maritime routes that connected the metropolis to continental American colonies. Until the mid-eighteenth century, however, the colony's economy was limited to the activities of its main ports, cattle raising, and small-scale tobacco production. Sugar production remained low during the sixteenth and seventeenth centuries despite the excellent conditions for its cultivation on the island. Black slavery was certainly important for the Cuban economy, but captives were employed mainly in the services sector of cities like Santiago and Havana. In the early eighteenth century, the economic and human landscape in Cuba was markedly different from the conditions produced by the spread of sugar production based on slave labor in the neighboring Caribbean colonies. The rise of a slave plantation economy on the island had been hindered by the broader Spanish structures of the Iberian Atlantic system: Castilian commercial regulations that supported the monopoly of Cádiz over the trade between metropolis and colonies, the lack of capital to finance the establishment of sugar mills, and, especially, the chronic shortage of slave labor.[85]

Inspired by the reformist projects that had marked the late seventeenth century, the Spanish Crown sought to stimulate the growth of the Cuban slave economy with the creation of the Real Compañía de Comercio de La Habana in 1739, which shared many similarities with an organization established in Venezuela the previous decade. However, unlike the Real Compañía Guipuzcoana de Caracas, which had been mainly financed by Basque merchants, almost half of the shareholders of the new company were based in Havana. Its privileges included a monopoly over the tobacco trade and the Cuban exports of sugar, timber, and leather. In return, the company had to supply the Armada de Barlovento, build warships for the Havana fleet, provide support for military prisons in Florida, and finally patrol the coasts of the island against the smuggling of goods and slaves. The company stimulated the establishment of new sugar mills on the island, but the lack of control over the slave trade continued to obstruct the effective growth of sugar production. The contraband slave trade continued—often under the auspices of Havana shareholders—but in numbers insufficient to satisfy the local demand and cheapen the cost of labor.[86]

The contrast between Cuba and the English and French Caribbean is noteworthy. The slave complex established by northwestern European powers in their Antillean possessions saw dramatic growth in the first half of the eighteenth century. The disruption of the monopolies of commercial companies—especially regarding the transatlantic slave trade—and the adoption of free-trade principles led to the rise of slave trade ports such as Bristol and Liverpool in the British case, a process that was soon replicated in France with ports such as Nantes and Bordeaux. The massive introduction of enslaved Africans quickly established a demographic pattern in the Caribbean islands of the Atlantic system of northwestern Europe, characterized by a ratio of slaves to whites that stood at (at least) four to one.

The period also saw the rise of Jamaica and Saint-Domingue. Jamaica had been taken from the Spanish in 1655, but its development had been obstructed during the second half of the seventeenth century by the resistance of Maroon communities, which had been formed shortly after the English invasion and strengthened by the slave revolts of the 1670s. The expansion of sugar plantations in Jamaica after 1715 stimulated the escalation of Maroon

attacks and slave flight. By the 1730s, Jamaica had become an enormous battlefield. The conflict only came to an end with the peace treaty of 1739, which
brought about the social stability necessary for the expansion of slavery on
the island. In a period of approximately fifteen years (1734–1750), the slave
population of the island climbed from 80,000 to 120,000, further doubling
before the end of the 1780s. Likewise, Saint-Domingue had been a Spanish
possession until 1697, when the western part of the island of Hispaniola
became French. As in Jamaica, the continuous war between France and England from 1689 to 1713 (with a short truce between 1697 and 1702) disrupted
the local sugar industry. After the Peace of Utrecht, however, the growth of
Saint-Domingue—especially its northern part—was remarkable. When a
peace treaty with Maroon communities was established in Jamaica, the
French colony already had a labor supply of approximately 117,000 slaves. It
is also important to note the different destinies of the sugar exported by the
two colonies, a consequence of the consumption patterns of their respective
metropolises. While Britain, which had been undergoing what scholars call
the "birth of the consumer society," received almost all the sugar produced
in the British Caribbean, the French market was not able to consume all the
sugar coming from the French colonies. Thus, starting in the 1720s, French
authorities stimulated the reexport of colonial products to the European
continent.[87]

The Caribbean slave economies grew increasingly dependent on supplies
from the British North American mainland. Since the 1660s, New England
had grown based on the export of basic supplies to the sugar colonies of the
Caribbean—timber, traction animals, grains, and especially fish. All of New
England's naval and commercial transatlantic activities had in fact been
based on the fishing industry during the eighteenth century. New England
was soon followed by the Middle Colonies (New York, New Jersey, Pennsylvania, and Delaware), which, despite having more diversified economies, also
depended on exports to the British Antilles. These exchanges were legal,
according to British navigation laws of the second half of the seventeenth
century. The same was not true of the contraband trade established between
North American settlers and the French colonies. This illegal commerce was
important for the French Caribbean islands, especially Saint-Domingue,
since it helped both to reduce the operating costs of sugar production by
providing access to cheap supplies, and to open the North American market

to the export of molasses (a product that had no demand in the French metropolis because of a ban on rum sales).[88]

The combination of economic competition in the Caribbean and conflicts over North American territories stimulated tensions between the British and French Empires in the New World. These culminated in the Seven Years' War (1756–1763), which set in motion the chain of events that ultimately led to the crisis of the Atlantic system of northwestern Europe. The consequences of the Seven Years' War redefined imperial identities and the politics of slavery in the Atlantic systems of both northwestern and Iberian Europe. The different impacts of the crisis, in our view, reinforce the case for the existence of a double temporality in the eighteenth-century Atlantic world.

Let's look first at the events in the Atlantic system of northwestern Europe between the 1760s and the 1780s. The Seven Years' War started in North America with conflicts along the Ohio River between Virginian settlers and Native Americans allied with the French. In the first two years after the official outbreak of the war, British troops commanded by colonists suffered a series of defeats, which led to a more direct intervention of metropolitan forces. Military forces sent from Europe were fundamental, for example, in the conquest of Québec in 1759. That same year also witnessed a shift in the American stage of the global war, now centered in the Caribbean. British economic power became evident in the large naval and land forces that made possible a series of remarkable conquests between 1759 and 1762 in Martinique, Guadeloupe, and, after two hundred years of resistance, Havana.

The impact of the conquest of Havana on Bourbon reformist initiatives is examined elsewhere in this work. For now, it is important to note that British soldiers became aware of the sheer size of the North American contraband trade with the French Caribbean that continued to take place in the context of war. With peace in 1763 came many different expectations. British authorities expected North American colonists to contribute to the maintenance of defense forces in an enlarged empire (that extended from Canada to the Gulf of Mexico) with their own funds, the management of tensions involving indigenous groups, and the support of imperial commercial regulations. In other words, colonists were counted on to help curb the contraband trade with rival colonies. However, North American colonists, feeling more British than ever, expected metropolitan support for the expansion into western lands without a rise in taxes. The new measures passed by London after 1765 went against the expectations of the colonists and started the crisis that in little more than a decade ended British control over half of its American empire.[89]

British imperial identity played a key role in the American Revolution, an identity that as we have seen had been shaped by the idea of freedom. In combination with the Atlantic republicanism that emerged in the seventeenth-century revolutions, the new British identity flourished in the slave colonies of North America, especially in the Chesapeake Bay (home of the first generation of US presidents, from George Washington to James Monroe). This master class—characterized by their residence in the New World and an attachment to their birthplace, unlike their Caribbean counterparts—developed practices based on the neo-Roman concept of freedom. They considered their active participation in decision-making spaces (colonial assemblies, county courts), their ownership of property, and their power to rule (over their captives) to be signs of their independence.[90] Metropolitan policies constructed negative views of North American inhabitants after 1763 precisely because of their involvement with black slavery, increasingly depicted as an institution that contradicted Britishness. Colonists responded by asserting their British identity and accusing Parliament of tyranny and corruption in their efforts to enslave the free English people of America. The references to freedom and slavery in their speeches were not simply rhetorical devices but a reflection of their material world.[91]

British colonists in the Caribbean shared the same political culture of their North American counterparts but followed a different trajectory. During the crisis that led to the independence of British possessions in North America, the Caribbean colonies remained faithful to the empire. Andrew O'Shaughnessy has methodically shown that the reason for this attitude derived from the fact that Great Britain continued to be the basic cultural, social, and political reference point for subjects in the West Indies. This was reflected in the high rates of absenteeism, in the rural and urban architecture, and in the attendance of the sons of Caribbean planters in metropolitan schools instead of North American ones. These close ties to Great Britain therefore hindered the emergence of a local sense of belonging among the small number of free whites resident in the islands. Moreover, the British Caribbean islands depended on the military support of the metropolis to counter the constant threat posed by external and, especially, internal enemies. The risk of large-scale slave rebellions, which was felt in all Caribbean islands, cemented the attachment to Great Britain.

In the context of proliferating slave revolts during the 1760s and 1770s, colonists in the British West Indies welcomed and financed the establishment of metropolitan forces in the islands. Unlike the situation in North America, British forces in the Caribbean never became symbols of oppression. Perceptions of the metropolis on an economic level were equally distinct. In the context of growing French competition, British sugar-producing colonies increasingly depended on the metropolitan consumer market. Colonists in the Caribbean also criticized the contraband trade from North America that supplied the rival French colonies of Martinique, Guadeloupe, and, especially, Saint-Domingue. Thus, it is not surprising that the harsher trade and tax policies implemented in the aftermath of the Seven Years' War were seen in North America as a direct product of the West Indian lobby in the British Parliament.[92]

The prosperity of Saint-Domingue, which had been growing since earlier in the century, certainly influenced political choices in the British world. Between the 1730s and the 1740s, the output of sugar production in the French colony grew from ten thousand to forty thousand tons per year, helping the colony become the world's largest sugar producer by the mid-eighteenth century. New investments after 1763 further accelerated production. Sugar mills in the North Province (which had been established earlier) increased the scale of their operations, while expensive irrigation systems opened the plains of the West Province to sugar production. In the 1780s, Saint-Domingue supplied over half of all continental European markets.

The economic geography of Saint-Domingue was marked by the contrast between plains and *mornes* (mountainous highlands in the interior). The combination of an irregular geomorphology in the mornes, heavy rainfall, and temperate weather left these areas mostly untouched by sugar producers. This in turn made the mornes more accessible to those with a modest amount of capital, and a number of free whites (many of them connected to the sugar-producing sector) who wanted to become slaveholders themselves increasingly came to occupy these areas after the 1740s. These settlers produced indigo and, especially, coffee. Production of the latter increased during the 1740s and 1750s, reaching approximately seven thousand tons one year after the end of the Seven Years' War. Then came the coffee boom, with production in Saint-Domingue increasing fourfold between 1763 and 1790. Requiring less capital than sugar production, the coffee economy attracted some of the wealthier *gens de couleur*.

The main engine of growth during this period was the rising demand in France and the rest of the European continent. The enormous success of sugar and coffee production in Saint-Domingue led observers to call the island "the pearl of the Antilles" in the 1780s. More accurate, however, would be to call it "the pearl of France," since the tropical products exported by the island generated a highly lucrative metropolitan reexport trade based in Bordeaux. The production of these commodities led to an unprecedented coerced migration of human beings. Around 480,000 enslaved Africans were disembarked in the French colony between 1761 and 1790, half of whom arrived in the 1780s alone.[93]

The economic growth of Saint-Domingue had another social aspect, which carried profound political implications. Unlike Martinique and Guadeloupe, Saint-Domingue did not have restrictions on manumission or on the inheritance rights of the children born of white fathers and slave women. This led to the emergence of a group of freedmen and free blacks of considerable wealth. The situation changed in the aftermath of the Seven Years' War with the adoption of new official policies limiting manumission rights, all of which had already been implemented in other French colonies. These new metropolitan attitudes led to the marginalization of wealthy free people of color (who had been profiting from coffee and indigo production), one of the key factors ultimately leading to the war.

After the loss of Canada and eastern enclaves, the French Empire was limited to Caribbean colonies and entrepôts on the coast of Africa. Following the relatively easy occupation of Martinique and Guadeloupe by the British, many in Paris started to question the loyalty of Caribbean colonists. The great migration of poor whites—the *petits blancs*—to Saint-Domingue after 1763 increased these fears. The economic frustration of the petits blancs and the success of a growing number of gens de couleur led metropolitan powers and local masters to develop new projects reconfiguring colonial identities designed to reinforce racial cleavages. Racial hierarchies provided symbolic capital to white settlers by producing political equality among actors who were socially unequal. New racial codes based on new concepts of "Frenchness" divided colonial society in the following two decades. Free persons of color were radically restricted from participating in colonial public life because of their African descent. Wealthy slaveholders born in Saint-Domingue, who bore little resemblance to their African parents and grandparents, were increasingly seen as being closer to the crowds of African captives than to poor, free whites. This new institutional racism emerged from the frustrations and expectations created by the Seven Years' War and paved the way for the revolutionary outbreak of 1790–1791.[94]

The birth of the antislavery movement in England—which indirectly contributed to the radicalization of slavery debates during the French Revolution—should also be understood as part of the impact of the Seven Years' War on the Atlantic system of northwestern Europe. As Christopher Brown argues, the origins of British abolitionism can be traced back to the imperial reconfiguration that occurred between 1763 and 1783. Critiques of slavery were not rare in Britain between the late seventeenth and mid-eighteenth centuries. These British criticisms, which did not question slavery per se (focusing instead on the activities of slaveholders and slave traders), were grounded in Britain's lack of experience with colonial slavery before the seventeenth century. This in fact helped create a divergence between metropolitan and colonial norms that proved decisive in the long run. Imperial identity itself stimulated views that depicted colonial slavery as the antithesis of Britishness. Despite the proliferation of antislavery critiques, the decentralized structure of the British Empire—based on the principle of local self-government of the colonies—left no room for metropolitan legal regulations over slavery in the colonies before 1776. Moreover, many people stressed the necessity of coerced labor for the economic health of the empire.[95]

The American Revolution transformed this milieu. The widespread use of antislavery rhetoric by both sides (British and North American) led to an unprecedented politicization of slavery. But the emancipation proposals that emerged during the imperial crisis still had to deal with the question of how to conceive an empire without slavery. The key issue was not only political but also constitutional. Who had the authority to eventually abolish slavery? After all, the legal framework of colonial slavery in the British Empire had been created without parliamentary interference. New World colonists had full autonomy to make decisions about their internal problems, especially those related to slavery. Thus, it is not a coincidence that antislavery critiques of the 1770s—some of them calling for the abolition of slavery as a whole—were part of a broader criticism of the unrestricted power of the American colonists. The imperial defeat in North America silenced these abolitionist proposals (because London could not immediately act against the Caribbean slaveholders who remained loyal to the empire) but allowed antislavery publicists and politicians in the metropolis to focus their attention on the transatlantic slave trade. Not only did Parliament have the authority to regulate the latter, but such an attack could also have the effect of weakening the political power of Caribbean slaveholders in the medium term.[96]

The secession of the thirteen colonies influenced the emergence of the British abolitionist movement in many different ways. It led to the revival, for example, of old plans for the colonization of Africa, now clearly marked by antislavery goals. In the 1780s, militants involved in the Sierra Leone experiment (which mobilized black troops and former slaves freed by the British during the war against the United States) argued that the British Empire could both compensate for its losses in the New World and demonstrate the superiority of free (over slave) labor on the African continent itself. Some characteristics of slavery in the Atlantic system of northern Europe also contributed to shaping the British antislavery movement. The failure of Protestant missions, especially in the Caribbean, led many in the Anglican Church to join the abolitionist cause. The principal names, Brown argues, came from the Teston Circle: James Ramsay, Thomas Clarkson, and William Wilberforce. Inspired by the missionary efforts of James Ramsay in Saint Kitts, where local masters and authorities opposed the conversion of black slaves, members of the circle added the topic of the material and spiritual condition of slaves in the West Indies to evangelical debates regarding the disciplining of subaltern metropolitan classes (through religious teachings and policies against vagrancy, blasphemy, and drinking).

In 1784, still affected by the traumatic reality of American independence, Ramsay published what became one of the main treatises of the abolitionist movement, *An Essay on the Treatment and Conversion of African Slaves in the British Sugar Colonies*. Ramsay's knowledge about the subject, and the nature of his accusations against Caribbean slaveholders and metropolitan powers for all the horrors experienced by enslaved Africans in the Antilles, incited British public opinion. The proslavery reaction was immediate and generated a debate through pamphlets and treatises that persisted until the foundation of the Society for the Abolition of the Slave Trade in 1787. Having Wilberforce as its main contact in Parliament and Clarkson as its primary national speaker, the society launched its first campaign against the transatlantic slave trade in 1787–1788 with petitions signed by thousands of people to pressure Parliament.[97]

Members of the society—most of them evangelical or Quaker—had good, albeit distinct, reasons for becoming involved in the struggle against the trafficking (the initial target of antislavery action because of the undisputable right of Parliament to regulate it) of slaves. According to the Teston Circle, the campaign would work as a Trojan horse, leading to a reform of social behavior in Great Britain based on new religious patterns. The Quakers (the great financers of antislavery publications) in turn believed that the campaign would provide them with a chance to engage in parliamentary politics without going against the principles of their sect, while also contributing to the creation of a new group identity based on a defense of the abolitionist cause. Clarkson, the first full-time antislavery militant, played a key role in uniting the two groups. He also brought many manufacturing entrepreneurs from northern England into the movement, who, like the Quakers, believed that they would thus earn a political voice.

Moreover, the public campaign against the transatlantic slave trade gave Britain the chance to recover its collective dignity and self-esteem, which had been dealt a blow by US independence. It could demonstrate the British commitment to the ideal of freedom while simultaneously distinguishing Britain from the radicalism of the North American rebels. In other words, abolitionism offered the opportunity for the British public to identify themselves as free Christians, providing moral capital to those who participated in the movement as militants or who simply supported it. The first (and decisive) victory of the movement was already won in the 1780s, being played in the realm of metropolitan public opinion. The second came after Parliament accepted the petitions sent by Wilberforce, which inevitably generated debates on the subject.[98]

The Quaker connections across the North Atlantic (described by David Brion Davis as the "Antislavery International") played an important role in the beginnings of the antislavery campaign in Great Britain and the United States.[99] Members of the sect had been preaching against black slavery in the North American political arena since the immediate aftermath of the

Seven Years' War. Moreover, British rhetoric in America—structured around the duality of slavery and freedom—led, as we have seen, to a politicization of the institution. This rhetoric, combined with the view that black slavery and the transatlantic slave trade had been imposed on the colonists by metropolitan powers and merchants, contributed to the emergence of interpretations that saw the foundation of the United States of America as an attack against all forms of slavery, metaphorical or real. State assemblies had already debated the status of slavery within their territories during the conflict against Britain, with many of them passing legislation to end the transatlantic slave trade.[100]

The greatest debate about the institution in the United States, however, occurred at the federal level, a relatively novel practice that influenced subsequent Iberian experiences. During the sessions of the Constitutional Convention of 1787, the issue divided the state delegates to the point where "it seemed that the issue of slavery would lead to the breakup of the convention."[101] Along with the composition of the Senate and the nature of elections and presidential powers, slavery is seen by many historians as one of the main topics of disagreement among the creators of the Constitution. There were three main points of discussion on the issue: whether slaves should be counted for purposes of political representation and taxation; whether Congress had the power to regulate commercial relations with foreigners, including those engaged in the transatlantic slave trade; and, finally, whether Northern states should return fugitive slaves to their original Southern owners. The successful conclusion of the Constitutional Convention depended on political compromises between state representatives that could (at least temporarily) overcome these regional divergences. The solution to the first point—the famous Three-Fifths Compromise—did not institute the principle of one vote per person, since the Constitution did not establish the criteria for voting in national elections, instead leaving the decision to the states.[102]

Thus, the delegates of 1787 left the decision about what place former slaves could occupy in the new political order to each individual state. The decision to prohibit Congress from regulating the transatlantic slave trade for twenty years (until 1808) was also a compromise between defenders of slavery and their opponents. As a result, slave states such as Georgia and South Carolina were able to postpone the prohibition of the odious commerce but not to eliminate the threat of its ultimate extinction. The same can be said of the fugitive slave clause, which was approved without major debate by Northern representatives under the claim that the Union was indissoluble.[103]

Despite the compromises established between May and September 1787, arguments continued until the ratification of the constitutional letter in June of the following year. The acceptance of the document by all states of the Union ultimately sanctioned slavery and provided the institutional framework for its subsequent expansion across the North American territory. This led a number of historians, whose interpretation can be traced back to Garrisonian abolitionism, to argue that the US Constitution was clearly a proslavery document. The ensuing defenses of slavery based on the compromises of 1787–1788 seem to confirm this point. Lately, a number of other scholars have argued, however, that while the Constitution of 1787 was indeed used by defenders of slavery to bolster their case starting in the 1830s, the document also had an antislavery interpretation that was similarly employed by the enemies of the institution.[104]

So far, our argument has been that the American Revolution, the racialization of social relations in Saint-Domingue, and the emergence of the British abolitionist movement were all part of the crisis that affected the Atlantic system of northwestern Europe in the aftermath of the Seven Years' War. Despite the latter's impact on the Spanish and Portuguese Empires, as well as the multiple interimperial connections created by the capitalist world-economy and international politics, it is clear that the historical time of the Iberian Atlantic system was different from that of its northwestern European counterpart. At the time, there was nothing in Iberian imperial identities or in the ideological program of the Second Scholastic that could lead to an imperial collapse or to a critique of slavery.

After the Seven Years' War, however, Iberian enlightened reformers developed more radical interpretations of these different historical times. The key issue in this change was the conquest of Havana by the English. The downfall of the Caribbean fortress shocked Madrid by demonstrating the weakness of Spanish power in the Americas. It was also a warning to Lisbon that the same could happen to Rio de Janeiro, which (like Havana to Spanish America) served as a protective wall for the riches of Portuguese America.[105]

The enlightened reformism of the Iberians between the 1760s and 1780s was influenced by perceptions of a disparity of power and temporal divergence in

relation to the powers of northwestern Europe, differences that were now interpreted under the dichotomy of backwardness and progress. After the end of
the global conflict and the return of Havana (in exchange for the definitive
cession of Florida to the British), Spanish enlightened men of letters continued
to explore the idea that their empire needed to be profoundly reformed, its
physiognomy transformed. Thus, restoration did not mean going back to the
grandiose times of Ferdinand and Isabella, as seventeenth-century arbitristas
had argued, but rather creating something new. Contemporary men of letters
argued that in order to answer the challenges of the moment, the spirit of conquest that had been at the origin of the Spanish Empire had to be replaced by
the ethos of commercial societies like Britain.

In order to achieve this transformation, traditional regulations were modified to promote free imperial trade. Shortly after the seizure of Havana,
Pedro Rodríguez de Campomanes—one of the main Spanish proponents of
reform—wrote that ending the fleet system and the monopoly of Cádiz
would allow Spain (and its overseas possessions) to become part of a single
and vast internal market that would in turn generate wealth and power for
the empire as a whole. More important, however, was the fact that the conception of time in these reforms was inspired by the modern concept of progress. "Progress . . . combined experiences and expectations," Reinhart
Koselleck argues, "both endowed with a temporal coefficient of change. As
part of a group, a country, or finally, a class, one was conscious of being
advanced in comparison with the others; or one sought to catch up with or
overtake the others." According to Spanish reformers, therefore, the solution
to Spanish backwardness was to be found in the acceleration of historical
time through an emulation of French and British experiences.[106]

Cuba occupied a central place in this new context, becoming a kind of
laboratory for Bourbon reforms in America already in the early years of the
reign of Charles III (1759–1788). One of the earliest reforms was the creation
of the Real Intendencia de La Habana in 1764 to promote the expansion of
the slave economy in the island. The monopoly of the Real Compañía de
Comercio de La Habana over the tobacco trade, sugar, timber, and other
exports was dismantled around that same time. The commercial regulations
of 1765 opened the Antillean (and, therefore, Cuban) trade to many Spanish
ports and initiated the end of the Cádiz monopoly, completed after the end
of the fleet system in 1778. The system of imperial *comercio libre* was

implemented, with individual merchant ships trading in the main ports of America and Spain. The Crown also tried to improve access to the transatlantic slave trade. The weakness of Spanish slave traders became clear during the occupation of Havana, when British slave traders sold more than three thousand African captives to Cuban masters in less than one year. Metropolitan regulations over the traffic continued until the late eighteenth century, but after 1763 the number of contracts for the introduction of slaves into the island significantly increased.[107]

Bourbon reformers constantly emphasized the importance of the slave trade to the growth of the Cuban export sector. Given the scarcity of labor in Cuba, they argued that the introduction of African captives was a fundamental part of the proper exploitation of the island's natural resources. Campomanes, for example, stated that the "trade in blacks in the West Indies is one of the objects of great attention there." The English and the French had shown how successful slave plantations could be. The Spanish, he argued, should improve the less explored regions of the empire (such as Cuba) by stimulating the development of a Spanish branch of the transatlantic slave trade, thus increasing royal revenue. A royal officer, Agustín Crame (a German military engineer hired by Charles III to reorganize Spanish defenses in the Caribbean), reinforced the pro–slave trade arguments of Campomanes in 1768 when he wrote that "to think about the transmigration of more Spaniards [to Cuba] would be an attack on the good economy. Transporting foreigners would be costly, complicated, and full of inconveniences. Even if everything went well, Europeans would never adapt to the rigors of rural labor that are still restricted to slavery. Who would come from Europe to become a simple journeyman comparable to an unhappy slave?"[108]

The Spanish enlightened reformers, however, undoubtedly believed that the plantation slave economies of the British and French Caribbean had to be emulated and installed in Cuba. There was, therefore, a key convergence between the proposals of the Spanish enlightened reformers and the goals of the Havana oligarchy. Both groups aimed at transforming Cuba into a new sugar island. Like the enlightened metropolitans, the Havana oligarchy—composed of landowning families, merchants, and colonial administrators who had been posted to the island since the last third of the sixteenth century—was clearly united by the late eighteenth century. This group went through an important transformation in the second half of the seventeenth century with the growth of matrimonial alliances involving peninsular military officers and bureaucrats sent from Spain by Charles III. The cohesion of this oligarchy and the crystallization of their economic goals became clear over the second half of the eighteenth century. After the creation of the Real Intendencia de La Habana in 1764, members of its Ayuntamiento demanded the abolition of the Cádiz monopoly, the ending of taxes on Cuban products in Spanish and American ports, the dismantling of monopolies over sugar, timber, and leather, the protection of Cuban sugar in the metropolitan market, and the liberalization of the transatlantic slave trade.[109]

Metropolitan and local interest blocs in Cuba agreed on the central role of the military. In the aftermath of the Seven Years' War, Bourbon reformers had in fact articulated the dire need for fiscal, economic, and military reforms. More revenue would improve the defense of the empire, but a new economic basis for the exploitation of colonial resources had to be developed, which would in turn strengthen Spanish control over its overseas possessions. According to the new policies implemented in Cuba after 1763, colonial militia units and regular troops were put in charge of the island's defense. In order to convince local elites to join the military service, the Spanish Crown granted concessions and privileges such as the *fuero militar* (commanding positions in militias) and, especially, ennobling titles to prominent local families, some of whom had already been involved in sugar production. At the other end of the Cuban social spectrum were the *pardo* (a racial term for the mixed-race population), and *moreno* (black) troops in the Havana region. This system of social stratification was a modified version of older strategies of mobilization: free men of color in militia groups had the right to the same fuero militar of white militia groups and were under the direct command of their equals, with white officers occupying only higher ranks.[110]

The impact of the Seven Years' War was not as dramatic in Portugal as it had been in Spain, but it had comparable consequences in the colonial world. The Pactos de Familia (August 1761) between France and Spain (already under the rule of Charles III) in the final few years of the war disrupted the policy of neutrality that had characterized the Portuguese Crown since the treaties of Utrecht, with both powers threatening the Portuguese Empire with their militaries. The change became clear after Spanish troops invaded the Portuguese metropolis in the second quarter of 1762. The battles lasted less than one year and did not pose a serious threat to Portugal's overseas possessions in America (despite some fears that Rio de Janeiro could fall into French hands), but the need for British support to expel the Spanish from Portugal—or to evacuate the royal family to Brazil in case Lisbon was conquered—clearly showed the economic and military weakness of Portugal. It is not surprising that the assessments of the all-powerful minister Sebastião José de Carvalho e Melo and his collaborators regarding the Portuguese situation within European imperial politics were very similar to those of contemporary Spanish reformers, all of them marked by the backwardness/progress dichotomy.[111] Similarly, reforms promoted by Carvalho e Melo, the future Marquis of Pombal, after 1763 resembled those implemented in Cuba around the same time.

The relocation of the capital of the viceroyalty of Brazil from Bahia to Rio de Janeiro in 1763 also indicated how the English conquest of Havana had an impact on the Portuguese Empire. The move was in fact part of a broader series of reforms that aimed at strengthening Portuguese control over its possessions in America and reversing the decline in gold mining profits. As had been the case in the Spanish world, Pombaline policies had fiscal, economic, and military purposes. Moves to strengthen the ties between metropolis and colony, therefore, reflected an attempt to regain control over Atlantic commerce from the British. Inspired by the mercantilist practices of the northwestern European powers, the Marquis of Pombal stimulated the individual accumulation of capital by Portuguese merchants in an attempt to maintain the wealth generated by colonial exploitation within the Portuguese imperial economy. The expulsion of itinerant traders (*comissários volantes*) from Portuguese America in 1755 similarly aimed at strengthening the great national merchants. In the 1750s, Pombal adopted fiscal policies to control production, prices, and transportation costs of products such as sugar, tobacco, gold, and diamonds. Export tariffs and freight costs were reduced and inspectorships were created to control the quality and prices of sugar and tobacco.[112]

The most fundamental Pombaline policy, however, was the creation of privileged trading companies. In 1755, the Companhia Geral de Comércio do Grão-Pará e Maranhão was founded, followed four years later by the Companhia Geral de Comércio de Pernambuco e Paraíba. Their objectives were clear, the first of which was to initiate a slave plantation economy in the northern region of Portuguese America, where the main production had been *drogas do sertão* (tropical forest products such as vanilla, sarsaparilla, cacao, and cinnamon) based on indigenous labor. The Companhia do Grão-Pará e Maranhão was created to facilitate the introduction of African captives in the region and stimulate the plantation production of rice, cotton, and other goods. The Companhia de Pernambuco e Paraíba had similar goals. The company was founded to help in the recovery of the decadent plantation economy of the northeastern coast of Brazil by importing large numbers of enslaved Africans, thus reducing the price of sugar and stimulating the exploitation of new products such as cotton and cocoa.[113]

In the case of the more prosperous zones of Portuguese America connected to Minas Gerais—Bahia and Rio de Janeiro—there was no need for trading companies. Pombal acted upon them by abolishing the fleet system in 1765—the same year Bourbon reformers abolished the system in Cuba—and officially allowing coastal trade in Portuguese America one year later. It was also in this context that administrators of the south-central captaincies were instructed to promote the cultivation of a diversified range of products, including coffee, tobacco, cotton, rice, indigo, silk, hemp, and wheat. Moreover, since Portugal was the only European empire with formal territorial possessions in Africa, the Pombaline administration sought to reorganize their control over Angola in order to improve the slave trade networks that supplied captives to Portuguese America. Here lies one of the main differences between Brazil and Cuba in the context of Iberian reformism: while the foundations of a Spanish transatlantic slave trade still had to be *created*, Portuguese colonialism in the South Atlantic sought to *improve* a business that already existed. It is also important to stress the central importance of slavery in the reforms promoted during the reign of José I. Despite the supposed antislavery nature of the royal orders of 1761 and 1773 (which, respectively, abolished the slave trade to the metropolis and established a free womb law for the gradual emancipation of slaves living there), they never posed any threat to slavery in the empire. Slavery in the British Empire, on the other hand, had been shaken by the James Somerset case of 1772 and growing tensions in North America.[114]

The efforts to improve slavery in Portuguese America and Cuba also shed light on another aspect of the Pombaline and Bourbon reforms: the place of free black and mulatto populations in these imperial orders. The participation of former slaves, freedmen, and free people of color in the military defense of Portuguese America against external (such as the expulsion of the Dutch from Pernambuco) and internal (such as the battles against the Maroon communities of Minas Gerais in the early eighteenth century) enemies already had a long history by the mid-eighteenth century. The Pombaline reform of 1766, which created new pardo regiments separated from the traditional black troops of Henrique Dias, did not significantly change the forms of administration of these forces. Privileges such as access to positions with salaries comparable to those of officers of auxiliary white troops remained open to pardos and blacks. In Cuba, despite the frequent mobilization of free men of color since the sixteenth century, the organization of pardo and moreno militias with privileges similar to their counterparts in Portuguese America occurred only after the fall of Havana. In both cases, these groups were generally seen as a fundamental part of the colonial status quo, showing the shared goal of these Iberian reforms to strengthen the identity ties of all sectors of the colonial population with the metropolis.[115]

It is important to stress some key features of this process in Portuguese America. Silvia Hunold Lara has argued that while enlightened reformism turned many formerly excluded groups (such as Brazilian Indians, Christianized Asians and East Africans, free blacks and freedmen who had been born in Portugal, and new Christians) into "vassals of the Portuguese monarchy," the same was not true of the many free blacks, mulattoes, and freedmen of Portuguese America. "Where slavery ruled the social order and was massively African, the growing numbers of free blacks and mulattoes led to increasing tensions in social relations." These tensions, according to Lara, emerged "in increasingly racialized forms: the discrimination against mulattoes (freedmen and free) developed alongside the tendency to associate all blacks, *pardos*, mulattoes, and *mestiços* to slavery under the label of *negros*." The growing number of former slaves had, therefore, "an eminently disruptive political potential" for colonial society as a whole.[116]

Lara reached this conclusion based on her study of discourses coming from the metropolitan sphere of imperial power, namely the speeches of royal administrators who relocated to the colony in the last decades of the eighteenth century.[117] If we look at social practices in Portuguese America, however, the picture that emerges is different. In Minas Gerais, for example, the first half of the century witnessed a constant debate about the social and political place of the growing population of former slaves and their free children. If voices contrary to the social and economic ascension of former slaves and their descendants managed to obstruct (through a royal order of 1726) their access to the higher positions of local chambers, proposals such as that of Lourenço de Almeida—which prohibited mulattoes from receiving inheritances from their white fathers—were rejected by the Conselho Ultra-marino under the argument that these individuals were fundamental for peopling the captaincy. Thus, the predominant position in imperial policies was that "the demographic and social expansion of the freedmen would be positive if accompanied by strategies of control and integration." Among these was the participation in brotherhoods and, especially, military regiments. Metropolitan debates about the benefits of segregated incorporation or institutional exclusion of former slaves continued throughout the eighteenth century. Social practices, however, were for the most part marked by inclusion, a characteristic that became widespread in the second half of the eighteenth century as a result of the pressures of freedmen and free people of color themselves, who sought to be integrated into the wider colonial slave society.[118]

In sum, the tensions that culminated in the crisis of the Atlantic system of northwestern Europe between the 1760s and the 1780s had no equivalent in the Iberian Atlantic system. While the political culture (based on Atlantic republicanism and new concepts of Britishness) that flourished in North America caused an imperial crisis and the subsequent declaration of independence of the United States, the ideals of good government inherited from the Second Scholastic pervaded the negotiations between colonists and peninsular authorities in the Iberian world. Emancipation was never a serious option in the latter, not even during the violent upheavals in New Granada and Peru between 1780 and 1783. While free blacks witnessed the extreme racialization of their position in Saint-Domingue, their counterparts in Portuguese America and Cuba were granted privileges in exchange for their contribution to maintaining the colonial order, thus avoiding the racial stigmatization of their social place. Finally, while the future of the transatlantic slave trade and black slavery was debated in the parliaments, constituent assemblies, and presses of Great Britain and the United States, the Iberian empires sought to expand the institution of slavery without any public discussion about its legitimacy in the colonial world. At this time, Portugal and Spain sought to emulate the practices that led to the material success of the

Atlantic system of northwestern Europe: a highly capitalized slave agriculture in colonial areas connected to the commercial growth of the metropolis. They nonetheless maintained the well-established patterns of segregated incorporation of both freedmen and free people of color.

The Revolution of Saint-Domingue and the Deepening of the Crisis

The crisis in the Atlantic system of northwestern Europe during the 1790s and 1800s deepened to such an extent that it ultimately extended into the Iberian Atlantic system. The impact of these events on the Portuguese and Spanish Empires will be discussed in the next chapter. For now it is sufficient to outline in a few pages the general forces unleashed by the French revolutionary process in the Old and New Worlds as well as their immediate implications for slavery in the Atlantic system of northwestern Europe.

The nature of political and ideological links connecting the American and French Revolutions is still the subject of debate among scholars, but there is a general historiographical consensus that French involvement in the first contributed to the start of the latter. The enduring financial problems of the French Bourbons, which had been exacerbated by the Seven Years' War, reached new extremes in the early 1780s. Louis XVI provided tremendous military support to the American rebels in their struggle against their common British enemy. In reaction to the poor situation of the royal treasury, the minister of finance, Charles Alexandre de Calonne (1783–1787), attempted to reorganize the fiscal basis of the kingdom by taxing the nobility and the clergy, both of whom reacted immediately. These failed attempts at reform were part of broader tensions that divided French society and played a decisive role in starting the revolution of 1789.[119]

On the other side of the Atlantic, metropolitan tensions combined with local ones in incendiary ways. As we have seen, the social standing of the gens de couleur in Saint-Domingue diminished during the 1770s and 1780s. At the same time, the collective ideals of autonomy of the white population became stronger. These were based both on the opposition to obstacles to free trade with foreign merchants (especially North Americans) and on the example provided by the independence of the United States. These ideals were also behind the opposition to the royal ordinances of 1784 and 1785 (which had established regulations for absentee-owned plantations and created institutional mechanisms to address slave complaints). Saint-Domingue planters reacted to these metropolitan initiatives, arguing that external interferences would inevitably undermine the slave order. The discussion led to the closing of the Cap-Français court in 1787 (one of the first to oppose orders coming from Versailles) and a ban on colonial assemblies in Saint-Domingue at the exact same moment that they had been allowed in Martinique and Guadeloupe. While the demands for autonomy among the white Saint-Domingue colonists became stronger in this context, soon turning into open rebellion, the large number of slaves—who continued to increase because of the active transatlantic slave trade—interpreted the episode as an indication that the king and the monarchy were on their side.[120]

The transition from the Estates-General to the National Constituent Assembly (which became the first European institution of this kind to accept the participation of deputies from overseas colonies) in France in July 1789 further stoked rising tensions between colonists and metropolitan authorities, whites and free people of color, and masters and slaves. These colonial cleavages penetrated the National Assembly, marking the participation of members of the Society of the Friends of the Blacks (Amis des Noirs) (which, inspired by its British counterpart, focused not only on the transatlantic slave trade but also on the civil and political rights of the gens de couleur) and defenders of the colonial lobby organized around the Massiac Club (who made up approximately 15 percent of the National Assembly). The latter managed to obstruct any debate related to the slave trade and slavery in the National Assembly and leave the power to decide on the political participation of blacks and mulattoes to the new colonial assemblies. The exclusion of the gens de couleur based on the racial arguments that had been spreading since the 1760s heightened the tensions in Saint-Domingue, culminating in the revolt of the free people of color in October 1790. The brutal repression of the associates of the mulatto leader Vincent Ogé, the proselytism of the Friends of the Blacks, and the many doubts regarding the loyalty of white colonists in Saint-Domingue pushed the National Assembly in May 1791 to grant political rights to blacks and mulattoes, as long as they were born of free parents and satisfied the income criteria. In August 1791, shortly after the arrival of this news in Saint-Domingue, the great slave revolt in the North Province of the colony started.[121]

The organization of the rebel slaves impressed planters and authorities and, more importantly, completely transformed the political balance of the colony. The colonists' leaders were fully aware of the existing imperial disputes and operated not only according to them but also in consonance with the demands of slaves. This explains, for example, the uprising in the name of the king (against the planters who had obstructed the ordinances of 1784 and 1785 and now commanded the local assemblies) or the alliance with the Spaniards from Santo Domingo. The deepening of the revolution in Europe also played a key role in shifting political relations in the Antilles. The large-scale slave revolt, the conflicts involving the citizenship of the gens de couleur, the collapse of the constitutional monarchy in France, the execution of Louis XVI, the proclamation of the Republic, and the arrival of an expeditionary force (commanded by a civil commission named by the new Legislative Assembly) with the goal of establishing the new republican order on overseas territories led the white planters of Saint-Domingue to seek British and Spanish support. These forces combined to heighten the impact of the French revolutionary events in the Caribbean, becoming enemies of the Republic and, especially, paving the way for the abolition of slavery. According to the Republican commissaries, the only solution to their complicated situation in mid-1783—when they were surrounded by British troops in the western and parts of the southern regions of the colony (which had approximately 250,000 black slaves) and black rebels and their Spanish allies in the North—was getting the enslaved population to support the Republic. This was the context of Léger-Félicité Sonthonax's proclamation in August 1793, which abolished slavery in the northern region of Saint-Domingue. Two months later, Étienne Polverel extended the measure to two other regions of the colony.[122]

The National Convention confirmed these measures after the Jacobin decree of February 4, 1794, which abolished black slavery in all French colonies without compensation for slave owners. No other European power had ever considered such a radical act. The decree sealed the alliance with the armed former slaves of Saint-Domingue, recognizing their victories in the battlefield. However, it also led to a problem that had barely been considered by the political imagination of the time: the conversion of the large mass of former captives into citizens. The North American experience of the previous decade did not provide an adequate precedent, since the US Constitution of 1787 had delegated the issue to the state level. According to the solution approved in August 1795 by the Constitution of the Year III, the ideal of ison-omy united the French national territory and, therefore, converted the colo-nies into departments and their inhabitants (including former slaves) into citizens with the same rights of those resident in France.[123]

Former captives faced multiple barriers to full citizenship. From the beginning of the revolution, many in the antislavery field had been arguing that Africans and their enslaved descendants would have to go through a long apprenticeship period that would prepare them for full freedom and citizenship. This idea defined the gradual emancipation plans of, for exam-ple, Nicolas de Condorcet. Those in the proslavery camp were preoccupied with maintaining both the racial order in a slave society and defending the supposedly innate inferiority of blacks and mulattoes, and they argued that emancipation would never arrive. Although not questioning the abolitionist act of February 1794, the Constitution of the following year seemed to acknowledge the truth of these views by establishing "special laws" for the administrative and judicial organization of overseas territories. The use of these "special laws" by the Massiac Club at the beginning of the revolution was based on the assumption that the laws of Europe could not be applied to the Antilles because of its climate and customs. Africans and their descend-ants, therefore, could not automatically become citizens. At most, according to proslavery defenders, they should return to their innate civil condition, which was slavery. While a considerable number of former slaves did enjoy citizenship rights through military service, most of those who continued to toil in the fields faced overwhelming obstacles to acquire such rights.[124]

Arguments against the conversion of slaves into citizens were utilized by the proslavery group, which had quickly reorganized during the battles between the British and the troops of Toussaint-Louverture in Saint-Domingue. Political dynamics in France, the victory of the black general over the British, and the consolidation of his rule in Saint-Domingue tempo-rarily cut short the plans to reinstitute slavery on the island. The moment for revenge came after the ascension of Napoleon Bonaparte and many former Caribbean slaveholders (including Bonaparte's wife) to power in 1799. A proj-ect to re-create conditions similar to those before the revolution was soon set in motion, starting with the Constitution of 1801, which officially trans-formed Saint-Domingue into a colonial territory subject to the "special laws" of the French Empire. The final Napoleonic effort to reenslave the black

rebels came with the expedition to Saint-Domingue of eighty thousand soldiers under the command of Charles Leclerc. However, the total war of 1802–
1803 led not only to Napoleon's greatest defeat before his failed invasion of
Russia but also, and more importantly, to the foundation of the second independent state of the Americas, Haiti.[125]

What impact did the Haitian Revolution have on slavery in the Americas?
This is an old subject of debate among scholars. The most common answer
stresses that the collapse of the largest sugar and coffee producer in the world
led to, first, new economic opportunities for rival slaveholders and, second,
a widespread fear of revolts in other slave societies of the hemisphere. These
discussions have reappeared during the two-hundredth anniversary of
Haiti's independence. Three main interpretations provide an overview of the
present state of the debate.

Reinforcing the classic interpretation, David Brion Davis writes that the
"Haitian Revolution was indeed a turning point in history. Like the Hiro-
shima bomb, its meaning could be rationalized or repressed but never really
forgotten, since it demonstrated the possible fate of every slaveholding society
in the New World." While the event was received as a warning in all slave
zones of the Americas, the growth of slavery in Brazil and Cuba indicated that
in some regions greed overcame fear. In the British Empire, however, the slave
revolution played a decisive role in ending the transatlantic slave trade. Seymour Drescher in turn relativized the idea of a turning point. The right question, he argues, is "whether the Haitian Revolution hastened or delayed slave
emancipation in the Americas." Criticizing the thesis of "the great fear," Drescher believes that fear did not stop the French plans for slavery nor influence
the British decision of 1807. Global antislavery pressure in the nineteenth century came from Great Britain and not Haiti, for political reasons that were
disconnected from an alleged fear of slave insurrections. Finally, Robin Blackburn defends the idea of a turning point by arguing that the Haitian Revolution destroyed the overwhelming obstacles of the 1790s to the abolition of
slavery. The event played a central role in ending the transatlantic slave trade
and setting in motion the abolition of slavery in British colonies, in the slave
emancipations of Spanish America, and in the reinforcement of "a process of
differentiation within the Atlantic world, dividing it more neatly into slave
and non-slave zones." According to him, the "Haitian Revolution, and prior
triumph of revolutionary emancipationism in Saint-Domingue, may have

helped to remobilize the slave regime where the slaveholders were strongest and conditions for slavery expansion most propitious—above all in Cuba, Brazil, and the U.S. South—but in other parts of the Atlantic world it helped to supply a context where significant further advances could be made."[126]

Blackburn's approach is a good example of how to avoid the risks of a conception of linear time, particularly pronounced in the arguments of Drescher but also present in those of Davis.[127] The Revolution of Saint-Domingue, an inseparable part of the French Revolution, can be conceptualized as the decisive moment of the broader formation of a new historical structure of Atlantic slavery emerging from the two previous coexisting ones. In other words, the decades between the 1790s and the 1820s represented the culmination of the crisis of slavery in the Atlantic system of northwestern Europe. This is clear in the effects of the Haitian Revolution on the British antislavery movement. If collective actions of slave resistance and the war against France paralyzed British abolitionists during the 1790s, the economic crisis of rival French colonies in the early 1800s, the failure of the Napoleonic expedition of 1802–1803, the independence of Haiti, and British naval control over the Atlantic paved the way for the acceptance of the abolitionist platform by metropolitan authorities. Thus, the Haitian Revolution was closely connected to the abolition of the transatlantic slave trade in 1807, an event that destroyed the prospects of British slavery's expansion.[128] Second, Saint-Domingue initiated a new pattern of slave resistance in which the actions of enslaved subjects in the Caribbean were directly connected to the dynamics of antislavery parliamentary politics in the centers of metropolitan power. This became clear in slave rebellions in the British colonies after the Napoleonic Wars (Barbados, 1816; Demerara, 1823; Jamaica, 1831–1832), each of them playing a fundamental role in the abolition of slavery in the 1830s.[129]

The decades between the 1790s and the 1820s, however, can also be seen as the starting point of a new historical structure of Atlantic slavery, a *new temporality*. In the context of the crisis of the Iberian Atlantic system, which had been particularly aggravated by the invasion of the peninsula by Napoleonic troops, the Brazilian Empire, the Spanish colony of Cuba, and the southern states of the United States participated in the establishment of this new structure. The following chapters will explore this process in the cases of Brazil and Cuba.

The Crisis of the Iberian Atlantic System and Slavery in the Constitutional Experiences of Cádiz, Madrid, Lisbon, and Rio de Janeiro, 1790–1824

The Saint-Domingue Revolution in the Brazilian and Cuban Historiographies

A crucial and enduring debate has emerged regarding the effects of the Saint-Domingue Revolution on the political dynamics of Portuguese America and the Spanish colony of Cuba. Cuban loyalty to Spain throughout the nineteenth century, when a number of independence movements and new republics emerged in different parts of Spanish America, has been interpreted since the 1820s as a consequence of the slavery issue. The idea that the expansion of slavery in the export sector became the main obstacle for Cuban slaveholders to embrace independence, fearful that the rupture with Spain could lead to a repetition of the revolutionary events and racial war that marked the founding of Haiti, appeared in the writings of many political groups on the island during the nineteenth century (defenders of the Spanish Empire, ideologues of independence, annexationists, and autonomists), making its way into the nationalist historiography of the periods before and after the revolution of 1959.[1] In a famous essay on the thought of José Antonio Saco published more than half a century ago, Manuel Moreno Fraginals analyzed the dilemmas of creating national sovereignty on the island using the expression "nation of plantation." A representative of old criollo groups displaced by the devastating expansion of sugar interests, Saco was among those who "did not want to transform Cuba into an island of sugar and slaves, aspiring for a nation and not a plantation."[2] The interpretation of Moreno

Fraginals was, in fact, connected to a broader topos of Cuban political and historiographical thought. His perspective juxtaposed the world of free peasants (the basis of nationality and independence) with the world of slave plantations (the basis of Spanish colonial domination and US neocolonial power), inspiring the famous counterpoint between tobacco and sugar made by Fernando Ortiz and, later, Juan Pérez de la Riva's idea of an "island with two histories."[3]

Historians have nonetheless explored reasons why Cuba persisted as a slave economy, besides the simple explanation that they feared slave revolts. According to José Antonio Piqueras, current explanations for Cuban loyalty explore three additional elements besides the slavery issue. First, Spanish military presence in Cuba had become stronger as a result of reforms implemented after the British occupation of Havana in 1762 and the strategic place of the island in the context of the independence wars on the continent. Second, the Saint-Domingue Revolution and the many Spanish defeats on the continent generated large flows of refugees to the island. Each of these new blocs strongly opposed independence and feared possible rebellions involving the black and mulatto populations. Third, the Havana oligarchy supported the reforms of Ferdinand VII, believing that Cuba would continue to benefit from changes, as had been the case since the Bourbon reforms. The articulation of these elements, however, was still produced by slavery. In the words of Piqueras: "Benefiting from the recent growth, criollo planters feared that a separatist insurrection and a subsequent violent Spanish response would destroy the wealth of the island, with slaves taking advantage of the situation to start a rebellion that would subvert the social order."[4]

Historiographical discussions about the impact of the Saint-Domingue Revolution on Brazil are more recent than discussions about the impact on Cuba, but they are equally important. Two important essays written by Kenneth Maxwell and Maria Odila Leite da Silva Dias were published during the 150th anniversary of Brazilian independence. Maxwell tried to explicate the connections between the challenges to Portuguese colonial rule over America in the 1790s and the imperial project established after the arrival of the royal family in Rio de Janeiro. In his view, the vassals residing in Minas Gerais who conspired against the Portuguese Crown between 1788 and 1789 wanted to create a republican government inspired by the US example (without fearing the slave system that supported them). After the failure of the plan and, especially, with the growth and spread of revolutionary ideas on both sides of the Atlantic, the political platform of slaveholders in Portuguese America started to change. The slave revolt in Saint-Domingue stimulated the rebirth of agricultural exports while leading to growing doubts about the benefits of adopting a republican platform in a slave society. Slaveholders' fears were partially confirmed by the conspiracy of 1798 in Bahia, which made clear the threat of racial polarization. Thus, the chain of events connecting 1789, 1791, and 1798 helped seal the alliance between the slaveholding settlers of Portuguese America and the metropolis. Embodied in these developments was a new idea of a Luso-Brazilian Empire, an idea developed by a group led by the minister and secretary of state of the navy and overseas dominions, Rodrigo de Sousa Coutinho. This alliance reached its peak when the center of imperial power shifted to America in 1808.[5]

A similar interpretation of the role played by Saint-Domingue in the politics of the Luso-Brazilian Empire was offered by historian Maria Odila Leite da Silva Dias, who specializes in the period after 1808. Concerned with the peculiarities of Brazilian political emancipation, especially its "moderate" nature (marked by the absence of significant military conflicts and the maintenance of the monarchy), Dias stressed the process of the "interiorization" of the metropolis in the colony. The establishment of the Joanine court in Rio de Janeiro and the "embedding of the Portuguese state in the Center-South" offered a safe exit to the proprietary classes of this region in the context of the imperial crisis that followed the Porto Revolution, a process defined by the establishment of alliances with their counterparts in the other provinces of Brazil. The pact was cemented, according to the author, by the threat of collective action against the order by blacks and mulattoes, both free and slaves. In her words, "the sense of social insecurity and 'haitianism' (i.e., the great fear of an insurrection of slaves or mulattoes, as exemplified by Haiti in 1794), should not be underestimated as typical elements of the mentality of that time, stereotyped reflexes of the European conservative ideology and counterrevolution. They acted as fundamental political forces and had a decisive role at a time when regionalisms and the diversity of interests could have divided the ruling classes of the colony."[6]

There has been a historiographical consensus in the past two decades that the fear of collective action involving slaves, and their eventual association with free blacks and mulattoes (a fear stimulated by the revolution in

Saint-Domingue), had a central role in the political decisions taken by social agents at the time of Brazilian independence.[7] Considering these two historiographical interpretations of Brazilian and Cuban slavery, the present chapter initially explores the impact of the Saint-Domingue Revolution on Portuguese America and on the Spanish colony of Cuba between 1790 and 1808. Based on the writings of enlightened Iberian men of letters and statesmen, our objective is to show how the forces unleashed by the crisis of the Atlantic system of northwestern Europe shaped the results of the events of 1807–1808, which represented a point of inflection in the historical structures of the Iberian Atlantic and linked the destinies of Brazil and Cuba. On the one hand, the Napoleonic invasion of Iberia, the arrest of the Spanish royal family, and the escape of the Portuguese royal family to America separated the trajectories of the two Iberian empires. In the Spanish case, the emergence of the *juntista* movement in the metropolis generated a quick response overseas, which paved the way for the independence movements of Spanish America. The Portuguese case in turn saw the establishment of the headquarters of the monarchy on the other side of the Atlantic and a number of measures, including the opening of ports to friendly nations, that completely changed the empire without generating immediate opposition to the House of Braganza. On the other hand, the abolition of the transatlantic slave trade to British territories by the British Parliament in 1807 led to the beginning of an international antislavery campaign the following year. In the next five decades, the main target of their actions became Portugal, independent Brazil, and Spain—or, more specifically, Cuba.

The following section of this chapter explores the political reconstruction of Brazilian and Cuban slavery in the context of Iberian constitutional experiences (1810–1824). As we have seen, after the 1770s the direct connection between colonialism and slavery that had been the basis of the Atlantic system of northwestern Europe came to an end. Colonial (as well as slave) relations entered a period of crisis, clearly expressed in the conflicts that pervaded the constitutional and parliamentary experiences involving metropolises, colonies, provinces, and states. Slavery was one of the main issues debated on these occasions. The answers provided by political actors in these instances were decisive for determining not only the different political arrangements in each region but especially the future of black slavery.

The constitutional and parliamentary experiences in the United States,

Britain, and France were closely observed by actors in Portugal and Spain, and their overseas territories. In the context of the crisis of the Iberian Atlantic system, these precedents provided general guidelines for the Spaniards and Portuguese within their respective constitutional processes. Historians, however, have not explored these issues. Synthesizing studies within an Atlantic framework, such as those by David Brion Davis and Robin Blackburn, have glossed over the theme of Iberian constitutional experiences, while specific studies have treated them in isolation from each other.[8] This chapter fills this gap by providing an integrated analysis of the arguments and strategies that supported the political project of Cuban and Brazilian slaveholding representatives in the Cortes of Cádiz (1810–1814), Madrid (1820–1823), Lisbon (1820–1822), and the Constituent Assembly of Rio de Janeiro (1823).

Two main themes connected to slavery were the subjects of debate on these occasions: the transatlantic slave trade and the rights of citizenship for freedmen and other African descendants. The solution found by deputies in Cuba and Brazil to the first issue was similar: silencing the discussion on the slave trade in constitutional debates while taking it to the diplomatic arena. On the second issue, their responses were distinct. While Cuban representatives agreed on restricting access for freedmen and African descendants to the rights of citizenship established by the Constitution of Cádiz (1812), deputies from Brazil in Lisbon and Rio de Janeiro defended the granting of such rights, as recognized by the Political Constitution of the Empire of Brazil (1824). Our hypothesis is that the differentiated impact of the Saint-Domingue Revolution on Brazil and Cuba played a central role in establishing these differences.

The Impact of Saint-Domingue on the Iberian Atlantic System, 1790–1808

Within the reformist scope of the Luso-Brazilian enlightenment, which aimed at revitalizing the economy of the Portuguese Empire—especially its American dimension—through the diversification of exports and the improvement of traditional sectors, the slave agriculture of the French and British Caribbean was taken as the example to be followed. As we have seen, the origins of these policies can be traced back to the Pombaline period. The fall of the powerful Portuguese minister in 1777 did not alter them. On the contrary, with the foundation of the Royal Academy of Sciences of Lisbon two years later (part of the recently established University of Coimbra), the ideals of Pombaline reformism penetrated the proposals developed by enlightened Luso-Brazilians during the last decade of the eighteenth century.[9]

In any case, there was no consensus regarding slavery among the members of the Royal Academy. We can see at least two different positions on the issue among the students of the University of Coimbra who had been born in Portuguese America. The first one, more critical, can be found in the writings of Luis Antonio de Oliveira Mendes. Writing about the economy of Bahia (the captaincy where he had been born) between 1789 and 1790 (thus before the slave uprising in Saint-Domingue), Oliveira Mendes assessed the condition of local export activities, which after a long period of crisis were recovering because of the new opportunities generated by the war of independence in the United States. Prospects in 1789, however, were not very promising given that sugar produced in Saint-Domingue dominated the open markets of Europe. Among his many propositions to stimulate the economy of Bahia, Oliveira Mendes suggested that slaves should be treated better as a strategy to make them work more, critically describing slaveholding practices in the state with terms such as "tyranny" and "great tyranny" (*tiraníssimos*). Still, what is striking in his account is his strong attack against the transatlantic slave trade between the Recôncavo and the Gold Coast of Africa.[10] Oliveira Mendes even considered that its suppression might be possible if masters decided to follow his suggestion to encourage marriages between slaves and more frequent employment of freedmen as wage laborers.

The second position can be seen in what may have been the first published account in Portuguese of the slave uprising in Saint-Domingue. In a speech to the Royal Academy (published already in 1791 as the third volume of the *Memórias Econômicas* series), José Joaquim da Cunha de Azeredo Coutinho stressed "the high prices of sugar in all of Europe because of the disgraceful revolution in the French colonies, our main competitors in this kind of agriculture." Citing the ideas of contemporary political economists on the advantages of a price system based on free markets, Azeredo Coutinho called for a reconsideration of price policies for American products, which had not changed since the Pombaline period. Such a change became all the more urgent since disturbances in the Caribbean had begun opening new opportunities in European markets. Although unable to foresee the end of French rule in Saint-Domingue as a result of slave action, Azeredo Coutinho believed that the moment was one of acceleration of historical time. In his words, "the unexpected revolution in the French colonies is one of those extraordinary impulses with which providence stops the ordinary order of things: now that those colonists have their hands tied in relation to agriculture, before they restart it, it is necessary for us to improve ours."[11]

Oliveira Mendes returned to the issue of slavery two years after Azeredo Coutinho published his account on sugar prices, renewing his critical remarks on the subject. This time, he discussed the conditions of the transatlantic slave trade, from the capture of slaves in Africa to their sale in Brazilian ports. Without mentioning the Caribbean events of 1791–1793, Oliveira Mendes described slaving practices in the Portuguese Empire in ways that put him very close to some of the most radical critics of slavery in the Atlantic world at the time. His terminology seems to have bothered the other members of the Royal Academy of Sciences in Lisbon, since it took eleven years for the text to be published (as part of the *Memórias Econômicas* series in 1812), crucially, with significant changes to its antislavery tone.[12]

Not that the *academy* was openly proslavery. In 1794, for example, the recently nominated bishop of Pernambuco, the same Azeredo Coutinho, published his *Essay About the Commerce Between Portugal and Its Colonies*, in which he stressed the centrality of the African slave trade for the Portuguese colonial system of the South Atlantic. Two years later, after reading about William Wilberforce's antislavery speeches in the British Parliament, Azeredo Coutinho felt the need to defend the legitimacy of the Portuguese transatlantic slave trade and the enslavement of Africans. This time, however, the bishop did not receive the support of the Royal Academy of Sciences, which refused to publish the piece. It would only come out in Britain in 1798 in a French translation. It is striking that Azeredo Coutinho did not mention Saint-Domingue in the text, something the British editor felt the need to do in a new preface in order to criticize the French Revolution, the antislavery campaign of the Amis des Noirs, and their consequences in the Antilles. It is clear that the publication of Azeredo Coutinho's account in 1798 served, above all, the pro–slave trade campaign in England, precisely when British troops were launching their final attack against Toussaint-Louverture.[13]

Despite some occasional comments about slavery by figures such as Oliveira Mendes and Azeredo Coutinho, historian João Pedro Marques describes a general silence in Portugal over the issue between 1790 and 1808. The reasons for this were the censorship—official or not—which seems to have affected both Oliveira Mendes and Azeredo Coutinho, and the sense of security among Portuguese authorities brought about by the relative geographical isolation of the South Atlantic in relation to the revolutionary epicenters of the Caribbean.[14] With the discussion blocked in the few spaces available for public debate in the absolutist Portuguese world, news of Saint-Domingue circulated mainly in the writings of metropolitan authorities.

Indeed, the sources explored by Kenneth Maxwell in his analysis of the impact of the Saint-Domingue uprising on political perceptions among slaveholders in Portuguese America are mainly letters exchanged between Portuguese authorities in the metropolis and overseas, without any reference to documents produced by colonists. One such letter, written on February 21, 1792 (and addressed to Martinho de Mello e Castro and other captaincy governors of Portuguese America), has been widely used by historians as evidence of the widespread fears of the possible impact that the Saint-Domingue Revolution could have on Brazil.[15] The letter authorized two French ships on a scientific expedition to stop at a Brazilian port, while instructing authorities to keep a close watch on their crews, keeping in mind rumors in Paris that revolutionary clubs wanted to "spread the abominable and destructive principles of Liberty." These principles—which had already fanned "the flames of revolt and insurrection, stimulating the uprising of slaves against their masters and stimulating a Civil War on the French part of the island of S. Domingos between some and others, where the most atrocious cruelties [were perpetrated], unknown even among the most barbarous and ferocious nations"—had also been rapidly spreading to continental Europe.[16] In other words, Portuguese authorities interpreted the revolt in Saint-Domingue as an integral part of the revolutionary process in France. This was the main reason why it was advised that the activities of any French person who eventually arrived in Brazil should be closely watched, not an alleged fear that the example of Saint-Domingue could disrupt the colonial slave society of Portuguese America.

That the anxieties of the Portuguese authorities lay more on the broader attacks on the structures of colonial power than on the specific fear of a large-scale slave revolt became evident in a famous piece written by Rodrigo de Sousa Coutinho between 1797 and 1798 on the reconstitution of Luso-Brazilian imperial relations. Considered in the historiography to be the most comprehensive Portuguese answer to the conjunctural crisis of the 1790s, this document shows that the great fear was the end of colonial ties with the motherland (*mãe-pátria*), as had happened in North America and had been defended in the conspiracy of Minas Gerais. At that moment, Saint-Domingue was not an example of such a rupture, since the former slaves remained loyal to the Republic of France. In his few references to slavery, dom Rodrigo made a few suggestions to increase the importation of enslaved Africans and the diversification of production in the American colonies.[17]

The suggestions of dom Rodrigo stimulated new efforts to improve slave trade networks in Africa as well as the publication of the series *O Fazen-deiro do Brazil* (organized by Frei José Mariano da Conceição Velloso), which made the latest writings from the British and French colonies on agriculture in the New World available to Luso-Brazilian vassals.[18] A letter to the governor of Bahia from 1799 dealing with the bilateral trade between the Recôncavo and the Gold Coast, for example, noted the decline of Dutch operations in that area ("given the difficulty of that nation after their sub-jection to the French to help the São Jorge Castle") as well as the operations of the French, "who have by themselves disentangled that trade, abolishing slavery." "Thus," the letter concluded, "this seems to be the perfect moment to give the Portuguese trade on that coast the consistency it has not had thus far." One possible strategy would be to "abolish the *Regimento das Arqueações*" of March 28, 1684, which had established a minimum amount of space allotted per slave onboard slave ships.[19] Ironically, the same indi-viduals who proposed the end of this seventeenth-century law in 1799 would later use it to defend the slave trade against the attacks of British abolitionists, arguing that it demonstrated that the Portuguese followed humanitarian principles in their slaving practices.

One interesting case that we can use to evaluate the impact of Saint-Domingue on Portuguese America during this period can be found in the seditious movement of 1798 in Bahia. Many historians argue that the "Incon-fidência Baiana" was marked by the participation of the subaltern sectors of the captaincy, who, inspired by the French, wanted to subvert the colonial order by ending Portuguese rule and establishing a representative republic based on equality before the law (thus eliminating social and racial distinctions). The participation of pardos and free blacks in the sedition supposedly frightened slaveholders. "To slaveholders," Kenneth Maxwell argues, "the words of Bahian mulattoes made the contagion of Saint-Domingue a concrete reality."[20]

Historian István Jancsó, however, has stressed one of the main problems in this interpretation: the range of participants in the sedition was larger than has been traditionally argued and included young members of the local elite. The repression carried out by the Portuguese Crown focused on the subaltern sectors, acquitting the sons of the local elite as part of the broader metropolitan project to reform colonial relations. It was in this context, specifically in the writings of metropolitan agents based in Bahia (such as the governor, Fernando José de Portugal), that the narrative of the event as a slave revolt emerged. In the words of Jancsó: "The violence of repression showed to those sectors of the colonial elites that were misled by political fantasies that their real interests lay in their connection to Lisbon," thus indicating that "this revolution, in case of success, would be led by poor unenlightened pardos, which would be the equivalent to a collapse of the social order, a new Saint-Domingue."[21]

In sum, the political impact of the Saint-Domingue Revolution on the Portuguese colonial world was relatively limited. It was the opposite in Cuba. People from all social sectors (masters, slaves, freedmen and free blacks in the cities and the countryside) on the Spanish island closely followed the revolutionary events in the neighboring French territories, despite the efforts of Spanish authorities to prevent news of the events from reaching the colony. Confidential letters by colonial authorities that were leaked by their messengers, personal reports from soldiers who fought republicans and rebel slaves, testimony from Saint-Domingue refugees, and news published by the *Gaceta de Madrid* kept Cubans updated about everything that happened on the neighboring island. Moreover, part of the Havana oligarchy had directly experienced the events as leaders of the Spanish military regiments sent to Saint-Domingue after 1793. The contrast with Portuguese America, where "news from Haiti" arrived through statesmen resident in Portugal, is clear. The absence of channels similar to those in the Caribbean made Saint-Domingue a distant example, with little influence over the political choices of Brazilian slaveholders.[22]

The impact of the Saint-Domingue Revolution on Cuba is clear in the writings of Francisco de Arango y Parreño, who was born into the creole elite of Havana in 1765. In the mid-1780s, after his parents sent him to Madrid to study law, he discovered the economic writings of Pedro Rodrí-guez de Campomanes, Gaspar Melchor de Jovellanos, Antonio Genovesi, and Ferdinando Galiani, and, shortly thereafter, the classic works of politi-cal economy, especially those of Adam Smith. Holding the title of Apoderado General do Ayuntamiento of Havana in Madrid after 1789, Arango wrote a number of texts incorporating the language of contemporary economic dis-courses that reiterated the historical demands of local elites in Havana to develop a plantation economy on the island. His activities in different instances of metropolitan and colonial power, and his remarkable intellec-tual output—as a number of historians have argued—were a fundamental part of the economic and social transformation of Cuba at the turn of the nineteenth century.[23]

In February 1789, shortly after becoming the representative of Havana interests in Madrid, Francisco de Arango sent his first request to the Bour-bon court for the cessation of the transatlantic slave trade to Cuba. At the time, he merely repeated an argument that had been previously made by some of the main figures of the Spanish enlightenment. "The experience of three centuries and reason before it," he argued at the beginning of his text, "has shown that the fruits of return and not the precious metals of the American colonies are the ones that reward in infinite ways their respective metropolises." Agricultural production in turn depended on the importa-tion of slave labor from Africa, a business that still did not have Spanish participation.[24] The request was fulfilled that same month with the *Real Cédula* of February 28, which authorized Spanish and foreign merchants to openly sell captives in Caribbean ports—Havana, Santo Domingo, San Juan, and Caracas—for a two-year period, open to renewal. In the following two years, Arango prepared other petitions requesting that the authoriza-tion be extended for a longer period than originally intended. Still inspired by the language of political economy, his arguments continued to explore the colonial experience of other European powers.[25]

News from the great slave uprising of August 1791 in the North Province of Saint-Domingue forced Arango to change the tone of his defense of the transatlantic slave trade. Within the new milieu of open rebellion, he had to convince the Spanish Crown that the conditions that had led to the revolt in the French colony were absent in Cuba. Especially noteworthy was his comparison between the violent treatment of slaves in Saint-Domingue and the allegedly benevolent nature of Cuban slavery.[26] In a memorial of November 20, 1791, the historical experience of Iberian slavery became ideological. With a particular reading of the debates that had been taking place in the Atlantic system of northwestern Europe since the 1760s, Arango argued that, unlike imperial rivals, the legislation and social practices of the Iberian world protected slaves and undermined the possibility of large-scale slave rebellion in Cuba. Thus, the ideological construction of the Spanish legislative framework depended on comparisons with other slave societies.[27] At the same time, the slave revolt was ascribed to a known space of experience in order to minimize its innovative potential. History repeated itself: Frenchmen were following in the footsteps of the ancients by getting close to "everything that is most barbarous in the legislation of Laconia and Rome to treat their slaves; thus it is not surprising that slave wars very similar to those that threatened Romans were seen taking place on the plains of Guarico [Saint-Domingue]." The revolt of Saint-Domingue was being interpreted with the assumption that the historical past could explain—and even project—the events of the present. According to this interpretation, which was very similar to that of Azeredo Coutinho, the slaves could never win this struggle, thus leading Arango to argue that it was "important to go very far and take full advantage of the period of inaction of the neighbor."[28]

The comparison with the English and French Caribbean was a central focus of Arango's best-known text, which he completed in January 1792. In it, the Cuban writer not only repeated his argument that the emphasis on mining had produced untold damage but also stressed the limited impact of the Bourbon reforms that had been promoted since 1763, which had yet to effectively stimulate sugar production in Cuba. The comparison with the commercial and productive system of the English and French indicated that Cuba in 1792 was "in the same distance of ten to one." The slave revolt in Saint-Domingue, however, opened a perfect opportunity to stimulate agriculture in Havana "to a level of power and wealth capable of sustaining competition, even after the recovery of our rival." If Arango still could not conceive of the possibility of a slave victory, he saw the event as the beginning of a new time—"the age of our happiness has arrived, the time without our illusions"—that could be accelerated by human actions. For those skeptical that Cuba could ever replace the British and French islands, Arango recommended that they look "at History. Search for Jamaica in it and see how it grew in few years; French Santo Domingo forming in less than thirty all the wealth they had before the insurrection of its slaves."[29]

The most important of Arango's proposals at the time was his promotion of direct slave trade between Africa and Cuba. Although halted by the Spanish Crown since 1789, the traffic continued to be controlled by the old English suppliers, who consciously limited the number of disembarkations in order to raise slave prices. According to Arango, traffic conducted by Hispanic-Cuban merchants could significantly reduce the cost of slave labor on the island. He also called for the loosening of restrictions over Cuban external trade, which he believed would facilitate the import of sugar machinery and the export of Cuban sugar to places beyond the imperial frontiers. Arango, however, was not proposing a system of total free trade in his *Discurso* of 1792 but rather a system of drawbacks to stimulate the reexport of Cuban sugar.[30]

After the radicalization of revolutionary events on Saint-Domingue (the Spanish and English invasion in 1793; the confirmation of the decree by Léger-Félicité Sonthonax abolishing slavery by the National Convention, which extended the decree to all the overseas provinces of France in 1794; the alliance of Toussaint-Louverture with the republicans; and the maintenance of Jacobin abolitionist measures by the Directory), the impact of slave actions on Arango's perceptions of time became stronger, as shown by a report presented by him to the Real Consulado de La Habana in June 1796 regarding the adoption of new rules to curb slave flights in Cuba. His suggestions followed the basic view that runaway slaves should be returned to their owners, preserving "the humanity . . . with all possible economy and convenience."

However, for Arango, the necessary steps were very different from those in other slave societies. Each social context is marked by specific circumstances that are in constant motion, thus demanding careful attention from the legislator. "On such an obscure and changing subject," Arango wrote, "there should never be general nor perpetual rules, since what yesterday may have been helpful can be very harmful today, and what is good and correct in Jamaica, e.g., might be damaging in another island or city."[31] For this reason, Arango believed that the regulations against *cimarrones* should be renewed and revised every ten years. There were no indications that the activities of cimarrones could have led to an open rebellion in Cuba at the time, but the large numbers of disembarked Africans on the island had the potential to change the balance of power.

Saint-Domingue was no longer seen as simply a repetition of past events (the slave revolts of the ancient world) but rather was representative of a new time, which in turn demanded new answers. The increasingly rapid transformations of the 1790s also stimulated Arango to articulate new requests for the liberalization of commerce. On April 20, 1799, the Spanish king, Charles IV, who had become allied to the French Republic during the war against Britain, issued an order prohibiting trade between the American colonies and merchants from neutral nations (practices that had been authorized by a royal *cédula* two years earlier).[32] Arango harshly criticized the measure in October 1799. Emphasizing that the growth of slave plantations had formed the basis of the Cuban economy since the 1760s, he argued that feeding the captives and exporting sugar depended on regular trade with merchants from neutral nations, especially North Americans. Cuban masters could not store their production indefinitely, given the dynamics of the world market and the risk of being excluded from the global circuits of tropical exports.

The context of revolution, moreover, was yet another reason to adopt the principle of a free market, since the program established in the early 1790s was not that effective anymore. The Saint-Domingue Revolution once again appeared in proslavery discourse as offering an ideal opportunity to accelerate the historical time: "Nobody can be interested in stopping the fast and incredible rise that, after the collapse of Guarico, has marked our agriculture. All Spaniards must, on the contrary, collaborate to our brief and happy occupation of the spot that had been previously occupied by unfortunate Santo Domingo in European commerce. This is the true interest of national commerce."[33]

In early 1803, Arango acquired firsthand experience in Saint-Domingue (which had previously never been visited by any Portuguese man of letters or statesman), which by then had entered an even more dramatic phase of radicalization and violence. In an official forty-day mission in April and May, he recorded the concerns and projects that had emerged in the context of the revolution started by the slaves of the French colony. Organized by the captain general of Cuba, the Marquis of Someruelos, the primary (and secret) objective of the mission was to evaluate the Saint-Domingue slave economy's prospects for recovery. Arango was haunted by the scale of human devastation caused by a decade of revolution and, especially, by the invasion of Napoleonic troops. The military victory of an army of former slaves, something unthinkable a few years earlier, had become an undeniable reality by 1803. Despite the efforts of Charles Leclerc and his powerful French army to destroy the resistance, Arango predicted that it was "almost impossible to put an end to the race of bandits." France continued to engage in the war only as "a matter of honor," without any chance that Saint-Domingue could become once again the slave colony that it was before 1791.

With the backdrop of this new reality, Arango continued advancing the proposals that he had been working on for over a decade. According to his plan, Spain needed to establish an alliance with Napoleonic France against Britain, despite all the problems that were part of this kind of deal ("I do not forget that this colossal nation that today is our ally can become our oppressor tomorrow"). Cuban sugar would then enter the French market—and, consequently, its reexport system—and an exclusively Franco-Spanish transatlantic slave trade to Havana could be developed. Spaniards would be able to take advantage of the French slave trade networks, while Napoleon would abandon the project to reestablish slavery in Saint-Domingue. The conclusion was clear: Cuba could become the largest producer of tropical goods in the world, but with even stronger foundations than its French predecessor had enjoyed. According to Arango, the crucial difference for the Spanish would be the relatively large white population in their colonies in comparison to those of their British and French counterparts.[34]

This ambitious plan depended on the French recognizing the "independence of the rebels of Santo Domingo." Events, however, did not follow the linear sequence anticipated by Arango. The former slaves of Saint-Domingue had already imposed a humiliating defeat on the French in 1803, ending the dream of a reconstituted French slave empire and, crucially, forcing Napoleon to sell Louisiana to the United States.[35] The Napoleonic invasion of the Iberian Peninsula in 1807 and the imprisonment of the Spanish royal family the following year finally put an end to any expectations of a Franco-Spanish alliance as envisioned by Arango after his visit to Saint-Domingue. Still, his 1803 plan indicates how the revolution initiated by slaves multiplied the number of alternatives available to contemporary actors and, as a result, their proposals for the future. In less than ten years, something unthinkable (the success of a slave revolt) had taken place, leading to the foundation of a sovereign state in the Caribbean under the control of former slaves. This unprecedented historical variable became a fundamental component of the political game.[36]

On the eve of the collapse of the Iberian Atlantic system, the example of Saint-Domingue was received in very different ways in Portuguese America and Cuba. Cuban slaveholders interpreted the revolution as "an unparalleled experience" that gave them the opportunity to build a more prosperous and stable economic and social order in the Spanish Empire.[37] Colonists in Portuguese America at first did not see the event as a rupture in historical time, but this also changed after the arrival of Prince Regent João in Rio de Janeiro in 1808. For Luso-Brazilian slaveholders, this meant the beginning of a new historical time that completely subverted the traditional order of things. Cuban slaveholders closely observed the policies taken by the Portuguese Crown, now based in Brazil, to resist British antislavery pressure and promote free trade. The collapse of Spanish colonialism in the 1810s (along with constitutional experiences in the metropolis and growing military conflicts in America) stimulated anxieties in Brazil about the process that transformed Saint-Domingue in Haiti.

The Crisis of the Iberian Atlantic System and the First Constitutional Experience: Cádiz, 1810–1814

When the Spanish Cortes gathered in Cádiz in 1810, the slave trade and slavery itself had become landmark issues in international politics. The campaign for the abolition of the transatlantic slave trade became a central part of the British struggle against the politics of Napoleon Bonaparte. After the collapse of the Peace of Amiens, which had been established between the two powers in 1803–1804, the subject reappeared in the British Parliament. In 1807, only a few weeks after the US Congress passed a federal law abolishing the transatlantic slave trade to the country, the British Parliament similarly abolished the slave trade between Africa and British possessions. At the time of the fall of Bonaparte in 1814, the issue had already become a priority in British diplomacy. The struggle against the slave trade united British public opinion while simultaneously contributing to the crisis of the French Empire.[38]

The meeting of the Cádiz Cortes in 1810 took place during a particularly turbulent time. The armies of Napoleon had occupied most of the Spanish territory, forcing the deposition of two kings while keeping one of them, Ferdinand VII, in captivity. The sovereignty of the Spanish nation, claimed by the Cortes, was associated with loyalty to the deposed and imprisoned king. An alliance with England in this context, an important step in resisting the invaders and concluding the constitutional meeting, could be reinforced with the adoption of antislavery policies.[39]

The issue was raised in the Spanish Cortes by José Miguel Guridi y Alcócer during the session of March 25, 1811. The New Spain deputy offered eight propositions that, in sum, called for the immediate abolition of the transatlantic slave trade, the emancipation of the future children of slaves, the reinforcement of the legal rights of slaves to manumission, and legislative measures to ensure the good treatment of slaves by their owners.[40] The proposal was clearly inspired by the antislavery laws that had been passed in the northern United States since independence.[41] Alcócer's proposal generated both surprise and panic in Cádiz, leading to the postponement of the debate, a discussion that the organizers of the Cortes tried to keep secret for one week. On April 2, the liberal deputy of Spain, Agustín Argüelles, presented a more moderate proposal that could be published. The new proposal called for the immediate abolition of the African slave trade to American provinces and the extinction of torture within the Spanish Empire. Supported by Mexia Lequeria, a deputy from Quito, Argüelles managed to make this proposition the center of debates in the plenary.[42]

The motion offered by Argüelles to extinguish the traffic required that the Spanish Council of Regency reveal the antislavery intentions of the Cortes to the British government so "that they could get in all extension the great object that the English nation proposed to itself in the famous bill for the abolition of the slave trade."[43] The reference was to the British Slave Trade Act of 1807 and the plans to extend it to other European countries and overseas. A decision from the Cortes (in the terms proposed by the deputy), therefore, would show the total commitment of Spain to these general objectives. In addition to the commercial treaty with the British that was being debated in secret sessions of the Cortes, Spain's antislavery posturing would ensure British support in the struggle against Napoleonic troops in Galicia and Asturias.[44] Argüelles, however, did not envision the end of slavery with these measures. Abolitionist policies would certainly affect the financial contribution of loyal Spanish regions in America such as Peru and Cuba to the Crown. But the end of the transatlantic slave trade would stimulate a gradual improvement of cultivation techniques in these slave regions, as had been the case in the British Empire.[45]

The arguments did not convince representatives from those regions. Already in the session in which Argüelles's proposal was first debated, the Cuban deputy, Andrés de Jáuregui, warned everyone about the risk of publishing the content of these debates in the *Diário de las Cortes*. According to the deputy, the island of Cuba, especially Havana, was going through a period of "great tranquility," while "sinister movements well known by H. M." had been shaking "a great part of America," a direct reference to the popular revolt of José María Morelos in New Spain and an indirect allusion to agitations in Caracas and Rio de la Plata. With a rhetorical and threatening tone, Jáuregui asked: "Are we going to expose ourselves to the transformation of internal peace in one of the most precious portions of overseas Spain?" He then concluded: "H. M. should remember the imprudent conduct of the National Assembly of France, the sad and fatal results that it has produced, even more in its exaggerated principles, no reflection . . . moreover, the impatience and inopportunity with which it has touched and conducted a similar deal."[46] Thus, the French parliamentary experience and its Caribbean consequences became tools in the hands of Jáuregui for the defense of the transatlantic slave trade and the Cuban slave order.

In a clear indication of the connections between the Cuban deputy in Cádiz and metropolitan authorities, a secret session of the Cortes on July 7 debated a letter from the captain general of Cuba, the Marquis of Someruelos, describing how Argüelles's propositions (published in the *Diário de las Cortes*) had generated a great deal of anxiety on the island. Pamphlets and newspapers denounced the risk of a revolution similar to the one in Saint-Domingue. Someruelos requested that the debates on the issue not be made public again. He also subtly observed that the revenue from taxes in Cuba was fundamental to winning the war against the French. Although based on slavery, this wealth played an important role in the financing of Spanish armies and was, therefore, more important than diplomatic support from the British.[47]

A longer response to the proposals of Alcócer and Argüelles came in the public declaration of the Ayuntamiento, of the Royal Consulate and the Economic Society of the Friends of the Country of Havana of July 20, 1811, written by Francisco de Arango y Parreño. The document synthesized many of the proslavery arguments that had been circulating in the Atlantic since the late eighteenth century and put forward an interpretation of the international politics of slavery and the constitutional and parliamentary experiences of Britain, the United States, and France.[48] Arango argued that the Cortes did not have the authority to deal with the issue of slavery, describing procedures in the United States and Britain, where the question had been exhaustively discussed for two decades with the active participation of slaveholders. In the treaties established between Britain and Portugal, "the Court of Brazil—despite being an English province today—did not do anything about the issue other than offering a vague and indeterminate promise to eventually abolish this trade."

In the Cádiz Cortes, however, not only were the provinces of America underrepresented but also Argüelles called for the immediate end of the traffic. In a series of rhetorical questions, Arango asked, could the Cortes interfere "in the sacred right of property acquired according to the laws of property, . . . whose inviolability is one of the great objects of every political association, and one of the first chapters of every Constitution? Could such thorny, respectable issues be touched when the larger interests of all the inhabitants of various provinces are carried with expertise; of various subordinate provinces, among many that are not, and that are in the list of those that have not completed their representation in Congress?"

Along with the primacy of property, economic weight, and the political loyalty of Cuba to Spain, the defense of the traffic presented by Arango in 1811 also made use of the events in Saint-Domingue. The author contended that the proposals of Alcócer and Argüelles threatened the Cuban economy by signaling to the slaves the possibility of an eventual liberation: "In the stupidity of the negro and solitude of our *haciendas*," he wrote, "is the most precise and fearful subordination. If Mr. Alcócer had seen with his eyes the fermenting produced by the announcement of happiness that would look for us, he would have feared, as did the judicious ones, that here would be lighted the fire that burned Saint-Domingue, if not with more violence, certainly with more guilt."[49]

The proposals of Alcócer and Argüelles were already dismissed in 1811 in the face of pressure from Cuban slaveholding representatives, who skillfully explored the themes of Cuban loyalty to the empire and the specter of Saint-Domingue to curb the antislavery impulse in Cádiz. The strategy to silence the debate over the transatlantic slave trade and slavery in the constitutional sphere (while relegating it to the diplomatic arena) successfully passed its first test in the Iberian world.[50]

The Cuban victory over liberals from the peninsula and New Spain was connected to another fundamental aspect of the Cádiz debates, namely the constitutional definitions of citizenship. Condensed in Articles 22 and 29 of the Constitution, they were the result of a long discussion spanning from September 4 to 14, 1811, marked by the defeat of a large number of American representatives in Cádiz. These articles established rigid criteria that denied citizenship to people of African descent in the New World and excluded them from the demographic census.[51] It is important to note that the approval of these definitions took place only a few months after the end of debates on the slave trade and, against the will of all other American representatives, had the support of the Cuban Andrés de Jáuregui.

The citizenship issue was one of the main points of contention between peninsular and American Spaniards after the first convocation of the Cortes. The decisions on citizenship and on the procedures for the election of deputies were based on the number of American representatives in the constitutional meeting. The problem had lingered since 1809, when the central junta called one representative of each viceroyalty (a total of nine Americans and thirty-six Europeans) to create a central government that could integrate Spanish America into the war against Napoleon. The sense of discontent generated by the imbalance in representation was intensified by the demands for the convocation of a constituent assembly.[52] The Cortes was then established in 1810 with the participation of American representatives (and endowed with constituent power).

The first decree for elections in America and Asia of February 14, 1810, however, claimed the integration of twenty-eight substitutes in an assembly with more than one hundred Europeans. This was the moment when protests in Caracas and Buenos Aires led to the *cabildos abertos* and the gradual rupture of ties with the Cádiz Cortes.[53] As a result, a decree of August 20, 1810, established that Indians and the children they had with Spaniards (*vecinos* and inhabitants within Hispanic territory) should be an integral part of the nation. Moreover, while elections took place in America, thirty substitutes participated in the sessions of the Cortes after September 23. In this way, a large number of the so-called castas, understood to be part of the population of free mestizos living in Spanish America, were integrated. One of the main issues during the first sessions of the assembly and in the decree of October 15 thus became the equality of European and American representation in the conformation of the Spanish nation.

Already in December 1810, however, American delegates presented an eleven-item manifesto to the Cortes that showed their dissatisfaction.[54] According to contemporary estimates, Spanish America had approximately fifteen or sixteen million inhabitants, of whom six million were Indians and another six million free mestizos, who were members of castas. The latter included not only those of indigenous and Spanish origin but also people whose ancestors had been African slaves. Representatives from New Spain, Guatemala, and Venezuela warned about the danger of excluding these people from the rights of citizenship. This would inevitably lead to divisions in what had been an undifferentiated and more importantly cooperative sector of the population of their regions, creating internal enemies in a period of consolidation of national unity. The American delegates hoped to integrate the castas in the project of establishing a constitution, which was being coordinated by a commission formed by Europeans and Americans, with Andrés de Jáuregui among the latter. The disagreements in the plenary reappeared here once the eleven-item manifesto became a focus of debate in August 1811.

It is important to note the sequence of debates during the first half of 1811. The proposal by Argüelles to extinguish the slave trade was presented in early April 1811, while the constitutional project was being developed. The debates about the inclusion of the castas into the electoral process had been interrupted on February 7. The abolition of the tribute collected from Indians—who were now citizens—had in turn been discussed since March 12. Argüelles offered a more moderate version of the proposition made by the Mexican Guridi y Alcócer (one of the main proponents of granting citizenship rights for the castas) to abolish the slave trade. To Alcócer, the combination of the extinction of the traffic with the emancipation of the future sons of slaves would broaden the basis for citizenship. Temporarily defeated, Alcócer still fought for his proposal, which clearly went against the interests of the slave regions of the empire, most notably Cuba. Perhaps he expected a

deal with the European Spanish (in defending the end of the traffic) or with
the Cubans, who until then had been silent on the issue of including the castas. In the case of Argüelles, however, the paramount issue of ending the
slave trade had no connection to the incorporation of the castas, since the
Spanish liberal never admitted the inclusion of the "descendants from
Africa" in his views of representation and citizenship.[55]

The conception of citizenship of the American delegates, including that of
Alcócer, was based on the notion of *vecindad* (rights acquired by local residents). The constitutional project established that the Spanish nation was
made up of the integration of Spaniards from both hemispheres. Alcócer
presented the hypothesis that the nation would be the collection of all vecinos of the peninsula and other territories of the monarchy, united into one
government and subject to the sovereign authority. He used the term *colec-
ción* (or agglomerate) to stress the diverse autonomous aspirations within an
empire that he understood to be Hispanic and global. In his view, self-will
and vecindad were more important than place of birth. The ties emerging
from the relations between vecinos included the castas and, ultimately, those
born in any other part of the world, as long as they opted to live within the
Spanish empire. Although his proposal would increase the number of American representatives at the Cortes, its ambition stretched even further. It
aimed to connect each of the different constituent parts of the empire, which
included Africans and Indians, and strengthen the internal ties of each provincial unit. In this conception, the integration of castas was an indispensable aspect of the unity and autonomy of these different parts. The proposal
also called for a federalist model based on the autonomy of provinces.[56]

During the sessions discussing the composition of the Spanish nation,
Arguëlles became the main opponent of the ideas put forward by American
delegates, arguing that they had misunderstood the meaning of the word
"citizenship." The modern understanding of the concept, first applied in
Spain, had no connection to the ancient concept of rights of the city or of the
citizen as a resident of the city. The new citizenship, in his view, was based
on the rationality of political principles, which should be the uniformly
applied to all parts of the empire. These definitions allowed the dissociation
between the individual and his place of residence (or even birth) in determining whether he was a citizen of the monarchy. Having access to this
right, therefore, depended on the capacity to contribute physically and

morally to the nation as a whole, qualifications that excluded African descendants at that time.[57]

The most systematic discussions took place between September 4 and 11, 1811, when Article 22 was passed, politically excluding the population of African descent. The debate restarted on September 14, when the issue of black citizenship resurfaced again and Article 29 was passed. The passing of both articles marked the victory of the commission responsible for the constitutional project and the defeat of American delegates. These debates indicate the unity of action and coherence of arguments among the representatives of different American provinces. There is a clear division between European and American Spaniards in the long speeches by representatives of both groups, with the exception of the Cuban Jáuregui, one of the American representatives who was on the commission (and a dissident among them). His only public intervention in the debates took place on September 25, when he supported the passing of Article 29.[58]

How can the behavior of the Cuban deputy be explained? Part of the answer can be found in the political discussions in Cádiz, but equally important were the profound transformations that had been taking place in Cuba since the 1790s. The most important request from Cuban slaveholders—silence over the slave trade and slavery—had already been fulfilled in April, and it seems likely that Jáuregui had already established an agreement with European Spaniards at that point. This would explain his acceptance of Articles 22 and 29 as proof of his cooperation with the Europeans. The choices of Jáuregui, however, were also an indication of the transformation of slavery in his home country.

As we have seen, although slavery did not represent the basis of social organization in Cuba before the third quarter of the eighteenth century, it had been important for the economy of the island, especially in the sector of port services in Havana. In 1774, for instance, the Spanish colony had a significant slave population (approximately 26 percent of all inhabitants in the island, estimated at 171,000 people) and a relatively large number of free blacks and mulattoes (17 percent of the total).[59] Although in smaller numbers, the latter had an important role at the time. The new militias of pardos (mulattoes) and morenos (blacks) established by the Bourbon reforms after 1763, for example, participated in the imperial conflicts related to the American Revolution. In the 1790s, the free black and mulatto units presented specific demands, such as better wages and access to higher ranks according to the racial lines of their groups.[60]

The Saint-Domingue Revolution and the transformations in Cuba that had been taking place since the 1790s threatened the position of these freedmen and their descendants on the Spanish island. In his 1792 text, which connected the economic opportunities opened by the Saint-Domingue Revolution to a broad reform program to stimulate slave production in Cuba, Francisco de Arango y Parreño called for the gradual dismantling of the pardo and moreno militias to ensure the internal safety of the island in the context of increasing importations of enslaved Africans. Arango believed that the veterans of these groups would leave the battlefield and join slaves to contest the slave order in Cuba because of their color identity ("they are all black; a little more or a little less have the same complaints and the same reasons to dislike us").[61]

Although supported by the Royal Consulate of Havana, Arango's proposal was not unanimously accepted among Cuban slaveholders or the captains general of Cuba at the turn of the nineteenth century, a consequence of centuries-old practices in the Iberian Atlantic system. His argument nonetheless contributed to the gradual decline of the prestige of black and mulatto militias while providing the framework used by Jáuregui during the Cádiz debates about castas.[62] The proposal combined a defense of the growth of the transatlantic slave trade and the tightening of racial barriers in Cuba, thus changing the social relations of slavery that had been in place before 1790. Denying the rights of citizenship to former slaves went hand in hand with the proposal to silence the debate regarding the slave trade and slavery at the Cortes.

Discussions about black slavery and the integration of castas in Cádiz reverberated in the Americas. The "racialization" of the theme of citizenship was one of the great impulses behind independence movements in Spanish America after 1810. It was not a coincidence that revolutionaries in the regions with the largest populations of free blacks and mulattoes developed their own myths about racial inclusion.[63] The deliberations from Cádiz were also felt in Cuba, although in the opposite direction after an episode that would reverberate for the remainder of the nineteenth century. The metropolitan debates of 1810 and 1811 about citizenship and slavery fueled the conspiracy of José Antonio Aponte, a free mulatto, artisan, and former captain of militias who, inspired by the examples of the black generals of Haiti, managed to gather slaves and free blacks and mulattoes in a broad revolutionary front against slave powers on the island.

The contestation of the slave order by subaltern groups in Cuba in 1812, which seemed to reproduce the events that had led to the Saint-Domingue Revolution, confirmed to the colonial elite that the decisions taken by their representatives in Cádiz had been correct. On May 23, 1812, Jáuregui and Juan Bernardo O'Gavan, a new delegate in Cádiz, presented a report to the Cortes about Aponte's conspiracy, reiterating Arango's arguments about the risks of the assembly dealing with the issue. Jáuregui and O'Gavan stressed that the greatest "threat to the island of Cuba was the free population of color in the city [of Havana], people with more skills than the slaves and a certain level of intelligence that had been use to promote the movement." The exclusion of the rights of citizenship to the castas, they argued, had been a correct decision. The next step for the Cortes would be to silence the discussion about slavery.[64]

In the greater context of the crisis of the colonial order on the American continent, the loyal island appeared to be a stronghold of European constitutionalism. In June 1812, the Cortes session started with Jáuregui saying that the Royal Consulate of Havana had sent a voluntary contribution of 200,000 pesos to help the monarchy. On September 9, Jáuregui had the pleasure of announcing that his country had been the first to register the publication and oath of the Constitution in America. With the convocation of the ordinary Cortes, on the island since July, Cubans started the electoral process for integration into the new legislature of 1813, thus showing their total compliance with the terms established in the constitutional text.[65] It was not a coincidence that one of the elected deputies at the time was the great ideologue of the Cuban slaveholding class, none other than Francisco de Arango y Parreño.

Slave Trade Politics under Absolutism, 1810–1820

In the meantime, the Portuguese Empire followed a different plan. At least during the 1810s, with the exception of the 1817 case of Pernambuco, the Braganzas managed to prevent the spirit of revolution from reaching their territorial possessions. The French invasion in 1807 forced the transference of the Portuguese court to Rio de Janeiro under the protection of the British navy, marking the end of the policy of official neutrality maintained by Portuguese diplomacy during the Napoleonic Wars.[66] A number of economic and political concessions followed, especially the opening of the ports to foreign nations in 1808 and the advantages given to the British with the Treaty of Friendship and Alliance of 1810. In this context, British diplomacy started to apply pressure for the Portuguese abolition of the transatlantic slave trade.

According to Article 10 of the Treaty of Friendship and Alliance, Prince Regent João, "being fully convinced of the injustice and impolicy of the Slave Trade and the great disadvantages which arise from the necessity to introducing and continually renewing a foreign and factitious population for the purpose of labour and industry within his South American Dominions, has resolved to co-operate with His Britannic Majesty in the cause of humanity and justice, by adopting the most efficacious means for bringing about a gradual abolition of the Slave Trade throughout the whole of his Dominions."[67] With those words, the Portuguese representative, Rodrigo de Sousa Coutinho, abandoned the pro–slave trade discourses that had circulated within the Portuguese Empire and joined the discursive field of the English antislavery movement. As historian João Pedro Marques argues, the absence of public debate about the theme in Portugal in the previous decades had led Portuguese diplomats to overlook the centrality of the slave trade issue in Britain.[68] In any case, dom João allowed his subjects to continue engaging in the slave commerce as long as it took place in Portuguese possessions in Africa.

British ships were already seizing Portuguese vessels in 1811, under the terms of the treaty that had been signed the previous year. By intercepting Portuguese slave ships going from North Africa to some regions in Brazil, however, the British overstepped the terms of the 1810 treaty. Portuguese authorities considered this encroachment not only to be interference in the internal affairs of the monarchy but also to pose a threat to the export economies of the main agricultural zones of Brazil, a view that was shared by the colonists. During that same year, Coutinho (now the Count of Linhares), signer of the treaty of 1810, wrote a letter to King George III with arguments that were quite similar to the ones being espoused by Arango at the Cortes of Cádiz at that same moment. His message was clear: the British anti–slave trade actions threatened the alliance between Portugal and Britain against Napoleon Bonaparte. Moreover, contradicting what he had written in

February 1810, Coutinho argued that enslaved Africans were an indispensable part of the imperial economy and that only after a very long period (much longer than the twenty-year period requested by Arango) could the transatlantic slave trade to Brazil be ended.[69]

The proslavery reaction of Coutinho, in fact, was part of a broader strategy to counteract British pressure. During the last year of his life, he established the political and diplomatic guidelines for the slave trade issue, a model that was later followed by João VI during most of his time in Rio de Janeiro. This strategy included the publication of pro–slave trade articles that employed arguments that were very similar to those outlined in the letter to the British king in the Brazilian press (the periodical *Idade d'Ouro do Brasil*, published in Bahia) and in Portuguese newspapers published in London (the periodical *O Investigador Português em Inglaterra*); the republication of a version of a 1793 text written by Luis Antonio de Oliveira Mendes as part of the *Memórias Econômicas* series, this time without the antislavery passages; and the promulgation of the Royal Charter of 1813 on the transatlantic slave trade, which aimed at legitimizing slaving practices in the Portuguese Empire by retrieving the 1684 legislation on the tonnage of slave ships (that allegedly proved that the Bragantine legislative tradition on the issue predated the supposed humanitarianism of British abolitionists by more than one century).[70]

The strategy employed by dom João was put to test in 1815 after the defeat of the Napoleonic troops and the beginning of the Congress of Vienna. While this generated new hope, it also raised new risks for the Braganza court. Great Britain began to pressure Portugal and Spain to abolish the slave trade to Brazil and Cuba, creating a common ground for both countries to defend slavery for the next fifty years. Portuguese representatives attempted to establish an alliance with their Spanish counterparts around one central idea, which had been developed by the Count of Linhares four years earlier and reaffirmed in many different instances since then: the slave trade could only be ended in the distant future, and British interference needed to be curbed by the Congress of Vienna.[71]

Portuguese emissaries were forced to negotiate directly with the British within the boundaries of this complicated milieu. With the treaties of January 21 and 22, 1815, the British promised reparations for the Portuguese vessels that had been seized in previous years, while the Portuguese agreed to abolish the traffic north of the equator. The treaties had only a minor impact on the Portuguese slave trade, since most embarkations of enslaved Africans to Portuguese America took place below the equator, specifically in the ports of central Africa.[72]

The Portuguese slave interests also won another partial victory in their alliance with the Spanish. One of the main British objectives during the Congress of Vienna was to convince each of the participating nations to sign a common decree to immediately make the slave trade illegal north of the equator while abolishing it entirely after a period of five years. All they could achieve in the end, however, was a declaration signed by all the present pleni-potentiaries condemning the trade as "repugnant to the principles of human-ity and universal morality" and calling for its abolition at a nonspecified future time. Politically strengthened but without achieving their initial objectives, the British diplomats learned a valuable lesson from the Vienna experience. It would be nearly impossible to impose an agenda against the traffic in multilateral forums, given that slave powers would inevitably estab-lish alliances among themselves. The better strategy would be to establish bilateral negotiations.[73] After that moment, Portugal, Spain, and, later, the Empire of Brazil would each have to face Albion alone.

With João VI living in Rio de Janeiro, Portugal passed its first test under the new rules of engagement. The Anglo-Portuguese Treaty of 1815 had also established the necessity of additional negotiations to ensure the application of its articles, but during that same year Portuguese authorities came to the conclusion that the imprecision of the document signed on February 22 pro-tected the traffic north of the equator. The growing number of seizures of Portuguese slave ships south of the equator by the British navy during the following year, however, made it clear that new diplomatic actions would be necessary to guarantee the safety of Atlantic trade. The negotiations con-ducted by Palmela in London starting in October 1816 had this objective, and they ended with the signing of the Additional Convention of July 28, 1817. Despite the fact that the mutual right of search and the establishment of mixed commissions to adjudicate seizures of slave ships could be interpreted as attacks on the sovereignty of Portugal, the Anglo-Portuguese Treaty of 1817 marked a monumental victory for the Portuguese monarchy and its project to expand slavery. By establishing the exact geographical African limits (all of them south of the equator) for legal slave trade ventures under the Portuguese flag, the document ultimately protected the transatlantic slave trade conducted within the Portuguese Empire so long as Brazilian ports were the only destinations. More importantly, the treaty of 1817 established an indeterminate future date for the extinction of the Portuguese slave trade.[74]

The platform presented by Rodrigo de Sousa Coutinho in an 1811 letter to the British king had been implemented. In the early 1820s, Portugal was the only European country with permission to legally engage in the transatlantic slave trade. The treaty with Britain was due, among other things, to the great efforts made by Portuguese diplomacy after 1814. Two months after the signing of the Anglo-Portuguese Treaty of 1817, Palmela already realized the magnitude of his achievement. In a letter dated October 8 to the king in Rio de Janeiro, he gave the news of the Anglo-Spanish Treaty signed fifteen days earlier and stated with pride that "after 1820 we will be the only nation capable of legally conducting the slave trade, and I believe this is one more reason that proves the convenience of the Convention of July 28."[75]

Indeed, Spain did not have much to celebrate. Given its context of imperial crisis, the variables in negotiations with Britain became much more complex. The defeat of Napoleon allowed Ferdinand VII to return to Spain and shut down the Cortes in May 1814. If the abrupt end of this first Spanish constitutional experience stimulated the independence movements in Spanish America, the ties between the Cuban slaveholding elite and the metropolis remained solid. The closing of the ordinary Cortes in 1814, in fact, gave the Cuban masters a sense of security. Just a few months earlier, in November 1813, deputy Isidoro de Antillón had criticized slavery in the plenary of Cádiz, leading to an immediate response from Arango y Parreño.[76] The former delegate Arango himself did not hesitate to already join, in 1815, a typical institution of the Spanish Old Regime that had been revived by the return of absolutism, the Council of the Indies. In his view, the closed councils of absolutist regimes could bring more benefits to the slaveholding interests of Cuba than the spaces of public opinion that followed from parliamentary politics and a free press.

The achievements of the Cuban slaveholding classes between 1815 and 1819 seem to confirm this view. In the words of Manuel Moreno Fraginals, "there was a period of harmony and happiness among the creole plantocracy between the end of the Cortes and the revolution of Riego." During those years, sugar mill planters acquired the right to freely expand into Cuban forests (as granted by a royal cédula of August 30, 1815), which until then had been strictly protected by the Spanish navy for military ends. They also saw the fall of the tobacco monopoly (July 23, 1817) and the establishment of a free-trade policy with foreign merchants (February 10, 1818). Finally, a royal cédula of July 16, 1819, allowed them to reformulate the entire agrarian structure of the island.[77] These measures created the institutional conditions that facilitated the growth of slave production in Cuba, changes that had been demanded by Cuban elites since the late eighteenth century. How can we explain all these successes in such a short period of time and in the context of absolutist restoration? A number of historians have provided the answer. In the 1810s, Cuba became indispensible for Spanish colonialism. While the wars of independence on the American continent undermined the empire, the growth of sugar and coffee exports from Cuba based on the continued disembarkation of enslaved Africans relieved the critical conditions of imperial finances.[78] Ferdinand VII rewarded the loyal Cuban slaveholders by satisfying their historical demands.

On one key issue, however, the Spanish Crown seems to have ignored the slaveholding interests from Cuba. Shortly after the Congress of Vienna, Britain began bilateral negotiations with Spain that revived the requests for both an immediate abolition of the slave trade north of the equator and its complete end in the near future. The Council of the Indies analyzed the British proposal in early 1816 and gave two answers: most counselors accepted the demands, while a minority called for the maintenance of the traffic for five more years, recognizing the impossibility of keeping it permanently. The Spanish Council of State embraced the proposal of the minority group and presented it in London in March 1816, adding a request for compensation of £500,000 (for the seizures of Spanish ships after 1810) and the payment of £1 million to finance European immigration to Cuba. British representatives immediately refused the proposal, aware that this capital would be used to finance the war against independence movements in America. Negotiations resumed in late 1816 based on a consensus around the necessary implementation of the mutual right of search and the establishment of mixed commissions (as had been the case in the Anglo-Portuguese Treaty). In this new round of debates, the Spanish offered a proposal stipulating the total abolition of the traffic in 1819 in exchange for £600,000. The British refused to pay more than £400,000. By mid-1817, Spain's dire situation had forced the country to accept the British offer, asking in return to change the date for the total abolition of the traffic to May 1820. These became the terms of the treaty signed in Madrid on September 23, 1817.[79]

Some documents, such as the proposal offered by the minority group within the Council of the Indies on February 15, 1816, indicate that there may have been a parallel compromise with Cuban slaveholders during the negotiations for the Anglo-Spanish Treaty. As we have seen, the counselors of the minority group diverged from the majority of the council, requesting that the slave trade be maintained for at least five more years (until 1821). While recognizing the impossibility of resisting British pressure, these counselors did not miss the opportunity to defend the legitimacy of the traffic and its centrality to the Cuban economy. The final document, allegedly written by Francisco de Arango y Parreño, presented an organic defense of slavery with references to the ancient world and to the benevolent nature of the institution in the Iberian universe, comparing the situation in Saint-Domingue with that in Cuba. The document's last words, however, indicate the possibility of a bargain. Realizing the inevitability of the end of the slave trade, counselors called for the implementation of free-trade policies in Cuba.[80]

A second document produced by Arango in the Council of the Indies explored the subject further, using the policies of João VI in Rio de Janeiro to pressure the Spanish Crown in their negotiations. According to Arango, the great rival of Cuba after that moment would be the former Portuguese colony. The "new situation of Brazil" had become, the previous year, a kingdom united with Portugal, "having at its service, without inconveniences nor obstacles, and at low prices, all the arms from Africa," with a merchant fleet "as considerable as economic" that also counted with "all the facilities and protection from the British." Finally, this new kingdom had access to "the free trade of all other known nations" and would soon change the structure of the world market for tropical products, especially sugar and coffee. There was only one option available to Ferdinand VII at that point, since he did not have access to the revenue from Mexico anymore: "Cuba, not for privilege but for straight justice and usefulness of the State, needs the advantages conceded to Brazil." Cuba could raise the revenue of Spain if allowed to freely trade with foreigners, a fundamental measure not only for the prosperity of the island but also for the "future safety and long union with the motherland."[81]

Cuban slaveholders constantly referred to the Brazilian example, especially after news of the Anglo-Portuguese Treaty of 1817 arrived on the Spanish island. On October 21, 1818, for example, the Royal Consulate of Havana sent a long representation to Ferdinand VII that had been signed by Andrés de Jáuregui, among others. The comparison between the content of the Anglo-Portuguese and Anglo-Spanish treaties caused, according to the signatories, "the most vivid and bitter feeling among the *hacendados* and merchants of this island." Portuguese America, a historical rival of Spanish possessions, changed its status when "the Court of Portugal transferred its residence to Rio de Janeiro, Brazil, [which] from its condition of Colony, became an American empire with possessions in Africa and Europe." The abundant natural resources of Brazil combined with the cheaper prices of slaves in the country (a consequence of its proximity to Africa) had been fully explored since 1808: a great flow of capital from British banks, companies, and commercial houses had been financing the expansion of sugar, coffee, and cotton plantations.

As long as Brazil and Portugal were part of the British informal empire, the Anglo-Portuguese Treaty of 1817 represented an action against Cuban agriculture. "England, which in September requested from Spain the total and absolute abolition of the slave trade by 1820, consents on that same month, actually, concedes to Portugal that it continues for the provision of its colony without limitation of time, until the will of its sovereign." Ferdinand VII inadvertently fell into the English trap. Skillfully using the thesis of Cuban loyalty to Spain in the context of a general collapse of its rule over America (and of the growing importance of its revenue for imperial finances), the Consulate of Havana called for the immediate annulment of the Anglo-Spanish Treaty in the face of the nefarious intentions of Britain.[82]

Conscious of the diplomatic risks involved with such a bid, the minister of foreign affairs of Spain ignored the requests of the Consulate of Havana. The Crown, however, had already been addressing some of the complaints from the Cubans regarding the treaty of 1817. The first measure was the royal cédula of February 10, 1818, itself, which allowed unrestricted free trade to Cuba. This was the formalization of a situation that had been actively practiced for two decades, but it is important to note that Arango connected one measure (the treaty with England) with the other (establishing free trade) in his reports of 1816. The second measure has left little documentation, despite its importance. Historian David Murray mentions an important source for this, an 1844 letter from the former captain general of Cuba, Miguel Tacón, to the minister of foreign affairs and the minister of the navy. Tacón admitted that in 1818 a royal order had been confidentially sent to the captains general of Cuba and Puerto Rico instructing them to turn a blind eye to the illegal importation of slaves, given their centrality to colonial agriculture.[83]

The immediate impulse to sign the Anglo-Spanish Treaty was clearly a product of the desperate efforts of Ferdinand VII to bolster the war against independence in America, as indicated by the Spanish requests for high reparations from the British. Portuguese diplomats in Madrid recorded the position of the Spanish monarch as early as 1817, when the operation to purchase Russian ships with the £400,000 compensation paid by the British only confirmed the rumors that had been circulating in the Spanish court.[84] The treaty of 1817 thus demanded a double alliance: with the English to reduce their pressure against the slave traffic and raise funds to fight against independence in the New World, and with the Cubans to preserve their loyalty during those turbulent times. For Cuban slaveholders, Brazil became the model to be followed, the center of a transatlantic empire with a monarch who protected slave trade interests. Thus, it was not a coincidence that the negotiation between Spain and Cuba involved the acceptance by the former of both legal free trade and an illegal slave trade. Even with the treaty of 1817, Cuban slaveholders still believed that their greatest gains came from the politics of absolutism rather than from the unpredictable game of parliamentary politics.

The discourse employed by Cuban slaveholders to articulate their political and economic demands in the short period between 1815 and 1819 dealt directly with the transformations that had been accelerating the historical time of Iberian America since 1808. This articulation combined two political alternatives that had been largely disconnected: first, Cuban loyalty to the metropolis in the context of crisis of colonial rule over America; and, second, the pact between the Portuguese Crown and American colonists that marked the transference of the Crown's headquarters to Rio de Janeiro. These two options, however, were different responses to a unified process—the general crisis of the Iberian Atlantic system—that included mutual influences.[85]

The Return of the Parliamentary Space: Madrid, 1820–1823

A third political option—independence—became available to Cubans after the beginning of the Liberal Triennium (1820–1823), when only New Spain,

Guatemala, Peru, Cuba, and Puerto Rico remained loyal to the Spanish monarchy. The risks that political radicalization in the metropolis could bring to the Cuban slave order, which had already been stressed by proslavery delegates during the Cádiz Cortes, resurfaced amid this new context. Besides some particular agitations in Cuba (including debates on the abolition of the traffic and independence conspiracies in 1821), the military mobilization of slaves, freedmen, and free people of color in the conflicts of the continent clearly demonstrated the direct relation between wars of independence and the destabilization of slavery to Cuban slaveholders.[86]

This second Spanish liberal revolution, which began in January 1820 with a mutiny of soldiers who refused to go to America to fight the insurgents, turned the slave trade into an especially acute problem within the internal political game. By reinstituting the Cortes—now based in Madrid—and the Constitution of 1812, the Spanish revolutionaries put the issue of the transatlantic slave trade to Cuba back on the table.[87]

The meeting of deputies in Madrid was different from its Cádiz counterpart in several key ways. It took place in the context of the defeat of Napoleon Bonaparte and the restoration of order according to the terms established in the Congress of Vienna. The king was present and forced to make an oath of allegiance to the Constitution. Finally, most of the American possessions of the Spanish Empire were gone. This Cortes did not have constituent powers, since its objective was to merely complete the work initiated in Cádiz. The polemical themes were the same, but the tone of the defense had changed. Americans requested an even larger representation at the Cortes but found an obstacle in the constitutional definitions that had already been passed. The same was true for demands to extend citizenship and electoral rights to the castas. Articles 22 and 29 of the Constitution of Cádiz were questioned during the triennium legislatures but remained unaltered. Those were the terms of the Constitution that delegates wanted to recover in their opposition to Ferdinand VII.

The participation of American representatives went through significant transformations. Their number had reached eighty in 1821, of whom 60 percent were representatives from Mexico.[88] The latter became the most important speakers at the Cortes of the Triennium until February 1822, when all representatives from dissident provinces in the New World were removed from the Cortes. From that moment until the end of the legislature (concluded in March 1823), overseas deputies came only from Cuba, Puerto Rico, and the Philippines. Thus, the first legislature of the Madrid Cortes was marked by the tensions and difficulties of the negotiations between liberals from Mexico and Spain. Most debates centered on disagreements about the level of autonomy that should be granted to the American provinces.[89]

Deputies from the loyal colony of Cuba actively participated in these debates, which revolved around two main issues between the call for elections, approved in May 1820, and the end of the second legislature: first, the liberal radicalization experienced in Spain and America, which demonstrated the general discontent with the aggressive policies Ferdinand VII had adopted since restoration in 1814; and second, the consolidation of independence processes, which put into question not only the rule of the monarchy but also the legitimacy of the Cortes and its call for Spanish unity.

Elections throughout Spanish America were largely defined by the ongoing revolution. Even in Cuba, the electoral process went through a radicalization that demonstrated that Cubans had a very specific set of priorities in this new liberal moment. In May 1820, the transatlantic slave trade was supposed to finally come to an end according to the terms of the Anglo-Spanish Treaty of 1817. The beginning of the Cortes and the inclusion of local representatives led to the rise of two opposite sets of hopes in Cuba: some expected to invalidate the treaty of 1817, while others sought to deepen the terms of the document in order to question slavery on the island. European liberals could not endorse either of these proposals, since the first one would complicate negotiations with Britain while the second one would inevitably generate conflicts with Cuban slaveholders. For these reasons, there was a general awareness that these tensions could ultimately lead to an eventual rupture with Spain, even in Cuba.

The problems with including Cuban deputies in the Madrid Cortes were symptomatic of these tensions. On July 5, 1820, the Cuban deputies residing in Spain—José Benitez y de la Torre and José Pascual de Zayas—were integrated into the Congress as substitutes.[90] The electoral process would then indicate titular members. On November 3, the same deputies became the official representatives of Cuba.[91] Elections in Havana, however, had indicated one more name to represent Cuba at the Cortes: Juan Bernardo O'Gavan. A Cuban representative at the Cádiz Cortes and signer of the 1812 Constitution, O'Gavan was also a canon of Havana Cathedral and a professor at San Carlos Seminary (the primary educational institution of the slaveholding oligarchy of Havana). The inclusion of this additional deputy, however, generated intense parliamentary debate. The session of February 1, 1821, received a request to cancel the Havana elections. According to the denouncer, while electoral instructions established the participation of ten voters in the last stage to elect the deputies of the province, twenty-one individuals had voted in a process full of irregularities.[92]

The debate on this issue divided Americans and Europeans. In the absence of Cubans (who were prohibited from participating in the discussions on the subject), Mexican deputies (who in turn defended the participation of the three Cuban representatives) represented Americans. It was generally assumed that the disproportionate number of voters had been a result of the integration of castas into the electoral process. In this context, Mexican deputies took the opportunity to revive the old American project of including the castas (and it is important to note that Cuban deputies, including O'Gavan himself, had opposed the inclusion of castas during the 1810–1812 debates). The European majority, however, was able to win the discussion and cancel the Havana election. The report from the Preparatory Commission of the Cortes was published on February 23, 1821. One week later, the men who had formerly been relieved of their duties—Benitez and Zayas—were readmitted into Congress after an order from the session president.

The reasons for the removal of O'Gavan are still unknown. The cancellation of the Havana election should have removed all three Cuban deputies. The exclusion of only one member of the delegation should have led to a new round of debates and explanations, but this did not happen. European liberals, who had been so obstinate in canceling the election before February 23, seemed to be satisfied when the Cuban group returned without Juan Bernardo O'Gavan. It seems likely that the positions of this important representative of the Cuban aristocracy were not well received at that moment.

After a few months of debate, the deputies at the Madrid Cortes were forced to discuss the treaty signed with Britain in 1817. In the session of March 23, 1821, shortly after the controversy about the integration of the Cuban deputies, the minister of foreign affairs of Spain, the Count of Toreno, recommended in the plenary "that a special commission be nominated to, according to Article 6 of the treaty signed by England and Spain, propose as quickly as possible the necessary measures to suppress the slave trade from

Africa that, in contradiction with this Treaty and to the disadvantage of humanity, continues to be carried out under the Spanish flag by naturals and foreigners, adopting the penal laws judged necessary to destroy such a shameful and inhuman traffic."[93] Toreno presented the proposal under the pressure of Henry Wellesley, a British diplomat in Madrid.[94] The deputies approved Toreno's indication, with Cuban deputies remaining silent on the issue. The president of the sessions became responsible for appointing the proposed commission.

O'Gavan then acted as the true representative of Cuban slaveholders, instructed as he had been by the provincial deputation of Havana to defend the "absolute equalization of the Spanish and Portuguese in the expressed traffic." Or, in other words, to nullify the Anglo-Spanish Treaty of 1817 and prepare a new document similar to the one signed by João VI in that same year.[95] Prohibited from talking during the Cortes debates, O'Gavan replied to Toreno's suggestion by releasing a pamphlet written and published in a few days while he was still in Madrid. Sent to the press on April 3, one day after the reading of a proposed anti–slave trade law elaborated by the commission (formed by three *peninsulares* and two Americans, both from New Spain), the document was the most sophisticated expression of the Cuban proslavery ideology until then, both a defense of the institution and a plan for the slave-holding elite's position in the political future of the island.

According to O'Gavan, a commission formed by the Cortes was not legit-imate because it did not include representatives from the overseas Spanish islands, an argument similar to the one made by Arango in 1811. Speaking as a representative of Cuba, or, in his words, the "country where I was born," O'Gavan did not consider himself to be a "defender of slavery" but of "labor, without which there is no production, nor population, nor force, nor wealth, nor any mode of perfecting the intelligence of men to stop them from falling into barbarity, stupidity, all sorts of disorders, all sorts of misery."[96] The "defense of labor" was a euphemism for the defense of Cuban slavery, an argument that O'Gavan developed largely by employing the proslavery ideol-ogy that had been circulating within the Atlantic system of northwestern Europe since the second half of the eighteenth century. His first point in the pamphlet justified slavery based on the climate of the tropics, an argument that could also be found, for example, in the writings of Montesquieu. In cold weather "the man is a slave of his necessities: nature surrounds him

everywhere and forces him to labor," whereas in warm weather "the legislator is called to perform the august functions of nature. The civil laws, religion, all institutions must with her stimulate man in every instant of his life,
compelling him to labor: without this there will be no social organization,
no means to perfect the human species."[97] Thus, it was the civil laws of states
in those tropical regions—including the colony of Cuba—that sanctioned
slavery, a minor evil given the "state of savagery" that inherently characterized the lives of Africans on their original continent.

In fact, O'Gavan argued, since African peoples lived outside civilized life
in a state of complete barbarity, the transatlantic slave trade brought great
advantages for them. Its civilizing effects became even more evident when
the conditions of black slaves on American plantations were compared to
those of the European working class. While the former were well treated and
protected by their masters from the cradle to the grave, the freedom of white
laborers in Europe was simply "the faculty to die of starvation." The best
indication of the benefits brought by the slave trade to Africans, according
to O'Gavan, could be found in the fact that "none of our freedmen ever tried
to return to the forests where they were born, to that country represented by
the Anglo-maniacs as inhabited by free and happy men."[98]

O'Gavan not only defended the legitimacy of the slave trade and slavery
but also attacked the treaty of 1817, which, according to him, had been an
imperialist imposition by Britain to weaken the rivals of its slave colonies in
the Caribbean and open markets for their colonial products from the East
Indies. He also stressed the political implications of the treaty, defending the
slave traffic by connecting it with the building of political order in the Spanish Empire:

> On this serious business [the slave trade] essentially depend the happiness
> and even the existence of the island of Cuba. Without the African arms
> necessary for the cultivation of its immense fields it would become a
> vast desert in a few years, and the vows of the eternal enemies of our
> agricultural and commercial prosperity and of our navigation would be
> fulfilled. . . . It is inevitable to remember that the island of Cuba always
> remained loyal to the motherland; it would be painful that laws passed
> without meditation destroyed this prosperity and pushed her to the
> common movement that today agitates the American continent . . . ; [the

Cortes has adopted] measures unfavorable to the system of union with the European provinces. The peoples from here and from there know very well what matters to their preservation and happiness. It should not be forgotten that in a short distance from that splendid island there is a wise government, liberal in principles and practices, powerful and active, that seeks to extend over her the beneficial hand, and attract her by all means to its systems of liberty and aggrandizement, offering abundant resources for its agriculture and commerce to a degree that Spain could never match.[99]

This passage lays out three political options available to Cuban slaveholders, all of which were connected to the imminent decision of the Cortes about the slave trade. If the "business" were preserved, thus maintaining the "happiness" and "existence" of Cuba, the colony would continue its historical experience of loyalty to the "motherland," Spain. If the laws passed without much "meditation" were effectively enforced, Cubans would follow the path of independence (an option criticized by the author, given the risks it would bring to the slave order as the examples of other Spanish continental colonies had shown), or call for the United States to annex them, a hypothesis that had been raised by Presidents Thomas Jefferson, James Madison, and James Monroe since the early nineteenth century and that was received with interest by certain sectors of the slaveholding oligarchy of Cuba.[100]

O'Gavan clearly preferred the first option, which, in fact, openly expressed the two grand objectives of the Cuban slaveholding oligarchy: union with Spain and the preservation of the slave trade. The implicit threat in his pamphlet apparently produced some results, since European liberals could not deal with such a significant loss in America. The minister of the interior intervened in the parliamentary debate and transferred the discussion about the special commission to the secret sessions of April 13 and 14, where it was properly buried.[101] Deputies of the Triennium in turn refused to approve any measure curbing the slave trade. This was another great victory for the Havana oligarchy and its project to expand slavery in Cuba. The treaty of 1817 would become a dead letter, and the unity of Spain would now be based on the complicity to maintain the prohibited commerce.

Alternative proposals of the period were all defeated. One example is the case of Félix Varela, a colleague and rival of O'Gavan at the San Carlos

Seminary. Also elected a deputy for Havana, Varela entered the Madrid Cortes on April 11, 1822, in the company of deputies Tomás Gener and Leonardo Santos Suárez, to join a second legislature. The Cuban delegation was completely replaced after that. Elections for the legislature of 1822 took place in the context of growing political radicalization brought about by the return of the constitutional regime. Among the many political groups (such as pro-independence groups influenced by Colombia and Mexico, annexationists trying to turn Cuba into a new North American state, and pro–Ferdinand VII absolutists) that emerged in Cuba, two became especially important: peninsular liberals resident on the island (whose basic platform was the strengthening of the central state and the creation of an integrated national Spanish market that protected their economic interests), and creole moderate liberals (who called for more provincial autonomy). The powerful Havana oligarchy, which had gained so much between 1814 and 1820, was then excluded from political control on the island. Without clear connections to any of these groups (and enjoying great intellectual prestige), Varela was elected as a sort of consensual candidate.[102]

Before occupying his seat at the Cortes (but already living in Madrid), Varela wrote a response to O'Gavan's pamphlet shortly after its publication, criticizing slavery and the laws that oppressed free people of color on the island. His targets were both the proslavery argument of O'Gavan and the restrictions on citizenship rights to castas that had been written into the 1812 Constitution. Employing the example of Saint-Domingue, Varela argued that the Constitution of Cádiz connected free blacks and mulattoes to slaves by creating a sense of common identity (against their white oppressors) among these subaltern sectors. To avoid such a dangerous situation, it was necessary not only to review the terms of the 1812 Constitution in order to extend citizenship rights to castas but also to guarantee the emancipation of all slaves. Varela attached a bill to his response designed to gradually abolish slavery in Cuba (in his view, the Anglo-Spanish Treaty of 1817 would already extinguish the slave trade).[103]

As historian José Antonio Piqueras has shown, Varela never published his response, which was only discovered in the late nineteenth century. Knowing the demands of his slaveholding constituents and having no political credentials for presenting his antislavery proposals in Madrid, Varela decided to remain silent on the issue. After the ending of the new Cortes in 1823, he went into exile and became a defender of the independence of the island.[104] Still, the slaveholding elite of Havana did not seem bothered by the end of another parliamentary experience in Spain.

This becomes evident in a piece written by Francisco de Arango y Parreño in September 1823 in response to an article from the Havana periodical *El Revisor*, edited by moderate liberals based in Cuba who considered the possibility of a political rupture after an eventual collapse of Spanish constitutionalism. The editors of *El Revisor* had translated an article by Dominique de Pradt stating the inevitability of Cuban independence. According to Arango, the independence option would be "unjust, impracticable, and ruinous." As part of his discursive strategy, he replied to each of the arguments in the article. Against the statement that most Spanish possessions in America had already been emancipated, he argued that the game had not been won in many parts of the continent and that even in places where independence was a reality, it had left a trail of destruction.

The exceptions were in those regions that did not engage in open wars of independence, which were Cuba and "privileged Brazil." Arango lucidly expressed how the slaveholding oligarchy of Havana interpreted the political cycle that had just come to an end. In his view, the end of the constitutional regime in Spain would not damage Cuba, but rather quite the opposite, since its great achievements had occurred "in the years before 1820, . . . when the power of the King was absolute." In the words of Arango, "the incredible growth of our fortunes" was the best indicator of the benevolence of the metropolitan government and the basis of the "pact that collectively forces Cuban society to respect the peninsula." This wealth, it is important to note, had been built based on the transatlantic slave trade, the commercial opening, and the stability of the internal social order. Finally, in this 1823 document, Brazil appeared as a successful example of an imperial transition that did not disturb slavery.[105]

Some of the reasons against independence presented by Arango at the end of the Triennium formed the basis of the option for political emancipation among the slaveholding classes of Portuguese America. The creation of a national state in Brazil as a monarchy (although defined by its constitutionalism) that maintained a territorial unity coincident with the old colonial frontiers and that refounded the slave order was a product of political dynamics generated by the transatlantic slave trade, the logic of commercial opening, and the necessity to safeguard the internal social order. This is why the *present* experience of Brazil, which prefigured a promising *future*, inspired Arango and his Cuban slaveholding allies in the development of their political projects.

The Constitutional Experience in the Portuguese Universe: Lisbon, 1821–1822

The Constituent Cortes of the Portuguese Nation gathered after January 1821 as a result of the revolution that originated in Porto in August 1820. Portuguese liberals demanded the return of King João VI, who had resided in Rio de Janeiro since 1808, and an oath of loyalty to the Constitution that was to be created in Portugal. The period between August 1820 and April 1821, when the monarch finally took the oath to uphold the Constitution and decided to return to Lisbon, was marked by deep uncertainties. Until that moment, Portuguese revolutionaries acted in consonance with the Spanish, who had been involved in the liberal reconstruction of their own monarchy since January 1820. Liberals from both countries envisioned a constitutional Iberian union in case the Portuguese king (with the support of the British) decided to stay in Brazil. Portuguese liberals initially feared that European rulers could become united in a defense of the order established by the Congress of Vienna and, for that reason, tried to establish an alliance with Spanish liberals.[106]

The Portuguese constitutional experience of 1821 and 1822, therefore, was profoundly shaped by decisions made in Spain. The Constitution of Cádiz, a symbol of a resistant liberalism, was revived in Madrid in January 1820 and became a reference point in Lisbon during August. It was sworn to by the king in Rio de Janeiro and acclaimed by the constitutionalist juntas of Pará (January 1821) and Bahia (February 1821). However, as we will later discuss, the Portuguese measures regarding the slave trade, slavery, and the rights of citizenship of freedmen and other people of African descent were based on different principles. After a period of uncertainty regarding the position of João VI, the Portuguese sought to maintain Luso-Brazilian unity and avoid the same type of rupture that was already apparent in the Spanish dominions. In the Portuguese case, this unity could only survive if slaveholding interests, predominant in all regions of Portuguese America, were not ignored.

Unlike the debates of the Cádiz and Madrid Cortes, Portuguese constituents never actually discussed the transatlantic slave trade. Cubans requested complete silence on the subject in 1811 and 1821, a request that was shared by Portuguese deputies in 1821 and 1822. After the beginning of the Porto Revolution and the establishment of the Cortes in Lisbon, its deputies had strong reasons not to meddle with the slave trade or slavery, institutions that had in fact been protected by the Anglo-Portuguese Treaty of 1817 (while having undesired consequences in the Hispanic world). Discretion was advised, especially for representatives elected in Brazil. An objective of the new Constitution, however, was to define the terms of access to citizenship rights. Silence also prevailed over this subject, but not completely, since the first decisions pointed to a different strategy from the one chosen by Spanish deputies.

After news arrived in April 1821 that João VI had joined the constitutional movement, Portuguese deputies adopted aggressive policies for the election of overseas deputies. They were favored by the approval of the Bases of the Constitution and by the decree for the election of overseas deputies, both of which passed in March. At the moment of elections, already with the acceptance of the Cortes by dom João, the Portuguese Constitutional Bases were finally established. The new text did not establish distinctions between free persons and slaves, nor comment on the latter's access to the rights of citizenship.[107] In any case, when sent to America, the Portuguese Constitutional Bases were accompanied by electoral instructions approved in Spain in 1812, but with one small (albeit significant) change. When adapting the Spanish electoral instructions to the Portuguese reality, Lisbon deputies excluded the restrictions to citizenship established in Cádiz (Articles 22 and 29). Thus, the first level of elections in Brazil included all the free black and mulatto population, turning the American dream debated in Cádiz during 1810 and 1811 into reality.[108]

It did not take long before the Cortes was forced to debate the subject of slavery in the Portuguese Empire. In a session on August 2, 1821, a few days before the arrival of first elected representatives from Brazil, deputy Anselmo José Braamcamp mentioned the issue in reference to the constitutional project. He stressed the division established between free and slave, an implicit distinction in the fundamental law. "I confess that is hard to approve this principle in an assembly where I see the most liberal ideas. All free men, says the article, and the word free I believe should be excluded from the article. We are forced to preserve slavery in the overseas possession, but I would like to see this sad reality indicated as an exception and not general rule, that should be regulated by all our newcomers. I wish this article indicated that, for now, while it is not possible to abolish slavery, we will make this difference."

Later, in the same session, deputy Francisco Simões Margiochi (also elected in Portugal) brought the subject up once again but went even further, proposing that slaves were considered citizens, arguing for the "Rights of Men," and demanding the establishment of mechanisms that prohibited the sales of captives. He admitted that the presentation of abolitionist proposals should be left for the future but proposed the immediate suspension of the citizenship of those who continued to sell slaves. Finally, he also suggested that the Brazilian delegation should be prohibited from occupying their seats in the Cortes in case they did not accept the antislavery principles offered by him. No Portuguese deputy supported Margiochi, as they preferred to wait for the arrival of the Brazilian deputies to decide on the matter.[109] Representatives from Pernambuco arrived a few weeks later, but the subject was never discussed in those terms.

The subject of slavery was very close to being revived after February 1822, when the deputies who had been elected in São Paulo arrived. On January 9, dom Pedro made the decision to remain in Brazil, a move that generated an open conflict between the governments in Rio de Janeiro and Lisbon. The Paulista representatives brought with them a platform that defended the unity of the Kingdom of Brazil, the presence of a prince in Rio de Janeiro (with the status of prince regent), and a complete restructuring of the Portuguese Empire. The document discussed the problem of slavery directly. In the *Instructions of the Provisional Government of São Paulo to the Deputies of the Province at the Portuguese Cortes, To Be Conducted in Relation to the Affairs of Brazil*, the following passage can be found: "imperiously requests equal legislative care for the improvement of the future of slaves, favoring their gradual emancipation and the conversion of immoral and brute men into active and virtuous citizens, watching the masters of these same slaves to ensure that they treat them as men and Christians . . . but all this with circumspection so that the miserable slaves do not claim these rights with tumults and insurrections that can bring scenes of blood and horrors."[110]

This passage, however, was never read nor mentioned in the Cortes. The general content of the program signed by the São Paulo junta was bravely defended by Antônio Carlos de Andrada e Silva at the Cortes.[111] His intransigent defense of the unity of the Kingdom of Brazil brought him the antipathy of most deputies elected in Portugal, the opposition of the Lisbon press, and total rupture with the Cortes. At no moment, however, did Antônio Carlos refer to the passage quoted above. During the constituent debates, São Paulo deputies attempted to establish alliances with representatives from other American provinces to defend the Kingdom of Brazil. Propositions for the gradual abolition of slavery, such as the one in the *Instructions*, could generate conflicts with representatives from those provinces, which completely depended on the slave trade and slavery. This was certainly one of the main reasons for the silence on the subject. Moreover, it is important to note that Antônio Carlos himself did not share the antislavery convictions of his brother, José Bonifácio de Andrada e Silva, possibly the author of the critiques to the institution present in the *Instructions*. In the debates regarding the commercial relations between Brazil and Portugal, Antônio Carlos stated very clearly that slave labor—cheaper than free labor—was fundamental for Brazilian sugar production and, therefore, to the success of the imperial economy.[112]

The strategy to silence the debate over slavery in the constitutional sphere, successfully employed by Cuban representatives at the Spanish Cortes, was reinforced in Lisbon by both the Brazilian and the Portuguese deputies, as illustrated by the destiny of a bill presented by the Bahian deputy Domingos Borges de Barros in a session on March 18, 1822. As we have seen, Borges de Barros had been one of the main members of the enlightened Luso-Brazilian group of Rodrigo de Sousa Coutinho. In 1822, however, he apparently changed his previous position. Given the similarities between his proposal and the representation about slavery presented by José Bonifácio to the Constituent Assembly of the Empire of Brazil in 1823, it is possible that he had been inspired by the antislavery passage of the *Instructions of the Provisional Government of São Paulo*, which had been excluded from the speeches of Antônio Carlos. The hypothesis seems plausible if we consider the emerging articulations between the delegations from São Paulo and Bahia.[113]

The Bahian deputy initially proposed measures to ensure the continuous flow of European immigrants into Brazil, including the creation of immigration commissions in America, the spread of Brazilian immigration agents through European countries, and promises that immigrants would receive special treatment from a legal perspective. Article 22 of the proposal clarified these objectives: "If the immigration of foreigners into Brazil is large during this initial period, the slave trade between that Kingdom and Africa will come to an end within six years after the promulgation of the Constitution of Brazil."[114] The proposal also had articles to "improve the fate of slaves," such as the possibility that a captive could purchase his manumission or request to change his master in case of mistreatment. The last item of the proposal would reward slave women with large numbers of children: "Masters should stimulate and favor marriage between his slaves. The married slave that presents six children alive will be emancipated, with the master supporting her as she raises her last son."[115]

What happened to the proposal offered by Borges de Barros? In the sessions of the following six months (which still included deputies from Brazil), it was not discussed even a single time. Moreover, Borges de Barros's modest regulatory proposals vanished in face of the broader objective of the proposal, measures such as making the influx of European immigrants a condition for the abolition of the slave trade, or stimulating the natural growth of slaves, which represented "the confirmation of the slave system, not its end."[116]

As had been the case in Cádiz, the slave trade issue was skillfully excluded from the Portuguese constituent debates. The issue of granting citizenship rights to freedmen was debated only when the draft of the Constitution was discussed and approved, this time without the antislavery speeches such as those given by Braamcamp and Margiochi in August 1821 (i.e., before the arrival of the deputies from Brazil).

Debates on the direct or indirect relationship between slavery and citizenship occupied few pages of the *Diary of the General and Extraordinary Cortes of the Portuguese Nation in 1821 and 1822*. The deputies elected in Portugal and Brazil split and then tried to agree on other themes, especially those related to the economic and political integration of the empire. On the issue of citizenship, it is striking that all deputies agreed on the adoption of inclusive policies, avoiding any notion of race in their arguments. Unlike the case of Cádiz, where debates on the issue of castas occupied long sessions during September 1811 and further stimulated insurgencies in the New World, the theme of citizenship did not play an important role in the independence of Brazil.

Very few racial terms appear in the pages of the *Diary of the Cortes*. During two years of daily debates, delegates never used the word *negro* in the singular form to describe a descendant from Africa. They used the term in the plural form, *negros*, only eight times, in contexts that largely lacked any political meaning. *Preto* appears only once in reference to Africans and *pretos* nine times. Other terms indicating African origin such as *mulato(a/s)*, *mameluco(a/s)*, *cabra(s)*, *pardo(a/s)*, *crioulo(s)*, *mestiço(a/s)* and *liberto(s)* were even less frequent. Finally, the idea of casta, so common in the Hispanic world, is not usual in the Portuguese vocabulary. The word was frequently used as a synonym for "type," yet it only appeared six times in association with social or ethnic differences. Thus, it is easy to see the political meanings expressed in these words. These terms were more clearly politicized in the sessions of April 17, May 22, June 26, and August 13, 1822. Particularly important here are the first and last sessions, when the criteria to define citizenship that would be included in the Constitution of the Portuguese nation were debated.

The right to vote was debated during the session of April 17. From the beginning, deputies employed a very broad definition of the issue, since the electoral instructions used in the composition of the Cortes did not make any reference to the existence of slavery or to the descendants of slaves. The text of the Constitution was to be defined in April 1822, with many proposals requesting the exclusion of certain sectors of society from political and electoral participation, including "vagrants," celibates older than age sixty and without children, illiterates, and, finally, freedmen and their children. On the seventeenth, a great debate regarding the inclusion of illiterates took place. The suggestion of a Portuguese deputy to exclude recent freedmen for two generations received little attention. The author of the proposal, José Campello de Miranda, received a series of replies from other representatives, especially from Brazil, ultimately joining the majority in their unanimous decision to extend voting rights to freedmen.

Not even Deputy Miranda offered a racial explanation for the exclusion of freedmen from elections. Fearing rancor, he explained that "the slave is always under the rule of his master and, therefore, to be truly free he has to rebel against the master, disobeying him. . . . Thus it is hard to believe that he has the same nobility of sentiments of any other Portuguese citizen."[117] The deputy not only ignored other possible forms of manumission but also distrusted individuals who were still close to the condition of slavery. In this way, he expressed his fears of this social condition, never raising any strictly racial reason.

The arguments against his proposal can be classified in three groups, all of them based on an interpretation of the historical experience of the Atlantic Iberian system: the inclusion of freedmen in productive activities, their demographic significance in the composition of the population of various Brazilian provinces, and the integration of this sector into public and military positions as a right acquired during the Old Regime. A deputy from Portugal replied to Miranda by emphasizing the diligence of freedmen: "The slaves get their manumissions by the gains of their industry, and in this case they will be useful citizens, since they proved that they love to work; or, by the spirit of humanity and generosity of their masters, and in this case they enter civil society after having witnessed good examples."[118] The Bahian deputy Marcos Antonio de Sousa argued that if Miranda's proposal were passed, there would be great agitation in Brazil, "where one-third of the population is made of freedmen and among them there are men of great integrity and probity." Antonio de Sousa also reinforced his argument by recalling past practices of the Portuguese empire: "The laws of dom José are still in vigor, which conceded to the freedmen to serve in public offices: the Marquis of Pombal knew that this measure was necessary for Brazil, and that these men should be employed for its good." Such a law, therefore, would generate "many intrigues" and "disagreements." The Cortes should instead legislate to "unite all citizens."[119]

Whether elected in Brazil or Portugal, deputies thought about the usefulness of incorporating this great sector of the Brazilian population. They were useful because they were productive and because they cared for the safety and management of public affairs in Brazil. For this reason alone they were citizens, which was a typical liberal argument. Moreover, deputies saw the reality of this situation entrenched in the social practices of the Brazilian population. The integration of freedmen and their descendants was an old reality, they argued, a structural reality of the social and political order of Portuguese America.

Representatives of Portuguese America stressed that the stability of the Brazilian slave society, already based on the cooperation of freedmen, could do without interference or support from the central government of Lisbon.

The argument was laid out on May 22, 1822, when the Cortes decided to send troops to Bahia against the vote of most representatives from Brazil. The Portuguese deputy José de Moura Coutinho argued that deploying military force in Bahia was, first and foremost, indispensable to repress ideas of independence, which were already present in many provinces. Second, it would safeguard the Portuguese and other European residents in Brazil. Finally, it could protect Brazil against slave uprisings.[120] The specter of Saint-Domingue was used here to frighten overseas deputies, reminding them of the intrinsic instability of all slave societies.

The reaction of the deputies from Brazil was immediate and continued during the sessions of the following months. Cipriano Barata (Bahia), José Ricardo Costa Aguiar de Andrada (São Paulo), and Antônio Carlos de Andrada e Silva strongly contested speeches like the one given by Moura, arguing that there was no risk of a repetition of the events of Saint-Domingue, given the large number of free persons who made up the Brazilian population. The tone of their arguments was either of indignation or derision. Indignation is clear in the words of Antônio Carlos:

> Some noble previous speakers complain, and in this space have confused everyone with the repetition of the same language: it is to safeguard Brazilians against blacks that the unsolicited, and hated, troops are sent. What an amazing audacity! Terrible mockery added to the most scandalous oppression! They believe we are so ignorant that we will receive as favors these insults and offenses! Don't we know better than anyone that slaves are not to be feared, that their number is insignificant compared to the free people, that the sweetness of domestic servitude among us has made our slaves friends before enemies?

Barata responded with a series of caustic comments: "Regarding the slaves, this deserves laughs. Don't be sorry for Brazil, Cortes. Don't feel pity for us. Poor slaves! It is better not to talk about this. Let's look at what really matters."[121]

The debate on citizenship resumed in different terms during the session on August 13, 1822. The main issue now was defining the qualifications required to become a Portuguese citizen, detailed in five different items in Article 21 of the constitutional project. The starting point was a broad, peculiar definition of the Portuguese Constitution: "All Portuguese are citizens." Unlike the texts adopted in Spain and France, or even the one passed in Brazil in 1824, the Portuguese never distinguished Portuguese citizens from those who were not.[122] Barata, however, did not like the terms and, shortly after the presentation of the article, made the only speech heard at the Cortes at that time about the racial differences of the Brazilian population. His goal was getting an explicit acceptance from Portuguese deputies that African blood would not exclude freedmen and their descendants from the status of citizenship. The speech employed almost all the terms for "African," "indigenous," and "Portuguese origin" described above.

According to Barata,

> I notice the word Portuguese. This word, Mr. President, can generate
> great jealousy among the peoples of Brazil. . . . I warn that the additional
> articles must be declared in the following way: of all Portuguese of
> all castas of both hemispheres. In Brazil we have white Portuguese
> Europeans and white Portuguese Brazilians; we have mulattoes that
> are the sons of all those Portuguese with black women, or the *crioulas*
> of the country or [those] of the Gold Coast, Angola, etc. We also have
> mulattoes, sons of the combination of the same mulattoes, and we have
> *cabras*, who are the sons of mulattoes with blacks. We have *caboclos*
> or natural Indians of the country, we have mixtures of these, i.e., the
> *mamelucos*, who are the product of the mixture between whites and
> the referred *caboclos*, and we have the *místicos*, who are the children
> of Indians combined with black people. Moreover, we also have black
> *crioulos*, who are born in the country, and finally we have the blacks from
> the Gold Coast, Angola, etc.

Cipriano Barata acknowledged that the third chapter of the approved project granted the right to vote to freedmen and did not exclude free people from access to political rights. Still, he warned that the word "Portuguese" "in Brazil is ambiguous," since it could suggest the exclusion of "people of color." Finally, he endorsed a different way of distinguishing citizens, based on the French revolutionary experience and later adopted by the Brazilian Constitution of 1824: "From now on I declare that it is better for Brazil to divide citizens between active and passive, according to abbot [Emmanuel

Joseph] Sieyès and other publicists, because this is more consonant with Brazilian affairs."[123]

A speech by a deputy from Portugal synthesized the different arguments laid out in the session: "Does the Constitution speak of blacks or whites when talking about the children of Portuguese parents? Don't they all understand each other? Does the color influence in any of these things?" Another deputy later stated: "This doctrine is not only typical of Brazil, but also of Africa and Asia, where there are freedmen who are not excluded from voting and the reason for this is that they are citizens." Finally, the discussion was concluded with the approval and immediate inclusion in the Constitution of Article 6, which noted the existence of a different kind of Portuguese/citizen: "the slaves, once they get a letter of manumission."[124]

Francisco Vilela Barbosa, a deputy from Rio de Janeiro, presented the article discussed above to the Cortes. He later raised this issue again when proposing that "all those who had been manumitted could not be elected, . . . not because they came from a miserable class . . . but because, having spent their time serving their masters, they could not have acquired the necessary knowledge and instruction for the complex performance of a representative of the Nation." According to him, "the sons of freedmen can be elected[;] having been born free and educated in freedom, they can have the proud and liberal sentiments with a precise instruction." Thus, despite the arguments of Barata, the deputy from Rio de Janeiro did not employ racial differences to distinguish the Portuguese. Rather, it was the lack of education that prohibited citizens from being elected. Vilela Barbosa received support from a Pernambucan deputy, who, referring to those coming from slavery, argued that "the despotism shackled them in everything, mainly closing the doors of the sciences for them."[125]

The right to elect freedmen seems to have been a more serious issue for deputies from Lisbon, since this debate lasted longer. Defenders of the exclusion of freedmen based their arguments on other ongoing experiences in the Atlantic. Fernandes Pinheiro, from São Paulo, justified his liberal affiliation: "And if someone here believes my ideas are not very liberal, please do me the justice of taking into consideration that in North America, especially in the states of Carolina and Virginia, of that country of freedom, many freedmen, by the way rich proprietors and producers, are not admitted nor called to Congress, nor to the specific assemblies of States, nor to primary assemblies, nor to electoral ones, nor to representative bodies etc." In other words, the proposal of Vilela Barbosa was more inclusive than the legal order of the land of the free. The Pernambuco deputy Manuel do Nascimento Castro e Silva recalled the specter of Saint-Domingue in reference to the lack of instruction: "Nothing more daring than ignorance. I know how to explain myself because I can already feel the horrors brought by the sinister consequences of such a deliberation, I can already see the sad scenes of the island of Saint-Domingue, because no one can ignore the influence that this class has on slavery—very easy to seduce."[126]

Arguments contrary to the proposal, however, laid out a different image: a large number of freedmen in Brazil were already part of the lettered sectors of society. Domingos da Conceição, elected in Piauí, asked the other deputies: "Had they been born slaves and after 40 or 50 years came to command a regiment as colonels or brigadiers, by then already considered citizens, would you like to prohibit them from serving as deputies at the Cortes?" Deputy Joaquim Teotônio Segurado in turn recalled that "there are many freedmen who are readily baptized as free and are called emancipated at the baptismal font," and that, therefore, they grow up as free men with access to education. Vilela Barbosa finally replied and tried to find a solution: "I agree that this exclusion is only applied to African freedmen and not to those born in the country, considering that many of these, as has been said, are educated by their masters in whose houses they were born; and many are emancipated at the baptismal font and sons of those same masters."[127] His indication was nonetheless rejected and, as a result, the Constitution of 1822 did not include any kind of restriction to the election of freedmen, whether they had been born in Brazil or in Africa.

It is possible to draw conclusions from the analysis of these sessions. Nonracial criteria defined the liberal conception of citizenship during this first Portuguese parliamentary experience. Liberals argued that citizenship should be granted to all free men who were productive and already integrated into the administration of public affairs. The unity between these Portuguese/citizens was seen as cultural and historical and should be maintained and extended through rational actions and education. The debates show that the development of this definition was a product of the image given by deputies from Brazil, perhaps representing another effort to preserve the unity of a disintegrating empire. While the theme was debated during 1822, a growing number of signs indicated that the union between the two kingdoms was no longer feasible.

It is interesting to note the affirmative quality of the definition of "Portuguese," which did not emerge in opposition to foreigners. References to the non-Portuguese residents of the empire, which had possessions on four continents, were rare. The definition of Portuguese/citizen was inclusive in many ways because it aimed at strengthening a fragile and collapsing identity. Thus, it established the identity of every Portuguese in the right to citizenship, the equality of the inhabitants of "both hemispheres," and, finally, the identity and possible equality of Portuguese individuals of many colors. After all, the Portuguese had to politically reinvent a multicontinental empire that, as we saw in the previous chapter, had been created in very specific ways during the fifteenth and sixteenth centuries. In the words of Antônio Carlos de Andrada e Silva, the deputies of 1821 and 1822 engaged in a "miracle of politics" to save a crumbling empire.

The Constitutional Experience in the Brazilian World: Rio de Janeiro, 1823

On the other side of the Atlantic, the task was different from the beginning. In the context of building a new identity, the definition of citizenship based on national boundaries required an opposition to the figure of the foreigner.[128] Still, the direct experience of the Cortes of Lisbon guided a large part of the constituent debates in Rio de Janeiro.

The criteria for citizenship in the Portuguese Constitution of 1822, for example, inspired the approach on the same issue in the draft of the Constitution for the Empire of Brazil, concluded on August 30, 1823, and submitted to the plenary the following month. According to the fifth article of this document, included in the chapter "Of the Members of the Society of the Empire of Brazil," Brazilians were "all the free men inhabiting Brazil and born in it" (paragraph 1), "all the Portuguese resident in Brazil before October 12" (paragraph 2), "slaves with letters of manumission" (paragraph 6), "children of foreigners born in the Empire, as long as their Parents are not in the service of their respective Nations" (paragraph 7), and "naturalized foreigners of any religion" (paragraph 8). In this last case, letters of naturalization were available to "every adult foreigner, resident in the Empire, possessing capital, properties, agricultural, commercial, and industrial establishments within it, or having introduced or practiced some trade or useful industry, or rendered important services to the Nation" (Article 6, paragraph 1).[129] The purpose of the text was to show that all Brazilians would be considered citizens, thus employing a solution similar to the one used by the deputies of Lisbon. Nationality became synonymous with citizenship, without any references to the issue of race.

The paragraphs related to this article were debated in the sessions between September 23 and 30, and from the very beginning were conditioned by the problem of slavery in the Empire of Brazil. Nicolau Pereira de Campos Vergueiro, a deputy from São Paulo who had been at the Lisbon Cortes, proposed an amendment that employed the terms of the Constitution of Lisbon and aimed to replace "members of society" with "citizens." All the representatives who supported or rejected his proposal referenced the servile status of a large percentage of the population of the empire in their arguments. Manuel José de Sousa França (from the province of Rio de Janeiro), for example, rejected the amendment and recalled that "according to the quality of our population, the children of blacks, captive *crioulos*, are born in the territory of Brazil but are not Brazilian citizens. We should make this difference: Brazilian is the one born in Brazil, and Brazilian citizen is the one who has civic rights."[130] João Severiano Maciel da Costa (from the province of Minas Gerais), trying to mediate an agreement between these parts, defended the existence of two kinds of citizens based on the difference between civil rights (restricted to those individuals who are "protected by the Law in the exercise and enjoyment of those rights, for which the preservation and safety the men have united in society: individual liberty, personal safety, right or safety of property") and political rights ("right of election, and of eligibility to have part in the Legislation of the country"), which in turn depended on the distinction between passive citizens (who enjoyed the first right) and active citizens (who had access to the second).[131] Following his logic, crioulo slaves, although born in Brazil (and therefore members of Brazilian society), could never be considered "civil Members of Brazilian Society."[132]

When proposing a separation between active and passive citizens, Maciel da Costa criticized the Constitution of Lisbon (approved in October 1822)—in his words, "the most deformed and contradictory known body"—for not distinguishing the two statuses. In this, he followed in the steps of Cipriano Barata, who had called for the extension of citizenship to freedmen while defending the distinction between active and passive citizens as appropriate for Brazilian society.

The amendment offered by Vergueiro to the title of the chapter "Of the Members of the Society of the Empire of Brazil" was defeated in the session of September 24. Immediately after the voting, however, Sousa França reintroduced the issue and, in an attempt to define who would have access to political rights, proposed a reformulation of Article 5 (from "are Brazilians" to "are Brazilian citizens"). The deputies who supported the new amendment used arguments similar to those described above, emphasizing (above all) the fact that slaves were not part of the social pact constituting Brazilian society.[133] This time, the amendment was quickly passed, unlike paragraphs 2 and 4 of Article 5, which dealt with the citizenship rights of the Portuguese residing in Brazil at the time of the proclamation of independence and of slaves who had received letters of manumission. These two themes occupied full sessions of the constituent assembly, a direct consequence of their relation to the construction of the new national identity in opposition to the old imperial identity, which involved Portuguese from both hemispheres and four continents.[134]

The relationship between slavery and citizenship was debated again in the plenary at the end of the session of September 27 and was debated exhaustively three days later. On the first date, only two amendments were presented. The deputy from Ceará, Pedro José Costa Barros, argued that only former slaves with jobs or established professions could obtain the title of Brazilian citizen. Sousa França in turn brought back a point that had been made by Manuel Caetano de Almeida e Albuquerque (Pernambuco) and José Arouche de Toledo Rendon (São Paulo) in a previous session. According to Sousa França, paragraph 6 of Article 5 could be approved without major problems in case

> our slaves had all been born in Brazil; because having the Right of
> territorial origin to be considered Citizens once the civil impediment
> of the condition of their parents was removed, the full enjoyment of
> this Right, which had been suspended by captivity, should then be
> restituted; but since this is not how it is, because a large part of our
> freedmen and slaves are foreigners from different Nations of Africa, and
> having excluded foreigners from the participation in the Rights of the

Brazilian Citizen, the conclusion is clear, if we are loyal to our principles, that the paragraph can only be passed in relation to *crioulo* freedmen, never to the African freedmen; because of foreign origin they should be encompassed by the general rule for foreigners; and the condition of captivity in which they came to our country does not lead to an exception in this regard. I offer an amendment for the conception of the paragraph in the following terms: "the freedmen that had been born in Brazil."[135]

Thus, Sousa França proposed a division based exclusively on birthplace, without making any references to race. It was because they were foreigners—and not for being black—that a manumitted African could not be considered a Brazilian citizen. Sousa França did not employ the repertoire of images and tropes—such as animality, a lack of mental faculties, or simply innate inferiority—that were hallmarks of the racist ideology of the Atlantic system of northwestern Europe.

The debate on the issue took place on September 30 and focused almost exclusively on the amendment of Sousa França, who further explained the reasons for his proposal. The main issue was that the rupture with the Portuguese Empire demanded a different solution to the problem than the one provided by the Lisbon Cortes. Although the inclusive policies passed in the Cortes were not directly connected to Portuguese Africa, Sousa França insisted that "they created a Constitution adapted to their possessions on the Coast of Africa, where the privilege of Citizen should inevitably be extended to the freedmen of the Nation, that they probably constitute most of the peoples; and we make a Constitution restricted only to our native Country. If I was a member of the Cortes of Portugal I would also vote for the affirmative on the same point that now I defend the negative."[136] While potentially "national" as part of the Portuguese overseas empire, the African had now become essentially a foreigner in the Empire of Brazil.

The priest José Martiniano de Alencar (Ceará) opposed the amendment because of "principles of universal justice." In his formulation, Africa appeared as a blank slate. Africans could not be considered foreigners in Brazil because they "never belonged to any Society." His central point, however, was another one. "If for principles of sane politics," he argued, "we should obstruct the commerce of slavery to then end it, it seems to me that we will reach this end more directly by conceding to the freedmen the privilege of Brazilian Citizen than by demanding certain conditions for this."[137] The antislavery speech by Alencar made clear that the objective of the decision taken by the Constituent Assembly of Rio de Janeiro to grant citizenship rights to African freedmen was to initiate the process of gradual emancipation of slaves in the Empire of Brazil, in order to create juridical, civil, and political homogeneity among the inhabitants of the new nation.

Such an interest becomes even clearer when we look at the members of the commission responsible for developing the constitutional project. One of them was the deputy for São Paulo, José Bonifácio de Andrada e Silva, whose antislavery opinions had already been expressed in the *Instructions of the Provisional Government of São Paulo to the Deputies of the Province at the Portuguese Cortes* but were developed further in his *Representation to the General Constituent and Legislative Assembly of the Empire of Brazil about Slavery* (concluded in 1823 but published only two years later). Bonifácio was one of the few people during that period who clearly and openly spoke about slavery. He not only called for the end of the traffic in five years but also defended the interference of public power in the domestic sovereignty of masters and the legal right of the slave to manumission as preparatory measures for an eventual emancipation.[138] It is possible that Bonifácio took on the primary responsibility for anything related to slavery in the commission of the constitutional project,[139] as indicated by the title of the project for the members of the society of the Empire of Brazil and the content of Article 254, which established the future creation of "establishments for the catechesis and civilization of Indians, slow and gradual emancipation of blacks, and their religious and industrial education."[140]

In sum, the defenders of the extension of Brazilian citizenship to African freedmen in the debates of September 30, 1823, also made direct criticisms of slavery. The debates on the issue in Rio de Janeiro had elements that were absent in Lisbon, with the discussion about citizenship rights leading to an open debate over slavery itself. The two deputies who quickly condemned or defended the amendment, José da Silva Lisboa (future Viscount of Cairu, deputy for Bahia) and João Severiano Maciel da Costa (future Marquis of Queluz, deputy for Minas Gerais) had opposite views about slavery and the transatlantic slave trade.

To defend his vote against the amendment, which had the objective of "making the Article simpler or broader, to end any doubt, declaring a Brazilian Citizen not only the crioulo that got from his master the letter of manumission, but also the one that acquired freedom through any legitimate title," Silva Lisboa presented a long antislavery defense that criticized the inhumanity of the slave trade while praising the champion of the British abolitionist movement, William Wilberforce. The example of Saint-Domingue was used in the same sense: "Where the cancer of slavery is embedded in the vital parts of the civil body," he declared, "only very slowly can it be disembedded."

For this reason, he viewed gradualism as the most adequate solution to the problem of slavery in Brazil. Silva Lisboa likewise established a direct link between the paragraph on the extension of citizenship rights to crioulo and African freedmen and the one dealing with the gradual end of slavery in the Empire of Brazil: "the illustrious Authors of the Project of our Constitution considered the Advices of Political Prudence; and, on this point, their system finds itself, I believe, so well connected that I do not have the adequate expressions to praise it. When I combine the article at hand with articles 254, 255, it seems to be that they completely address the objections that have been insistently raised, establishing the basis of regulated benefits for slaves, only proposing their slow emancipation and moral instruction."[141]

In opposition to Silva Lisboa, Maciel da Costa argued that the destiny of freedmen was a "thorny issue, about which have vacillated enlightened and human Nations that, like us, have them." Like Sousa França, he noted the foreignness of African former slaves and added the issue of "public safety, this first Law of States that is superior to everything." If the assembly had agreed to stipulate a series of clauses for the concession of citizenship to other foreigners, Maciel da Costa was shocked to "see that the African, by obtaining his letter of manumission, which is a title that simply allows him to own himself and his time, moves ipso facto into the bosom of the Brazilian family, to our brother, finally." The rigid criteria for granting citizenship to foreigners in Article 6 would be ignored in the case of Africans. To prove that the amendment of Sousa França was not exclusionary, Maciel da Costa established a comparison with the United States. Even if the amendment were passed and the crioulo freedmen were distinguished from Africans, the deputies of the Empire of Brazil had gone much farther than their US counterparts, who prohibited the civil and political participation of black people based on explicitly racial criteria.[142]

In a subsequent speech, Maciel da Costa also laid out his view of the transatlantic slave trade (which was also the opposite of Silva Lisboa's): instead of justifying it as a duty of conversion (a central topos of the slaving ideology of the Portuguese Empire), he laid out what would become the main form of defense of the transatlantic slave trade to the Brazilian Empire in the ensuing three decades.

> Foreigners from other Nations come to this country carried by the necessity to make fortune, the Africans come because their barbarous compatriots sell them; and Brazil is not a more natural country of some than of others, and can only be adoptive by the general means recognized by Nations. That we owe Africans their admission into our family as compensation for the evils that we have inflicted on them is something new to me. We are not guilty of the introduction of the Commerce of men; we receive the slaves we pay for, take from them the labor that we also take from free men, and give them the support and protection compatible to their state; the deal is closed. That they are not barbarians, because according to historical relations, there are already regular Societies among them, as my illustrious friend [José da Silva Lisboa] says, I appeal to the testimony and experience of those that receive them here from the Ships that carry them. Finally, Sirs, political safety and not philanthropies must be the basis of our decisions on this issue. Philanthropy has already led to the loss of the very prosperous French Colonies.[143]

The emphasis on the distinction between Brazilian and African freedmen was, therefore, based on two arguments: first, the transatlantic slave trade to the Empire of Brazil would not come to an end anytime soon, constantly introducing foreigners into the national territory; second, and directly connected to the first reason, to follow the principle of public safety, "the first Law of States," it was necessary to adopt measures of social control such as the distinction between Brazilian and African freedmen. Since the former could become citizens, they would more eagerly defend the order than the latter.[144]

The plenary approved the position of Silva Lisboa, but the argument of Maciel da Costa became the real winner behind the curtain. On November 12,

1823, when the Constituent Assembly was debating Article 24, Pedro I dissolved it and created a new commission with ten members, making it responsible for preparing the final text. Six former constituent deputies became part of the new commission, among them Maciel da Costa, who signed the Constitution passed on March 24, 1824, in the position of secretary of state of the affairs of the empire. This Constitution, the only one passed during the period of black slavery in Brazil, excluded African freedmen from citizenship but not crioulos. It also eliminated Article 254 of the draft of the Constitution of 1823.

If there were certain continuities between the solutions to the problem of citizenship in Lisbon and Rio de Janeiro, the transatlantic slave trade generated very different responses in these two spaces, as the terms of the debates about political rights in the latter indicate. As we have seen, the Additional Convention of July 28, 1817, designated the slave trade in the South Atlantic as an internal business that operated within the Portuguese Empire, providing a shield against British pressure. In this context, Portuguese deputies could avoid such a delicate issue and exclude it from the Lisbon Cortes during the 1820s. After the independence of Brazil, however, the Convention of 1817 could not be employed to defend the transatlantic slave trade anymore, since the collapse of the Portuguese Empire politically split the close connection between Portuguese America and Africa. One possible strategy to re-create the diplomatic protection of the traffic in the South Atlantic would be to incorporate Angola into the Empire of Brazil. This was precisely what two deputies elected by the African province to the Cortes of Lisbon suggested. Before arriving in Portugal, Eusébio de Queirós Coutinho and Fernando Martins do Amaral Gurgel e Silva stopped in Rio de Janeiro, where they defended (to the local press) the incorporation of Angola into the recently formed General Constituent and Legislative Assembly of Brazil. The following year, the movement for incorporation into the Empire of Brazil became stronger in Benguela.[145]

The stronger reactions to these projects did not come from Portugal, which lacked the military strength to stop an eventual integration of Angola into Brazil, but rather from Great Britain. After 1822, the British foreign policies regarding the old colonies of Iberian America began focusing on the transatlantic slave trade. Between 1822 and 1827, for example, the British foreign secretary, George Canning, sent officials to Buenos Aires, Montevideo, Valparaíso, Lima, Cartagena, Mexico City, La Guaira, Veracruz, and

Panama, instructing them to gather information about three fundamental issues: first, if the respective countries had declared independence; second, if they would keep it; and, third, if they had interrupted the slave trade. France supported and financed the new absolutist restoration of Spain in 1823, refusing to sign commercial treaties with the new American republics that emerged from Spanish America.

Canning, on the other hand, playing a sort of sheriff in international politics, openly revealed his intentions: "I resolved that if France had Spain, it should not be Spain 'with the Indies.' I called the New World into existence to redress the balance of the Old." Economic reasons could be naturally found in the strengthening of the British credit system: "Spanish America is free; and if we do not mismanage our affairs sadly, she is English."[146] Independence, access to the world market, and participation in the British credit system had a price for Hispanic countries: the end of the transatlantic slave trade. Between the end of the traffic and the end of Spanish absolutist rule, the new American republics did not hesitate to follow the rules of the game. The exception, as we have seen, was Cuba, whose slaveholding elites remained loyal to the absolutism of Ferdinand VII in order to take advantage of its diplomatic body, now strengthened by the support of France.[147]

Brazil entered this new milieu after its independence, having to face the British antislavery policies. Canning repeatedly offered political recognition of the new nation in exchange for a bilateral treaty for the total suppression of the transatlantic slave trade.[148] But, unlike with the Hispanic cases, both the ending of the traffic and the recognition of independence against absolutism were fundamental issues in Brazil: the country needed the support of Britain in order to be recognized and gain access to the global circuits of goods and capital, but could not envision successful participation in this commercial world without the transatlantic slave trade. This dilemma defined the historical narrative of the Empire of Brazil until 1850.

The problem was discussed in the Constituent Assembly of 1823, with Carneiro de Campos recommending the creation of a special commission to establish a treaty with the British ambassador that would recognize independence, in exchange for a commitment to abolishing the traffic of slaves within one year.[149] The issue was discussed in a secret session in which all deputies agreed to delegate negotiating power to the executive; request that the future treaty with Britain not establish the end of the slave traffic in less than four years; ensure the recognition of independence; and, finally, allow Britain to protect the constitutional and representative regime of Brazil, avoiding absolutist coups, republican outbursts, and separatist actions that could eventually emerge (even as a reaction to the end of the traffic).[150]

The decision of the deputies to take the slave trade issue from the plenary to the diplomatic arena derived, to a large extent, from experiences in other parts of the Atlantic. Those experiences demonstrated the dangers in debating the theme in parliamentary spaces, and, in fact, a certain anti-slavery impulse that could be found among a considerable number of Brazilian constituents. For example, the heavily anti–slave trade proposal of José da Silva Lisboa on the citizenship of African freedmen was passed on September 30, 1823. Behind the scenes, however, the platform of Silva Lisboa was defeated, with the Constitution of 1824 completely ignoring the problems of slavery and the slave trade. If the omission helped legitimize the institution on a national level ("projecting it over contemporaneity"[151]) it also gave Pedro I exclusive power to deliberate on the slave trade for the following two years. In the Anglo-Brazilian diplomatic negotiations of 1824 and 1825, Brazilian officials continued to maintain that the slave trade could not be abolished in less than four years, but the limits of their actions became increasingly evident.

Even before formally recognizing the independence of Brazil, which depended on the signing of a treaty to abolish the odious commerce, Britain had already showed its force to the new empire. According to Article III of the Treaty of Peace and Alliance (signed between Pedro I and João VI in August 1825 for the Portuguese acceptance of Brazilian emancipation), "Your Imperial Majesty promises not to accept proposals from any Portuguese colony to reunite themselves to the Empire of Brazil."[152] The objective was clear: stopping Angola from becoming a province of Brazil and the transatlantic slave trade from becoming an internal affair of the new national state. The collapse of the old Portuguese Empire thus paved the way for British pressure and, ultimately, for the end of the traffic itself.

The Iberian Constitutional Experiences and Slavery in the Nineteenth Century

The parliamentary actions of deputies from the metropolis (and overseas) during the Iberian constituent assemblies were shaped by the range of experiences generated by the crisis of the Atlantic system of northwestern Europe. Events such as the development of the Constitution of the United States, the British campaign for the abolition of the transatlantic slave trade, and, especially, the Saint-Domingue Revolution constantly informed the arguments and strategies of political actors in Cádiz, Madrid, Lisbon, and Rio de Janeiro. On these occasions, Cuban and Brazilian representatives defended a clear platform for the protection of slavery and the slave trade with some success, since these issues did not become the object of new legislation.

As we have seen, the strategy employed by Cuban and Brazilian deputies in their respective constitutional experiences in Iberia was simply to silence all debate on the issue of the slave trade. Pointing to the French case as evidence, Cubans argued in Cádiz and Madrid that public discussion of the problem would bring the revolutionary events of Saint-Domingue to the Spanish colony (as demonstrated by the conspiracy of José Antonio Aponte). They also explored the US and British cases to defend their position that the question could not be debated in the legislature for at least two decades. The same topos of a long expiration date was present in the writings of Rodrigo de Sousa Coutinho, who established the procedures to deal with the issue during the Joanine period. Between 1821 and 1823, in face of the polarization that divided the Spanish Empire, the slave trade issue was not even discussed in the Cortes of Lisbon or in the Assembly of Rio de Janeiro. Deputies of Portugal and Brazil simply ignored proposals such as those offered by Domingos Borges de Barros and José Bonifácio de Andrada e Silva.

The future of slavery in Cuba and Brazil faced a decisive moment during their respective constitutional experiences. Moreover, some of the elements that influenced the establishment of an empire in Brazil after independence also pushed Cuba to remain a Spanish colony. In both cases, these options were conditioned by the maintenance of slavery. The pamphlet by Juan Bernardo O'Gavan was clear in this sense. As long as the metropolis supported the maintenance of the slave trade to Cuba in face of British diplomatic pressure, Cuba would remain a province of Spain; if, however, the Cortes decided to legislate on the issue, Cuba would not follow the path of independence that had been taken by the old Spanish colonies but rather would look to the United States for annexation. The processes of independence in Spanish America—and all the military conflicts and internal disorders, and, especially, the gradual emancipation of slaves that accompanied them—were interpreted as complete anathema in Portuguese America. The space of experience in Spanish America played a formative role in horizon of expectation of the creators of the Brazilian national state, who sought to reestablish the previous imperial and slave order under the new basis of a constitutional monarchy.[153]

Cuba and Brazil experienced the different results of a single historical process that began in 1790 with the Saint-Domingue Revolution and its uneven impact on slavery throughout the Americas, which became more intense after 1808 with the collapse of the Iberian Atlantic system and the beginning of the international antislavery campaign of Britain. The colonial continuity in Cuba and the adoption of a constitutional monarchy in Brazil were different answers to a single set of forces, both sharing the ultimate objective of entering the nineteenth-century world economy with a model based on the intensive exploitation of slave labor.[154] But if the strategies employed by Cuban and Brazilian deputies in the Iberian constitutional experiences to re-create slavery and the transatlantic slave trade were very similar, they were profoundly different on the issue of granting citizenship rights to freedmen and other African descendants. While deputies from Cuba agreed on restricting the political rights of these groups (as outlined in the Constitution of 1812), deputies from Brazil defended and passed the concession of these rights in Lisbon and Rio de Janeiro.

Why did Cuba and Brazil diverge on the issue of citizenship? The difference is even more striking given the fact that both countries were demographically similar (despite the differences in scale) in the early nineteenth century, each having large numbers of free people of color. Possible explanations for the differences in these solutions can be found, first with the position of Cuba in the Spanish Empire and the weight of all the Brazilian captaincies in the Portuguese empire, and second with the uneven impact of the Saint-Domingue Revolution on both places.[155]

In the early nineteenth century, Cuba was the only genuine slave society of Spanish America (to use the classic concept of Moses Finley), where slaves formed the basis of the economy and of the power of local elites.[156] There certainly were important slave enclaves in other Spanish colonies, but the institution was not the basis of social organization in those places. This characteristic of the Spanish island, moreover, was recent. For two centuries,

Cuba had been a society with slaves but not a slave society. The transformation started in the second half of the eighteenth century, particularly after the beginning of the Saint-Domingue Revolution, when Cuban producers took advantage of the opportunities brought by the collapse of the French colony. Only then did Hispanic Cuban merchants decide to engage more directly in the transatlantic slave trade. Finally, in the 1790s, the economic heart of the Spanish Empire was not Cuba but New Spain and Peru. It was only with the deepening of the crisis of the Iberian Atlantic system in the 1810s that Cuba and Spain became increasingly dependent on each other.

Saint-Domingue, however, did not mean only new economic opportunities for Cuba. Because of the geographical and human idiosyncrasies of the Caribbean, which, according to Sidney Mintz, constituted an authentic *oikoumene*,[157] the specter of Haiti haunted or inspired the inhabitants of Cuba, whether we consider metropolitan authorities, slaveholders, free people of color, or slaves.[158] For this reason, Cuban slaveholders radically reconfigured the strategies of social control after 1790, especially with the establishment of new criteria for the social and political incorporation and exclusion of former slaves. In the face of the support offered by the metropolis for the transatlantic slave trade (against British pressure), and for the internal safety of the island (against eventual uprisings of racially subaltern groups), the Cuban slaveholding oligarchy did not hesitate to sacrifice the citizenship rights of free blacks and mulattoes in Cádiz and Madrid.

The contrast with Brazil is clear. The colonies of Portuguese America had already exhibited the key characteristics of slave societies since the sixteenth century. Practices related to slavery consolidated over time and helped cement the unity and even identity of the Luso-Brazilian colonists. Among these practices, it is important to note the combination of a large transatlantic slave trade based on Brazilian ports and high rates of manumission. As many historians have shown, manumissions in Brazil had followed the same pattern since the seventeenth century: the chances of being manumitted increased the further a slave was removed from the experience of the Middle Passage. At the turn of the nineteenth century, this free and freed population, removed from the transatlantic slave trade for one or more generations, represented one of the greatest backings of the Brazilian slave society, but also a history of demands that been progressively politicizing the social place occupied by them. The sedition effort of 1798 in Bahia may have been the most radical moment before 1808, but it is important to remember the nature of demands in Minas Gerais before and after the conspiracy of 1789, in which representatives of free pardos, blacks, and mulattoes emphasized their indispensible role in supporting slavery in the colony when presenting their pleas.[159]

In the years immediately following the arrival of the royal family in Rio de Janeiro, slaveholders did not correlate the politicization of former slaves to a possible repetition of the events of Saint-Domingue. The South Atlantic was a historical-geographic space apart from the human flows of the Caribbean oikoumene and, therefore, was detached from the black revolutionary epicenter. The dissemination of news from Haiti in Brazil was successfully blocked, circulating almost exclusively in the writings of men of letters and statesmen.[160] The Pernambucan Revolution of 1817 initiated the transformation of this context, which became particularly strong during the constitutional experiences of 1821 and 1823. It led to a redefinition of imperial identities and generated more intense debates among deputies from Portugal and Brazil about the risks brought by the example of Saint-Domingue.[161]

The eventual solution—a highly inclusive definition of citizenship—is surprising at first, leading some historians to dismiss it as empty rhetoric.[162] Such an interpretation, however, is inadequate, as shown by the speech of the priest Venâncio Henriques de Rezende, deputy for Pernambuco in the Assembly of Rio de Janeiro. In his view, popular mobilization in Brazil forced deputies to adopt broad criteria for the concession of citizenship rights: "At the present time great importance is given to this word, that there should be great jealousy, and displeasure, if a class of Brazilians believed that there was an effort to make this title exclusive to another class. In this they do not want to claim all political rights, because they recognize that not everyone is capable of everything; they do want, however, to be recognized as Brazilian citizens."[163] The "class" referred to by Rezende was the enormous mass of free blacks and mulattoes born in Brazil, who had been increasingly participating in the conflicts that defined the crisis of Portuguese colonialism in America.

The speeches of Rezende and other Brazilian deputies indicate the growing awareness among contemporary political actors of the institutional dynamic of Brazilian slavery, based as it was on a complex combination of social incorporation and continuous production of inequality. The inclusive definition of citizenship in the Brazilian Constitution of 1824 was conceived as a condition for the maintenance of the internal order and, ultimately, the expansion of the transatlantic slave trade itself, thus being much more than mere rhetoric. The question of the political participation of freedmen and their descendants was at the center of the debates on citizenship and the reproduction of slavery.[164] Thus, it is not surprising that, unlike the US Constitution of 1787, the Brazilian Constitution of 1824 was never used to criticize slavery, only to defend it.

Slavery and Parliamentary Politics in the Empire of Brazil and in the Spanish Empire, 1825–1837

⸻ ❖ ⸻

THE REFOUNDATION OF the Brazilian slave order by the imperial Constitution of 1824 and the reestablishment of the informal pact between Ferdinand VII and Cuban slaveholders (after the restoration of absolutism in Spain in 1823) combined to create a new institutional framework that allowed new economic expansion in the Iberian Atlantic. In response to the growing demand for primary products in the industrial regions of the North Atlantic, coffee production in Brazil and sugar production in Cuba underwent dramatic growth between 1820 and 1835. The Spanish island more than doubled the volume of sugar exported to the world market, going from 50,000 annual metric tons to 115,000, while international production as a whole increased by only 38 percent. Brazilian coffee exports in turn went from 13,000 annual metric tons to 60,000, surpassing other competitors from America (Jamaica and Cuba) and Asia (Java). Free trade, urban growth in the industrial centers, and the period of peace after the Congress of Vienna provided the context for the economic growth of Brazil and Spain-Cuba during the nineteenth century.[1]

A different force also intertwined the political destinies of these two empires. With the growth of slavery based on the slave trade, Rio de Janeiro and Madrid became the main targets of the anti–slave trade policies of Great Britain. In 1825, George Canning sent ambassadors to Brazil to intermediate the acknowledgment of independence by the Portuguese in exchange for the definitive abolition of the transatlantic slave trade. After intense negotiations, the Empire of Brazil became part of the "club" of free nations, and an

Anglo-Brazilian Convention was established in 1826 to abolish the slave trade by 1830. Canning also offered military and diplomatic support to Ferdinand VII against external threats to Cuba but expected either the recognition of the new Hispanic republics or the fulfillment of the anti–slave trade treaty of 1817. The tensions between the expansion of slavery based on the slave trade, the maintenance of the political unity of the empire, and British diplomatic pressures profoundly marked the history of both Brazil and Cuba until at least 1850.[2]

Despite the two main common forces shaping Brazil and Cuba—a world market and British antislavery diplomatic pressure—the two regions followed radically different political paths. The year of 1826 marked the end of the last cycle of liberal revolutions that had led to independence movements in Spanish America. While representatives from former Spanish colonies gathered at the Congress of Panama in search of mutual help against the former metropolis, deputies from all Brazilian provinces began the regular activities of the imperial Parliament. Cuba, in contrast, not only remained a Spanish colony but also adopted the system used in besieged towns, which granted extraordinary powers for captains general to preserve the social control and political status of the island. Such a regime produced a state of siege *tout court* over time, without freedom of the press or procedural safeguards. It was a regime that significantly helped to preserve the contraband slave trade from the very beginning. The Empire of Brazil in turn opted for the foundation of a new constitutional order in which freedom of the press and parliamentary sovereignty produced a remarkable public sphere.

It was within these different contexts that Brazil and Spain-Cuba had to adopt a realpolitik approach against British anti–slave trade pressure in order to protect the development of their respective slave economies. With these institutional asymmetries, the construction of pro–slave trade politics in both regions followed almost opposite paths between 1825 and 1835, becoming similar only in the years after this initial period.

Parliamentary Brazil: Public Sphere and the Slave Trade, 1826–1835

None of the constitutional regimes that dealt with the issues of the slave trade or slavery reached an absolute consensus over them. These questions had already divided national deputies in the Empire of Brazil in 1826 (the

first year of the Parliament) during negotiations with Britain over the establishment of an anti–slave trade convention between the two nations. As we
have seen, the Constituent Assembly granted the power to decide the future
of the slave trade to the executive, only requesting a period of at least four
years for the eventual abolition of the traffic. The decision, however, was contested on both sides of the Atlantic. While Canning rejected the treaty as too
confusing, Brazilian congressmen considered putting the slave trade issue
again under the control of the Chamber of Deputies. On May 19, José Clemente Pereira, elected in Rio de Janeiro, presented a bill postponing the date
for the abolition of the slave traffic to January 1, 1841. The text did not char-
acterize the traffic as piracy nor future seized Africans as "free," but rather
as "freed." A commission that examined the bill, however, reduced the period
from fifteen to six years, arguing that the trade was "improper for a free and
civilized people" and expecting that its extinction would lead to larger flows
of free workers and modern machinery to Brazil. This was the first of many
divisions over the issue in Parliament.[3]

The dispute within the Chamber of Deputies was solved by external pressures. On November 26, 1826, the British ambassador pulled out an agreement with the Brazilian executive that established the abolition of the
transatlantic slave trade in a period of three years and turned it into a crime
of piracy, with the eventual possibility that Brazilian slave ships could be
condemned in British courts. Ratified by Pedro I, the convention was submitted to the Chamber of Deputies, although it could no longer be rejected
or changed. Still, given the report from the Commission of Diplomacy and
Statistics of July 16, 1827, deputies engaged in the first great public debate
about the transatlantic slave trade and slavery in Brazil over three entire sessions (July 2, 3, and 4).[4]

The commission, composed of five members, approved the treaty—"the
lights of the century did not allow the continuation of such a commerce"—
and called for a law regulating the execution of the penalty of piracy. However, two members of the commission, Luiz Augusto May (deputy for Minas
Gerais) and Raimundo José da Cunha Matos (deputy for Goiás), opposed the
argument and voted accordingly. May, editor of the well-known periodical
A Malagueta, noted that the Constitution of 1824 (Article 102, paragraph 8)
established that treaties vital to the country could only be ratified *after* the
approval of the legislative body. Since suppressing the slave trade would

inevitably reduce commerce and the circulation of currency, such a decision could never be taken without the consideration of national representatives. His rejection, therefore, was based exclusively on procedural issues. Cunha Matos in turn not only mentioned procedural questions but also discussed the slave trade itself, returning to some of the themes that had been debated in the Cortes of Lisbon and in the Constituent Assembly of Rio de Janeiro. His ideas prefigured the pro–slave trade arguments of politicians, state officeholders, and slaveholders until 1850, when the traffic was finally suppressed.[5]

Cunha Matos was a man of many faces. Having engaged as a soldier in the battles against revolutionary France during 1793 and 1794, he then worked as the *provedor da fazenda* (royal administrator) and provisional governor in São Tomé and Príncipe for almost twenty years. In 1817, he finally established himself in Portuguese America, where he helped suppress the revolution of Pernambuco and was nominated *governador das armas* (governor of arms) in Goiás after independence. An active deputy during the first two Brazilian legislatures (1826–1829 and 1830–1833), he then became a member of the National Auxiliary Society of the National Industry (Sociedade Auxiliadora da Indústria, or SAIN) and the Brazilian Historical and Geographic Institute (Instituto Histórico Geográfico Brasileiro, or IHGB), of which he was a cofounder. During the debates of the 1820s, Cunha Matos was proud of having witnessed the "embarkation of the miserable black slaves, of those men that are bought or seized in [African] wars." Thus, he considered himself the most apt to judge the diplomatic dealings.[6]

According to the deputy, the definitive extinction of the slave trade would lead to a great crisis in Brazil since it would affect commerce, the navy, fiscal revenues, and agriculture. Without the importation of slaves and the growth of agriculture associated with it, the states could not pay for public servants nor finance the war that was then being fought over Cisplatine Province (which was in the process of becoming Uruguay). Perhaps his most remarkable argument, however, was the association he made between the inclusive criteria for Brazilian citizenship in the Constitution of 1824 and the defense of the slave trade and slavery itself. For Matos, the convention would curb "an enormous recruitment of black people that, with the mixture with other *castas* over time, would reach the state of giving us active citizens and intrepid defenders of our nation."

In consonance with Article 6 of the Constitution, we can observe in the expressions "mixture of other castas" (*mistura de outras castas*) and "over time" (*decurso do tempo*) an indication that the descendants of Africans would become citizens after manumission and gain the ability to become active in civil society, join the army, and hold public office. While the slave traffic demographically increased the number of slaves, the latter would soon become free people of color, without whose active participation in society Brazil's material progress would descend into barbarism: "There are immense places where now only blacks and pardos can live with impunity, [but] these places, today wealthy and peopled, will become deserts, home of beasts and birds, [if] only there is a lack of people of black or pardo color to inhabit them."[7]

Matos's arguments generated immediate reactions from the Chamber of Deputies. A bishop from Bahia—one of the authors of the report—ridiculed the pretense of viewing Brazilian slavery as beneficial for Africans and their descendants: "I believe, Mr. President," he said, "that none of the Africans thanked the illustrious deputy for this act of compassion and humanity, that has taken them from the company of their wives, their children, and their nation." Another deputy rejected the idea that only black individuals could inhabit territories with a torrid climate: "Do not say that slavery is typical of warm countries, where the indirect weakness of fiber needs rest and repose; because such an inclination is typical of all men and all countries." Even the young Bernardo Pereira de Vasconcelos—future leader of the Regresso cabinet and defender of the contraband slave trade—noted the international isolation of Brazil on this matter and the positive example of Haiti: "Ah! Sirs, let's copy the Americans; Brazil is today the only country in the globe that continues to engage in this commerce; let's change our conduct in relation to Africans, in every sense our equals, as proven by the Haitians." Coming from Vasconcelos, the future ideologue of a slave trade empire, the statement may at first seem sardonic, but there is no evidence that the deputy defended the traffic during the debates of 1827.[8]

By seriously discussing the slave trade itself, the deputies implicitly accused Pedro I and his cabinet of incompetence for signing such a damaging convention. Not surprisingly, the emperor immediately prohibited the publication of the votes and of the speeches made by Cunha Matos and May in *Diário Fluminense*, the newspaper responsible for publishing the parliamentary debates. The two deputies nonetheless decided to individually publish their defenses.[9] Moreover, criticisms of slavery and the slave trade in the public sphere could have negative consequences for both slaveholders and slaves. For this reason, deputies concerned with the preservation of the institution focused purely on procedural issues in the last two days of discussion.

Already raised by May and Matos, who envisioned the end of the slave traffic only "when the free, sovereign, and independent Brazilian nation decides so," procedural issues became the central focus of the speeches made by the São Paulo deputies Francisco de Paula Souza e Melo and Nicolau Pereira de Campos Vergueiro. On the concession to the executive made by the Constituent Assembly in 1823, Paula Souza acknowledged that it was "true that the Assembly authorized, but it was to abolish the traffic only after a certain period (that it indicated)" and "only if England recognized our independence and ensured our system of constitutional-representative-monarchical government. And did the minister do this?" Supported by Vergueiro, the deputy criticized the characterization of the slave trade as a crime of piracy in the text. In a liberal state, the creation of laws was a prerogative of Parliament:

> Is it possible to make laws through treaties in a representative government with the division of powers? Wouldn't such a treaty be nullified by the law of nations? And if that is the case, what are we going here? Why did Brazil cross the turbulent sea of a revolution that gave it a representative government? . . . If that is the case, if a minister can make and unmake laws through a treaty, then close the doors of the rooms of senators and deputies, this form of government is permitted and let's again embrace the proscribed absolutism.[10]

Along with the Paulistas, Clemente Pereira reiterated that the treaty was an attack against the "interests of the nation, its honor and dignity, sovereignty and independence." This phrase, frequently repeated in the assembly, suggested that the executive had taken away the intent of national representation. But why did they use these terms? Brazil still did not have a law specifying possible crimes against the nation by cabinets or ministers, but the Chamber of Deputies would pass a bill for such a law in July 1826 (one of the requirements of the Constitution of 1824). Already in its first chapter, the bill established that statesmen responsible for *treaties* against the monarchy, the life of the emperor, or "the independence, integrity, defense, dignity, or interest of the nation" would be accused of *treason*. Moreover, ministers who "usurped any of the attributions of the legislative or judiciary powers" would equally be accused of treason.[11] The penalties were harsh, going from the loss of job, honors, and graces to perpetual prohibition from holding public office to, in the worst case, the death penalty.

By arguing that the treaty violated national interests by ending the slave trade in such a short period, tarnished dignity because it was the product of British threats, and usurped legislative attributions by passing laws without examination by national representatives, the deputies implicitly defended the punishment and even execution of the minister. In the face of these tensions, the Senate made some quick changes in the bill of law in order to save the minister responsible for the treaty, a senator himself. The terms "interests" and "dignity" were excluded from the first article, and the crime of usurpation was assigned to a different category of offense, one with lighter penalties than that of treason. Among the deputies, José Custódio Dias (representing Minas Gerais) deplored the amendments: "A law that would honor the nation will be vilipended by fetid amendments." And, significantly, Clemente Pereira added: "The nation, trusting to the discretion of the ministers the celebration of treaties, demands from them that they do not compromise their honor, dignity, and interests."[12] The deputies nonetheless passed the amendments proposed by the Senate in order to have a law of ministerial responsibility as soon as possible.

The focus on procedural issues in the debates efficiently ended the tensions that had divided the deputies on the slavery issue. Only the group that supported the convention, a loyal group connected to the emperor, and a few antislavery deputies rejected the accusation that the executive had disrespected the sovereignty of the National Assembly. Thus, although the Chamber of Deputies had decided to postpone the discussion about the treaty, the Convention of 1826 contributed to the rising parliamentary opposition to Pedro I. Vergueiro criticized the convention again during the debates on the budget for foreign affairs of 1827. The following year, José Lino Countinho, who had previously been a critic of slavery, used the treaty to attack the cabinet: "The last ministry was criminal for many other acts; we will settle the account. I am the first to declare that I will accuse the minister responsible for the treaty on slavery. We should all go after him."[13] In 1830, Paula Souza made strong general accusations against the government:

It will be necessary to employ the language that has been used here, in speeches that have shown that the government has been stupid, that it has ceded for weakness; and aren't we witnesses that the minister of State has said here that for weakness he has agreed to the treaties? Two or more times he has said so, once regarding the treaty on slavery, and the civilized peoples know better than ourselves that the government of Brazil has offended the national honor and stupidly acted, and shouldn't we express our opinion, that the government of Brazil has established treaties that vitally violated the Constitution of the State?[14]

During the process that led to the abdication of Pedro I, the Convention of 1826 seems to have helped the Chamber of Deputies in its struggle against the centralized conception of state, as articulated in the Constitution of 1824 (and which would only be redesigned after the passing of the Additional Act of 1834). The rejection of the centralized administration and the resentment of external interferences culminated in the Law of Regency of July 14, 1831, which established that future international treaties would have to be approved by the assembly. Combined with the Law of Ministerial Responsibility, this measure created a context similar to that of the US republic: the slave trade was now an *internal* issue regulated by legislative power. Unlike Spain, Brazil would never establish another anti–slave trade convention with Britain.

Still, the emergence of a public sphere in the empire allowed the circulation of texts, proposals, reports, and articles against slavery and the slave trade at a moment marked by the expected abolition of the slave trade, September 1830. This was according to the terms of the Anglo-Brazilian Convention, and radical political disputes generated by the abdication of Brazil's first emperor. The national law of November 7, 1831, prohibiting the transatlantic slave trade can help us understand this antislavery moment. The law is frequently considered both an outcome of British pressure and a cynical strategy of the great slaveholders who supposedly controlled Parliament, *uma lei para inglês ver*.[15]

The Brazilian law of 1831, however, exceeded the Convention of 1826 in several different ways. In the convention, the only criminals were the crews of slave ships, while freed Africans were only those belonging to seized slave ships, without any stipulation that the Brazilian government should expand these original provisions. The law of November 7 in turn established that all transgressors, from the ship's crew to the planters who purchased the captives, would be prosecuted. It also allowed anyone to report to the police not only illegal disembarkations but also the presence of Africans who had already been illegally disembarked anywhere. Finally, all Africans illegally disembarked in the country should be considered free, and it is important to note that the word "free" had important ideological and juridical implications. Unlike the term "freed," used in Clemente Pereira's proposal, it assumed that the slaving practices in Africa were not legitimate and allowed the use of Article 179 of the Penal Code, which condemned to prison an individual responsible for reducing a free person to slavery. In sum, by declaring the illegality of the slave trade on sea, on the coast, and in the interior of the territory, the Brazilian law widened the scope of influence of the convention. By defining the proprietor as a criminal, it created new punishable conducts.[16]

Senators were aware of all these differences when they debated the bill for the 1831 law. A number of senators reacted immediately after a member suggested that the first article (on the freedom of Africans illegally disembarked) retroactively included all individuals disembarked in the country since September 1830 (when the 1826 Convention had taken effect). The measure would free between fifteen thousand and sixty thousand Africans—there were variations in the estimates during the debates—and lead them into "a Revolution, since it is only necessary that one knows how to read so that, after reading this provision, mention it to all the others."[17] The amendment was defeated, but the fact that the first article—which was very similar to the defeated amendment—was passed without major debate indicates that senators did not envision their coexistence with a large mass of Africans illegally disembarked with a law declaring that they were free. Had they foreseen the dramatic growth of the contraband slave trade in the ensuing two decades (responsible for the disembarkation of approximately six hundred thousand people), it seems unlikely that they would have passed such a law. The article challenged the right of property and legal security of the contraband slave trade by undermining public and private control over slaveholdings. As Senator José Teixeira da Mata Bacelar argued, the convention established penalties for transgressors, while the law of 1831 granted freedom to Africans who were illegally disembarked. Such freedom was incompatible with the contraband trade and for this reason should be projected into the future, not the past.[18]

Parliamentary debates at the beginning of the regency took place within the parameters set by the law of 1831. Denunciations of the persistence of the slave trade appeared in the Chamber of Deputies and in the Senate in debates about the establishment of the navy, in additional proposals to curb the traffic, and in ministerial reports.[19] In a circular letter of 1832, the minister of justice, Diogo Antônio Feijó, requested the distribution of posters with the penalties, fines, and risks attached to the violation of the 1831 law. His priority was denouncing "the horrible crime of selling or buying free men."[20] This was best represented by the circular letter sent by Aureliano de Souza Coutinho (minister of justice after Feijó) to the justice of the peace of Vassouras in 1833: "Not only do they commit a crime with this commerce, but they [the proprietors] promote and create an abysm in their own future. . . . Because Africans, when ladinos and aware that they are free, will not stop fighting to escape a captivity that is illegal."

His logical conclusion was that neither "the law nor the government, in these cases, will protect the property of the masters."[21] Between 1831 and 1835, the contraband slave trade operated in defiance of decisions made by the national state, with the indictments of slaveholders responsible for the purchase of illegally enslaved Africans, who in turn were considered free. It is estimated that the number of slaves illegally disembarked in the country from the beginning of the Regency until 1834 may have reached over forty thousand.

Two landmark slave revolts took place within this context. In 1833, dozens of captives rose up at parish of Carrancas (part of the comarca of Rio das Mortes, in the southern part of Minas Gerais), where the highest ratio of slaves per free persons in the province (approximately 60 percent) and an equally high number of Africans within the slaveholdings (56.25 percent of the total of black slaves) could be found. Slaves owned by the liberal deputy Gabriel Francisco Junqueira killed his son at Campo Alegre plantation and then moved to Bela Cruz, where they joined other captives and killed the proprietor, José Francisco Junqueira, along with his mother, wife, daughter, son-in-law, and two grandsons—a five-year-old and a two-year-old. Nine members of the Junqueira family were slaughtered in the uprising, leading to an immediate and violent repression that culminated in the hanging of sixteen rebels. Even more explosive was the Malê revolt of January 1835 in Salvador, the capital of Bahia. The ratio of slaves (42 percent of the population) and Africans (63 percent of the slaves) was extremely high there. Almost six hundred captives fought in the streets of Salvador for nearly three hours with the intention of moving into the countryside, where they expected to join other slaves and strengthen the resistance. Repression was once again rapid and bloody: approximately seventy slaves were summarily shot and more than five hundred were punished with the death penalty, torture, or deportation to Africa.[22]

These two insurrections had an immediate impact on the public sphere. The Carrancas revolt was connected to political convulsions related to disputes between moderates and *caramurus*, as the supporters of Pedro I were known. In March 1833, supporters of the former emperor took over Ouro Preto, the capital of Minas Gerais. To stop imperial troops, they strategically spread a rumor that, although the emperor had freed the slaves, their masters had kept them illegally enslaved. The fuse was lit, and on May 13 the revolt started in the plantation of the liberal deputy, where slaves shouted: "You usually do not talk about the Caramurus, we are the Caramurus, we are going to devastate everything."[23] The following month, Parliament debated new measures to prevent the restoration of Pedro I: the centralization of the National Guard, the creation of a municipal guard to increase the protection of localities, strict control over the press (with the explicit censorship of any references to Pedro I), and the establishment of rigorous punishments for rebelling slaves. The objective was to ultimately hinder alliances between external enemies (such as the former emperor and his supporters) and internal ones, namely slaves. The first article of the law against slave revolts clearly referred to the massacre of the Junqueira family and created criminal types in toto based on the violent behavior of the insurgents: "Slave men and women who kill, wound, or physically injure his or her master, administrator, overseer, or their wives and children will be punished with the death penalty."[24] The bill, however, only became law after the Malê revolt.

The effects of the slave revolt in Bahia were qualitatively different. In its wake, part of the press published articles criticizing slavery, the slave trade, and the African presence in Brazil. At the court, the *Jornal do Comércio* reprinted a text from the *Aurora Fluminense* written by Evaristo da Veiga and published its own piece condemning slavery on moral, political, and

economic grounds. The following year, *Diário da Bahia* published three articles about the lack of ties between slaves from Africa and the national state.
In the legislative arena, the municipal chamber of Itaparica submitted to the
Provincial Assembly of Bahia a bill to "bring slavery to an end" and "anni-
hilate with this same step the hopes of the contraband."

The text called for the emancipation of all slaves by 1875, the passing of a
free womb law in 1855, and the deportation of all freed Africans. In May 1835,
the Provincial Assembly of Bahia itself submitted a petition to the Chamber
of Deputies in Rio de Janeiro requesting the peremptory prohibition of the
commerce between the empire and Africa with the objective of avoiding the
"events that have shed blood on the streets of the capital of this Province."[25]
The struggle of slaves clearly paved the way for antislavery speeches in the
press and in institutional spaces such as the Provincial Assembly, which had
recently been created by the Additional Act of 1834.

Moreover, twelve different proposals about slavery and the slave trade
were submitted to the Chamber of Deputies between the end of the slave
trade and 1836. Eleven of these became public between 1834 and 1836, a relatively high number, and ten were submitted after the Malê revolt. The Bahian
Antônio Ferreira França submitted four proposals ranging from the establishment of a free womb law to a deadline for the end of slavery in the country. João Barbosa Cordeira, deputy for Pernambuco, suggested that all men
should be considered free upon reaching the age of thirty (and women after
twenty-five), while Antônio Luís Patrício da Silva Manso (a mulatto chief
surgeon born in São Paulo and deputy for Mato Grosso) offered a proposal
with 166 articles to remodel the empire's entire labor system. In 1836, Henriques de Rezende called for closer supervision of the trade with Africa, and
Martim Francisco Ribeiro de Andrada, elected to the Chamber of Deputies
that same year, suggested that slaves should not be sold without the presence
of the justice of the peace.[26]

These proposals, however, were not merely reactions to slave actions. During the elections for regent of 1834, Feijó became the first statesman to publicly condemn the persistence of the contraband slave trade, perhaps
inspiring the indignation of other opponents of the traffic. In his newspaper
O Justiceiro, he published an article describing slavery as an abstract and
practical evil, which led some to interpret the article as an antislavery piece.
The priest, however, added that

[Brazilians] consider slaves indispensable to life. Agriculture in Brazil is in its infancy: . . . if the land needs cultivation, the slave, forced to perform excessive work, . . . soon loses [his] life and impoverishes the master. . . . Well, in this state of backwardness of our agriculture . . . to end the traffic of black Africans all of a sudden is to demand the impossible. At first it seemed that at least morality would win, although [practical] interests would lose; on the contrary, everything got worse.[27]

The priest defended the necessity of slavery and the slave traffic in Brazil at that particular historical moment, inverting three specific arguments that had circulated earlier: illegally disembarked Africans should still be slaves; their purchasers were not guilty; and the law of 1831 should be revoked. "Hundreds of slaves [it is important to note that the author did not use 'free men' as before] enter the plantations of our farmers every day, and, with the evil growing as it does now, it is inevitable that the law will be revoked and the authorities will give up." In the final version of the proposal, Feijó restated that the law of 1831 needed to be revoked and that the obstruction of the slave trade only helped English warships. He suggested that the struggle against the traffic should return to the terms of the Convention of 1826, and that Brazil should follow in the steps of Spain, which did not help chase slave ships or allow interventions in the property of hacendados. The Spanish Crown had signed the Convention of 1817 but did not pass any kind of subsequent law to widen the freedom of Africans or the punishment to individuals involved in the illegal traffic.

The actions of Feijó as a candidate, however, did not match his actions as regent. Once elected, he did not help build pro–slave trade politics in Parliament. On the contrary, his ministers (all of them selected based on broad coalitions) openly defended the pursuit of slave ships, as indicated by eight governmental resolutions against the traffic issued during this period. Up to that moment, for example, suspected slavers were supposed to be seized by the police and inspected by the justice of the peace. In order to avoid corruption, the minister of justice, Francisco de Montezuma, ordered that two experts of the navy, the customs officer, and the attorney general should accompany the justices of the peace during their inspection of suspected slavers. The foreign minister, Manoel Alves Branco, in turn, signed the additional articles to the Convention of 1826 in 1835, which, if approved by

Parliament, would allow the seizure of vessels equipped for the slave trade (and not just those having enslaved Africans on board).[28]

The struggle continued through academic works outside Parliament. Francisco de Sales Torres Homem published an antislavery article in Brazil's first magazine devoted to the romantic movement, in 1836, the first year of the magazine's existence. Then came Frederico Leopoldo César Burlamaqui's famous *Analytical Memoir About the Commerce of Slaves and Domestic Slavery*, published by the Sociedade Defensora da Liberdade (Society in Defense of Liberty), which was directed by Evaristo da Veiga.[29] Although none of the speeches made by Evaristo da Veiga about the slave trade have been found so far, his antislavery crusade inside and outside governmental institutions was constantly referred to in Parliament. In later debates in the 1830s, Deputy Saturnino de Souza e Oliveira stated that "Evaristo raised his voice to stigmatize this traffic not only in the House but also in the press and in his society in defense [a reference to the Sociedade Defensora da Liberdade]; and although unhappy with the existing stipulations, he declared himself to be ready to support new stipulations that could produce the effect of ending the traffic more quickly."[30]

The future of the slave trade was unclear in a milieu marked by the passing of a severe national law, collective slave actions, antislavery articles and proposals in the public sphere, and a hesitating executive. In fact, only the rise of a different group of statesmen (the Regresso cabinet), and their alliances within the institutional context of liberalism, created the conditions for the protection of the contraband slave trade by the Brazilian state. The shift was so radical that Alves Branco later apologized for having signed the Additional Articles with Great Britain. "The opinion of the country," he argued, "was not favorable to the traffic back then." The corollary of his excuse was that the opposite was now (in the 1840s) true.[31]

Cuba "Under Siege": The Captain General and the Contraband Slave Trade, 1825–1834

Unlike Brazil, the Spanish Empire had already developed pro–slave trade politics by the early 1820s. Between 1789 and 1818, Cuban slaveholders supported Madrid in an informal pact with the Spanish Crown in return for free-trade policies and other measures to stimulate slave agriculture in the island. After 1820, this pact had to be transformed to include the political and institutional protection of the slave trade by Madrid. Cuban slaveholders actively participated in this rearrangement, which permitted the emergence of the contraband slave trade to the Hispanic Caribbean, the longest lasting illegal traffic in enslaved Africans in history.

At the center of this new configuration were the extraordinary powers of captains general, the so-called facultades omnímodas, granted in the context of growing activity by free people of color and slaves and the international conjuncture created by the last cycle of independence movements in Spanish America. According to historian José Piqueras, the turbulent Liberal Triennium (1820–1823) led to a polarization in Cuba between the Ayuntamiento of Havana, dominated by radical constitutionalists and peninsular liberals at the time, and the Deputación Provincial de La Habana, composed of representatives of hacendados from rural districts. The escalating politicization of free blacks and mulattoes, who had been excluded from electoral processes by the Constitution, became one of the main points of contention between the two organizations. In this context of rising tensions, a secretary of the captains general denounced to the government that some individuals had organized "elections to the Ayuntamiento" and sold "public roles to the populace and to the people of color." Planters from Havana and Matanzas lamented the circulation of "disorganizing ideas" in a country where "the elements of its population are the most varied" and "the horrible lesson given by Santo Domingo" was still fresh.[32]

The subject was debated again in 1823 after the Deputación passed a memorial to the minister of overseas affairs requesting the institutional strengthening of the position of captain general. Presented by Joaquín Gómez, the slave trader with the eighth largest volume of trade in Cuba at the time (and growing by the day), the text warned about the dangerous situation of Cuba: an island surrounded by dissident provinces that wanted to wrest it from Spain. If that were to happen, the country would collapse, an inevitable result considering its heterogeneous population. In an allusion to the participation of blacks and mulattoes in the public sphere, which had been haunting Cuban slaveholders since the Aponte rebellion, the memorial noted that the interests of slaves and free people of color—two thirds of Havana's population—"are in manifest opposition to that of whites and, since they acquire instruction and importance every day, [those people] inspire fears and require all vigilance accompanied by extraordinary mea-sures." According to the petition, the Cortes should grant extraordinary powers to the captain general, "making him the center of the conservation and union of the island of Cuba to the Metropolis" whenever the Deputación declared it to be urgent.[33]

The wars of independence in Spanish America that coalesced during the second constitutional moment did indeed agitate the Spanish colonies. Located between the Yucatán Channel and the Straits of Florida, Cuba became the base for Spanish naval and military operations against Mexico and Colombia until the last recolonizing effort of Ferdinand VII in 1829. At the same time, the island's substantial sugar and coffee production provided great revenue for the metropolis, which used this capital to pay for its troops and other war expenses. For these reasons, Hispanic American revolutionar-ies supported Cuban proindependence activists in their plans to emancipate the island, which was in fact agitated by conspiracies that included La Cadena Triangular (1823), Soles y Rayos de Bolívar (1823), and Águila Negra (1828).

Cuban planters in exile for treason, such as the Iznaga family, repeatedly met with Simón Bolívar between 1824 and 1827 to plan the emancipation of the island in what would eventually be a concerted action involving Mex-ico, Colombia, and Cuban patriots. Félix Varela got in touch with these figures from the United States. In New York, for example, he met José María Heredia—a participant in the Soles y Rayos de Bolívar conspiracy—and supported them, with reservations at first but then explicitly in his newspaper *El Habanero* (1824–1826).[34]

After the decisive Spanish defeat at Ayacucho in December 1824 and recurrent news of an imminent invasion of Cuba, the cabinet of Ferdinand VII granted the wish of the hacendados by issuing the Royal Order of May 1825. The order gave extraordinary powers to the captain general—powers that were only granted to local authorities in a state of siege—in an effort to preserve political dependence and social peace on the island. Thus, the high-est authority of Cuba received "unlimited authorization" to fire employees and deport people of any "destiny, position, class, or condition"—from nobles to freedmen and slaves—under the slightest suspicion of misdeeds, without the need of a trial or due process. The captain general was also empowered to suspend any metropolitan orders or legal measures related to any area (such as trade, agriculture, jurisprudence, military activities, or contraband). The régimen de las facultades omnímodas lasted until the end of the Ten Years' War in 1878 (on the eve of abolition), ultimately giving total control over the political, economic, military, and judiciary administration of Cuba to the captain general.[35]

Although frequently represented as despotic and restrictive of local liberties, this regime may have also been an institutional instrument to determine local rules in Cuba, eventually even against certain metropolitan decisions. A quick comparison with a proposal about the local administration of Caribbean colonies at the Madrid Cortes during 1823 reinforces this point. The document, written mainly by Varela, had certain points in common with the petition sent by the Deputación in 1823 and the Royal Order of 1825, such as the power of the *jefe político* to suspend laws and fire officials. It is important to note that not *all* powers, in this case, would be concentrated in the hands of a military chief. Moreover, the main terms of the proposal were rejected at the Cortes, which considered them to be violations of parliamentary sovereignty. But Varela's proposal, the petition presented by Joaquín Gómez at the Deputación, and the Royal Order of 1825 had an underlying common denominator: all power on the island should be concentrated in the hands of a single individual. The difference was that, for Gómez and the royal order, this power should be granted to the captain general.[36]

After its formal establishment in 1825, the régimen de las facultades omnímodas became inextricably linked with the preservation of slavery and the contraband slave trade. The Council of the Indies stipulated in 1819 that the captain general would take on the primary responsibility of implementing the terms of the Anglo-Spanish Treaty of 1817. Thus, his powers became associated from the very beginning with limiting the impact of the treaty on Cuba. Captains general used the power they had acquired after 1825 to suspend metropolitan orders that would have enabled disembarked slaves to claim their liberty, orders intended to forestall a British attack on Madrid. Shortly after the Royal Order of January 1826 was issued establishing that Africans who had been illegally disembarked could claim their liberty, captain general Francisco Dionisio Vives reported to Madrid that the treaty of 1817 was not valid on land and that he would not help find enslaved Africans illegally disembarked on the island. In 1830, Vives also refused to publish in Cuba's official newspaper a royal order for the more effective application of the 1817 treaty, which had been passed under British pressure. In the ensuing decade, Miguel Tacón (captain general between 1834 and 1838) also refused to publish the anti–slave trade convention of 1835 in the official newspaper, irritating the British consul on the island. Captains general and the Cuban slaveholding elite became so interconnected over the years that the latter frequently decided who would become the former.[37]

Besides ensuring the contraband slave trade and maintaining ties to Spain, the captain general also took on the primary responsibility for maintaining internal social order, an issue that could generate as much tension as the other two. Besides the "efforts from the American Continent," Vives made reference to the even greater dangers of the "doubly threatening enemies [who] exist inside our homes and within our families." Not only had slaves been insubordinate, but freedmen apparently also wanted to follow the "path offered by the pernicious example and language used in the aforementioned recognition [the French recognition of Haitian independence in 1825]."[38] The warning had some truth to it. One month earlier, around four hundred captives from approximately twenty coffee plantations rebelled in Guamacaro, Matanzas, leading to the death of sixteen white men, women, and children and the destruction of property (houses, equipment, and part of the harvest). The punishment carried out by the governor of the province, Cecílio Ayllón (the future Marquis of Villalba), was also bloody, leading to hundreds of deaths during the suppression of the rebellion, the execution of twenty-three slaves, and the sentencing of many others one hundred lashes.[39]

That same year, Ayllón instituted a Reglamento de Esclavos in order to organize the "administration within rural properties to better guarantee the safety of the fields." The new regulations were immediately implemented in Matanzas. Divided into four parts, the Reglamento dealt with safety measures, rights and duties of masters, criminal law, and vigilance. Ayllón believed that the Guamacaro revolt was part of a broader plan involving free people of color from Havana and Vuelta Abajo, who had been supplied with gunpowder and bullets by slaves. Thus, it is not surprising that the main point of the new rulings was to cut all communication between slaves and the world outside the plantations. Free blacks and unknown whites were prohibited from entering the stores established on the plantations to sell goods to slaves or from sleeping at the barracks. The plantation gates were to be locked after nine o'clock, while white overseers were to make sure that all slaves remained within their *bohíos* (slave quarters). Estates with more than thirty slaves were to replace the separate bohíos with a single slave house made of masonry, with two areas organized by sex and a single entrance lockable with chains.[40]

The Reglamento can be considered the first explicit effort to use the construction of barracks as a strategy for controlling the movement of slaves. Similar instructions appeared in the *El vademecum de los hacendados cubanos* (1831) by Honorato B. de Chateausalins, *Observaciones sobre los ingenios de esta isla* (1836) by Andrés de Zayas, and *Bando de gobernación y policia de la isla de Cuba* (1842) by Captain General Gerónimo Valdés. Barracks became a common feature of the Havana-Matanzas-Cárdenas landscape. Many of the captives were indeed incarcerated, and urban slavery clearly became more rigid over time.[41]

The threat that the events that had occurred in Saint-Domingue could be repeated in Cuba led to tensions regarding Spain's foreign policy. Although Madrid had decided to grant extraordinary powers to the captain general in an effort to reinforce the stability of the island and maintain hopes to reconquer Colombia and Mexico, many were opposed to these measures. Shortly after leaving the Intendencia de Hacienda of Cuba in November 1825, Francisco de Arango y Parreño argued that the regímen de las facultades omnímodas was not sufficient to assist with the expeditions against the former colonies. He believed that several factors worked against them: the island could not resist a naval blockade; Hispanic Americans were eager to help in the emancipation of Spanish possessions; the British were inclined to recognize the emerging republics; France had recently recognized Haiti; and fanatics and slaves were ready to take advantage of the turmoil brought by an eventual civil war in a slave society. In such a context, Arango believed that Spain should withdraw from the world created by the independence movements of Spanish America and focus on the example given by the French Empire in the late eighteenth century. Cuba—wealthier than Saint-Domingue in 1790—could give more to Spain than the French colony had ever given to Louis XVI, Arango argued, as long as Ferdinand VII accepted the loss of the old colonies.[42]

In the event of an abrupt end of peace, the "youngsters, the adventurers, the poor, the people of color, the slaves" would quickly join the revolt. The best example of this could be found in "the regrettable state of Venezuela," which, after both the patriotic and royalist armies had employed slaves during the wars of independence, had passed a free womb law in 1821. Even worse was the general dissatisfaction of the great landholders with the recolonizing efforts of Spain. Although still trusting the loyalty of these "good vassals," Arango argued that they might eventually support secession if Madrid refused to accept the British offer to maintain the colonial status of Cuba in exchange for the recognition of the new American republics: "Let's not deal with the evil ones. What strikes me, and cannot strike H. M. any less, is the clamor of the good ones, who—persuaded that this cannot continue within the peaceful domain of the King, our lord, if the declared guarantee is not readily adopted—consider that [the guarantee] being despised, only the useless ruin of this country is possible."[43]

On the other side of the Atlantic, Félix Varela agreed with Arango on two central issues: first, that the hacendados would prefer independence after realizing the incapacity of the Spanish government to ensure the order of their slave society; and second, that a Hispanic American invasion could quickly occupy the island without leading to a war, since the existence of slavery would turn such a conflict into a social revolution. Valera had witnessed not only the opposition of Cubans and peninsulares to antislavery measures during the parliamentary sessions of 1821 and 1822 but also the use of these measures as an excuse to increase the island's control over separatists.

These issues may partially explain his concern with the preservation of slavery on the island. Also important was the fact that the Madan family had supported Varela during his exile. They were an important family of slave traders and property holders in Matanzas, and they were associates of the New York trading house Goodhue and Company. Varela, however, reached conclusions directly opposed to those of Arango. Seeing the emancipation of the island as inevitable, he called for the support of secessionist troops and a subsequent regime change in the island. In sum, independence without revolution—the same strategy employed in Brazil at the time—was in his view the best way to preserve slavery. But after the US government declared its support for Spanish sovereignty over Cuba, Varela realized that the interimperial rivalries between France, Britain, and the United States was one of the main obstacles to the political emancipation of Cuba.[44]

France and Britain explicitly declared their support for Cuba's colonial status, but the Spanish Empire definitely got the upper hand after US president John Quincy Adams stated in a speech to Congress in 1826 that the country would not accept an invasion of Cuba by Hispanic American troops. Adams believed that the result would inevitably be either the total devastation of the island or its annexation by France or Britain. In such a context, the United States would spare no effort to maintain "the present state of things, the tranquility in those islands, and the peace and safety of their inhabitants." Enthusiastically received by Cuban authorities, who immediately published it in *Diario de La Habana*, the speech temporarily discouraged partisans of independence.[45] During the 1820s, therefore, three main Cuban problems were temporarily solved: the slave trade was put under the control of the all-too-powerful captain general; vigilance over slaves was doubled; and Spanish sovereignty on the island was protected by inter-imperial competition.

The gradual establishment of this new order was accompanied by reforms in Cuba's tax-collection system. The Cortes had approved a reform of the customs in 1820, which established duties that could reach 83.5 percent of the value of foreign products carried by non-Spanish vessels. The goal was to integrate the peninsular national market and strengthen the merchant marine. After widespread rejection in Cuba, the new tariffs were readjusted to between 20 and 37.5 percent, depending of the assessment of local authorities. Moreover, after 1825 the *superintendente general de la hacienda*, Claudio Martínez de Pinillos, revolutionized the Cuban fiscal system by setting tariffs proportional to the value of the product. Since 1792, these tariffs had been calculated based on fixed prices, which remained unchanged by variations in the world market. This strategy was adopted by the Crown to stimulate agricultural production.

The change produced immediate results. Cuba sent 19,549 pesos fuertes to the peninsula in 1824. The following year, this sum rose to 114,919 pesos fuertes. In 1827, it broke a new record with the remittance of 1,027,836 pesos fuertes. The independence of Mexico, which cut off the main source of revenue of the Spanish metropolis, forced the Crown to strengthen the tax-collection system in Cuba in order to deal with the public deficit. The long period between 1825 and 1851 (with Pinillos as superintendent) demonstrates that most peninsulares, Cuban merchants, and hacendados generally accepted the new fiscal model of the empire.[46]

Still, some individuals rejected the new model. In 1827, Arango was part of a junta that protested against the new fiscal measures. Their report was originally intended to discuss the creation of a commission to gather data about the technological advances of Jamaican sugar production, but Arango and the other signers instead described the conjuncture of the world economy in the aftermath of the Congress of Vienna. They concluded that only new governmental policies, and not technological advances, could save the Cuban economy. According to the junta, the gap left by the collapse of Saint-Domingue had already been filled by the emergence of new world producers, namely Cuba, the Philippines, India, and, especially, Brazil. The latter, having an autonomous government that responded to local demands and a cheap supply of enslaved Africans, had become the main potential rival of Cuba. With the forces of supply and demand driving coffee and sugar prices down, the junta called for the end of all export tariffs for both products in order to make Cuba competitive in the European market.

It is important to note that Arango does not mention the contraband slave trade as one of Cuba's comparative advantages, which might indicate that he no longer considered the traffic a viable political and social alternative for the development of the island. The junta believed that the expansion of importation rights could compensate for the government's eventual losses caused by the measure. In this new system, consumers would take on primary responsibility for paying duties, thus relieving production and stimulating new investments with the capital liberated by the coffee crisis, which Arango considered inevitable (despite the fact that the number of slaves employed in coffee production was equivalent to those working on sugar plantations).[47]

The report did not lead to the end of export taxes but it did curb their indiscriminate rise. In the period before the great fiscal reforms of the 1850s, the tariffs were only 3 percent for Spanish vessels and 6.25 percent for foreign ones.[48] Moreover, the text anticipated that the new conditions of markets for tropical products would demand constant growth in productivity from producers in order to remain competitive in the world economy. In the context of the nineteenth century industrial world economy, Brazilian coffee production surpassed its Cuban counterpart, while the rise of sugar production in Cuba led to the decrease of its Brazilian counterpart. Coffee plantations and sugar mills competed for access to land and labor on the Spanish island, but the frequency of hurricanes tended to favor sugar production in the long run, since sugarcane could be grown faster and showed more resistance to these climate conditions than coffee trees. In Brazil, these two sectors did not compete for lands or slaves, and coffee trees grew without the dangers of the Caribbean's hurricane seasons.[49]

With the growing social, political, and fiscal stability of the island, Dionisio Vives allowed the publication of a few newspapers and magazines in Puerto Príncipe, Trinidad, and Matanzas. At the turn of the 1820s, a group of young men of letters who had been directly or indirectly involved in the Liberal Triennium—Domingo del Monte, Blás Ossés, José de la Luz y Caballero, and later José Antonio Saco—joined the Sociedad Económica, where they started a Permanent Commission of Literature and published *Revista Bimestre Cubana* to discuss aesthetic issues. After Saco became the main director of the magazine, however, its focus shifted from reviewing fiction to books about the economy, politics, and social issues. In the liberal moment that followed the death of Ferdinand VII in 1833, members of the commission received permission from the Crown to found the Academia o Instituto Habanero de Literatura. The new institution, however, was immediately opposed by slaveholders; the general superintendent, Martínez de Pinillos; and other members of the Sociedad Económica, especially Juan Bernardo O'Gavan and Ramón de la Sagra. The dispute was discussed in newspapers and pamphlets, ultimately leading to the dissolution of the academia and the exile of José Antonio Saco in 1834.[50]

What caused the quarrel? It is clear that several factors were behind the dispute, from literary controversies to occasional critiques of public health measures taken by Pinillos. The main reason behind the escalation of tension, however, was connected to events taking place in the Brazilian Empire and in Europe. The Anglo-Brazilian Treaty of 1826, as we have seen, established an expiration date for the slave traffic in 1830 and stimulated the passage of an even harsher slave trade law by the Brazilian Parliament on November 7, 1831. The international isolation of Cuba thus led Arango y Parreño to send a report to Madrid in August 1830 calling for the end of the contraband slave trade to the island. In May 1832, Arango formally submitted his plan, accompanied by a political justification: "Today we find ourselves in the notable, not to say shameful, position of being the only ones carrying such a nasty commerce. Our last partners were the French and the Brazilians." He noted, however, that France had established a treaty with Great Britain in 1831 while Brazil had also prohibited "this commerce at the insistence of England and, although the intervention of [England] [creates the] inevitable certainty that the prohibition will be carried out in [Brazil], we know that a decree was published there applying the penalty of Article 173 of their Penal Code to the introducers of negroes and the fine of 200 pesos for every slave disembarked to those responsible for their introduction."[51]

Arango operated behind closed doors throughout 1832, in tune with the absolutist government, but Saco brought the issue to Cuba's small public sphere by reviewing Robert Walsh's *Notices of Brazil* (1830) in *Revista Bimestre Cubana*. The first thirty pages of his review dealt with general issues such as the liberalization of trade, freedom of the press, public health policies, payment of the clergy, education, public libraries, and the artistic, military, and scientific academies. Each of these issues was compared to its counterpart in Cuba, which had "in Brazil its most formidable rival." It is clear that during this period, the Empire of Brazil provided a great example for Cuban men of letters—both proslavery and antislavery ideologues such as, respectively, Arango and Saco—of the successful transition from a backward colony to a politically and materially advanced national state.

The article's main points appear in the discussion about slavery and the slave trade in its last twenty pages. Like Arango, the young critic Saco considered the Anglo-Brazilian anti–slave trade treaty as definitive: "Since March 23, 1830, has been forever abolished in Brazil a commerce that, degrading the human species, has already destroyed one of the Antilles and left another one on the brink of ruin." Saco focused on the problem in Cuba, particularly the "demographic composition of the island" and "abolitionist militancy." The demographic censuses and estimates of 1775, 1791, 1811, 1817, 1825, and 1827 led to the conclusion that the numbers of blacks and mulattoes was growing more rapidly than the white population. It is ironic that the census of 1827, which had been prepared as part of a strategy to stabilize the slaves' social order, inspired an antislavery text. According to Saco, the census had mistakenly described a population that was 56 percent black versus 44 percent white, hiding the presence of five hundred thousand people of color (62.5 percent) in contrast to only three hundred thousand whites (37.5 percent). He then cited the defense of the slave trade in the *Real Consulado* of 1811 written by Arango, who called for its end only when the population of blacks and mulattoes surpassed the number of whites.[52]

After indicating a similar growth of the population of African descent in the Caribbean, Saco warned that the combination of contemporary political circumstances and this demographic imbalance would inevitably lead to social conflict. He enumerated "philanthropic laws imposed by some European nations; societies composed of distinguished Bretons; periodicals published to deal exclusively with this issue; long parliamentary debates that incessantly reverberated on this side of Atlantic; predictions, at times imprudent, from some religious sects; political principles that, with the strength of the thunder, proclaim themselves in both worlds; and recent commotions in many parts of the archipelago." There was no solution other than the immediate suppression of the contraband. Again, the reasons for its end were not connected to economic motives or anxious philanthropy but to the political conjuncture: "Everyone knows the efforts that for interests and humanity England has done to carry out its treaties. It is not the only one working for the abolition of the traffic since France has also been making efforts to extinguish it." At the same time, Saco argued that the government should create a fund to explore the possibilities of employing free labor in sugar production.[53]

The review by Saco was the first text to openly criticize the contraband slave trade, generating angry responses from hacendados and slave traders. In a letter from 1832, Arango y Parreño mentioned the "bloody war that the black interest has declared against those who, full of good intentions, wanted to open the eyes of these obstinate blind people." He added: "Since everyone knows my opinion on this issue, I will not be surprised if they bite me in their conversations or letters and give to me, in this incident, a part I did not have." Fearful of even worse repercussions, Arango recommended caution for those presenting his anti–slave trade proposals that same year, but emotions were still running high. After all the controversy generated by the academy of literature, pro–slave trade figures such as Pinillos and O'Gavan asked the captain general for the deportation of Saco from Cuba.

Their request was fulfilled in 1834 in yet another example of how the facultades omnímodas could help the contraband slave trade. With a lamenting tone, Arango recognized that, although only the captain general could curb the traffic, he had also become a key part of its continuation, pointing out "the close [relations] that he has with some who have defended the continuation of the traffic in blacks and who openly purchase great quantities of those fraudulently disembarked. I fear, therefore, that the cooperation of this Chief is not very effective if the ministry does not recommend him the business in terms that can scare him."[54]

The transition from a legal slave trade to an illegal contraband slave trade in both Cuba and Brazil was analogous to the transformation of an economically oriented business into a politically protected activity. These new activities demanded state actions that were in direct opposition to the international order, but not everyone agreed with this configuration. The views of Arango, Saco, and other critics of the contraband slave trade must be understood in light of the demographic balance—as constantly noted by them—and the new political meaning of the illegal traffic. Combined with events in the British Empire, these views forced defenders of the slave trade to react in unison with their government. In Cuba, the régimen de las facultades omnímodas, which contributed to the consolidation of the contraband slave trade, became fully established, as indicated by the deportation of Saco in 1834. In Brazil, the Regresso created the political configuration necessary for the rebirth of the slave trade.

Great Britain in Action: From Abolition in 1833 to the Treaties of 1835

Before 1833, the only great slave emancipation in the western hemisphere was the Haitian Revolution. The violence that pervaded that process and its revolutionary context, however, transformed the most remarkable event in the history of slavery into a "nonevent" for European and American statesmen at the time, who refused to view it as an example that could be followed by civilized nations. Witnessing the decline of the French colony, a contemporary observer noted that "such cheapness of labor is by no means to be expected from the voluntary industry, however great, of negroes in a state of freedom, as now excites the enterprise and splendidly rewards the success of the planter, in places where slavery in established." This negative perception of abolition would soon go through a radical shift with the second greatest emancipation in Western history, now carried out from above by the British Empire and presented to the world as the result of a philanthropic and well-calculated policy.[55]

Popular demand for great institutional reforms in Britain—such as the end of religious discrimination in elections, changes in the representative system, and the emancipation of slaves in the Caribbean—increased in the late 1820s. The great innovation within the antislavery movement was the call for immediate instead of gradual abolition, as demanded by the Antislavery

Society after 1830. An intense popular mobilization and the reform of the representative system—eliminating the rotten boroughs and diminishing the power of the West Indian lobby—forced the Whig government to present a proposal for abolition in May 1833. After three months of debate, the law was passed and its implementation expected for August 1834. The always perceptive Alexis de Tocqueville noted the novelty of the event: "We have seen something unprecedented in history: slavery abolished . . . not gradually, slowly, over the course of those successive transformations . . . but completely."[56] Abolition in Saint-Domingue had definitely been a precursor, but it did not set a precedent as the British experiment could do.

The French thinker was not alone in his views. Many contemporary actors understood the British case as a kind of laboratory for the future of the abolitionist movement and slavery in the Americas. "You reinforce the chains of slaves in other lands," an abolitionist warned the emancipated slaves, "if you confirm the accusation that when you are not forced to work as they are, you will be as lazy as they are." Although commissions formed to assess conditions in the aftermath of abolition continued to state the superiority of free labor in tropical plantations, British statesmen feared that the colonies could not compete with the production from slave societies such as Brazil and Cuba, both still taking advantage of the illegal disembarkation of enslaved Africans. It was not long before both powers realized that slavery and the slave trade could soon come under British attack again, as indicated by the Brazilian consular agent in London. "Besides the machinations of the so-called promoters of the freedom of negroes," he wrote in 1833, "we will have against us those from English colonists themselves, who are expected to work to deprive us from the benefits that we could possibly receive from their disgrace."[57]

Indeed, after including equipment clauses in its treaties with the Netherlands (1818) and France (1831 and 1833), the British government pressured for the inclusion of similar clauses in treaties with Spain and Brazil. These clauses significantly expanded the evidence that might justify the seizure of suspected slavers such as hatches with open gratings, divisions in the hold or on deck, and a larger quantity of food or water than would be necessary for the consumption of the crew alone. After the conventions with France, British diplomatic pressure became so intense that both the Spanish and Brazilian ministers of foreign affairs, Francisco Cea Bermúdez and Bento da Silva

Lisboa, called for the adoption of the equipment clause by their respective
governments, sending requests to the Chamber of Deputies in Rio de Janeiro
and to a special commission in Madrid (which did not have a representative
system).[58]

The different political configurations of Spain and Brazil, however, dictated the rhythm of negotiations. Civil war in the wake of the death of Ferdinand VII in 1833 restricted the Crown's ability to maneuver, and so it
accepted the inclusion of an equipment clause in exchange for British support against the Carlist opposition. Extra provisions to the 1817 treaty were
added in 1835 amid protests from Havana. In Brazil, social disturbances such
as the Malê revolt also influenced the cabinet to sign the Additional Articles,
which included an equipment clause, but the ascendancy of legislative power
over international issues blocked their ratification. In this particular case,
the constitutional regime based on the separation of powers became an
obstacle for antislavery measures. Moreover, a quick comparison between
the two conventions illuminates the differences between the contraband
slave trade in Cuba and Brazil, and also how those involved in these processes perceived these distinctions.

The sixty-four-page Anglo-Spanish equipment treaty replaced the original convention of 1817, updating the procedures for the seizure of vessels and
operations of mixed commissions. The ten-year experience with the contraband slave trade also led to the inclusion of new articles. The first article read:
"The Slave Trade is hereby again declared on the part of Spain to be hence-
forward totally and finally abolished in all parts of the World," thus prohibiting the intercolonial traffic that had been implicitly allowed by the treaty of
1817. Perhaps influenced by the Brazilian law of November 7, 1831, which punished all individuals involved in illegal disembarkations, the British pushed
the Spanish government to promise to promulgate "a penal Law, inflicting a
severe punishment on all those her Catholic Majesty's Subjects who shall,
under any pretext whatsoever, take any part whatever in the Traffic in Slaves."
The treaty also established nine different situations that justified the seizure
of suspected slavers and made Great Britain responsible for the *emancipados*,
newly emancipated Africans, found aboard slave ships, which in turn
required captains general to provide data about their situation to mixed
commissions every semester.[59]

Signed in late July 1835, the five-page Anglo-Brazilian Additional Articles are much simpler. They do not use abolitionist language (such as "inhuman traffic," a phrase used in the preamble of the Anglo-Spanish Treaty), nor do they make reference to the treatment of emancipados or to the necessity of a new penal law against slave traders. The Additional Articles merely reproduced the equipment clause that had been included in the Anglo-Spanish Treaty. These differences between the two conventions can be traced back to the different moments of the rise of the contraband slave trade in the two countries. While the traffic to Brazil only reappeared in the 1830s, its Cuban counterpart had been explored by the Spanish state since the early 1820s—and even openly defended by the Council of State in 1829, whose 1828 project to recolonize Mexico depended on the wealth of the island. Thus, British pressure over Spain would naturally be stronger.[60]

These differences, however, vanished in the following years. With the British Empire becoming the greatest political and economic power in the world, the "unprecedented" emancipation of slaves in their Caribbean colonies—in fact, the final moment of the crisis of slavery in the Atlantic system of northwestern Europe—significantly transformed the perceptions of international politics among the main remaining slave powers: the United States, Brazil, and Cuba. Paranoia and conspiracy theories gradually appeared in these regions in reaction to British diplomacy and abolitionism.

The Brazilian representative in London suggested that the government should be "more vigilant so that the same [abolitionist] doctrines that today are ruining the majority of proprietors in the English colonies are not introduced in Brazil." All Englishmen, from nonconformists to investors in the West Indies, would try to "destroy the system of slavery that still exists in Brazil and that will ruin said [English] colonies after the emancipation of their slaves." In Cuba, Miguel Tacón adopted measures to isolate the island from the "English experiment," such as prohibiting the entrance of abolitionist emissaries, sending a spy to Jamaica to observe abolitionist activities, and imprisoning non-Spanish black sailors. The politics of slavery had changed its tone, becoming louder.[61]

Regresso: The Construction of the Politics of Slavery in Brazil, 1835–1837

In 1834, the same year that slavery was abolished in the British Empire, Brazil held its first elections for regent, the principal executive power. A great dispute emerged between two main groups: on the one hand, Evaristo da Veiga from Minas Gerais and Diogo Antônio Feijó from São Paulo, and on the other, Honório Hermeto Carneiro Leão from Minas Gerais and Holanda Cavalcanti from Pernambuco. It was during this first electoral race that Feijó called for a revocation of the slave trade law of 1831 in the press as part of his platform, which may have helped in his victory. Ironically, his partner, Evaristo da Veiga, was one of the most vocal critics of the slave trade, and his cabinets could never reach a consensus about the issue. Feijó introduced the pro–slave trade discourse into the public sphere but could not do the same in parliamentary politics. The individuals who managed to do this were precisely the ones who would replace him in the government.[62]

The proslavery alliances in Parliament can be traced back to the politicians who actually lost the elections for Regent. Carneiro Leão, Bernardo Pereira de Vasconcelos, Rodrigues Torres, and Paulino José Soares de Souza became the founders of the Regresso, later called the Saquarema Party, the Party of Order, and the Conservative Party. Their agenda was based on both an interpretation of the recently passed Additional Act and Penal Code reform, and an articulated defense of the contraband slave trade and the status as property of slaves illegally disembarked (especially those owned by sugar and coffee planters in Campos dos Goytacazes, the Paraíba Valley, the southern part of Minas Gerais, and the Bahian Recôncavo). Increasingly active in Parliament between 1835 and 1841, Vasconcelos and his entourage formed a compact parliamentary majority that completely remodeled the judiciary of the empire. And this was not their only victory.[63]

On July 24, 1835, while the Chamber of Deputies discussed a bill from the Senate to stop the contraband, Vasconcelos abruptly called for the revocation of the law of 1831, starting a series of pro–slave trade initiatives in the Brazilian Parliament.[64] However, other deputies ignored the proposal, and his speech was not even published in the periodicals responsible for publicizing parliamentary debates—probably because it went against the current public opinion at the time. Vasconcelos decided to publish it on the pages of his newspaper, *O Sete de Abril* (April Seventh):

This Mister Deputy said that the enslavement of Africans was not as odious as represented by other Misters; that it is adapted to our customs, convenient to our interests, and undeniably advantageous to the same

Africans, who improve their condition; and supported his arguments with the opinion of ancient philosophers and the examples from all civilized and noncivilized nations, concluding that the abolition of the traffic was not the object of the law, but that it should be left to the time and progress of the country: when the traffic was not convenient to the public and private interests anymore, then they would be their loudest enemies.[65]

Such an open proslavery argument had not circulated in the Brazilian public sphere since the opposition of Raimundo José da Cunha Matos to the Anglo-Brazilian Treaty of 1826. By stating that slavery was well adapted to "our customs" and convenient to "our interests," Vasconcelos sheltered the institution from critiques in the spheres of morality and political economy, many them of shared even by Feijó. The adjective "advantageous" (*proveitosa*) in turn qualified the impact of Brazilian slavery on the African. "Advantage" is associated with profit and, in this sense, complements the sentence "Africans, who improved their condition," alluding to the material and social gains of Africans in a representative monarchy. Finally, it is important to note that the deputy connected the traffic first to "public" and then to "private" interests, indicating that it would be more crucial to the former than to the latter. Much more direct than Feijó had been in 1834, Vasconcelos did not hesitate to describe the Brazilian state as the greatest beneficiary of the largest contraband slave trade of the nineteenth century.

When the interpretation of the Additional Act was introduced in Parliament in 1836 and elections for the next legislature began, Vasconcelos again called for the revocation of the law of 1831. During a session on the empire's budget for the following year, the deputy discussed the revocation in less abstract terms, inverting two popular arguments of the period. Instead of criminalizing the proprietors, as established by the 1831 law, he called for their amnesty. Instead of classifying the contraband as immoral, he criticized the law that prohibited it.

Vasconcelos differed from Feijó in two key ways: first, Vasconcelos argued that the "speculators without conscience" were not the slave traders but those who denounced illegal disembarkations in order to receive rewards; and second, he no longer expressed any formal condemnations of slavery. The arguments put forward by Vasconcelos revolved around the redemption of proprietors, attacks against the 1831 law, the condemnation of those attempting to free illegally disembarked slaves, and an association between the wealth generated by slaves and the patrimony of the Brazilian national state:

> [Vasconcelos] has to show that this law of 1831, more specifically its six first articles, can only serve the oppression of citizens and the interest of some speculators without conscience; that he has noted facts that cannot continue to occur without great losses to morality and public and private interests; that one of the articles, which he proposes the revocation of, authorizes any person to arrest any African, without a special warrant from authority, which has led to great inconveniences and great embarrassments to many people; however, he does not want to risk the future of such an important project and because of this he does not want it to be submitted and voted by the House if it is a matter of deliberation or not; he requests its submission to the Commission of the Constitution. The following project of the illustrious deputy is read: "The Legislative Assembly decrees: Sole article. The first six articles of the law of November 7, 1831, which declared Africans imported to Brazil to be free, are revoked."[66]

Less than a month later, the General Assembly received a representation from the Municipal Chamber of Valença in Rio de Janeiro that was similar to the proposal of Vasconcelos.[67] The signers warned that the "most respectable and interesting part of the population of the Empire," out of necessity, had disobeyed the national law and did not have the protection of their slave property. They concluded that the prohibition of the traffic encouraged immorality and, in a daring move, threatened to engage in armed resistance to avoid the alienation of their property: "The execution [of the law] would lead the people to a rebellion and formal disobedience, because this respectable majority of your fellow citizens will try to maintain their fortunes, accumulated with so much fatigue and sweat, intact by any means." Only the revocation of the law would prevent the "loss of many families" and "enormous disgraces throughout the Empire." Even before reaching the Chamber of Deputies, the request appeared—along with a similar one from the Provincial Assembly of Rio de Janeiro—on the pages of the newspaper owned by Vasconcelos.[68]

Around that same time, also on the pages of *O Sete de Abril*, Vasconcelos linked the reform of the judiciary to the slave trade. According to him, Great Britain had instilled in Brazil the desire to have institutions similar to theirs, by any means necessary, without respecting the particularities of custom, habit, and local need. He then added:

> Of the English it is the institution of the jury, and we use it in such a way and risk it in such a way that, instead of reaping the benefits that this powerful Nation has reaped, we demoralize the institution and manage to gather a shout in unison against it everywhere. Of the English it is the great institution of the judges of the peace: and what has it produced among us? What a long string of evils, what a litany of complaints, what a sum of abuses, what great number of errors, of ignorance, of frauds, and vexations![69]

He then criticized the Brazilian state for broadening the anti–slave trade convention of 1826 with the passing of a complementary law: "A law ten times harder is made, even more fatal than the famous Treaty," he complained, "a law passed in the effervescence of passions, in the delirium of the Revolution, in the exaltation of the Parties, in the dislocation of all things, and in the dreams of all ideas." According to him, the individual to be condemned was neither the slave trader nor the planter who disobeys the law, but rather the informer authorized by the law, who denounces and "gives to the theft the color of virtual, to the crime the gesture of lawfulness."[70] Vasconcelos later explained that the national prohibition had "dispositions in discordance with the principles of Law" because it authorized anyone to denounce the illegal ownership of Africans. "It is generally admitted in the courts," he explained, "that every *boçal* African is free: any person or bailiff enters the house of a citizen and tells him: 'These slaves of yours are free Africans. They will soon go to the deposit.'" While the law stated that the boçal (African-born) was free, he argued, the "principle of property was based on the assumption that he who owns the thing, in case of doubt, must be considered its owner." Between the assumption of freedom and the assumption of ownership, the state should choose the latter and protect the illegal property.[71]

On June 17, 1837, Vasconcelos lamented the fact that the proposal to revoke the 1831 law—which he affectionately called "my darling" (*meu mimoso*)—did not garner the attention of the House.[72] A few weeks later, the deputy angrily reacted to the minister of justice, Francisco de Montezuma, who had been cracking down on the slave traders. "It does not seem very coherent to want . . . to curb the arrival of Africans," he said. "And what will be the consequence to our industry? Although the English execute this treaty that they imposed by violence, abusing their prepotency, for us to join the English in their speculations, gilded with the name of humanity, is not reasonable nor does it coadunate with the grievances of the Brazilian heart produced by so much violence."[73]

At the same time, municipalities and provincial legislative assemblies contributed to the growing proslavery effort that had begun at the center of the parliamentary regime. Municipal chambers such as those in Barra Mansa, Valença, Vassouras, and Paraíba do Sul—all of them expanding centers of coffee production—as well as the provinces of São Paulo, Rio de Janeiro, Minas Gerais, and Bahia, sent more than twenty petitions for the revocation of the law of 1831.[74] In 1839 and 1840, the Chamber of Deputies and the Senate received two representations from Minas and two from Bahia calling for a reform of the Penal Code and the Additional Act as well as the revocation of the 1831 law. Saquarema politics reverberated in the wealthiest corners of the empire.[75]

In July 1837, the Marquis of Barbacena, an associate of Feijó, tried to pass an anti–slave trade proposal that revoked the 1831 law but incorporated the equipment clause of the Additional Articles and interdicted the introduction of any Africans in Brazil, even as free laborers. The objectives of the marquis are still unclear, since documents on this issue are scarce, but it is possible that Barbacena was trying to weaken the Regressista opposition and preserve Feijó's position in the last days of his term. After passing the Senate, the text divided the Chamber of Deputies in discussions that, significantly, did not include the main figures of the Regresso. The exception was Sebastião do Rego, who offered as an alternative the short and direct proposals of the leader Vasconcelos as an alternative. Moreover, some of the petitions submitted to the chamber in tune with the Regresso platform called for the approval of the passage of Barbacena's proposal dealing with the 1831 law, ignoring the rest. After replacing Feijó in the executive on September 19, 1837, the future Saquaremas dealt the last blow to the bill, hindering its discussion in the chamber. How can we explain the behavior of these pro–slave trade defenders?[76]

After rising to power, the Saquaremas used their "compact majority" to pass the reforms of the judiciary without making reference to the proposals of Vasconcelos and Barbacena to revoke the 1831 law. Instead, they developed politics in the executive that favored the contraband slave trade without engaging in parliamentary debates. Shortly after becoming a minister, Vasconcelos restored the old regulations of the 1831 law in place of the ones used by Montezuma to seize more than thirty suspected slavers in Rio de Janeiro. The examination of suspected vessels was again assigned to lay judges (and it is ironic that the greatest opponent of the justices of the peace, Vasconcelos, favored the noncentralized judiciary as a strategy to help the contraband slave trade). After having been harshly questioned three times by Montezuma in the chamber, Vasconcelos hypocritically replied: "These providences of Mr. Montezuma were easily circumvented because the ships did not enter the ports—the ships received the goods they needed just outside the ports; and the traffic continued in the same way, with the difference that it was now slightly more costly and accompanied by other types of illicit traffic."[77]

The Saquaremas also changed the organization of naval forces, a fundamental component of the enforcement of the Anglo-Brazilian Treaty and the 1831 law. Since the regency of Feijó, ministers of the navy had invariably been officers of the army or high-ranking men of the armada, but the conservatives nominated Rodrigues Torres—a planter, mathematician, and politician—for the position. The liberal opposition immediately asked if Torres had issued the instructions authorizing imperial ships to seize slavers. "Two are the kinds of services, in my opinion, that must be demanded from the naval force among us today," he answered. "The first is to help in the pacification of the provinces that are now in tumult; to protect and guarantee the public order in those where it has been maintained for now. The second kind of service is to protect commerce and curb the contraband, about which some illustrious deputies have complained in this House. Well, the first kind of service is, today, the most important." By publicly announcing that the main purpose of the navy at that moment was not to police the coast, the minister indicated that the contraband slave trade could still be safely conducted.[78]

The Saquaremas tried to impose a "gag rule" on parliamentary debate, as illustrated by an intervention of Carneiro Leão in 1839. After listening to the complaints of Martim Francisco Ribeiro de Andrada about how distinguished

personalities had been protecting slave traders, the future Marquis of Paraná
praised the gag rule and the persecution of abolitionists in the United States,
calling for similar measures in Brazil. "With the growing wrath of abolitionists
in 1835 and 1836 in that country," he argued, "states with slaves opposed them,
and the people in the states without slavery understood this, considering that
the interests of states with slaves had been threatened, and that they should not
be mere spectators, but take the initiative to punish abolitionists. There were
insurrections in New York, Philadelphia, and other states without slaves."[79]
With control over parliamentary debates regarding the slave trade, members
of the Regresso started to act in other spaces of the public sphere. In 1838, they
published a pro–slave trade pamphlet written by José Carneiro da Silva, future
Viscount of Araruama and a famous Saquarema leader from the province of
Rio de Janeiro (titled *Memoir About the Commerce of Slaves, Which Aims to
Show That This Traffic Is a Good and Not an Evil for Them*). The following year,
Vasconcelos sponsored the publication of Carlos Augusto Taunay's *Manual of
the Brazilian Planter*, which contained proslavery passages.[80]

Slave actions in the public sphere and in macropolitics had unprecedented
effects in this new correlation of forces. In November 1838, hundreds of slaves
from two plantations owned by the *capitão-mor* Manuel Francisco Xavier in
Pati do Alferes (a parish in Vassouras) ran away into the dense Atlantic forest
in the middle of the night. Apparently, their goal was to establish a Maroon
community in the mountains of Rio de Janeiro, but authorities also feared
that they could join the slaves of the National Gunpowder Factory in Estrela,
Rio de Janeiro. The repression carried out by the National Guard six days
after the flight of the slaves led to the death of six captives in combat and the
recapture of almost all the runaway slaves. Those who opposed both the contraband slave trade and the growing African presence in the country never
mentioned the case in Parliament. In the press, a few slaveholders accused
each other of slave mismanagement. Even Vasconcelos seems to have taken
advantage of the event. "The entire province shook," he wrote in *O Sete de
Abril*; "If the effort of Pati was frustrated, others can have worse results."
Vasconcelos and his associates frequently referred to the dangers of slave
revolts in order to justify the centralization of the judiciary defended by them
in Parliament.[81]

The politics of slavery created by the Regressistas entailed criticizing the
1831 law in Parliament while they were in the minority and protecting the

traffic (without revoking the law) when in power. In pamphlets, newspapers, municipal and provincial representations, and Parliament, they created a powerful consensus within the liberal state that made the 1831 law ineffective without revoking it, which prevented political debate and diplomatic tension related to the issue. In a sense, political enunciations became positive law, turning the 1831 law into a dead letter, giving legal security to the illegal slave properties of planters, and denying the support of the state to illegally enslaved Africans for their legitimate claims to freedom. Having presented their proposals in Parliament, the Regressistas convinced slaveholders that they were protected by the imperial state against any eventuality. The illegality of their slave properties had been "suspended."

Noting the immediate consequences of these proslavery politics for the slave trade, judiciary reform, and partisan disputes, the liberal opposition frequently discussed proposals regarding the 1831 law. "It is necessary to take a decision about this law," Antônio Carlos de Andrada e Silva said. "It is like a sword of Damocles hanging above the heads of all deputies, it is properly an elective machine: let's end this once and for all." Montezuma in turn argued that the "party that rose to power on September 19, it is true, turned this into its political lever," promising "that this law would be revoked, that the law of the Senate would be passed." While in power, the cabinet and its "seventy votes up" received support for all of its principles, and "if it did not have more it was because it did not demand and proclaim. Good lord . . . !!," but "for what reason wasn't the law of November 7 revoked?"[82] Indeed, the protection of the contraband connected some regional representatives to the party of the Regresso, located at the core of the nation-state. In Rio de Janeiro, such support was so evident that even the well-known "elections of the truncheon" (*eleições do cacete*), carried out under the control of the liberal cabinet, led to the selection of six Saquaremas and only four liberals. After the change in government, the liberal champion Martim Francisco wrote sardonically to Antônio Pereira Rebouças: "The Portuguese and Africanist party won: God willing, it is for the happiness of Brazil." The second sentence was unclear, but the first could not be more precise.[83]

The "Africanist party" also managed to impose their own concept of state during the 1830s. The program of moderate liberals—initially embodied in the Penal Code of 1832 and in the Additional Act of 1834—strengthened lay magistrates and broadened the administrative duties of provinces. In opposition to the unitary state of Pedro I, the constitutional reform of 1834 established provincial legislative assemblies and granted the power for provinces to create courts below the High Court (similar to courts of appeal) and a police administration managed at the municipal level. Some of the most important innovations among the lay magistrates were the new powers of the justices of the peace and the jury. According to the Constitution of 1827 and relevant legislation passed in that year, justices of the peace were to be elected locally and occupy their position for one year. They had multiple responsibilities on the parish level, from conducting pretrial actions (such as small hearings) to maintaining social order. The Penal Code of 1832 extended their term to four years and made them responsible for bills of indictment. During those years, these lay magistrates had unprecedented power in Brazil.[84]

Already after 1835, however, lay magistrates became the subject of controversy because of disputes between clans for control over the strategic position of justice of the peace. Moreover, the growing number of revolts—Farroupilha, Balaiada, Cabanagem, and Sabinada—led imperial politicians to develop strategies to strengthen the presence of the government in multiple localities, especially those under rebel control. The goal was to prevent the acquittal of rebels by popular juries controlled by justices of the peace. The first effort carried the decentralizing mark of moderate liberals, with provincial assemblies trying to weaken the power of the justice of the peace by transferring some of his duties to newly designated mayors between 1835 and 1837—specifically in São Paulo, Pernambuco, Alagoas, Sergipe, Ceará, Paraíba do Norte, and Maranhão.[85]

The main solution, however, came from the Regressistas in two steps. First, their interpretation of the Additional Act in 1838–1840 eliminated the provincial capacity to create judicial offices below the High Court and propose candidates for high-ranking police positions. Second, the reform of the Code of Criminal Procedure in 1841 established three principal changes: the pretrial and trial functions of the justice of the peace would now be overseen by the mayor; this commissary would also be a part, along with the parish priest and the justice of the peace, of the electoral commission that qualified citizens to vote during elections; and, finally, all police and judicial positions in the empire (such as county judges, municipal judges, chiefs of police, and attorneys), with the exception of the justice of the peace, would answer to the minister of justice. This conservative solution differed from its liberal counterpart because the provinces in this case did not have the power to decide who would occupy positions in the judicial system.

The virtual control over the judiciary and the police by the executive branch could potentially lead to the use of overwhelming force not only against provincial revolts but also against the contraband slave trade (as would actually be the case in 1850). At this point, we can see the clear articulation of Brazilian institutional developments and the dynamics of the illegal traffic: both in their discourse and their practices, the Regressistas convinced planters and their representatives that they would not fight to end the contraband slave trade. Thus, the pressure against the 1831 law gained renewed strength in 1836 after the Regressistas put forward their interpretation of the Additional Act, and elections for the legislature sanctioned the centralization of the judiciary. Historian José Murilo de Carvalho argues that the centralization of the justice system was only passed by Parliament because of the corporatism of the magistrates. We could add, however, that such reform could only be passed because the Saquaremas assured planters that the new justice system would never prosecute them for the illegal property that they had accumulated through piracy and theft.[86]

Finally, the rise of the Regresso had a direct impact on the growth of the contraband slave trade. When presenting his proposal to revoke the slave trade law in 1836, Vasconcelos apparently submitted it to the Commission of the Constitution to prevent debate in the plenary and to avoid risking premature defeat. At the time, a perceptive deputy from Pernambuco warned other representatives that the mere presence of the proposal in the House would work as a promise to revoke the law and stimulate the growth of the contraband. In the following year, the same deputy noted that "in the north, in [the deputy's] province, the importation [of Africans] was very rare; but . . . since the appearance of the indication to revoke the law of 1831 some have spread the rumor that the law had been abolished, and the importation of Africans was not surprising anymore."[87] The proposals of Vasconcelos and Barbacena remained shelved for more than ten years in the assembly, as noted by historians, but they were never forgotten.[88]

The corollary of all this could not be more perverse. Approximately 2,000 slaves were disembarked annually in Pernambuco between 1831 and 1836. Between 1837 and 1840, this number rose to almost 6,000. During those same periods, the number of disembarked slaves in Bahia rose from

3,300 to 3,600, despite the impact of the Malê revolt. In the Southeast, the growth is indisputable: vessels disembarked almost 46,000 enslaved Africans in the region between 1831 and 1835. In 1836 alone, the number of disembarkations was 46,000, and they reached a total of approximately 161,000 in the following four years.[89] As Montezuma cried, if the Regresso did not get more it was "because it did not demand and proclaim. Good lord . . . !!" Instead of the lord, however, the deputy could have cried for the help of Great Britain, whose intervention seemed more likely and possible in the following decade.

The Reopening of the Parliament in Spain and the Problem of Citizenship, 1834–1837

By granting the rights of citizenship to free people of color and freedmen born in the Empire of Brazil, the Constitution of 1824 created a powerful consensus on the issue in that country. Even the reform brought by the Additional Act of 1834 and the growing liberal pressure—which even called for women's suffrage and land reform—did not consider any kind of change to Article 6 of the Constitution and its crucial first paragraph defining citizenship without any reference to race. The *Historical, Political, Civil, and Natural News* (*Notícia histórica, política, civil e natural*) published in 1833 synthesized the reasons for the consensus among politicians of all stripes on the constitutional definition of citizenship: "In face of the equality of rights for all colors," the author argued, "the spirit of rivalry that existed between them, and that could have been so harmful, is gradually being extinguished. The distinction now is between Citizen and Slave."[90]

A similar consensus can be seen in the so-called mulatto press. A number of newspapers with titles related to skin color such as *O Filho da Terra*, *O Mulato*, *O Brasileiro Pardo*, *O Cabrito*, *O Meia Cara*, *O Crioulinho*, and *O Crioulo* began to appear. Historians have generally considered them to be the political initiatives of pardos and freedmen, but it seems possible that these newspapers were published by radical liberals or conservatives opposed to the regency, which was under the control of moderate liberals at the time. Among their accusations against the government, they occasionally mentioned discriminatory practices in nominations for public and military positions, and they spread rumors that the rights of citizenship would be taken away from blacks and pardos. "We do not know the reason why moderate whites have declared war against us," *O Mulato* argued. "In elections," the writer continued, "there is not one representative of our colors, in public offices and everywhere else they have excluded us."[91] In the end, even these accusations only called for the observation of the Constitution in order to establish nonracialized equality among free persons.

The only official measure that could, in fact, justify the assertions of the "mulatto press" is paragraph 13 of the decree of October 25, 1832, regarding the National Guard, which had been created in the previous year. The decree established that members of the militia—active citizens despite the color of their skin—could only elect second-degree electors for official positions, a strategy intended to prevent freedmen from ascending to higher-ranking positions than those occupied by free men.[92] The article was passed without much discussion, despite the complaints of the mulatto deputy Antônio Pereira Rebouças. Members of Parliament believed that the absence of distinctions based on color among the members of the National Guard represented an advance over colonial militias (and their segregated black, pardo, and white battalions). In the words of Raimundo José da Cunha Matos, one of the greatest defenders of the slave trade during the debates of 1827, with the "law that created the National Guard, all colors became mixed and there are no distinct bodies of whites, pardos, and blacks; the rights are equal."[93] The Constitution of 1824 and its emphasis on the legal equality of races, therefore, temporarily resolved the problem of citizenship and color. The issue would resurface again only at the peak of social and political crisis.

The case of the Spanish Empire was markedly different. The restoration of absolutism between 1823 and 1834 solved problems related to plans for independence and the actions of free persons of color with the establishment of the régimen de las facultades omnímodas. The convocation of the General Cortes in 1834, however, started a process that would reestablish the representative system in Spain and generate debate over the issues of slavery, citizenship, and political representation. During the parliamentary debates, liberals from the peninsula, surprisingly, defended the absolutist solution that granted extraordinary powers to the captains general and denied constitutional guarantees to the inhabitants of Cuba. Such behavior can only be understood by looking at the events that reorganized political institutions on the peninsula.

At the beginning of the Carlist wars in 1833, regency councillors drafted the future Royal Statute, a moderate constitutional text that would take effect in 1834. To ensure the support of American inhabitants for the process that had begun in Europe, the text established that "a special clause will determine the number of Procurators of the Kingdom and Substitutes [Procuradores do Reino e Suplentes] that should be chosen in the Spanish provinces of Asia and America."[94] The decree of the Royal Statute established on May 20 the terms of electoral participation for Americans: procurators would be elected by an extremely reduced number of representatives who had been chosen based on their wealth (in other words, they were elected by towns completely controlled by local oligarchies).[95] Between July 1834 and May 1836, some of the famous sugar- and coffee-producing families of Cuba sent André Arango and Juan Montalvo y Castillo to represent Havana, Juan Kindelán and Prudêncio Echevarría y O'Gaban to represent Santiago, and José Serapio de Mojarrieta to represent Puerto Príncipe on the peninsula.[96] Cuban procurators had effectively surpassed Juan Bernardo O'Gavan despite his ties to the two main authorities on the island—Captain General Miguel Tacón and the superintendente general de la hacienda, the Marquis of Pinillos—and all the electoral restrictions established by the Royal Statute. After the defeat, Tacón openly criticized Montalvo, calling him a subversive and separatist in his letters to the peninsula.[97]

A liberal uprising in August 1836 would change things again. The victory of the progressives led to another convocation of the Cortes, which in turn called for the enactment of the 1812 Constitution of Cádiz in place of the Royal Statute. Thus, the Cádiz Constitution was adopted for the third time in Spain, with the Cortes becoming responsible for its application. The calls for constitutional equality between Spaniards on both sides of the Atlantic became stronger in this new context, with an extension of the convocation to the Spanish domains in America, namely Cuba and Puerto Rico.

The reception of the initial news in Cuba—namely, the uprising in Málaga and the creation of one of the first autonomous juntas by the liberal movement—only confirmed the loyalty of the island to the government. The fears expressed by Captain General Tacón, however, led to some particular developments. According to the voting criteria of the Cádiz Constitution, an electoral college composed of twenty-four people under the control of the local cabildo was supposed to select the representatives of Havana. However, the governor attempted to manipulate the process in every possible way and caused a crisis after rejecting the electoral list prepared by the college. New elections took place, with voters continuing to support the oppositionists Domingo del Monte and Nicolas Escobedo in spite of Tacón's political stance. Conflict spread throughout the island, leading to a change in the electoral law: the Council of Ministers reduced the number of Cuban deputies to the Cortes from eight to three. Another meeting of the Electoral College took place in November 1836 as a result, maintaining the appointment of Escobedo against the expectations of the captain general and the metropolitan government.[98]

Two other Cuban provinces still had the right to send their representatives to the Cortes—Puerto Príncipe and Santiago. Puerto Príncipe elected Tacón's closest deputy: Francisco de Armas. Opposition to the captain general, however, reached its peak in Santiago, where José Antonio Saco—the intellectual successor of Félix Varela, who had been forced into exile by Tacón—was elected.

At the same time, the city of Santiago also witnessed one of the most serious conflicts of 1836. On hearing the news about the successful revolution in Spain, the governor of Santiago de Cuba, General Manuel Lorenzo, swore to uphold the Cádiz Constitution and initiated the electoral process in the eastern part of the island before knowing the official position of the captain general. He celebrated both "authentic liberalism" and loyalty to the queen regent. Meanwhile, Tacón's actions led to the establishment of strong opposition in the government between September and December that had the support of prominent residents of Santiago.[99] The captain general called for Lorenzo's deposition and the exile of the rebel leaders, describing their activities as illegitimate. In late 1836, the situation escalated to a naval blockade of the eastern part of the island and military conflict.

Tacón sought to maintain government control over the entire island by any means necessary. Apart from a military victory over Lorenzo, the captain general also tried to reverse the electoral defeats through actions in Madrid. The metropolitan government acknowledged Tacón's demands, changing the rules of the game in April and finally suspending the application of the Cádiz Constitution in overseas territories in August 1836.[100] At the same time, Tacón received support and honors from the Ayuntamiento in Havana, now controlled by the sugar aristocracy.[101] During the turbulent year of 1836, therefore, we can see the complementary actions of two main groups articulated through the figure of the captain general: Spanish liberals, who feared that disturbances in Cuba could lead to the loss of Cuba, and the Cuban sugarocracy, who feared that liberal constitutionalism could eliminate the privileges of Cuban slaveholders.[102] These two groups, however, were ideologically distinct. While part of the Cuban slaveholding class clearly had proslavery concerns, Spanish radicals condemned slavery and considered it incompatible with the liberal regime. In their defense of the empire, these two sectors developed together a new colonial status for Cuba that excluded those groups who saw in the Constitution the possibility to become integrated into the state while remaining influential in local government.

This alliance had already been defined when the Cortes convened in the metropolis. Most Cuban deputies sent to Spain were oppositionists, despite Tacón's efforts. During a secret session on January 16, 1837 (three months after the beginning of the debates), the deputy Vicente Sancho presented a proposal that would guide discussions about Cuba until the end of the parliamentary sessions. Viewed by historians as one of the liberals involved in the 1836 insurrection and an outspoken critic of slavery, Sancho described the dangerous situation in Cuba, as exemplified by the case of Santiago.[103] He then called for the formation of a special committee with members of the Commission of Overseas Affairs (Comisión de Ultramar) and the Commission of the Constitution to assess the situation in the overseas provinces.[104] As a member of the Commission of the Constitution, Sancho directly participated in the preparation of the draft that would be debated at length in the Cortes.

On February 12, 1837, the commissions released their report. Taking the January debates (which had taken place in secret sessions) regarding the participation of overseas representatives in the Cortes as their starting point, the commissions supported the proposal offered by Sancho. Their arguments had three main points. First, a regime of special laws was the only way to properly govern those provinces and keep them attached to the metropolis (the term "metropolis" had been avoided in previous constitutional debates). Second, the overseas populations were composed of "elements" different from those of the peninsula and, for this reason, required their own specific laws. Finally, the periodical change of overseas representatives at the Cortes could not take place at the same pace as with their peninsular counterparts because of the distance of the overseas provinces. According to the commissions, this would inevitably lead to a predominance of overseas representatives based in Europe, who were therefore distanced from their constituents back home. For this reason, special laws were necessary to satisfy the demands of the overseas possessions.[105] Spain seemed to be following in the steps of the Napoleonic experience.[106]

The demand for special laws was the implicit result of two different decisions. In his original comments, Sancho had mentioned the inconvenience of Cuban participation in the Cortes and noted that the *present* conflict in the eastern part of the island had been generated by the actions of Lorenzo. His assessment, however, called into question not only the present but also the future participation of Cuban deputies in the Spanish Cortes. Moreover, he argued that the decision should be applied not only in Cuba but also in Puerto Rico and the Philippines. In other words, based on an isolated event in time and space, the commission had developed a plan for all overseas territories of the empire.[107]

Since the proposal only prescribed rules for the future, it was not supposed to have any effect over the 1836 sessions or on the representatives selected by Spanish "inhabitants of both hemispheres," as established by the Constitution of 1812 and the regent queen. Still, members of the commission proposed that deputies who had arrived in Madrid in January should be excluded from the Cortes. Although the commission defended the "necessity of Special Laws" as a central part of its argument, the order of their priorities was to first, prevent the entrance of the deputies elected in opposition to Tacón and his supporters in Cuba and Spain; second, ensure that this threat did not reappear in the following sessions of the Cortes; and, finally, demonstrate concern for legal order throughout the entire empire, and for this reason, call for the development of "Special Laws." By avoiding the use of the word "colony" and announcing the formal equality of all Spaniards (as defined by the Constitution), the commission reinforced the idea that all Spaniards were subject to a single body of law. However, by defending, as we have seen, the importance of the "metropolis" maintaining total control, the commission reintroduced the vocabulary that had been regularly avoided during the parliamentary debates of the 1810s and 1820s.

The discussion continued into the sessions of early 1837. A number of arguments in favor of and against the proposal were presented in sessions until

June, when it finally passed.[108] These debates, however, took place without the participation of overseas deputies, thus enabling the commission to achieve its major objective: to exclude Tacón's opponents. Protests began immediately. Representatives from Cuba submitted a complaint about their exclusion to the Cortes in the session of February 27, 1837. Moreover, they argued that the same body of law that applied on the peninsula should also be applied overseas, and they rejected any other solution. The argument was articulated by José Antonio Saco in a famous piece in which he criticized the position of the Cortes and expounded the radical perspective that would guide his actions in the following years. The text was submitted to the Commissions of the Constitution and Overseas Affairs, but it was never returned to the Cortes.[109]

The *Diário de Sesiones de las Cortes Constituyentes* describe secret sessions, as had been the case in most parliamentary discussions about overseas problems, but they also reveal shifting views about certain issues. Now, not only were the definitions of citizenship marked by a clear racial divide, but so too were the institutional relations between Spain and Cuba. The debates around Sancho's proposal, in fact, indicate the abandonment of the formal equality that had been maintained between the Spanish on the two sides of the Atlantic, which had been a central aspect of the Cádiz Constitution. This equality, as we have seen, allowed the inclusion of American representatives in the Cortes in the debates between 1810 and 1814. The main objective of these policies was to guarantee Spanish unity against the Napoleonic invasions and avoid the complete collapse of the empire.

Building a national state of Atlantic dimensions was a bold move, especially because of the failure of the earlier French effort to achieve a similar goal. Thus, constitutional equality between Spaniards (free and vecino) was tied to the objective of creating similar institutions on both sides of the Atlantic and ensuring subsequent economic integration. These objectives were accompanied by a centralizing agenda, with the Cortes responsible for defining the economic union and political parity of the empire. At that point, the American representatives expressed disagreement with this conception of centralization and European national integration. According to them, true equality should be accompanied by provincial autonomy in America. The particular needs and objectives of these provinces could not be satisfied by the central government. Liberals from the peninsula (such as Agustín Argüelles) never accepted these proposals during the 1810s and 1820s.[110]

A different liberal conception of the relations between Spaniards appeared in 1836–1837 as a result of earlier reflections on and influences of the French Revolution. The idea of constitutional equality between peninsulares and Americans was replaced by a permanent perception of heterogeneity.[111] The goal now was to create new legislation that reflected the different social conditions between Spain and the overseas territories, and, perhaps more importantly, within colonial societies themselves. These concerns had already been raised in the constitutional experiences of the 1810s and 1820s, especially regarding the issue of citizenship. Now, however, these distinctions were central to the definition of the relations between Spain and Cuba—as well as, by extension, Puerto Rico and the Philippines.

The report of the commission also indicated that the extraordinary economic growth of Cuba was based on a population of 704,437 inhabitants, a large number of whom were slaves and former slaves.[112] The report then referred to Articles 28 and 29 of the Constitution to defend the position that national representation in the Antilles was limited to inhabitants whose parents were of Spanish ancestry, which meant less than half the population.[113] "Where there are such marked differences in the population," the report argued, "the law cannot be the same for the provinces that do not have them or the convenient modifications must be established." The conclusion was that "it is important to later distinguish how Spaniards of different colors will be represented . . . so that the Cortes can forever eliminate any possible source of harm."[114]

The old liberal Argüelles—a former member of the Cádiz Cortes—presented the best defense of the differentiated treatment. On March 10, 1837, he referred to the constitutional debates of 1812 and "the evils caused by philanthropic deliberations from that moment." He now lamented the fact that he had personally agreed to the independence of American countries after previously having legislated for unity. In his view, the lesser evil for Cuba would be to ignore the existence of an independence movement, since this could lead to the same tragic destiny of Haiti. Argüelles then described with many details all the proclamations of independence in America and asked himself about Cuba: "With so many distinct and varied elements in the population, should we close our eyes to experience? Without considering the sad results, are we going to blindly follow the theory of equality?"[115] He later referred to the proclamations of independence as acts of treason against the Constitution of 1812 and asked: "How can we talk about unity and equality between Spaniards now? Separation is a fact and everyone that participated in that moment cannot forget this."[116] Moreover, Argüelles argued that the measure had been constitutional: "The government has called Cuba and the other overseas provinces to the Cortes. Just laws, however, must accompany circumstances, and now the Constitution of 1812 is only valid for Europe: this is how the Commission has thought. . . . Liberty is an idealized form for happiness and there are a thousand ways to get it. The proposed article is valid for the pacification and prosperity of those provinces."[117] He then concluded that after the passing of the article related to the special laws—understood as constitutional and pacifying—there would be no need for the presence of overseas deputies at the present Cortes.

In another section, Argüelles discussed the social heterogeneity in the constituent parts of the empire: "Here slavery is not discussed. Does this exist in the peninsula? I would like to reconcile the Constitution of 1812 with present circumstances but that is impossible. The Constitution is presently only applicable in the peninsula. . . . There exists a strong element of destruction: slavery." He revived and radicalized an important argument of the debates of 1812, when slavery became a reason for limiting the participation of American deputies in the Cortes: "When they wanted the population to be the basis of elections, then, knowing that they would provide the majority and be able to transfer the seat of the Spanish empire with one single election from here to Mexico or Peru, deputies of that period, circumspect and prudent, said no, because the population of 17 or 18 million mentioned by you is not homogeneous and proof of this is the fact that not a single one of you does not have Spanish origin."[118] The implicit conclusion was that the American deputies there were trying to govern and control the others.

Despite these opinions, Argüelles still opposed the transatlantic slave trade. During the Cádiz debates, he asked, "Despite the mixed commission in Havana to make the treaty, despite all the care that I suppose authorities in that island have had to curb the traffic, it is clear that they could never stop it." Tables assessing the numbers of slave disembarkations in the island were presented in the plenary, which led him to provocatively ask, "Isn't it necessary that in the special legislation adopted for the internal government all measures dictated by prudence are taken to decrease or eliminate this threat? . . . Could they ever think like anthropologists and suffocate these generous ideas that had been spreading among all castes around the earth?"[119]

As noted by Argüelles and other deputies in 1836 and 1837, the existence of slavery and African descendants overseas led to the parliamentary decision to significantly reduce the demographic basis for the American representation in the Cortes of Cádiz. While American representatives from many parts of the hemisphere struggled to integrate the *castas pardas*, Spanish liberals and Cuban representatives, as we have seen, joined forces against such a project. Inspired by the historical experience of the Iberian Atlantic system, deputies from New Spain, Guatemala, and Peru sought to broaden the electoral basis and the number of American representatives in the Cortes, arguing that the inclusion of the castas pardas as Spanish citizens would help to maintain peace and political control in their provinces. The opposition of peninsulares and their Cuban allies to the proposal became one of the main obstacles to the union between Europeans and Americans at the Cádiz Cortes.

In 1836 and 1837, the situation had not substantially changed. American representatives in Madrid came only from Cuba and Puerto Rico. Spanish constituents feared the loss of these last imperial possessions, as shown by Argüelles's arguments. Some of the anxieties described by him did not exist anymore, such as the possibility of an American majority in Congress transferring the "capital of the empire to Mexico, Peru," or even Havana. Thus, the concern with the electoral basis in America had disappeared and could no longer justify the exclusion of the castas pardas from citizenship. Moreover, according to Argüelles, the deputies in the Cortes were primarily interested in maintaining internal order. On the issue of excluding castas pardas, Cuban representatives had always supported Spanish liberals.

Thus, other fears accompanied liberal arguments about slavery and the inclusion of people of African descent during 1836 and 1837, arguments that also influenced the problem of castas pardas. The idea of casta, a typical category of the Old Regime, was gradually replaced in the liberal vocabulary by the idea of race.[120] On March 9, Deputy Villa defended the necessity to differentiate Spaniards: "I wish, gentlemen, that we could go back to the years of Ferdinand and Isabel. . . . The peaceful and timid inhabitants of Cuba, of whom we only have a vague memory, were replaced by European and African races and produced a third one, all of them worthy of the attention of the Cortes. Can we forget any of them when passing legislation in the Cortes?"[121]

In the opinion of Vicente Sancho—shared by Argüelles—Cuba had changed after the 1810s. The population of African descent had increased significantly since the 1810s, sought to control the island, and, for this reason, supported the independence movement. Sancho insisted that such a view had been confirmed by recent events. According to him, many proprietors in the eastern part of the island ignored the Constitution because they did not want to grant any rights to the population of African descent (and such rights had been granted by the Cortes only in a few exceptional cases): "They cannot be lovers of freedom as Europeans are." In Havana, the government could control revolts, but in the eastern part of the island proprietors feared that those who favored independence would give weapons and money to blacks and mulattoes. Even whites in America, therefore, were different from their European counterparts.

According to Sancho, Cubans nonetheless saw these rare cases (when blacks and mulattoes were included in the constitutional order) as excessive. Moreover, the deputy also argued against the participation of overseas representatives in Parliament. A deputy from Cuba, in his view, represented a very different reality from that of Spanish representatives. Thus, could the representative system function in the same way throughout each of these different parts of the empire? Or, in other words, could the electoral rules developed for Spain also be applied in Cuba?[122] Cubans had to deal with the problem of slavery and, therefore, did not talk about freedom like Europeans did.

According to Sancho, two bodies of laws in the Spanish Empire had emerged as a result of the different constituent realities of the monarchy as exemplified by the distinct qualifications for citizenship. While a vecino resident in any part of Spain was considered a citizen, residents in America had to prove that they did not have African ancestry. Sancho made use of the ideological justifications of the Atlantic system of northwestern Europe—remarkably expressed by Montesquieu in his writings on the differences of climate, customs, and production—to explain the existence of two different legislations in the Spanish Empire and the impossibility of a single representative system. The latest events in Cuba seemed to confirm the opinion that divisions and revolts could compromise election results and the terms of elected deputies. The results of elections under these conditions, in Sancho's view, were not the true expression of the opinions and needs of the people. For this reason, the presence of these deputies at the Cortes was an impediment to the development of an authentic system of national representation.[123]

Finally, Sancho also criticized Article 258 of the Civil Code for establishing that not only the Civil Code itself but also the Penal Code would be the same for the entire monarchy, "without the problems resulting from variations introduced by the Cortes according to particular circumstances." He then added that "the civil codes, sirs, cannot be the same in both places. In America there is slavery and this changes all social laws, the relations between father and son, mother and whoever will be born. The Penal Code is the confirmation of the Civil and stipulates the penalties of those who commit offenses. Thus, as a consequence, it is also different. Could a citizen from Andalusia, surrounded by voluntary servants, and a mill owner from the island of Cuba, surrounded by 500 or 400 slaves, be considered in the same manner? Could the same Penal Code protect both? I do not think so. What about the procedures? I believe they must also be different."[124] The difference was in the existence of slavery and, for this reason, he asked, "And can we destroy it? Is it in our power to do it? Ask those from Cuba if they want it?"

Thus, in Sancho's opinion, the application of the Constitution in America depended on the existence of both a national representation composed of legislative bodies that could receive the deputies elected by overseas provinces, as well as local legislative bodies similar to those in Europe that could ensure the application of the law. And even if these conditions were established, the difficulties in creating an electoral body in the terms proposed by the Cortes could not be ignored. The following passage synthesizes his thought: "The Constitution that we are developing cannot be applied in the overseas provinces.... And what Constitution could be applied in America? Let me be clear: none! Constitutions are created to guarantee the rights of men. Which ones? Liberty and equality. In those countries these words, so great for us, are words of extermination and death. How can we say that everyone is equal in a country where half of the people own the other half? To talk about liberty there is to place the dagger in the hands of the negroes. And how could weak Europeans, irritated by the heat, offer any resistance to the children of the sun?"[125]

The problem of regulating the government of the island remained. The return of the Cádiz Constitution put the legislation regarding provincial deputations back on the table, which had stimulated the calls for autonomy by Mexicans and other American representatives in Cádiz and Madrid in 1821 and 1822. This legislation established that the captain general should be deposed and replaced by a provincial deputation selected in local elections. This time, however, the debate was marked by racial arguments regarding the inapplicability of the Constitution overseas. The goal was to overthrow the article about provincial deputations.

In March 1837, Deputy Villa derived some unexpected conclusions from the special laws for overseas territories. "Since the fundamental laws offered to the peninsula are not applicable to overseas possessions, since they should not be treated as colonies; since we think that it is fair that these provinces get the same benefits of liberty while compatible with their state, I don't see a way of governing them other than granting that power to their inhabitants, i.e., to a provincial deputation, elected as they think best, that consider the economic direction of the islands, leaving the central government to the executive authorities that the supreme government of the nation assign to them. This is an old project: it has been announced in this place and put into practice in the States of the West by a nation that loves liberty as much as Spain does."[126] In this clear reference to the British Empire, the transference of economic decision-making power to the provincial deputations would allow for faster and more efficient action, which could in turn generate more economic growth and free the central government to take care of the general problems of the nation. After adding this, Villa said that he would support the proposal offered by the commissions, as this would make the Spanish Empire consonant with modernity.

The following day, Villa received a reply from Agustín Argüelles: "Mr. Villa must know that the inhabitants of America were never ruled by laws similar to ours and that after declaring the equality of rights we have denied them a municipal and provincial government."[127] He then noted that the peninsulares had refused to grant autonomy to the provincial deputations of America after the parliamentary debates of Cádiz. In his view, the American calls for a federalist model for the empire stimulated the emergence of independence processes. For this reason, Europeans had rejected these proposals in 1810 and 1821 and were expected to do the same now, considering the dangerous situation in Cuba. In the March 25 session, Argüelles brought the question back for debate, this time associating it with slavery: "Overseas, freedom struggles against slavery and this is the difference: the property in slaves does not follow European principles. A provincial deputation in Cuba will not be like those from Europe, since property is distributed differently there. That province stands over a volcano. . . . Let's avoid Saint-Domingue since the same race and the same hatred exist there."[128] To prove his point, Sancho asked about the possibility of organizing local powers in tune with Europe. "Here we depend on the ministers, and what ministers will be there? There will be viceroys or governors, but will we put this power in the hands of an ambitious man? Of an [Agustín de] Iturbide, who will have the glory of calling himself an emperor? Or of a coward, who, unable to resist the threats, would one day proclaim independence?" Considering the impossibility of applying the Constitution overseas, any change on the island would be a step toward independence. "Cubans hate political innovations."[129]

Several European deputies criticized the general proposals of the commissions in the Cortes. The strongest criticisms, however, came from the deputies who had been expelled from the Cortes. The most important came from José Antonio Saco, with the *Examen analíctico del informe de la Comisión especial*, written at the beginning of the debates and published in 1837 by Tomás Jordan. Its central argument was on the issue of political rights in a slave society. If American peoples were heterogeneous, why had they been called to participate in the creation of the first liberal Constitution? To answer the question, Jordan discussed the issue of political rights in liberal regimes. First, he argued that political rights should be distinguished from civil ones: the first were exclusive to the population of European origin, while the second were common to all free men. According to these principles, Cuban society was not exceptional. In most countries where liberalism had been implemented, the majority of the population did not have the right to vote.

His argument regarding the possibility of liberalism in slave societies was based mainly on the British example, and for this reason it was very similar to those defended by Villa during the Cortes debates. The generation of 1810 had already considered using the colonial assemblies of the British Caribbean—with their governors assigned by the Crown—as a model for the slave societies of the Spanish Empire. The situation, however, was different now. After the beginning of the abolitionist process in the British dominions in 1833–1834, defenders of Cuban autonomy had to search for less dangerous examples. In the words of Saco,

People will say that I'm a partisan of the English nation and that I openly want Cuba to become one of the satellites moving around that planet. Those saying these things are wrong and those who judge me in this way do not know me. If the Spanish government got to the point of cutting the political ties that connect Spain to Cuba, I would not be vindictive to the point of suggesting the union of my country with Great Britain. I would then give her an autonomous existence, an independent existence. . . . But if, forced by circumstances, I had to throw her into the arms of strangers, no one could receive her with more honor or glory than (the arms) of the Confederation of North America.

The arguments of José Antonio Saco presaged those of the annexationism that would become stronger in Cuba after the constitutional definitions of 1837. In the following decades, the proposal to join the states of North America represented a zeitgeist of opinion for Cubans during the long process of establishing a liberal order in a slave society. It also stimulated the emergence of a great debate. The constant threat of abolishing the slave trade and the dangers of a slave revolt—which the Constitution of 1837 did not dissuade— stimulated the search for alternatives to a Spanish union that, in fact, excluded Cubans. Saco expressed at that moment a liberal tendency that would become more radical in the following years and oppose metropolitan actions.

Saco's opinions were an expression of the broader creole opposition to the political arrangement of 1837. In general, this opposition consisted of a refutation of the notion that the existence of slavery in Cuba called for special laws, especially the loss of rights of active citizenship because of the peculiarities of the population. According to him, the "diversity of interests and diversity of representatives should always exist in national assemblies. The homogeneity of one population cannot be found in a single skin color."[130] Imperial unity should be based on a common past and shaped by the defense of the shared interests of the nation. It nonetheless presupposed certain differences between Europe and America. This was very different (if not completely opposite) from the arguments made by figures such as Argüelles and Sancho, who defended the search for protection against internal enemies for the sake of the survival of Spanish national sovereignty. Ramón de la Sagra synthesized the arguments of integrationists from the peninsula: "On the island of Cuba they are not exactly a people or, in other words, there is a large number of political minors, deprived of a larger or smaller number of rights. There are no more than two races, the white and that of color."[131]

British Abolitionism, Second Spanish Empire, and the Brazilian Regresso

Hispanic Cuban and Brazilian political actors reacted in unique ways to the great transformations of slavery in the Atlantic world between the rise of independence movements in Iberian America and abolition in the British Caribbean. The dangers of imperial fragmentation, the recurrent fears of slave revolts, the eventual implementation of the representative system, the problem of citizenship and slavery, the British pressure against the slave trade, and, finally, the beginning of abolition in the British Empire in 1833 were some of the issues shared by both empires. Political agents in the Spanish and Brazilian Empires searched for solutions that preserved the social order, political organization, and economic growth. Because the variables described above played different roles in the Caribbean and in the South Atlantic, Brazil and Cuba followed different strategies.

The concentration of political and military power in the hands of the captain general in Cuba provided stronger tools against slave revolts and independence movements after the Liberal Triennium (1820–1823). As we have seen, the measure was adopted as a result of the combined efforts of a coalition of Cuban groups who were opposed to the enlargement of the public sphere during the Madrid Cortes. After the reopening of the representative system during the following decade, the régimen de las facultades omnímodas could be extended because of the actions of Cuban slaveholding classes and most metropolitan deputies against groups calling for the implementation of a Constitution. Ironically, the need to preserve imperial unity, slavery, and the contraband slave trade led to an alliance between slaveholding anti-constitutionalist groups in the colony and constitutionalist antislavery politicians in the metropolis. Although the former had mainly economic concerns and the latter essentially wanted to save the Spanish Empire, they shared the common objective of making the political system more predictable in order to avoid social disruption.

These two groups managed to guarantee the coexistence of a representative government on the peninsula with the exclusion of deputies from the colonies, the nonapplication of the Constitution overseas, and the extinction of colonial deputations. The principle of racialized citizenship became the basis of the political configuration that the Spanish Empire developed after 1837. This political arrangement was so stable that not even the constitutional changes of 1845, 1856, and 1869 were able to shake its foundations. In other words, many of the nineteenth-century inhabitants of Cuba, Puerto Rico, and the Philippines waited for reforms or special laws that never came. In the absence of a definition, the colonial possessions remained outside the sphere of the law, so to speak.[132]

The principles adopted in 1837 led to new tensions but also provided the basis for the modernization and economic growth of Cuba. They marked the construction of what some historians call the "Second Spanish Empire," the reinvention of the Hispanic state in the nineteenth century context of a free-market global economy based on the adoption of the technologies of the Industrial Revolution, the exploitation of slave labor, and the maintenance of the contraband slave trade.[133] Politics in the Second Spanish Empire was characterized by the lack of parliamentary representation, the principle of racialized citizenship, and the division between "constitutional zones" (metropolitan provinces) and "nonconstitutional zones" (overseas provinces). Since the pact had slavery and race relations at its center, constitutionalists in the colony associated the limitation of their rights with the institution of slavery. The critique of the imperial pact by Saco and his group became associated with antislavery discourses.

The Empire of Brazil in turn embraced the great governmental reforms that had formed the core of independence, not having pro–slave trade politics a priori. The division of powers, the definition of general, provincial, and municipal jurisdictions, and the defense of a public sphere (without censorship during the 1820s) were central to the anti–slave trade treaty of 1826, which became another important variable in the state-building process. Only by the mid-1830s, after the great reforms of the Additional Act in 1834 and the beginning of abolition in the British Caribbean, did a clear political alignment between Brazilian slaveholding classes (interested in the reopening of the slave trade) and a faction of imperial statesmen (the leaders of the Regresso) appear. The former ensured the expansion of the slave economy (especially in the coffee-producing and mining areas of central and southern Brazil), while the latter developed the juridical apparatus of the empire. Such a configuration became as solid and entrenched as that of the Second Spanish Empire.

The defense of the contraband slave trade in both regions, however, would soon confront a major obstacle. After the end of slavery and apprenticeship in the British Caribbean, new pressures on the British government came from an even more internationalized abolitionist movement and from former British slaveholders, who had been experiencing an unprecedented crisis generated by the end of their traditional labor system. The Brazilian and Spanish Empires, therefore, had to resist the escalation of British pressure by using their respective institutional structures and their own accumulated experience confronting the dual problems of race and political representation. Each empire would reinvent, in its own way, the relationship between liberalism and slavery.

CHAPTER 4

The Politics of Slavery in the Constitutional Empires, 1837–1850

THE PROSLAVERY COMPACTS established in the second half of the 1830s led to an effective association between capital and politics in the Brazilian and Spanish Empires. Between 1823 and 1835, the Cuban treasury accumulated around 5 million pesos every year, of which 10 percent was sent to Madrid, first as *remisiones de fondos* and later as *sobrantes de Ultramar*. With the growth of colonial production and the fiscal reforms implemented by the peninsular government during the following decade, the money sent to Madrid rose by 600 percent per year (from 500,000 to 3 million pesos). Part of these resources financed the participation of the constitutional monarchy in the Carlist wars.

The situation in the Empire of Brazil shared many similarities with the Spanish context. With the growing number of regional revolts (Farroupilha, Sabinada, Balaiada, and Cabanagem), the government increased public expenditures from 12,000 contos in 1834 to 24,000 contos in 1839, of which 54 percent was spent on defense. However, a comparable growth in imperial revenue, which went from 14,000 contos in 1834 to 24,000 contos in 1844, was spurred by the growth of agricultural exports. The expansion of slavery and the contraband slave trade significantly contributed to stabilizing the constitutional regimes of the Brazilian and Spanish Empires.[1]

The intensification of the transatlantic slave trade in turn led to the rapid deterioration of relations with Britain. Led by the Agency Committee, the abolitionist movement pressed the British government to abolish apprenticeship in 1838 instead of 1840 and launched an international campaign to abolish slavery in other countries. In the words of the abolitionist newspaper *Reporter*, the "Frenchmen, the Dutchmen, the Danes, the Spaniards, the

Brazilians, and the North Americans felt the influence of slavery in the British colonies. . . . They consider us conquerors; they can foresee their destiny." Besides the domestic motivations, the internationalization of the abolitionist movement was also the result of the successful reopening of the slave trade to Brazil. The yearly mean of disembarked slaves in all the Americas tripled because of the numbers of disembarkations in Brazil, which rose from twenty-nine thousand between 1831 and 1834 to seventy-seven thousand between 1836 and 1839. Thus, two associations were created in Britain at the turn of the decade to fight the odious commerce: the Society for the Extinction of the Slave Trade and for the Civilization of Africa of Thomas Fowell Buxton, and the British and Foreign Antislavery Society of Joseph Sturge. While the former believed in a gradual replacement of the illegal commerce in slaves with the trade of legal goods, the latter called for the abolition of slavery in all countries as the only way to suppress the traffic as a whole. A fundamental step in this campaign was taken in 1840 when the first World Antislavery Convention convened in London, which received delegations from many countries, especially France and the United States.[2] An efficient Atlantic network of militants and informants gradually emerged in the main slaveholding regions of the Americas, contributing to the rise of global public opinion against the institution of slavery.

Abolitionists did not have the power to directly make governmental decisions in Britain, but their militancy influenced the choices of foreign affairs ministers, who also had to deal with pressure from former Caribbean slaveholders. One of the consequences was a series of anti–slave trade treaties signed by the Foreign Office during 1839: with Chile on January 19, Venezuela on March 1, Argentina on May 24, Uruguay on June 13, Haiti on December 23, and a number of African potentates on various dates. Before 1841, Mexico and Texas also signed similar treaties while France, Austria, Prussia, and Russia signed the Quintuple Agreement of 1841, which described the transatlantic slave trade as piracy.[3] Two years later, the second World Antislavery Convention called for the abolition of slavery in the newly independent state of Texas in order to limit the expansion of North American slavery. The British Foreign Office favored the action but did not explicitly support it. In this context, US statesmen successfully negotiated the annexation of the territory into the United States, knowing what was potentially on the horizon: Cuba could be next.[4]

Britain was compelled to adopt an interventionist—albeit cautious—attitude toward the Brazilian and Spanish Empires while absorbing pressure from former Caribbean slave owners, an internationalized abolitionist movement, and the surge of US expansionism. These actions influenced the perceptions of the dangers of slave revolts shared by slaveholding classes, and they impacted slave actions as well. Slaveholders in Brazil and Cuba searched for solutions to these tensions in their respective institutional settings. In Spain, the colonies were excluded from the representative system in order to protect slavery. In Brazil, the slave system depended on the contraband slave trade, which was created by proslavery alliances in the imperial Parliament. Sharing similar objectives, Cuba/Spain and Brazil developed their own politics of slavery.

Contraband and the Reinvention of Politics in the Second Spanish Empire, 1837–1841

After the rise of Regressistas to the Brazilian executive in September 1837 and the beginning of a new legislature in May 1838, the number of antislavery proposals in Parliament and anti–slave trade pamphlets in the public sphere significantly decreased. Slaveholders in the Paraíba Valley, Norte Fluminense, Minas Gerais, and the Bahian Recôncavo defended the continuation of the slave trade and threatened to offer armed resistance against attempts to emancipate Africans who had been disembarked illegally in the country. A minister described how newspapers in Rio de Janeiro—now completely allied to slave traders—refused to publish articles against the contraband. "There was an effort to publish a writing at this Court," he said in 1840, "establishing a public opinion about the traffic in Africans, and it seems that two newspapers did not want to include it in their columns." That same year, Rio de Janeiro publisher J. E. S. Cabral released *Representation to the General and Constituent Assembly of the Empire of Brazil about Slavery* by José Bonifácio, but this was an isolated episode that did not generate debate or change the course of events.[5]

Slave trade alliances in turn were so strong that they even affected other parts of the Old World. On December 10, 1836, a decree from the Portuguese Crown sought to regulate penalties for slave traders and the seizure of suspected slavers. It incorporated an equipment clause similar to those used by

Spain in the treaty of 1835 and Brazil in the Additional Articles (although the latter never passed the Brazilian Parliament). Portuguese historians have interpreted the decree either as a sincere effort to suppress the contraband, as a scheme to protect the contraband, or as a strategy to assert Portuguese sovereignty in response to British pressure.[6] Despite the original intentions of the government, it is clear that the measure had an impact over the slave trade to Brazil and Cuba.

In 1837, the general receiver of public revenue (*recebedor geral das rendas públicas*) and the European inhabitants of Mozambique petitioned the governor general of the eastern coast of Africa, the Marquis of Aracaty, against the application of the decree. According to them, the suppression of the slave trade would ruin not only the subjects of the Crown who had invested in the only profitable business operating in the province but also the public servants and magistrates who depended on public revenue (which in turn depended on the exports of enslaved Africans). After receiving the petitions, Aracaty wrote to the Crown that coercion could lead to both an economic collapse and a political crisis. "Because of this," he wrote in November 1837, "I declare that agreeing to such powerful arguments, based on a rigorous examination of the petitions that were presented to me, compelled and subjected to the imperious law of necessity, superior to other laws, I admit and accept the said petitions."[7] Thus, political configurations within Brazil, Portugal, and Africa ensured the continuation of a large-scale contraband slave trade in the South Atlantic.

The British reacted quickly. The 1839 Palmerston Act unilaterally extended to the Portuguese flag the practice of seizing suspected slavers based on their equipment. The Foreign Office also reinterpreted the treaty of 1826 to authorize seizures of vessels equipped for the traffic. By seizing vessels without slaves on board, the British put into practice the policies that should have been implemented by the Additional Articles. The effects were immediate. Between 1831 and 1838, the British navy seized only one slave ship flying the flag of Brazil off the coast of Africa. From late 1839 to late 1840, however, that number rose to fourteen embarkations. Slave traders lost more than 150 ships on both sides of the Atlantic, while the number of slaves carried to Brazil dropped from fifty-five thousand in 1839 to twenty-five thousand three years later.[8]

The year 1837 was also critical in the Hispanic world. The main characteristics of the Second Spanish Empire took shape that year: the exclusion of colonial representation from the Spanish Parliament, the indefinite suspension of the Constitution overseas, the protection of the contraband slave trade, the racialized concept of citizenship, a protective tariff system in peninsular Spain, and the unrestricted inclusion of the colonial economy into the global free-market economy. Such a configuration contributed to the emergence of an antihegemonic movement that associated the exclusion of Cubans from Spanish parliamentary politics with the existence of slavery and the slave trade in Cuba. Thus, at the center of their demands were the implementation of liberal institutions in the colony, the immediate end of the contraband slave trade, and, ultimately, the gradual abolition of slavery itself. Although a great number of historians link this conflict to an opposition between creole and peninsular interests (the latter described as the only side responsible for the events of 1837), the political-ideological groupings remained as complex as ever. As we have seen, slaveholding classes from the western part of the island were instrumental in the creation of the Second Spanish Empire.

At the turn of the 1830s, Great Britain found itself in a major diplomatic crisis with Spain after nominating the Scottish abolitionist David Turnbull to the post of superintendent of liberated Africans and, later, British consul in Havana. The first position had been created after the treaty of 1835 to supervise the transportation of liberated Africans to the British colonies. Turnbull was sent to replace Richard Robert Madden, an Irish abolitionist connected to Thomas Fowell Buxton, who had also participated in the protests against apprenticeship in the British Caribbean. While in Cuba, Madden did not limit his activities to his institutional duties. He contacted a number of hacendados who, dissatisfied with the pact of 1837, were willing to provide him with information on the contraband slave trade. In a questionnaire (which included seventy-three questions) sent to Domingo del Monte y Aponte, one of the opponents of the new political regime, Madden inquired about the profits generated by the traffic, the manufactures used in it, the national flags that protected it, the final destiny of the capital accrued from it, the role of captains general in its continuation, its contribution to the growth of slavery, the mortality rates of the Middle Passage, and the condition of emancipados.[9]

Del Monte came from a family that had worked in the Spanish administration of Santo Domingo, from where they had left to move to Cuba along with four thousand other colonists after the beginning of the Haitian

Revolution in the 1790s. He was one of the disciples of Félix Varela, who had been part of the group around José Antonio Saco, including José Francisco Ruiz, Manuel González del Valle, Gaspar Betancourt Cisneros, Félix Tanco, and José de la Luz y Caballero, president of the Real Sociedad Económica de Amigos del País. Having graduated with a law degree, del Monte married the daughter of the wealthy Basque slave trader Domingo Aldama Arechaga but became a critic of the contraband slave trade. According to him, the traffic was responsible "for our political oppression" and for bringing "great and odious obstacles to the progress of the civilization of our race in Cuba." In the *tertulias* organized in his house, he sponsored the production of three antislavery novels: *Petrona y Rosalía* (1838) by Félix Tanco, *Cecília Valdés* (1839) by Cirillo Villaverde, and *Francisco* (1839) by Anselmo Suárez y Romero. This literature aimed to demonstrate that slavery was morally degrading for masters.

Del Monte answered the questionnaire sent by Madden at the peak of his antislavery activities in 1839, unhesitatingly accusing Spanish metropolitan interests and the captains general of Cuba of protecting the contraband slave trade. "Has the Spanish government," Madden asked, "enough power to suppress it on this island?" "More than enough," del Monte replied. "Do they wish to suppress it?" "No." "Did General Tacón seek to suppress it?" Madden insisted. "No; on the contrary, he was the one that protected it the most." Before Tacón, del Monte explained, the bribes went mainly to the employees of governors. "Tacón organized it in a way," he concluded, "that directed its totality to his hands."[10]

Although abolitionists like Madden and opponents of the Second Spanish Empire like del Monte condemned the contraband slave trade for very different reasons, their alliance generated some important antislavery material, which was subsequently used by the first World Antislavery Convention. The relationship between these two groups also created the conditions for the unpredictable, incendiary actions of David Turnbull. Having traveled through Cuba in 1838–1839, Turnbull developed a plan to quickly and definitively destroy the contraband slave trade. As he explained in his book *Travels in the West*, published in 1840, instead of patrolling the seas for slave ships—in his view an expensive and inefficient policy—Cuban demand would come to an end after the emancipation of all Africans illegally disembarked on the island against the Anglo-Spanish treaties of 1820 and 1835.[11]

He argued that the powers of the Mixed Commission of Havana should be extended, granting judges the ability to investigate the legal status of Africans and use them as witnesses. The burden of proof would be exclusively placed on the slaveholder. According to Turnbull, such a policy would undermine the legal security of slave transactions: "[It is] only by making him insecure, in possession of his illegal purchase, that the buyer and owner of an enslaved African will abstain from paying the price."[12] Turnbull was trying to establish in Cuba the same concept that slaveholders and statesmen were trying to destroy in Brazil.

Conscious of the aggressive tone of British diplomacy after 1839, Turnbull presented his project to the first World Antislavery Convention, received reviews in a few newspapers, and managed to personally deliver a copy to the British secretary of state for foreign affairs, Lord Palmerston, who used it in his diplomatic negotiations with slave societies in the Americas. Turnbull became the British consul and superintendent of liberated Africans in Havana in November 1840, quickly renewing the alliances that had been established by Madden. He allegedly created two committees—one of whites and another of free people of color and freedmen—to prepare for the independence of the island and the emancipation of slaves. At the same time, the British representative in Madrid submitted the project to the recently elected government of Baldomero Espartero while abolitionist agents dispatched to peninsular Spain published an anonymous article criticizing the contraband slave trade and calling for the gradual abolition of slavery. *El Corresponsal* published the article on December 24, 1840. According to Domingo del Monte, its anonymous author was Ramón de la Sagra.[13]

After news of the publication of the antislavery article arrived on the island, the Junta de Fomento (Development Board), the Ayuntamiento de La Habana (Municipality of Havana), and the Tribunal de Comercio (Tribunal of Commerce) immediately submitted memorials to the regency. The arguments employed by protesters and their effects, however, differed from previous ones because of the conditions established by the Second Spanish Empire. On February 19, 1841, the Count of O'Reilly (Manuel O'Reilly Calvo de la Puerta), the Count of Casa Bayona, Félix Ygnacio de Arango, and Francisco de Céspedes submitted a motion to the Ayuntamiento to denounce the article to the government. Two weeks later, a text written by the first two petitioners, along with José Agustín Govantes and Ramón de Armas, was finally passed. The Ayuntamiento officially criticized the contraband slave trade but defended slavery, explicitly using racial terms: "It is not the desire to perpetuate slavery, it is not the wretched love of wealth, which must perish with the slaves which compose it, on which the opposition to emancipation is founded. The preservation of the existence of the white class is that which can and ought to prevent it." More revealing of their proslavery stance, however, was their subtle criticism of the exclusion of Cubans in the pact of 1837:

> However petty, still the only semblance of representation which
> these faithful inhabitants enjoy, the municipality proposes with all
> the warmth which justice inspires, and with all the confidence which
> the wisdom of a just Government authorizes, to demonstrate the
> impossibility of resolving the emancipation of the slaves of this island
> without compassing its destruction. . . . It is painful to observe that
> the circumstances which have served as a pretext for denying to the
> provinces of America the right of representation and other social
> guarantees, are not taken into account when the emancipation of slaves
> is in question.[14]

Besides the use of the derogatory terms "petty" (*mesquino*) and "semblance" (*simulacro*) in reference to the level of representativeness of the Ayuntamiento, the association of parliamentary exclusion with the problem of slavery indicates the dissatisfaction of its members with the events of 1837. The authors then exposed the imperial pact of political exclusion in exchange for the preservation of slavery in order to demand the fulfillment of the latter (since Cuban deputies had already been excluded from the Cortes). The actions of the Ayuntamiento are not surprising. As we have seen, its members had opposed the captain general in the elections of the 1830s and written—with a contribution from del Monte—the *Proyecto de Memorial a S. M. la Reina*. The latter condemned the restriction of political freedom imposed on the island for the preservation of slavery, citing the United States as a successful example of the combination of constitutionalism and slavery.[15]

The memorial from the Tribunal de Comercio, which included the proprietor, Wenceslao de Villa Urrutia, was more attuned to imperial politics. Also lamenting the exclusion of Cuba from constitutional politics, the authors of the protest, Jorge P. de Urtétegui, Nicolás Galcerá, and Alejandro

Morales, began with an assessment of the arguments about an alleged incompatibility between a representative system and the slave order. "An imprudent speech delivered in the extraordinary Constituent Cortes of 1811," they warned in reference to José Miguel Guridi y Alcócer and Agustín Argüelles, "which did not refer to the abolition of slavery, but to the suppression of the Slave Trade, so alarmed the authorities and corporations of this island," later leading to the "horrible conspiracy [of José Antonio Aponte in 1812] . . . , which, if it had once been installed, would have produced a general conflagration of the property, and the universal massacre of the white population."

Reticent in the early nineteenth century, the public sphere's speeches had become incendiary in the global context of internationalist abolitionism: "At that period the sect of Abolitionists in England . . . had not yet established those societies which now, by means of their agents and their money, are endeavoring to undermine all those countries where slavery exists." Moreover, the United States could use the same argument about slavery in Cuba that they had been using to justify their intervention in Texas. Could the country, they rhetorically asked, "look with indifference at a similar change in its neighborhood on the island of Cuba, without finding a motive, or at least a pretext, for putting in practice in Cuba the same maxims which have guided its conduct in Texas[?]" After accusing Turnbull's book of inflaming the population of the island, they called for the abolition of the contraband slave trade as a necessary step to protecting slavery and indefinitely postponing the issue of emancipation.[16]

The Junta de Fomento addressed a memorial on February 27 (also as part of this wave of protests in 1841). The memorial was signed by thirteen members of the junta, among them the Count of Villanueva (Martínez de Pinillos), the Count of Barreto (José Francisco Hipólito Barreto), and the great landowners the Marquis of Real de la Proclamación (don Manuel Recio de Morales y Sotolongo) and Salvador Samá, both registered among the owners of the fifty largest mills on the island in 1860. Like the memorial of the Tribunal de Comercio, the authors from the Junta de Fomento emphasized the incompatibility between a slave society and the expansion of constitutionalism in the public sphere, and they denounced the publication of antislavery texts as an attack on one of the informal rules of the Second Spanish Empire: "The mere idea that the discussion of so dangerous a question is tolerated in Madrid in newspapers, which are afterward circulated here with profusion, which are already within the reach of our freed men, and which, before long, will become known to our slaves in town and country, has been sufficient to excite the distrust and alarm of capitalists and proprietors as to the future fate of the island."

In a free-market economy marked by competition and the mobility of capital, the legal security of slave property was a precondition for future investments. In the absence of this legal security, legal resources would inevitably move to countries with more stable institutions. The memorial also mentioned the racialization of social relations, arguing that an eventual emancipation of the slaves would lead them "to robbery and other vices, and there not being a sufficient number of whites to keep them in subjection, a degree of rivalship and hatred would be provoked, such as can only issue in a great war of colors." Finally, the authors of the text approved metropolitan policies against the contraband slave trade but demanded both the promotion of white immigration to the island and the end of debate about slavery in Spain. Otherwise, the memorial concluded, they would seek independence:

> That the Regency in its profound penetration condescend to consider that in the question of negro freedom, there has been but one feeling or opinion since the arrival of the publications in question from Madrid, which is, that the island would be irrecoverably lost by it to the mother country and to its inhabitants, who would prefer any extreme to the calamity of sacrificing their fortunes, endangering their lives, and remaining in a state of subordination to the negroes.[17]

These efforts achieved a great deal of success. On June 15, the Spanish government officially delivered the British project to the captain general, Gerónimo Valdés, soliciting reviews from corporations and individuals. As we have seen, Cuban institutions had interfered in resolutions from the Crown, as in the cases of the *Representación de la Ciudad de Habana a las Cortes Españolas* of 1811 and the 1823 petition submitted by the Provincial Deputation of Havana, which requested the concentration of power in the hands of the captain general. However, the request for reviews from its subjects by the Crown—a decision taken from the top down—was an unprecedented political act within the Spanish Empire. Spanish statesmen had informally created political representation in a nonrepresentative regime through ad hoc consultations with colonial subjects. Landowners and merchants on the island in turn quickly understood that new political concept and sought to make it mandatory. The Junta de Fomento became the main participant in the colony during this new cycle of exchanges taking place in 1841.

Six days after the arrival of the royal order to Valdés, the Junta de Fomento, presided over by the Count of Villanueva at the time, debated the British proposal in a plenary, prepared a memorial, and nominated an extraordinary commission to analyze the issue point by point. Villanueva divided the arguments into social and legal spheres. "If the English inquisition [i.e., the British judges responsible for verifying the origins of slaves] penetrates into these plantations flying the flag of freedom," he explained, "so that the negroes covered by the convention flock to her, it would not be long before she snatched all individuals of the same race, whose stupidity does not reach the succession of times nor does it penetrate into the difference of rights between fellows of the same castes and of one single color."

As in previous reports from Cuba after the Haitian Revolution, freedmen appeared as potential threats to the slave order, even when they were granted some privileges and rights. The legal arguments of Villanueva in turn were very similar to those employed in Brazil to revoke the slave trade law of 1831: international treaties were only valid on the high seas and could not be extended into the national territory. In his opinion, all articles of international treaties

> deal exclusively with the fact that vessels containing negroes bought on the coast of Africa are found off the coast of Africa, in the Spanish colonies or in the Middle Passage, as expressed by Article 9. Other than these three cases, there is no infraction, a felony is not committed nor can a penalty be applied. Neither the English nation nor the Spanish have the power to declare the freedom of slaves found on the island of Cuba who had been introduced there after the year 1820.[18]

The Junta de Fomento nominated the Marquis of Arcos (Ignacio Peñalver y Peñalver), Evaristo Carrillo, Narciso García y Mora, and Tomás de Juara Soler for the commission. The first was a member of one of the greatest sugar producing families of Cuba, who increased their wealth by lending money to other planters and merchants and by making investments in Madrid. The commission released the very long report "Informe de la Junta de Fomento" and an opinion in the name of the Real Consulado (Royal Consulate), both on September 28. By the end of 1841, the Junta de Fomento had produced four proslavery texts, indicating the ubiquity of the institution in debates on the problem of slavery.[19]

The authors of the "Informe de la Junta de Fomento" employed some of the proslavery arguments from other contemporary texts, including the inevitable economic decline, the potential war between races, and the restricted jurisdiction of the Anglo-Spanish treaties of 1817 and 1835. These arguments were developed within a global framework, making reference to the destabilizing effects of emancipation on the British Empire and of internationalist abolitionism. When Alcócer and Argüelles prepared their texts in 1811, the report explained, "we had not encompassing us millions of free persons of color, . . . nor had a powerful, persevering, and astute nation declared itself their ally and protector; in fine, that did not pass beyond a domestic question. . . . In what a different situation we now find ourselves!" Since Great Britain had turned abolition in the British West Indies into a model to be followed by other slave countries, the authors deliberately ignored the Haitian Revolution—because of its "casual and unpremeditated" character—to concentrate their efforts on the British abolitionist process.

With references to Tocqueville, Adolphe Granier de Cassagnac, and the political economist John Ramsay McCulloch, they stated that the "opinion in Europe respecting the emancipation of negroes did not accord with the result which it has had in the English colonies. Distinguished writers studied the question, and, justly distrusting theories, came to consult facts." The consequences of abolition in Jamaica invalidated abolitionist intentions: "Your Excellency, the nation, the whole world knows it: misery substituted for abundance, and even opulence; assassinations, robberies, incendiarism, desolating those fields before cultivated with so much diligence and intelligence; the products in sugar and coffee diminishing." If Western states, without exception, had recast the Haitian Revolution as a "historical nonevent" because of its "unpremeditated" character, Cuban proprietors and, by extension, slave powers in the Americas attempted to do the same with British abolition despite its planned character. It was not the nature of the event but rather its consequences that were allegedly uncontrollable.[20]

More important than gathering arguments to invalidate the new convention with Britain was the necessity to establish the future terms of debate about slavery and the contraband slave trade. At the end of the report, the commission connected parliamentary speeches with slave actions and sugar production in the British Empire between 1807 and 1839, warning that in the "history of English colonies . . . each negro insurrection has coincided with the multiple motions submitted to Parliament, from the prohibition of the traffic, to the debate and passing of the emancipation bill." From this followed the dramatic drop of 73 percent in the annual mean of Jamaican sugar production between 1802–1806 and 1835–1839. "These numbers are louder than all the arguments," they argued, "and not only prove the sad consequences of emancipation, but also the sinister influence that certain questions produce in countries where slavery exists, and that may stimulate hopes of freedom in the near future among this class." According to the authors, the institutional stability of slavery was not compatible with the freedom of expression characteristic of the representative regime—which may indicate that the pact of 1837 was well received by the Junta de Fomento. The group noted the unprecedented actions of the metropolitan government, which had asked for orientation from its Cuban subjects and sought to extract a governing rule for the future: "Finally, it will close its report, proposing: 1st. That Her Majesty be beseeched to deign make not the least alteration in the negro question, in any respect whatever, 'without hearing distinctly, as she has been pleased to do, these authorities and corporations,' who will always explain what may be needful with zeal and loyalty."[21] Suspicions that the junta supported the compromise of 1837 are confirmed by another report prepared by the commission, this time in the name of the Real Consulado. In this one— as a strategy to preserve the stability of the island—the authors call for the application of the "Special Laws that were promised to us in the Constitution of the Monarchy and that these, for our construction, must be as unpopular as possible." Thus, no constitutionalism tout court was allowed.[22]

These two documents—especially the first one—helped build, without a law or statute being passed, one of the strongest possible foundations for the Second Spanish Empire. As we have seen, the report of the Junta de Fomento of September 28, 1841, sought to make official the Crown's political practice of listening to a restricted group of Cuban subjects before making any decision about slavery-related issues. The intentions of the junta were clear. Each audience was like having a Cuban deputy in Parliament, with the advantages that in this case, local opinion was expressed directly, representatives did not have the chance to form alliances with opponents of the junta (as could be the case in distant peninsular Spain), and debates took place outside the public sphere. With this political arrangement, which was strengthened or guaranteed by the promised special laws, the opinions of the Cuban slaveholding classes could be taken into consideration without the need for elections or freedom of the press. Through their accumulated experience, colonists and metropolitan authorities sought to establish forms of political representation in a nonrepresentative regime.

The Real Sociedad Patriótica and an individual from Matanzas also submitted reports to Gerónimo Valdés. Both reports generally stated the necessity to resist British pressure and at the same time "[close] the doors everywhere to the new introduction of Africans," since this commerce had already been prohibited "by our government and by all nations of Europe and America, except for Brazil." The passage also reveals just how widespread the perception was that the contraband slave trade to Brazil was being protected by the state itself.[23] As in the memorials of the Ayuntamiento, the Tribunal de Comercio, and the Real Consulado, the authors defended white immigration to minimize the effects of suppressing the contraband slave trade. Two dissident texts supported the proposals of Turnbull outside this controlled form of communication. One of them, signed by the "Hijos del país" (sons of the country), called for a free womb law, the emigration of Africans, and radical British intervention in the island. The other, written by del Monte, correlated the end of the contraband slave trade to political reforms introducing freedom of the press and representative institutions. Both were presented directly to Turnbull, never appearing in Cuba or in the Spanish public sphere.[24]

Divergences in the colony immediately reverberated in Spain. During that same year, the Countess of Merlin, doña María de las Mercedes de Santa Cruz y Montalvo, a Cuban creole who had resided in France for many years, published *Los esclavos en las colonias españolas*. Initially published in *Revue des Deux Mondes* because of its comparisons between the Spanish and French slave systems (as part of the abolitionist campaign in France), the book was immediately translated and published in Madrid. In the context of growing British diplomatic pressure, it quickly acquired the status of an important proslavery and Anglophobic piece. The book was, in fact, associated with a more moderate group of Cubans opposing the new institutional configuration of the Spanish Empire. The Countess of Merlin was very close to the traditional Montalvo and O'Farrill families, and she was connected to reformists such as Saco and del Monte.

Like the memorial of the Ayuntamiento de La Habana, *Los esclavos en las colonias españolas* explicitly defended slavery (with references to the war between races, economic decline, the failure of the British abolitionist "experiment," and Cuban paternalism) while rejecting the contraband slave trade. The argument was in consonance with the general perception that the metropolis tolerated the illegal traffic—"an attack against natural rights"—as an exercise in political control. "Forgetting about colonization, the growth in the number of slaves is tolerated," she cautiously warned, a policy that was "unfair and damaging . . . to the true interests of the metropolis, to which the island of Cuba is intimately connected by ties of a common race, customs, religion, and sympathies: whenever the government proves to be benevolent, Cuba will be faithful." The author also praised the then-exiled Saco, a "notable patriot," and criticized the attitudes of Tacón and the corruption of colonial authorities. "Governors, with the presence of police officers, should not authorize the disembarkation of slave cargoes," she argued, in a comment that was similar to one of the answers given by del Monte to Madden's questionnaire (which she probably knew).[25]

Although different discourses continued to appear, the publication of *Cuestión importante sobre la esclavitud* by Mariano Torrente in November 1841 marked the end of a cycle of responses to the regency. The author, who had worked for eight years at the Havana customhouse, published a few other studies about the colony (including the proslavery piece *Slavery on the Island of Cuba* in 1853) and acted in the Spanish Parliament as a defender of slavery, the slave trade, and the political arrangement of 1837. His position becomes clear in *Cuestión importante*, in which he describes the proposals to abolish the contraband slave trade and introduce white colonists as "utopias." He also refers to the "delirium" of "certain reformists, guided by a holy zeal," in a possible reference to del Monte and Saco.

Considering the traffic as a means of saving the lives of Africans condemned in their countries of origin, Torrente described as illogical "the established principle that the island of Cuba wishes to suppress the traffic,

because I cannot believe that men would want something that hurts them."
However, the author was likely aware of the Cuban votes to extinguish the
traffic, since he not only asked the Spanish press to stop publishing antislavery texts but also tried to make Baldomero Espartero change the way the
issue was being debated: "The ministers of the Crown have enough light and
a great amount of data to plausibly contest all diplomatic notes that might be
addressed to them about the issue of slavery without the need to ask for
reports from those who have more than once firmly and decisively stated
their opinion."[26] Despite the persistence of the traffic, Torrente noted that it
had lost a good part of its political legitimacy after the establishment of constitutionalism in Spain.

The general idea underlying these defenses was that Great Britain had
been conspiring to destroy Cuban slavery after the economic decline caused
by emancipation in the British Caribbean in 1833. The secret actions of the
British, according to this view, would inevitably lead to a war between races,
economic collapse, and the independence of the island or its annexation to
the United States. Colonial corporations considered stopping the slave trade
in order to end diplomatic tensions and their effects on the slave order, calling for new policies to stimulate other forms of immigration to the island.
This did not mean, as historian Jean-Pierre Tardieu believes, that they
wanted to end slavery and "gradually prepare the integration of freedmen
into the future systems of production that depended, moreover, on European
immigration. The teachings of Baron Humboldt and Francisco de Arango,
therefore, had not been forgotten."[27] This argument may apply to the men of
letters associated with Saco but not to the members of the Tribunal de Comercio or the Junta de Fomento. When these groups talked about an eventual
emancipation of slaves, it was to postpone it to a politically indeterminate
future. In other words, they openly rejected it.

As we have seen, Cuban colonists tried to make official the unprecedented
practice of colonial consultations started by the Spanish government. They
had some success, since a number of future consultations took place. The
problem is that they could not completely control the reception and interpretation of their proposals. After receiving the reports, Gerónimo Valdés submitted them to the metropolitan cabinet accompanied by an appendix that
he drafted on November 3, 1841. In his view, the oft-mentioned European
immigration was not suitable for the island for political and economic

reasons. According to him, not only did the tropical sun discourage whites from working, but more importantly, many colonists wanted to increase immigration to raise the number of whites on the island, to the point of saying "without risk an everlasting good-bye to Spain." As the contraband slave trade challenged metropolitan sovereignty in the colony and white immigration undermined the loyalty of the colony to the metropolis, the only solution was to follow the US example and stimulate the natural proliferation of slaves. Such a solution could ensure the self-sustained growth of slavery without generating international tension, and also maintain a demographic composition unfavorable to independence movements.[28] But diplomatic negotiations, reports, and reviews would not be enough for such a change. New legislative action was also necessary. This is precisely what Brazil and Cuba attempted to do during the 1840s.

Imperial Conflicts and Legislative Action, Part I: Great Britain and Spain, 1841–1845

In September 1842, Gerónimo Valdés explained to the Spanish government that he had prosecuted the slave trade since he had arrived on the island in May 1841 to protect himself from Santander merchants involved in the traffic. Many historians have reproduced this image of Valdés as a staunch opponent of the slave trade and have described Espartero's government as having anglophile inclinations. However, it was only after January 1842 that British agents based in Cuba noted the beginning of anti–slave trade actions by the captain general. It seems more likely that Valdés had not tried to suppress the traffic before having interacted with Cuban families, receiving reports from colonial corporations, and, as a consequence, becoming convinced of the benefits of stimulating the natural growth of slaves. His first efforts against the traffic did indeed start in 1842, including the release of four circular notes to other officers demanding the fulfillment of the Anglo-Spanish Treaty by his subaltern officers (which led to the capture of a few illegally enslaved Africans), the seizure of a Spanish slave ship (the second since 1820), and the prohibition of the Cuban practice of purchasing foreign ships and registering them as Spanish.[29]

Valdés also prepared a survey addressed to the great Cuban hacendados with the objective of regulating relations between masters and slaves, improving the "health of servants," and stimulating "their reproduction, with the just labor that is owed to their master." The questions dealt with subjects such as feeding, dressing, amount of labor, *conucos* (land and animals owned by slaves), infirmaries, housing for married slaves, and health care for pregnant and parturient slaves as well as their children. On February 23, the survey was sent to the Marquis of Arcos, Rafael O'Farrill, the Count of Fernandina, Domingo Aldama, Joaquín Muñoz Izaguirre, Jacinto Gonzáles Larrinaga, Joaquín Gómez, Wenceslao de Villa Urrutia, Sebastián de Lasa, Ignacio de Herrera, José Manuel Carrillo, and Juan Montalvo. Half of this select group had already considered suppressing the contraband slave trade. Villa Urrutia and the Marquis of Arcos had signed the reports of 1841, while Montalvo, O'Farrill, Aldama, and Fernandina had signed the anti–slave trade petition of the following year. Valdés probably got carried away with this informal consensus, but he was completely wrong to believe that this level of support for government action regarding slavery could be found among the broader slaveholding class. Only one-third of the interviewees did not explicitly object to government intervention in domestic affairs, while the majority considered the traffic a political issue disconnected from the administrative and social control of plantations.[30] The conduct of the captain general already indicated the unpopularity of the plan: instead of consulting with colonial corporations, as requested by the reports of 1841, Valdés only met with the select group of proprietors mentioned above. He knew that ignoring contrary votes from colonial corporations, especially after 1837, would result in great political costs for the Spanish Empire as a whole.

The historical experience of slavery in the Americas had been defined by the autonomy of masters in the administration of their captives and their integration into civil society. These practices were refashioned in the context of enlightened reformism and representative regimes to prevent the local disturbances—and, ultimately, the abolition of slavery—that could be encouraged by public interventions in the private sphere. Interference from the French Crown in the administration of Saint-Domingue plantations in 1784–1785—which gave slaves the power to complain about mistreatment—and, especially, the British amelioration proposals of the 1820s, were seen as persuasive examples of how intervention in the private sphere was the first step toward abolition. Moreover, three events involving Great Britain, the

United States, and slaves in the early 1840s further stimulated the animosity of Cuban colonists and Spanish authorities.

Working both as consul and superintendent of liberated Africans, David Turnbull had the means to carry out his official and unofficial intentions. The Anglo-Spanish Convention of 1835 had established that the captain general had to submit reports documenting the condition of emancipados "every six months" to the Mixed Commission "with the object of showing the existence of negroes who had been emancipated because of the present treaty, their deaths, the improvement of their situation, and the progress of their religious, moral, and industrial education."[31] In his role as superintendent of liberated Africans, Turnbull witnessed the captain general assign many emancipados to Cuban plantations for indeterminate periods, where they worked under conditions analogous, if not identical, to those of slavery. Likewise, as British consul, Turnbull had the necessary diplomatic immunity not only to perform his official duties but also to act on his personal convictions.

After arriving on the island, Turnbull received from Madden a list of rowdy freedmen, unruly slaves, liberal creoles, and paid informants. Supported by this network, he convinced a few free people of color to live in the British West Indies ("a land of true freedom"), rescued seven British blacks who had been illegally enslaved, and helped free a number of emancipados found in conditions of forced labor. His boldest action, however, was an attempt to gather free people of color and white proprietors together in a general insurrection against the Spanish government and slavery. Turnbull never admitted his involvement or elaborated on the case in his correspondence, but he did mention it in a letter to the abolitionist Joseph Sturge. "All this [his deeds] has served to inspire the Slaves of this island with Hope," he argued, "which next to the positive enjoyment of Liberty, is perhaps the greatest good which could have been obtained for them. Above all the rich Creoles have arrived at the conclusion that their own freedom, that is their expectation of sharing in the management of their own affairs, is inseparably bound up with the extinction of the Slave Trade and the personal freedom of the Slaves now existing on the Island." Putting aside the overstatement in the expression "the rich Creoles," the quotation indicates how the British consul mediated the alliance between hacendados and free people of color toward support for political reform on the island and, eventually, the abolition of slavery. It is impossible to determine the names of all the planters who conspired with Turnbull, but there is no question that former students of Félix Varela such as Domingo del Monte, José de la Luz y Caballero, Félix Tanco, and José Luis Alfonso were among them.[32]

While Turnbull remained laconic about his deeds, his assistant, Francis Ross Cocking, who also had connections to Tanco and del Monte, was much more outspoken about the alleged actions of his mentor. According to Cocking's testimony, he and Turnbull attempted to take advantage of the political dissatisfaction among creoles by connecting them to antislavery freedmen. Two committees—one of whites and the other of free men of color—were created to fight for political independence and gradual emancipation. However, there were two major obstacles. In mid-1842, Turnbull was removed from his post as consul and, fearing for his life, decided to move to the Bahamas. At the same time, Cuban proprietors opposed to the political pact of 1837 increasingly believed that they could gain political rights without threatening the social order by allowing the island to be annexed to the United States. In any case, evidence that Turnbull and Cocking had indeed organized—or more likely participated in—an insurrectional network can be seen in the fact that the free men of color stuck to the plan, spreading delegates across the island and looking for foreign help. In April 1843, the pardo leader Juan Rodríguez met with the new British consul, Joseph Tucker Crawford. He requested the military support that had been previously promised by Turnbull. Crawford ignored the plea but did not discourage the expectations and projects of Rodríguez and others.[33]

Since the late 1830s, slave revolts in the western part of Cuba had grown larger in size. In January 1838, twenty-nine slaves of the San Isidro de Manacas estate in Trinidad killed their overseer and traveled to the El Quemado estate, where they were joined by sixteen other slaves and set the place on fire. They then moved on to the Santa Isabel estate, owned by Pedro Gabriel Sánchez, where they killed the overseer, burned down properties, found weapons, and were joined by other slaves. After hiding for a few nights in the mountains, they attacked the Mainicú estate, destroying part of the property; they were joined by yet more slaves. Efforts to subdue the insurgents went on for months without success, with the authorities finally ending the revolt by capturing the leaders on May 14 and sentencing seven slaves to death by shooting. One month later, however, a free pardo, also in Trinidad, denounced a conspiracy involving escaped slaves from various local estates who planned to take over

Trinidad and declare the emancipation of all slaves in the region. Subsequent investigations discovered connections between the new plan and the rebel slaves of January. Five more men were then sentenced to death.[34]

The patterns of resistance and expectations of slaves seemed to be the main problem for authorities and masters. These rebellions and conspiracies had been sparked by mistreatment and abuse (disproportionate punishment, excessive labor, insufficient food), but they were not simply a struggle to improve immediate conditions. In their testimonies, captured insurgents talked about their desire to "kill all whites, except for the women . . . , [and] destroy and set the estates on fire," because they felt that they were not inferior to the blacks of Saint-Domingue, who had expelled their masters and taken over their lands. A series of conspiracies in Havana, Cienfuegos, Trinidad, and Matanzas stoked the fears of slaveholders in 1839. In the ensuing two years, small insurrections took place such as those on the Arratía estate in Colón and the Perseverancia coffee plantation in Cárdenas, both located in Matanzas Province. The large number of rebellions and conspiracies between 1837 and 1843 has led historian Gloria García to describe this as the "period of great uprisings."[35]

The cycle of revolts influenced how slaveholders perceived relations between slaves, proprietors, and free people of color, especially after news of the end of apprenticeship in the British Caribbean arrived in 1838. While planters in Cárdenas linked the preservation of the social order with improvements in the slaves' diet and the protection of their conucos, the governor of Matanzas, Antonio García Oña, called for the passage of a new reglamento for his jurisdiction. Among the new repressive and control measures were the suppression of religious education for slaves and their children, permission to use hunting dogs without muzzles to control slaves, a prohibition on taverns located outside the villages, the absolute exclusion of free people of color from any administrative position on the plantations, and the mandatory use of bells on any estate with more than twenty-five slaves as a strategy to facilitate communication in case of rebellion. The captain general, Gerónimo Valdés, did not pass these new regulations proposed for Matanzas since he had been working on his own reglamento that would be valid for the entire colony and officially interfere in the domestic sovereignty of the slaveholders.[36]

The idea of annexation to the United States grew popular among Cuban slaveholders during this same period. As we have seen, the US decision to abide by the status quo in Cuba in the 1820s dampened the popularity of independence plans among creoles. There were indeed good reasons—economic, geopolitical, and regional—for certain groups in the United States to closely monitor events in the Spanish colony. Even before the liberalization of trade in Cuba in 1818, the United States had been gradually replacing Spain as the colony's main commercial partner, providing technology, credit, and transport. In the 1840s, the United States was responsible for 39 percent of all external trade with Cuba, compared to 34 percent with Great Britain and 27 percent with Spain.

This trend was also apparent in the growing number of US commercial houses in Havana, especially from New York, which accumulated capital by extending credit and shipping sugar to US ports such as New Orleans, Savannah, Charleston, Baltimore, Philadelphia, New York, and Boston. Many of these houses also participated in the contraband slave trade by providing bills of exchange, ships, and liquidity. For this reason, more than one thousand US citizens lived in Cuba, many of them as great landowners—leaving aside absentee slave owners who lived in the United States but had large amounts of capital invested in Cuban plantations. One indication of this massive US presence is the fact that a US citizen was primarily responsible for the foundation of the important village of Cárdenas in the 1820s.[37]

Some historians associate US expansionism toward Cuba with the slaveholding interests of the US South. According to Eugene Genovese, Southerners feared that Spain could abolish slavery on the island. John McCardell has argued that the driving force behind territorial imperialism was the need to maintain political balance between the number of Northern and Southern representatives in the US Senate, since such a balance had become impossible in the House of Representatives, where free states were now overrepresented as a result of massive immigration to the North.

Other historians have argued that annexationism transcended economic particularities and the regional anxieties of the slaveholding class. Tom Chaffin, for example, considers it to be a multifaceted phenomenon connected to "southern and Cuban planters, steamship and rail magnates, New York and southern mercantilists, and others with vested financial interests in Cuba, its slavery, and trade."[38] It is possible to argue that linking annexationism with the origin or geographic basis of its supporters misses the central point that most of its leading proponents had capital invested directly in plantations (whether in Cuba or the US South) or indirectly via external trade (involving goods produced by slaves). Although it was not the only issue at stake, slavery was central to annexationist sympathies. As Chaffin recognizes, the simple fact that the movement never presented an emancipation plan made it somewhat proslavery.

For this reason, the annexationist *New York Herald* described in October 1841 the Spanish request for colonial reports on the British proposal for the emancipation of slaves illegally introduced into the island: "It is easily to be seen, that England aims at the heart of our southern states, and is determined to possess herself of Cuba." Two Southern congressmen immediately reacted to the news and questioned the capacity of the Spanish to maintain its sovereignty over the Caribbean, while expressing their desire to incorporate the island into the United States. The Spanish consul in Washington in turn immediately warned Valdés that the United States would only respect Spanish sovereignty in Cuba if Spain continued to resist British pressure. Around that same time, the ardent annexationist Alexander Everett, who had already been to Cuba twice in the service of the US government, investigated the perceptions of Cuban slaveholding classes about an eventual annexation to the northern neighbor.[39]

Cuban historians have also offered different interpretations of the relationship between annexationism and social groups. Some scholars have described annexationism in Cuba as a protonationalist movement of independence, while others, such as Raúl Cepero Bonilla, have emphasized its connection to the problem of slavery. María del Carmen Barcia and Eduardo Torres-Cuevas have developed a more complex explanation centered on three geographically distributed annexationist groups: the Havana Club in the western part of the island, which aimed at creating a large slaveholding region integrated to the US South; Las Villas, also a proslavery group, located in the center of the island; and the Puerto Príncipe faction in the East, which called for the replacement of slavery with a free labor system. Historian Manuel Moreno Fraginals in turn considers annexationism the most aggressive aspect of Cuban reformism because of its frequent threats of secession. According to him, the three groups were unified behind a single project under the leadership of José Luis Alfonso and Gaspar Betancourt Cisneros. Based on the ideas of these leading figures, Moreno Fraginals tracked four primary objectives of the movement: suppressing the contraband slave trade, encouraging white immigration, eventually abolishing slavery with compensation to slave owners, and creating institutional mechanisms for the political participation of creoles.[40]

This interpretation is mostly correct but has the flaw of reducing annexationists only to the followers of Alfonso and Cisneros. A number of proslavery hacendados apparently also supported the annexationist movement in reaction to British pressure and the actions of Valdés. According to a report of December 1842 from the new British representative in Havana, Joseph Crawford, the local "American party" had among its members the Count of Fernandina, Wenceslao de Villa Urrutia, the Marquis of Arcos, Salvador Samá, and Joaquín Gómez.[41] If Crawford's assessment is correct, one of Moreno Fraginals's arguments is flawed—after all, these were great slaveholders who never called for the gradual end of slavery. His broader idea— that annexationism was used as leverage to gain political and economic benefits—is nonetheless accurate.

The survey submitted by Valdés in early 1842 as part of the preparation of the Reglamento de Esclavos was openly questioned by eight of the interviewees (two-thirds), while the other four—Jacinto Gonzáles Larrinaga, Sebastián de Lasa, Joaquín Muñoz Izaguirre, and Domingo Aldama Arechaga—made a few objections but agreed to answer it. Those who openly objected to the survey provided evasive and confusing replies or simply refused to provide answers at all. In the same year as the survey, the British consul described three members of this latter group—the Marquis of Arcos, the Count of Fernandina, and José Manuel Carrillo—as supporters of the annexationist movement. It seems likely that their general dissatisfaction with slave revolts, British pressure, and the impending government intervention in domestic affairs influenced their decision to embrace annexationist plans.

The reply from the Marquis of Arcos is a lesson on how to politely respond to a superior order without obeying it. In the first page and a half (out of five), he seemed to be formally answering the questions. A closer investigation, however, reveals that he refused to objectively describe the amount of clothes provided to slaves, the number of hours they worked, the exact size of their infirmaries, and whether separate bohíos were provided for married slaves. Arcos's vague answers not only failed to provide the parameters for the legislative action envisioned by Valdés but also reflected, in his words, the impossibility of "standardizing practices that are so detailed that they change according to circumstances." They provided a subtle critique of the captain general's plans to interfere in domestic affairs. The remaining pages of Arcos's reply of May 19—three months after Valdés had submitted the survey—openly criticized the initiative based on theoretical, geopolitical, and historical arguments.[42]

According to the marquis, assessing the limits of a master's power had been a difficult task at all times. The subordination of a large group to a minority was only possible because of the "moral strength" of the master over the slave as the sole authority. Thus, sharing power with laws and fiscal agents transformed the rule of masters into a source of injustice, abuse, and hatred in the eyes of the subaltern. This principle became even more problematic in the context of Turnbull's actions, emancipation in the British Caribbean, and the anti–slave trade efforts of Valdés: "The protection that [slaves] know the British government grants, the efforts of their consul [Turnbull] to gain the loyalty of some, the emancipations that are taking place [the end of apprenticeship in the West Indies], the definitive end of the contraband [Valdés's measures], all these circumstances put them in a state of excitement so dangerous that it should receive attention from the government to search for an antidote before it has to take action that could stimulate it even more."

Historical experience had shown that such interventions in constitutional regimes paved the way for general emancipation, as had been the case with reforms in Great Britain after 1823 and subsequent abolition in 1833. Finally, Arcos argued (based on the conditions generated by the pact of 1837) that parliamentary exclusion to protect slavery increased Cuban power over the institution's future course: "Just as the inhabitants of this island are deprived of all political rights, which (absolutely speaking) a representative government cannot deny without injustice, and they are denied because it is said that it is not convenient, so no concession should be granted in favor of slaves that, innovating the rules that govern them, can lead to ideas of insubordination among them, because the masters and reason and experience say that it is not convenient."[43]

Wenceslao de Villa Urrutia was even more passionate in his response. Generally remembered by historians for having pioneered the vacuum pan on his plantation, which significantly increased the volume of sugar produced, Villa

Urrutia became an important figure in Cuban politics, participating in colonial corporations and advising the Spanish government on delicate issues such
as the Reglamento de Esclavos of 1842 and the slave trade law of 1845.[44] His
report stated that Valdés's intended reforms would create "embarrassing difficulties to the government" because they would put "in great danger the tranquility of the island, immediately producing unrest, then disobedience and
perhaps later the insurrection of slavery in the fields." Villa Urrutia did not
even reply to the later questions of the survey, stopping on the third one.
According to him, "it would be impossible to describe the obligations because
of all the individual circumstances." He also considered it unfeasible "to establish the faults, demand the fulfillment of responsibilities, and impose the penalties for transgressors." Thus, two-thirds of the report (just like that of Arcos)
was a critique of the proposal of a new reglamento.[45]

In his view, neither ancient nor modern nations such as Greece, Rome,
England, or France had satisfactorily defined the scope of the master's power.
In the absence of positive models, he believed that the matter should be regulated by practices and customs. The best example could be found in the
experience of the Spanish Empire itself, whose ordinances recommended
basic precautions for issues such as religious instruction, feeding, clothing,
elder care, and marriage without interfering with the master's authority over
the slave. Moreover, new regulations would inevitably lead to tension between
masters and government authorities, with corrupt fiscal agents either protecting or prosecuting planters according to the value of the bribes. For these
reasons—the irreducibility of masters' practices to legal norms, the existence
of well-established regulations, and the potential tensions between authorities and hacendados—proprietors in Havana, Santo Domingo, Caracas, and
Louisiana managed to suspend the application of the royal cédula of 1789.
After making references to Turnbull and British abolitionism, Villa Urrutia
raised a point (in the context of growing annexationist pressures) that had
the effect of a secessionist threat to the captain general:

> The Senate of the United States has just included the word "slaves" in one
> of its minutes related to the servants of American citizens, always absent
> in its Constitution and in all documents of the legislation and the federal
> government, with the sole objective of making the powerful nation that
> is now trying to undermine and destroy slavery in certain countries

understand that the Congress of the United States considers it a legal institution with all its consequences, and that they are ready to maintain it and defend the property that comes from it against all kinds of attack. A timely and exemplary action of national dignity and patriotism that not a single abolitionist vote dared to contradict! True Spaniards also own these qualities, and the hope of Cuba is that H. E. belongs to this number.[46]

The complementary opinions of the Count of Arcos and Villa Urrutia were expressions of the politics of the Spanish Empire and its representative system in the metropolis. Colonists would only support their own exclusion from Parliament if they were granted the power to decide on the future of slavery in their colony. Violations of this tacit agreement could lead to the annexation of the island by the United States. In a context marked by the abolition of slavery in various countries and growing antislavery liberalism, annexationism is central to understanding how the nation-state became a fundamental part of the continuation of the slave system over time. If Spain could not play this role, many colonists believed that their northern neighbor could easily replace it.

In late 1842, despite significant opposition, Gerónimo Valdés published the Reglamento de Esclavos as an annex to the *Bando de governación y policia de la isla de Cuba*, a broader legal code. Scheduled to come into force in January 1843, the new legislation represented a departure from other texts about the management of slaves, such as Cecílio Ayllón's *Reglamento de esclaves*, the article by Andrés de Zayas, *El vademecum* by Honorato B. de Chateausalins, and Antonio García Oña's proposal. Its articles also reinforced the need for *barracónes* (prisonlike barracks) to ensure control over the movement of slaves and restrict their communication with the outside world. But, unlike Ayllón's regulations and García Oña's proposal, they established a minimum allotment of food and a maximum number of working hours in the fields for slaves. Valdés's regulations included measures to stimulate the natural growth of slaves such as granting separate bohíos to slave couples, allowing slaves to choose their partners, ensuring the nursing of infants, and providing general assistance to sick children. It also revived a controversial norm of the royal cédula of 1789 that limited the number of lashes for disobedient workers to twenty-five.

Articles 34 and 35 were a bit more unusual, establishing the initial value of the *coartación* (the slave's process of self-purchase from his or her master) at fifty pesos and codifying the custom that allowed *coartado* slaves to change masters in case of mistreatment. If the broader objective of these regulations was to stimulate the natural growth of slaves, the introduction of manumission in Articles 34 and 35 seems counterproductive. In the turbulent context of the 1840s, however, the dynamics of manumission—which had become widespread in the Iberian world as an efficient strategy to control and discipline slaves—could be used to defend an alleged benign nature of slavery in Cuba. Thus, the inclusion of these articles in the regulations may have been connected to the need to reinforce social control and ideological justifications.[47]

The Reglamento de Esclavos of 1842 did not represent a total defeat for the Cuban slaveholding classes. According to historian Manuel Lucena Salmoral, the new regulations were to a large extent a repetition of the *Reglamento sobre la educación, trato y ocupaciones que deben dar a sus esclavos los dueños y mayordomos de esta isla*, which had been inspired by the royal cédula of 1789 and established in Puerto Rico in 1826. But a few important innovations in the Reglamento of 1842 were in response to the reports of hacendados. The maximum number of working hours for slaves in Puerto Rico during the harvest and grinding season was thirteen hours per day, while the annual quota of clothes was established at three sets of clothing and two shirts. The most relevant regulation, however, remained outside the legal scope. The Puerto Rico Reglamento called for inspections to be carried out by judges or people nominated by them who would have to "visit and inspect the plantations three times a year." Its Cuban counterpart, however, abstractly transferred these duties to itinerant judges whose *instrucciones*, included in the same *Bando de Gobernación*, did not allow them to "introduce themselves in rural establishments, nor in the domestic administration of slaves, nor in any kind of direct or indirect survey, except to report to this superior political government any violation that comes to the attention of said authorities."[48] The domestic administration of slave affairs was thus protected in the new regulations.

Valdés tried to find a middle ground between proprietors and the general government of the island, but such a balance was destroyed by unexpected events. On March 27 and 28, 1843, only three months after the Reglamento de Esclavos came into force, over one hundred slaves from one of the largest Matanzas plantations—the Alcancía estate, owned by Joaquín Peñalver—killed the engineer and two of his assistants, set the cane fields on fire, and left the estate to search for support from other slaves in the surrounding plantations. Slaves from the La Luisa, Trinidad, and Las Nieves estates, the Moscú coffee plantation, and a railroad in Bemba (present-day Jovellanos) joined the insurgent group, making the total number of participants approximately 460 individuals. The uprising led to the destruction of many properties and the death of 7 men. The suppression of the movement led to the death of 120 slaves in battle and the execution of 7 others by firing squad. Other insurrections and disturbances, which together involved a total of 300 slaves, also took place in the Majagua and Santa Rosa estates of Domingo Aldama, the Ácana and Concepción estates in Sabanilla, and the Arratía and Flore de Cuba estates in Guamacaro, all of them in the Matanzas region.[49]

The tensions of the period were reflected in the excessive reaction of colonial authorities and in the links between some of these revolts and the conspiring groups of free people of color who had previously been in contact with Turnbull. According to Turnbull's assistant, Francis Ross Cocking (in his later testimony of 1846), and the pardo Juan Rodríguez (in a meeting with the British consul at the time), some slaves had decided to rise in revolt before the beginning of a planned war for independence, leading to the Alcancía incident. On November 5, 1842, the situation grew worse. Slaves from the Triunvirato estate in Sabanilla, Matanzas, set the property on fire and escaped toward Ácana, where slaves involved in the previous conspiracy were imprisoned. After arriving there, the slaves killed three white women, two men, and one child, wounded many others, and set the buildings on fire. Other slaves joined them, and together they went to Concepción, which had also witnessed some recent disturbances. After repeating their actions there, they took over the San Miguel, San Lorenzo, and San Rafael estates, where García Oña's troops killed sixty rebels, wounded another seventeen, and arrested around seventy.[50]

Frightened by the frequency, intensity, and brutal character of the revolts, a group of ninety-three slaveholders and merchants from Matanzas, including Domingo Aldama and José Luis Alfonso, submitted an anti–slave trade petition through García Oña to the new captain general, Leopoldo O'Donnell, who had replaced Valdés after the fall of Baldomero Espartero in Spain. The widespread racialized perception of Cuban society, further confirmed by the census published in 1842, appeared in the text: "The persistent use of this ominous contraband . . . has accumulated on the territory of this island a population of color whose ascendancy reaches today, according to official statistics, the excessive totality of 660,000, of which 498,000 are slaves." The rest of the petition discussed the uprisings of March in Alcancía and November in Triunvirato, the extermination of more than three hundred slaves in the subsequent repression of these revolts, and the expedition organized by Thomas Fowell Buxton to the Niger River in 1841. The issue of the contraband is approached from an economic perspective, since it had already been solved in terms of the "political existence of the country," "indisputably much superior to all others." García Oña refused to submit the petition to O'Donnell, leading Alfonso to request another petition from the Count of Fernandina, Juan Montalvo, and Rafael O'Farrill. This one would be submitted directly to the captain general.[51]

At the same time, a slave woman belonging to Esteban Santa Cruz de Oviedo, owner of the La Santísima Trinidad estate (also in Sabanilla), denounced a conspiracy involving slaves from various plantations whose objective was to exterminate all whites. Authorities immediately interviewed a number of individuals. A summary judgment on December 21 led to the sentencing of sixteen individuals to death and dozens of others to prison; the executions were carried out in front of more than one thousand slaves. Directly influenced by this new conspiracy, Alfonso prepared the anti–slave trade petition five days later. He generally presented the same racialized perception of Cuban society that divided the island between blacks (regardless of their status) and whites, warning about the complexity and recurrence of revolts. He also denounced the language employed by the insurgent slaves and praised the system of natural growth of slaves in the United States.[52]

The solution offered by O'Donnell, however, was to intensify the repression. After personally visiting Matanzas, the captain general permitted the use of extrajudicial processes to interrogate suspects. Between January and March 1844, investigations led to searches, imprisonment, torture, confessions, and the sentencing of almost three thousand people in what became known as the Escalera Conspiracy, a reference to the place where the victims were tied up and beaten. The numbers are astounding: slaves from more than 230 plantations experienced the horrors of arbitrary trials. Incomplete statistics point to a total number of 96 whites, 783 slaves, and 2,187 free people of color as victims of interrogation, imprisonment, ostracism, or execution. In the end, 78 people were sentenced to death, another 1,292 were jailed, and 430 blacks and free mulattoes were expatriated. Among the free people of color sent to the gallows were the poet Plácido (the pseudonym of Gabriel de la Concepción Valdés); the mestizo Santiago Pimienta, who owned seventeen slaves; Andrés José Dodge, a dentist who had studied in London; Jorge López, a lieutenant of the pardo militia; and Miguel Román, owner of an academy of arts. Of the group of whites, which included José de la Luz y Caballero, Félix Tanco, and Domingo del Monte, fourteen were declared guilty. Two were sentenced to exile and one to death.[53]

According to historian Robert Paquette, despite the indiscriminate use of torture, the testimonies from different places reveal that "the government had caught a revolution in the making." This was a consequence of specific conspiracies of various groups that in the early 1840s—for local and international reasons—converged in a loose and temporary alliance between liberal creoles and free pardos who sought independence and the end of slavery. After the withdrawal of whites and the hesitation of pardos, the slaves, who had much less to lose, supposedly initiated the series of revolts in 1843. The trials of the following year targeted mainly free people of color, considered by many to be the only dangerous elements capable of leading slaves into a social revolution. But the chief goal of the repression was to weaken three social groups that had been growing restless: plantation slaves, free blacks or mestizos, and reformist men of letters with antislavery views. According to Aline Helg, after the Escalera Conspiracy, Cuba could not have a "mulatto escape hatch" as in Brazil, where Brazilian pardos could become high-ranking military officers, administrators, and even national representatives.[54]

The series of slaves revolts in 1843 and the Escalera Conspiracy were the culmination of tension generated by the political-legal order that emerged from the constitutional experience of Cádiz (and had been proposed by Francisco de Arango y Parreño already in the 1790s). This arrangement created extremely unfavorable conditions for free people of color in Cuba. These revolts and conspiracies, however, also helped consolidate the new politics of the Second Spanish Empire, which had first appeared in the consultation requested by the regency in 1841. Cubans interpreted their exclusion from Parliament in 1837 and the suspension of the Constitution overseas as part of an informal agreement that gave them more power to decide on the future of slavery in Cuba. In this context, the promulgation of the Reglamento de Esclavos appeared to be a violation of this arrangement, since it was widely opposed by Cuban slaveholders. For this reason, Leopoldo O'Donnell already sought to undo the actions of Gerónimo Valdés during the trials of 1844 not only in the legal arena but also in practical terms.

In a letter dated February 29, O'Donnell requested a report about the Reglamento de Esclavos from the Junta de Fomento. This was the opposite of what Valdés had done: while the regulations had been written without the participation of colonial corporations, their revision would begin with them. Contemporary political actors noticed the change. "What powerful reason [that] could motivate the creation of these regulations without the knowledge of the corporations," representatives of the Junta de Fomento argued, "against the good of the country and ignoring the vote of the people most identified with it because of their character and roots, the commission was not able to find out."[55]

The authors of the report recalled that "the most respectable people in the country in all respects" had warned that new regulations would lead to "the saddest consequences," especially because they brought innovations similar to those introduced in the British Caribbean before abolition and revived some of the measures of the suspended royal cédula of 1789—a direct reference to the votes of the Marquis of Arcos, Villa Urrutia, the Count of Fernandina, Carillo, and Izaguirre. The problems in the statute, they argued, were twofold. The articles that followed the recommendations of the reports were unsatisfactory because they transformed concessions from masters—employed to reinforce hierarchy within the units of production—into rights of slaves, who were eager to use them against their owners. Other norms, such as that restricting the number of lashes, dangerously limited the power of masters over their slaves.[56] The Junta de Fomento then concluded that it was "impossible to govern the race of color with contemplative measures from now on. It is necessary to vigorously employ an open and energetic regime of superiority and power in which whites and, especially, masters are surrounded by a prestige that can balance moral and physical power." Instead of reforming or revoking the Reglamento of 1842, however, the best solution was to simply be silent about it, thus avoiding the deterioration of diplomatic relations with Britain, the dissatisfaction of slaves, and the persistence of debate about the issue.[57]

The adjustment of the captaincy general of Cuba and slaveholding classes also appeared in the wording of the resolutions. In the presence of O'Donnell, the Junta de Fomento prepared one set of rules for colonial authorities and another for proprietors. The first called for the immediate departure of emancipated Africans once they received their manumission letters; the deportation of any free black without a profession or property; the reinforcement of obstacles against the entrance of foreigners of color; the prohibition of the employment of people of African descent in pharmacies (fearful that they could poison whites); strict vigilance over black tenant farmers (suspected of organizing slave insurrections in rural zones); and the restriction of the number of taverns, permitting only those with substantial capital (and thus not needing to do business with slaves to remain open).

Instructions to proprietors in turn established that the amount of working time, food quotas, clothing allotments, and health care for the sick would be decided according to the "prudent judgment" of the masters. Free people of color were excluded from administrative positions on plantations and prohibited from leaving the plantations in groups, while each productive unit had to be at least 5 percent white. The circular notes submitted by O'Donnell to the authorities and the hacendados used conciliatory language, reflecting the restoration of the political pact. Those resolutions were only taken after O'Donnell had received "indications from various people who love the country," and after "enlightening discussions generated by this important question at the Junta de Fomento." Similar expressions emphasizing the control of the slaveholding classes over the future of Cuban slavery continued to appear in circular notes over the following months.[58]

During the violent repression of January 1844, O'Donnell released a note based on a royal order of June 2, 1843, asking for instructions on the passage of a slave trade law, as requested by the Anglo-Spanish Treaty of 1835. Metropolitan authorities wanted to know some of the characteristics of the new law, such as its procedural aspects and the penalties for disrupting legal commerce. The main reason for the royal order was British diplomatic pressure.

After the cessation of the Carlist wars, which had been frequently used as an excuse, Spain could not postpone the fulfillment of the treaty anymore. At least this was the interpretation of the Brazilian consul in Madrid, according to whom "the English government has lately complained so frequently that the cabinet of Madrid, threatened with the interruption of diplomatic relations with London and, in fact, not having any more pretexts to postpone the fulfillment of a commitment solemnly contracted, was forced to take a step that they knew would be unpopular."[59] But this was only part of the reason. Besides international pressure, Cubans themselves had called for the fulfillment of the treaties in 1841 in order to prevent the forced emancipation of slaves illegally introduced on the island. Moreover, the traumatic uprisings and conspiracies of 1843 must have contributed to the decision to quickly pass the new slave trade law.

Two months after the treaty of 1835, the Spanish government submitted a supplemental bill to the *procuradores del reino* (Lower House representatives), but the dissolution of the Cortes, the reform of the Cádiz Constitution, General Manuel Lorenzo's rebellion, the parliamentary exclusion of the overseas representatives, and the Carlist wars combined to indefinitely postpone its discussion.[60] In 1843, after having reestablished the balance of the political pact of 1837, metropolitan authorities did not dare to repeat the mistake and decided to follow the proposals of the Junta de Fomento (i.e., to confer with Cuban slaveholders before making any decision related to slavery). Thus, before submitting a proposal to the Cortes, the captain general had to form "a junta of enlightened proprietors and natives of this island or long-time resident peninsulares" to "deliver to H. M. the indicated report, which should be accompanied by others submitted by proprietors, authorities, corporations, and other people considered apt."[61] Eager to include Cubans in the decision-making process, O'Donnell broadened the colonial representation that could be consulted, requested reports from four individuals (Domingo Aldama, Ignacio de Herrera, José Pizarro y Gardín, and Wenceslao de Villa Urrutia), four corporations (the Tribunal de Comercio, the Ayuntamiento de La Habana, the Real Sociedad Patriótica, and the Junta de Fomento), and three public institutions (the Superintendencia General Delegada de la Hacienda, the Audiencia y Cancellería de Puerto Príncipe, and the Audiencia de Puerto Príncipe).[62]

Although all informants shared the common goal of ending the contraband slave trade, they disagreed on a number of issues. Aldama and Herrera, for example, approved the proposal for a new penal law, but Pizarro and Villa Urrutia rejected it under the assumption that Parliament would incite slaves and free people of color to rebel. According to them, the contraband needed to be suppressed by the captain general himself through the facultades omnímodas or by the queen through the *leyes de Indias*, in both cases circumventing the Cortes. Villa Urrutia expected that a deputy could offer "any plan for emancipation, and in this case not only the interests of the island, but of all the state could be affected." He also recalled the "inopportune, improper, and impolitic publication" of the Reglamento de Esclavos of 1842, "despite the very precise warnings of its bad effects made by many people [including Urrutia himself]." The slaves, he explained, "cannot know a relation with society other than the one tying him to his master, and this principle, adopted in the United States of America and in Brazil, is what guarantees the safety of the country there." While Aldama defended the economic superiority of free labor, Villa Urrutia stated that slavery would continue to exist through the movement of slaves from coffee plantations and old estates—incapable of competing in the international market—to the new establishments and all their advanced technology, which Urrutia himself had employed on his own properties.[63]

The reports from colonial corporations and public institutions also had many similarities. The Sociedad Patriótica, which had previously criticized the contraband slave trade, described the 1841 report as prophetic because of the recent slave revolts and conspiracies. According to them, suppressing the contraband was the first step toward the abolition of slavery and its replacement with white immigration. They argued that transgressors of the slave trade law—crews, ship owners, and investors—should be sentenced to ten years in jail in Africa. Repeat offenders should be sentenced to life in prison. The Junta de Fomento, in turn, defended the economic benefits of slavery and contraband, only agreeing on the political obstacles to their continuation. The "changes in the [abolition] debate in Europe," the "crazy efforts" of "abolitionist societies," British diplomatic pressure, and the turbulent Caribbean context (i.e., the proximity to countries that had experienced abolition such as Jamaica and Haiti) made the continuation of the slave trade impossible.

The Escalera Conspiracy had taught everyone two important lessons: first, that the contraband slave trade should be abolished, and second, that the law abolishing it should not allow interpretations that favored slaves (in a reference to the Reglamento of 1842). The report considered the penalties applicable to the crews of slave ships but not ship owners or investors (i.e., merchants and planters). A report from the Tribunal de Puerto Príncipe was even more incisive. It concluded that the law should not be extended to slaves already living on the island or to future disembarked slaves. The permission "to start posterior investigations would be a very appropriate means . . . of disquieting the existent slavery." Finally, the Tribunal de Comercio and the Audiencia de Puerto Príncipe defended the continuation of the slave system, arguing that its problems could be solved by white immigration and the natural growth of the slave population.[64]

After receiving these reports, O'Donnell formed the Junta de Autoridades y Propietarios, whose basic proposals included the establishment of six-year sentences for the principal crew members on slave ships (without making reference to merchants or planters involved in the violation) and the passing of the new regulation as an additional clause in the treaty of 1835 to avoid legislative debate at the Cortes. Joaquín Gómes, one of the members of the junta, also underlined the necessity of prohibiting investigations on the plantations in search of slaves illegally introduced after the new regulation was enacted.

Each of these documents was compiled and submitted to the Cortes to guide the parliamentary debates. The debates and final wording of the so-called Penal Law of 1845 show the great control Cuban slaveholding classes came to possess over slavery. The new regulation prescribed a six-year sentence in prison for masters of slave ships but did not punish ship owners or investors in slave ventures. Thus, the 1845 law violated the provision of the treaty of 1835 that established the necessity of a penal law for all "subjects who shall, under any pretext whatsoever, take any part whatever in the Traffic in Slaves." Article 9 in turn ensured "that under no circumstances, and at no period, can the proprietors of slaves be proceeded against, or disturbed in their possession of them [the enslaved Africans], under pretext of their precedence."[65] At this point, the Spanish Empire was able to legally ensure the same things that Brazil had to guarantee through parliamentary speeches and political alliances. To revoke the 1831 law would have inevitably led to the deterioration of relations with Britain.

The most significant connection between Cuban reports and the conduct of Spanish deputies can be found once again outside the legal body. The government did indeed not try to regulate the contraband slave trade with a decree, a supplemental regulation, or the leyes de Indias, as requested by some of the signers of the reports. But the issue was discussed at the Cortes with the utmost discretion. Soon after the project was presented to the Senate, two deputies abstractly discussed the principles underlying the problem. This was the usual procedure, since the first assessment of a text must always be theoretical. Shortly after these introductory speeches, the minister of state, Francisco Martínez de la Rosa, began warning that slavery and the contraband slave trade were issues beyond the scope of that debate. He then requested that senators skip the first stage of legislative discussion and start a concrete examination of the articles:

> The question of slavery, although the preceding gentleman has said a few words about it, must be totally excluded; and whatever is the opinion of the individuals about such a delicate matter, it can not be touched without leading to very serious inconveniences. The government of H. M. is resolved to defend, by every means at his disposal, the peaceful possession of the loyal inhabitants of the Antilles, defending their properties and preventing any pretext, whatever it is, from disturbing them in the enjoyment of their legitimate rights or from threatening the existence of those wealthy possessions, a very important part of the monarchy. Thus the question of slavery is completely removed because, despite a few points in common, it is not necessarily connected to the question of the traffic in blacks nor with the question of the penal law necessary to stop it or punish it.[66]

Forced to give up on their analysis of the project, Spanish representatives must have noted the irony of the situation of role reversal in legislative practices: around half of the pages of all colonial reports offered an abstract analysis of the issue. Once again, Cuban slaveholders had the last word on issues related to slavery. The same discretion marked the inclusion of Article 9. The legislation initially did not openly say that plantations were beyond the scope of police investigations. During the debates, however, one senator suggested the isolation of plantations from investigations in order ensure the peacefulness of Cuban slaveholders. There were some misunderstandings between the cabinet and the proposer of the amendment, with the first fearing that the proposal itself had already revealed the negligence of the government in such a fundamental discussion. Ministers achieved a victory in the plenary, but after all articles were passed the following day, the amendment was quickly included in the legal body.[67] It seems that an agreement outside the Cortes was reached to include the amendment. This was the safest way to make politics in a public space.

The law was sent to Cuba accompanied by the following note: "Far from trying to disturb the created interests or threaten the legitimately acquired properties, the law clearly tries to express that damaging investigations against slave owners cannot be started."[68] The captain general had to then convince Cubans that the government had been an exemplary partner. It was not that the government was simply fearful of disappointing its overseas subjects. In fact, government procedures after 1841 reveal how exclusion from Parliament and the suspension of the Constitution in 1837 led to a more informal system of politics. These practices in turn created channels of representation in a nonrepresentative system. Thus, although they did not participate in the Cortes, Cuban colonists found ways to influence parliamentary politics about slavery without being encumbered by some of Parliament's characteristic disadvantages.

But where did all this power come from? It certainly did not come exclusively from slavery. Metropolitan actors learned that the politics of the Second Spanish Empire left some room for reformist critiques such as the ones put forward by José Antonio Saco's decisive pamphlet, *Paralelo entre la isla de Cuba y algunas colonias inglesas* (1837), or by *Proyecto de memorial a S. M. la Reina*, which encouraged calls for Cuban independence or its annexation by the United States. The reaction to these critiques did not take place in the discursive field of theory or ideology but in the practices of governance. Strengthening ties to colonists by establishing procedures similar to those of constitutional regimes across the Atlantic (although without passing statutes or laws to regulate them) gradually became necessary not only for the maintenance of slavery but for the security of the Spanish Empire itself.

All these events had a great impact on the Cuban economy. Approximately 39,000 slaves were carried from Africa to the island during the first half of the 1840s, a relatively high number. The annual mean, however, had been declining since 1842, probably as a consequence of the proposals defended by Turnbull in Britain. After the Penal Law of 1845, the number of slaves disembarked in Cuba dropped to 400 in 1846, then rose slightly to 1,500 in 1847, 2,000 in 1848, 7,600 in 1849, and 3,100 in 1850. The annual mean of disembarkations during this period was 2,900 per year. Perhaps the argument of Laird Bergad, Fe Iglesias García, and María del Carmen Barcia that these "tendencies were less related to institutional factors, such as the treaties to ban slaving or British efforts at enforcing them, than to the demand for slaves in the island's various economic sectors" is excessively economistic.[69]

On the contrary, demand remained high and led to the movement of slaves from coffee plantations to sugar-producing estates, as anticipated by Villa Urrutia. Moreno Fraginals estimated that around fifty thousand captives were relocated to sugar-producing estates between 1844 and 1848, marking the end of Cuban coffee production (and the predominance of its Brazilian counterpart in the world market). By the end of this period of retraction, Cuba had been experimenting not only with the migration of Canary Islanders but also with the employment of coolies—contract laborers from China, India, and the Philippines. The reduction in the numbers of slaves arriving via contraband trade was a consequence of a conscious political decision.[70]

Imperial Conflicts and Legislative Action, Part II:
Great Britain and Brazil, 1841–1845

A number of events—the campaign for the immediate abolition of apprenticeship, the creation of new antislavery societies (the Society for the Extinction of the Slave Trade and for the Civilization of Africa as well as the British and Foreign Antislavery Society), the organization of the first World Antislavery Convention, the launching of the Niger expedition with the great meeting at Exeter Hall, the assignment of Turnbull to Cuba, and the 1839 Palmerston Act against Portugal—each reverberated in the Empire of Brazil. Although the country had not directly experienced some of these pressures, the recent unilateral seizures of Brazilian ships equipped for the slave trade clearly showed that this was about to change. Moreover, the commercial and anti–slave trade treaties of the 1820s, which had been occasionally used to protect the country from these pressures, would expire in, respectively, 1844 and 1845. In any case, the contraband slave trade after 1831 had always been considered a temporary measure whose success depended on international forces that were beyond the control of statesmen and planters. Aware of this global political context, the individuals responsible for reopening the slave trade started to formulate a new strategy.[71]

In the second half of 1841, an anonymous proslavery article in a Rio de Janeiro newspaper called for the immigration of free Africans to Brazil. In "Reflections About Slavery," the anonymous author, signing as J. A. L. G., cited Voltaire's comparison between a slave and a soldier. The first "had the advantage of not risking his life like the warrior, spending it in the arms of his wife and children." The author then argued that Dutch jurist Hugo Grotius "approves the enslavement of blacks and considers them to have better conditions than most of the wage workers of Europe, who many times have nothing but a black old piece of bread to feed themselves and their large families." Finally, he contrasted the benefits of the civilized Brazilian Empire with primitive African customs: "I will add that it is more philanthropic to employ blacks as slaves than let them kill each other as prisoners of their enemies, which happens whenever they do not have the expectations of selling the prisoners."[72]

The second half of the article pointed to a new phase of British abolitionism. The author noted that the British Empire had been fighting African slavery "only on the sea, only on the coast," in reference to the violent incursions of its navy. The intention was to eliminate Brazilian commercial competition in order to favor the East Indies, "where coffee, sugar, and other kinds of spices and drugs are cultivated; where workers, most of them Indians, work hard to receive four *vinténs* or one *tostão* a day, to their satisfaction." He then acknowledged that the violent actions of the English ("the lords of the seas") could not be defeated, warning that not even Napoleon at the peak of his power managed to do it after the continental blockade: "Napoleon fell! And the English cabinet won!!!" In his conclusion, the author explained: "Since we do not want to be defeated, covered in mud and misery, let's search for a middle ground between the philanthropic English cabinet and our own interests."

The author offered a proposal to encourage the immigration of European colonists and, especially, free Africans into the country with the help of private companies.[73] And the demand was apparently not limited to Rio de Janeiro. Shortly after the publication of the article, the president of Minas

Gerais Province urged the Provincial Legislative Assembly to request from the government "some company that proposes to bring them free Africans, to be employed under supervision in the construction of roads and exploitation of mines for a certain number of years."[74] As had been the case with the slave trade problem, their greatest representative in Parliament, Bernardo Pereira de Vasconcelos, immediately embraced the ideas of the conservatives from Rio de Janeiro and Minas Gerais. In contrast with the Second Spanish Empire, political procedures in Brazil involved all spheres of the representative system—press, provincial assemblies, and Parliament.

In discussions in the Council of State (Conselho de Estado) in 1842, Vasconcelos offered a proposal to solve not only the labor problem but also the issue of land access. Inspired by reports of Edward Gibbon Wakefield that were being publicized by Rio de Janeiro newspapers at the time, the proposal defended several points: that *terras devolutas* (government-controlled public lands) had to be purchased; those already in the hands of planters should be taxed regardless of whether they were in use; the revenue from taxes and sales should be used to import free colonists; and immigrants could only purchase or rent land after three years of residence in the empire. The proposal had a twofold objective. On the one hand, it aimed to solve disputes between *posseiros* (squatters) and proprietors, a long-term problem generated by the disordered settlement of the territory during the colonial period that had been aggravated by the lack of new land regulations after independence. On the other, it would bring free laborers to facilitate the expansion of the agricultural frontier, generating more revenue and in turn allowing new investments on immigration flows in a virtuous circle.[75]

Historians have explored the history of the Land Law of 1850 in two principal ways. Some scholars have discussed the reasons behind the law, describing the chaotic settlement patterns in Portuguese America and independent Brazil as well as the growing desire for an immigration system of white colonists to stimulate the growth of agriculture.[76] Others have looked at its effects during the second half of the nineteenth century, such as the tension generated by the demarcation of terras devolutas, the appropriation of large tracts of land under the protection of the law, the consolidation of a land market, and the subsequent rise in the value of plantations and extension of land-mortgage credit.[77] These interpretations are fundamentally correct, but they share the common view that the law was an effort to bring Brazil from a backward slaveholding past into the modern world of free labor. Thus, they miss the connections between the law and, first, the dynamics of the nineteenth-century contraband slave trade and, second and more importantly, the project to bring in not only European families but also free laborers from Africa. The passage of the Land Law of 1850 can be interpreted as a proslavery reaction in the diplomatic arena to the new phase of British abolitionism.

Only one month after the Regressista Rodrigues Torres submitted the proposal to the Chamber of Deputies, Vasconcelos stated in the Senate that Africa had civilized America. "Africans have contributed to increasing or have produced the wealth of America themselves," he argued, continuing, "Wealth is synonymous with civilization in the century we live in; thus, Africa has civilized America."[78] Manoel de Oliveira Lima, Otávio Tarquínio de Souza, José Murilo de Carvalho, Ilmar Rohloff de Mattos, and Luiz Felipe de Alencastro, among other scholars, have already referred to that statement as one of the most significant defenses of the contraband slave trade made in Brazil after 1822.[79] They may be right, but this is only half of the story. An examination of the speeches made by the senator during the 1840s about the proposal—which, after passing the Chamber of Deputies in 1843, remained shelved in the Senate because of the liberal administration between 1844 and 1848—shows that the Regresso praised the contraband slave trade in order to defend its transformation into free African immigration.

In his lengthy proslavery speeches, Vasconcelos argued that the accumulation of wealth in the history of the New World always depended on forced labor and that, of all its variants, slavery was the least harmful alternative. "What I wished," he said in a challenging tone, "was that the noble senator had looked at the history of the colonies and told me: —This colony prospered without slaves." According to him, every time the British rejected the institution, they had to search for "the convicted of England," who were also "subject to punishments as severe as if they were Africans when they do not work."[80] The Anglo-American War of 1812 in turn interrupted Irish immigration into the United States, leading US authorities to search for "Germans, and they imported them to these states that do not allow slaves. Without ceremony the Americans sold these Germans in public auctions in the presence of Quakers." The crux of his argument was that the end of black slavery could lead to worse forms of exploitation of whites themselves.[81]

The senator then imagined the unlikely scenario of a radical reduction of the contraband slave trade as a result of policing activities off the coast, antic-ipating the reasons for the development of a new project to solve the problem of labor supply. After saying that "according to the news I have been given, not one single slave has entered Brazil this year," Vasconcelos heard from angry members of the opposition comments such as "you are mistaken; only in Santos more than four thousand had entered." His reply, ironic as usual, was that "with respect to figures, there is nothing easier than increasing them, we just need to add a digit." The senator swore that he was not a sup-porter of the contraband—since that would be "against the laws ruling this country, and there is a law prohibiting this traffic"—and warned about the eventual collapse of the country if new measures to replace the traffic were not taken: "Let's take a look at any of our great agricultural establishments; what do we see? Three or four hundred slaves of the masculine sex and a very small number of slave women. . . . There is no hope that these arms can be reproduced, and then what will result from this? . . . Aren't we, therefore, in danger of becoming barbarous?"[82] European colonization in this context was not a sensible alternative. A hardworking, free white man from Man-chester, the heart of the world economy, would become lethargic in the vast unoccupied lands of Brazil. The only solution here was the use of some coer-cion to organize labor, as suggested in the following passage:

A cousin of the present first minister of England, Robert Peel, a great capitalist, got a great extension of land in that part of the colony of New Holland called Swanriver; he carried his immense wealth in workers, cattle, seeds, and tools there to establish a principality. Those who have seen this colony and have written its history attest that shortly after arriving in his destiny in 1829 he was immediately abandoned by the laborers he had hired; his cattle died, the machines stayed on the beaches and became useless, and in a few days the great English capitalist did not have a single person to bring him a glass of water or make his bed![83]

All this happened because the "European has a habit that cannot be extir-pated, which is that of being a landowner." The fact that the most notable people on his continent were great landowners stimulated in the youngest children the desire to also become one of them one day. Once in America, this desire became stronger because of the easy access to fertile land.[84] How could the accumulation of wealth in the country be preserved without relying exclusively on the contraband or on European immigration? According to Vasconcelos, Africans lacked the cultural factors that generated the independent nature of Europeans. They were the most adequate solution. Moreover, they could bear the heat of the tropics:

> [The government should end the traffic by] selling the *terras devolutas* and using the capital to import free laborers. . . . I was always inclined toward Africans, understanding that they are the most useful arms Brazil has. . . . The present [liberal] administration hates African arms, liberalism believes such arms are not supposed to be used anymore; well, I do not venture into the secrets of liberalism: but what I believe is that many provinces will be reduced to misery in a short period of time if the government does not open its eyes, if it does not quit being so liberal, and exclusivist liberal. How can there be culture in Pará? Will free arms come? From what part of the world? The European can work under the sun of the tropics, the sun of Pará? . . . Where will arms come from to cultivate the lands of Pará, Maranhão, and other provinces that are in identical circumstances? . . . I wish the Mr. minister of the Empire could tell me if there wouldn't be a way to import Africans not as slaves. I believe that without the help of African arms, many of these provinces whose representatives today believe this is . . . I don't know . . . inhumanity, I can't recall the expressions very well, introduce in Brazil black arms, that many of these provinces will be abandoned.[85]

These words have already been interpreted as a defense of the slave trade, but they were also a positive assessment of the effects of African labor in Brazil. This labor had been ensured by the slave trade until then and should now be replaced by a system of colonization, as proposed in the debates over the Land Law.[86] Immigrant supporters of the liberal party such as José Pedro Dias de Carvalho, Nicolau Pereira de Campos Vergueiro, and Antônio Pedro da Costa Ferreira reproached Vasconcelos with the argument that the law should only deal with "white colonization, entirely removing the colonization of Africans from it [the country]."[87]

The conservative strategy may have been influenced by the approaching expiration date of the Anglo-Brazilian commercial treaty, whose renewal had in fact been debated between 1841 and 1844. British duties for non-British sugar (sixty-three shillings per hundredweight) were much higher than for that imported from the British Caribbean (twenty-four shillings per hundredweight). This was a rich market that Brazilian producers wished to enter with privileges to compensate for Cuban competition and the growth of beet sugar production. In order to open the market to the Brazilian Empire, the London government demanded new efforts against the slave trade: Brazil should sign an anti–slave trade treaty similar to those signed by Britain with Spain in 1835 and Portugal in 1842. The reply from two leaders of the Regresso was significant: the Empire of Brazil would happily accept the new treaty as a condition for revising the commercial treaty as long as the British allowed the importation of free Africans into the country.[88] Thus, the Land Law bill was being used not only to deal with the global expansion of abolitionism but also in diplomatic relations between the two countries.

Their hopes, however, were soon dashed. Aware of the limitations of its power over Cuba, Britain intensified its pressure on Brazil, demanding measures for the gradual emancipation of slaves. This more aggressive tone infuriated Brazilian and even US politicians. A US special envoy to London wrote to the Brazilian government that the United States expressly condemned the aggressive conduct of Britain. "The procedure of the English government of trying to tempt Brazil and Cuba into emancipating their slaves," the Brazilian envoy argued, paraphrasing a US consular agent, "very much annoyed the American government, which considered this procedure an illicit intervention that England claimed in the internal affairs of other peoples."

Shortly after that, Secretary of State John C. Calhoun provided some advice in a letter addressed to the Brazilian government: "It is our established policy not to interfere with the internal relations of any other country, and not to permit any other to interfere with ours." He then continued: "Brazil has the deepest interest in establishing the same policy, especially in reference to the important relation between the European and African races as it exists with her and in the Southern portion of our Union. . . . The avowed policy of Great Britain is to destroy that relation in both countries and throughout the world."[89] Indeed, the Brazilian Empire did not accept anything related to emancipation in their dealings with the British. After one year of discussions, the Anglo-Brazilian negotiations for a commercial treaty, an anti–slave trade convention, and an emancipation plan came to an end in late 1843 without an agreement.

The Brazilian debates and strategies related to the Land Law—which was finally passed in 1850 without achieving its original objectives—were responses to the same international conjuncture that had also been influencing events in Cuba. Like the Cuban slaveholding classes, who proposed and regulated the end of the contraband slave trade in a delicate international context, Brazilian planters and statesmen sought alternatives to the simple continuation of the contraband slave trade. Brazil and Cuba developed different political configurations in this context, but both were inspired by the British solution to the labor problem after the end of slavery in the British Caribbean. The British government had been encouraging other forms of immigration and labor to replace the slave trade and slavery. By 1839, more than twenty thousand Asian workers had arrived in the West Indies, despite accusations from abolitionists that this system of contract labor was the continuation of the slave trade under a new name. Large numbers of Asian contract laborers continued to arrive in the Caribbean and the Mauritius islands, perhaps as many as two hundred thousand between 1838 and 1861.[90] In the context of a growing number of slave revolts, Asian contract labor appeared to be a good alternative for Cuban planters after the passing of the Penal Law of 1845. Slaveholders sought ways to reduce the African component of the population, which they increasingly considered dangerous.

Unlike Cubans, who experienced the tensions of a racially polarized society, Brazilians explored a different aspect of British immigration policies. After 1841, the year that "Reflections About Slavery" was published, the number of Africans liberated by the Royal Navy or shipped from Africa as free colonists to British colonies increased significantly. By 1867, more than thirty thousand Africans had been transported to Jamaica, British Guiana, and Trinidad. Thus, it was no coincidence that the president of Minas Gerais Province requested from the general government the means to finance the immigration of Africans, just like the British and their "method of purchasing colonists on the coast of Africa, who then become free and are taken to cultivate their colonies."[91] The only reason the Brazilian government did not fulfill the request was because of British resistance to it. The failed attempt to develop an alternative form of African immigration ensured that the contraband slave trade would remain strong for many years.

The great round of Anglo-Brazilian diplomatic discussions during

1841–1844 led to increasing radicalization on both sides. In 1844, the Brazilian liberal cabinet raised customs duties for British manufacturers, who until then had been protected by the commercial treaty. Great Britain in turn passed the so-called Aberdeen Act in 1845, empowering British courts to adjudicate Brazilian vessels unilaterally seized by the Royal Navy.[92] The Brazilian Empire had three options at that point: sign a treaty to suspend hostilities with Britain, as Portugal had done in 1842; pass a penal law capable of suppressing, or at least reducing, the contraband slave trade, as Spain had done in 1845; or protest the measure, seek diplomatic support from other countries, and allow the slave trade to continue.

Unlikely though it may seem, Brazilian statesmen opted for the contentious third option. Far from being the result of political incompetence, the decision was an expression of the powerful alliance that had been established between slave traders, planters, and politicians in the second half of the 1830s. Thus, we may ask, why did the Portuguese and Spanish governments not risk such a bold move? The former did not have slaveholding classes, the key force behind the construction of the contraband slave trade. The latter was restrained by a politically constructed view of Cuban demographics developed in the first half of the nineteenth century. In the absence of similar limiting factors, the contraband slave trade to Brazil basically became a unique business in the immediate years after 1845.

Unlike in the Spanish Empire, the debates about the slave trade in Brazil—although involving mainly foreign states—pervaded the main spheres of the representative system. Shortly after the passing of the Aberdeen Act, two important documents were released: the Protest of the Imperial Government Against the Aberdeen Act (Protesto do Governo Imperial contra o Bill Aberdeen) by the minister of foreign relations, Antônio Paulino Limpo de Abreu, and the book *England and Brazil: The Slave Traffic* (*Inglaterra e Brasil: Tráfego de escravos*), anonymously signed by "a deputy." Since the texts are related to, respectively, a liberal ministry and the conservative Saquaremas, they reveal the great impact of the Aberdeen Act on national sovereignty and honor. The two groups, which had been divided on the contraband slave trade issue, found themselves on the same side. Still, the arguments reveal the different relations of each party with the contraband slave trade.

The Protest of the Imperial Government Against the Aberdeen Act was submitted to different Brazilian embassies—including those in the United

States, Portugal, Spain, France, and Great Britain—in a desperate effort to create an international consensus in favor of Brazil. The representative in Madrid managed to have it published in Spain's leading newspaper, *La Gaceta de Madrid*. In the 1850s, Brazilian congressmen praised the document—also reproduced in Henry Wheaton's highly respected work on international law—as a great diplomatic move by the Brazilian government.[93] The main objective of the document was to prove to other nations that Great Britain could not unilaterally define the slave trade carried by Brazilians as piracy. Limpo de Abreu approached the issue in two principal ways. First, he discussed the terms of the Anglo-Brazilian Treaty of 1826. According to Article 1, he wrote, only the Brazilian government had the right to legally treat the slave trade as piracy. The article should, therefore, be understood as a piece of legal fiction—the decisions of the mixed commissions, which did not condemn suspected slavers for piracy, clearly proved this point.

Limpo de Abreu also argued that, according to the letter of the treaty as well as ipso facto, the contraband slave trade could not be considered piracy by the law of nations. The minister then offered four kinds of arguments: one analogical ("the traffic does not threaten the maritime commerce of all peoples as does piracy"), one historical ("not long ago the same England did not repute itself defamed for dealing in African slaves"), one referring to authority ("Russia, France, Spain, Portugal, the United States of North America, Brazil, and other powers have not abolished slavery yet"), and, finally, one logical ("until today the traffic had only been considered piracy in bilateral treaties, another piece of evidence that it was not seen as piracy in the law of nations"). In the epilogue, he reinforced the feelings of justice and philanthropy of the Brazilian Empire, calling for a new Anglo-Brazilian treaty to replace the "abusive, unjust, and offensive" act.[94]

In December 1845, *O Brasil*'s printing works, the press of the renowned newspaper owned by the Saquarema Justiniano José da Rocha, published the anonymous *England and Brazil: Traffic of Slaves*. The book was a collection of approximately twenty articles that had been published under the title *O bill de lord Aberdeen* (*Lord Aberdeen's Bill*) in *O Brasil*. This was the lengthiest Brazilian document written about the most important diplomatic friction experienced by the country in the nineteenth century. Still, it has been mentioned only once in the historiography on the subject. In *The Abolition of the Brazilian Slave Trade*, Leslie Bethell made reference to the book in a footnote, attributing its authorship to Justiniano José da Rocha—a lawyer, journalist, Saquarema politician, and owner of the newspaper that had published it. Perhaps Bethell reached this conclusion after checking the entry "Justiniano José da Rocha" in the *Diccionario bibliographico brazileiro*; the author of that work, Sacramento Blake, included *England and Brazil: Traffic of Slaves* among the books authored by Rocha. The problem is that Blake also attributed its authorship to J. M. Pereira da Silva in a separate entry of the *Diccionario*.[95]

The monumental *Diccionario bibliographico portuguez* of Innocencio Francisco da Silva can help us solve this problem. Its tenth volume, of 1833, attributed the authorship of two anonymous publications to J. M. Pereira da Silva, *Imperialism and Reform* of 1865 and *England and Brazil*. The editor added that the latter "had never been included in the list of works of Mr. Pereira da Silva and for this reason some still doubt that it is his; however, it was affirmed to me that it was his. The illustrious author, if [he] happens to read these lines, should elucidate this point." The following volume of the *Diccionario bibliographico portuguez* included a protest from Pereira da Silva, but against the attribution of the authorship of *Imperialism and Reform* to him. His silence about *England and Brazil* indicates that he was very likely the author of the book.[96]

The biography of João Manoel Pereira da Silva (1817–1898) is almost synonymous with the history of the Conservative Party. The son of a Portuguese merchant who relocated to Rio de Janeiro after the arrival of the royal family in 1808, Pereira da Silva studied law in Paris and returned to Brazil in 1838, where he acted as a lawyer at the court, became a successful merchant (also involved in illegal operations), and helped consolidate the Regresso. Shortly after arriving he joined the Conservative Party, and by 1840 he had already appeared as part of the Provincial Assembly of Rio de Janeiro. Three years later he was elected to the General Assembly. These were the first steps of a successful political career that later included his election to the Senate and activities as a councillor of state.

According to Sacramento Blake, Pereira da Silva never wavered in his political loyalties for more than fifty years, from 1838 to 1889. He also became an important author, writing biographies (*Plutarco brazileiro*, 1847), novels (*Manuel de Moraes*, 1866; *Aspazia*, ca. 1870), historical studies (*História da fundação do império do Brasil*, 7 vols., 1864–1868), and political memoirs (*Memórias de meu tempo*, 1896). A member of the Instituto Histórico e Geográfico Brasileiro, the Historical Institute of France, and the Academy of Arcadia in Rome among other institutions, he contributed to the emergence of the romantic movement in Brazil, occasionally contributing to the famous magazine *Nitheroy* in Paris and meeting with figures such as Domingos José Gonçalves de Magalhães, Manuel de Araújo Porto-Alegre, Francisco de Sales Torres Homem, and Cândido de Azeredo Coutinho.[97]

The articles written by Pereira da Silva and published in *O Brasil* were compiled into a book in order to, according to the preface, contribute to the dispute with Great Britain the "meditated reading that [it] deserves." According to the editor, the book was a response to an article in the *Times* that had openly connected Brazilian statesmen to the slave trade: "We will have the occasion to see where this frenzy of inhumanity and injustice, stimulated by this brutal avarice that searches for profits in the most barbarous sources, will take these imprudent and mad politicians." The article continued: "Infamous bunch of thieves of the sea. . . . Rio de Janeiro is where these evil men belong to." What primarily outraged the Saquaremas were not so much the accusations of their involvement in the slave trade, but the comparison of slave traders with buccaneers and pirates. Like the Protest of the Imperial Government by Limpo de Abreu, the primary goal of *England and Brazil* was indeed to prove that the slave trade could not be defined as piracy. For this reason, the book included a disclaimer that it should be considered a "commentary and development of the protest recently submitted by the imperial government to England." The two documents, however, are not identical. The proslavery perspective is much more evident in the articles of Pereira da Silva.[98]

Like Limpo de Abreu, Pereira da Silva distinguished the slave trade from piracy for reasons ranging from abstract precepts in the law of nations to the text of the Anglo-Brazilian Treaty of 1826. One of his main arguments, however, focused on the liberty provided by the balance of three powers in a modern nation-state. The same subject had been debated in the assembly in 1827:

> According to the principles that underline the representative system, according to the principles of our constitutional law, its disposition [of Article 1 of the 1826 Convention] is nothing but a promise, made by the Executive, to start and promote or recommend to the general legislative

assembly the creation and promulgation of a law considering and treating as pirates . . . the Brazilian subjects involved in the slave trade. At the time of the conclusion and celebration of the Convention of 1826, we were already living under the influence of a representative system, the Constitution that governs us had already been passed, and the executive power was not responsible for passing penal laws or measures of this nature.[99]

Pereira da Silva also tried to demonstrate that slave trade activities were not, ipso facto, piratical. He noted that slavery had been allowed to exist in the eastern part of the British Empire, in French Algeria, in the French Caribbean, in the colonies of Portugal, in the Low Countries and Denmark, in Brazil, in Venezuela, in New Granada, and in Texas. Finally, he noted that in the United States the institution not only existed but also expanded every year. "In 1830, the number of slaves [in the United States] was 2,009,042," he enthusiastically argued; "however, in 1810 they were 1,191,364 and in 1790 only 697,697." His arguments became increasingly trenchant. He maintained that not only slavery, but also "the traffic of slaves is until today allowed by some powers: we will not mention what is done in great numbers through almost all of the Levantine lands, belonging to the Barbary States, we will only deal with what happens in the dominions of European and American powers. Let's start with France."[100]

The Saquarema author used international treaties, travel accounts, and official correspondence to demonstrate that the slave trade continued to be tolerated in the African parts of the French and Portuguese Empires, Constantinople, Hungary, Bucharest, Croatia, and Russia, among other places. He continued his argument with some particularly harsh words for Africans:

If the commerce of slaves is still allowed and tolerated in many places and possessions of different civilized nations, if at the Levant it is carried on with so much strength and vigor and in a way that does not spare Christians or the Moor, nor the Abyssinian or the Nubian, nor the white color of the inhabitants of Wadey and Fazzen, and even less the white complexion of the beautiful ladies of Circassia and the unmatched beauty of the maidens from Georgia, if men and women are sold by all costs in the *Bazzares* of Constantinople and in the markets of Smyrna, Benghazi,

Algiers, Oran, Bona, and others, how can England want to repute an offense against the nations that, by their own deeds, they admit?

[England] has acted only in favor of Africans; only to their benefit they have offered their charity, applied all their thoughts, attention, care, solicitude, and efforts. . . . Neither the miserable Bohemian nor the Hungarian, nor the captive of Russians nor the ladies from Georgia or Circassia or Abyssinia nor the Indian . . . nor the destiny of the white or the Christian or of any other slave deserved the beneficial attention of Great Britain . . . only the African.[101]

Pereira da Silva also repeated conspiratorial ideas about abolitionists as the agents of imperial projects and colonial interests. According to him, the presence of Royal Navy ships off the coast of Africa had the goal of maintaining the British navy—which dominated the global circuits of free trade—in action after the end of the Napoleonic Wars. The reason why the slave trade was tolerated by the British in all places except Brazil, Cuba, and Puerto Rico was because they wished to protect agriculture in the peripheries of the British Empire: "Thus, according to England, the only infamous, inhumane, and punishable slave trade is the one supporting the cultivation of the lands of countries in America!!"[102]

The widespread perception that emancipation in the British Caribbean had been a social and economic failure, a perception shared by many Cuban slaveholders, was also used by Pereira da Silva. In his words, Great Britain had discovered that, because "emancipated slaves, dominated by an endless idleness, refused and escaped work, the agricultural establishments were consequently deteriorating, the emigration of white men increased, properties had their values extremely lowered." The government then smartly raised import taxes on goods produced by slaves and promoted the "import to their colonies of negroes rescued from slavery by the mixed commissions in their dominions."[103] The author was clearly resentful of the unsuccessful round of diplomatic negotiations of 1841–1844.

The Saquarema deputy also made a few comparisons to show that the slave trade carried by Brazilians was not as harmful as that allegedly practiced by the English. First, according to him, only Brazilians knew the destiny of the slaves carried across the Atlantic. Using a personal pronoun to merge the Conservative Party, slave traders, and the nation, he argued: "We . . . do not take the slaves we buy to any strange market," but the British were responsible for "the exclusive provision [of slaves] to the dominions of Spain." The slave trade would not be problematic as long as nations only carried slaves to their own territories. The argument expressed the conviction that the slave-producing center (Africa), as historian Luiz Felipe de Alencastro argues, had to be intimately connected to the center of slave-produced goods (Brazil).[104]

The migration of Asian contract laborers to British plantations is described like a travel account about the slave trade, starting with the initial pillage in the interior of the Indian subcontinent, moving on to a description of the barracks on the coast and the ocean crossing, and concluding with their miserable conditions on New World plantations. The argument was based on the writings of the abolitionist Thomas Clarkson, texts of missionaries in Berbice (British Guiana), reports by governors from Caribbean colonies, and other works that, although written with the intent of improving British administration, were widely used by proslavery militants in Brazil. In the conclusion, the author also addressed convict labor. Once again the defense of the slave trade was accompanied by disdain for Africans:

> Like robbing children, Coolies are taken from their homes and from the arms of their families, put in prisons within warehouses and there maintained until the ship leaves. . . . Embarked by force, and sometimes by mistake and allurement, they are packed in the hold of ship, closing the hatchways. . . . After arriving at Port Luiz or any other of some British colony . . . [they] don't have the freedom to choose either the person they will have to serve, or the labor they are going to have to perform, they are given to whoever wants them, according to their physical qualities. . . . Deprived of their families, under the rigors of a severe discipline, having to work in the harshest conditions for miserable salaries, they live like slaves. . . . Few Coolie women are imported by merchants. . . . The mortality [rate] of these Indians is similar to that of slaves. . . . And what is the destiny of the convict in English colonies of the Pacific? Is it different from that of a slave? Certainly not; equal in everything, even when they run away, they are whipped by the police!! . . . The only difference we find is that convicts are Europeans and English, and our slaves are generally Africans. This is the profound and entrenched hatred that the very humane Great Britain has for slavery.[105]

The comparative exercise offered by Pereira da Silva also encompassed the conditions of Brazilian freedmen. In *Lettres sur l'Amérique*, Michel Chevalier stated that US slaves worked less and were better fed and treated than most European peasants, an argument that was later repeated by the Brazilian deputy. Pereira da Silva then subtly compared the inclusion of freedmen's political rights in the Brazilian Constitution to their exclusion in its US counterpart: "If this happens in the United States, despite the proverbial oppression of pardos and free blacks themselves, how could this bad treatment [exist] in Brazil if such an oppression does not exist?" On slaves liberated by the mixed commissions, he argued that "the condition of these freedmen in Brazil is today equal to that of our white servants, and it is certainly better than that of workers in the manufacturing establishments of England and of most peasants in Europe. If our slaves generally live a better life than this miserable people . . . how could these freedmen, who are considered and treated as such by our authorities, not be well nourished?"[106] The deputy then exclaimed: "What a sad picture Ireland offers us! Slaves do not suffer that much!" Ironically, he expressed his philanthropic sentiment: "Humanity also needs some compassion over the sad conditions of the poor classes of England. How they live there! How they educate the children of workers! What a miserable state of things! How immoral!"[107]

The pro–slave trade policy of the Brazilian state combined with the unpredictability brought about by the Aberdeen Act stimulated the growth of the contraband slave trade. It is estimated that the number of slaves disembarked in Bahia rose from 20,000 between 1841 and 1845 to 45,000 in the ensuing five-year period. The approximate number of enslaved Africans disembarked in the central southern region, especially in the Paraíba Valley and Minas Gerais, went from almost 100,000 in the first half of the 1840s to 210,000 in the second. Such dramatic growth was also spurred by the dynamics of the world market. Great Britain had reduced its import taxes on coffee to less than 50 percent and decreased the taxes on slave-produced sugar from sixty-three shillings to twenty-three, coming very close to the fourteen shillings taxed on British Caribbean sugar. Cuba, which had also been favored by this reduction in taxes, witnessed a large migration of slaves from coffee plantations to sugar mills, instead of any growth in the transatlantic slave trade. In fact, the reduction of the contraband slave trade to the Spanish colony after the Escalera Conspiracy led to a concentration of the illegal business in

Brazil, to such an extent that even the great slave trader Francisco Ruviroza y Urzellas transferred his operations from Havana to Rio de Janeiro.[108]

In the following years, however, the favorable conditions of the world economy were not matched by a favorable international political configuration. The Empire of Brazil gradually became diplomatically isolated, an isolation that could only be overcome with the definitive end of the illegal trade in enslaved Africans.

The End of the Contraband Slave Trade to Brazil: Geopolitics and Slave Agency, 1846–1853

Despite the Brazilian effort to denounce the Aberdeen Act, or the "Algerian Law" as the British foreign secretary Lord Aberdeen himself nicknamed it, Great Britain had the total support of France and Portugal to seize vessels flying the Brazilian flag. Around 40 percent of the ships that passed by the port of Luanda between 1845 and 1860 were warships—half of them British, 25 percent Portuguese, 15 percent French, and the rest belonging to the United States. Shortly after the passage of the Aberdeen Act, the governments of London and Paris sent 3,000 and 2,500 men, respectively, to Angola. In 1846–1847, French ships departed from Luanda eighty-seven times while English ships departed from the same port fewer than sixty-six times.[109]

These operations reverberated immediately in the Brazilian Chamber of Deputies. João José de Oliveira Junqueira, elected from Bahia, exclaimed: "The country of gentlemen, the country of glory, the country of the Bayard, the Montmorency, the Lafayette," had accepted "to seize our ships!!" Another deputy added the arrival of a new enemy besides France: "France followed in the same steps [as England], started to similarly insult and harm us. And then Portugal! . . . Even Portugal! . . . is seizing our ships."[110] The former metropolis now allegedly refused to receive Brazilian consuls in Luanda while maintaining a British vice-consul in the city. The resentment of the Brazilian deputies was reflected in broader society. Around that time, Baron Forth-Rouen saw inside a church in Salvador an ex-voto of Jesus Christ protecting a Brazilian slave ship against the attacks of English and French warships.[111]

This was the backdrop—Brazilian protests ignored by other nations, large numbers of slaves disembarked, and parallel talks between Brazil and Great

Britain—when the liberal cabinet in Rio de Janeiro, on May 31, 1848, ordered the seizure of slave ships and cancelled its instructions to the Brazilian consul in London that had requested him to obtain British approval to transport African colonists to Brazil. Moreover, the new government also revived the Marquis of Barbacena's proposal of 1837, making it more rigorous before submitting it to the Chamber of Deputies. In taking these unprecedented steps toward the suppression of the slave traffic, the new cabinet may have been influenced by Brazil's growing diplomatic isolation and by the immediate abolition of slavery in the French Caribbean in March 1848.[112]

The new orientation was therefore a result of the cumulative effects of the Aberdeen Act and the new place of slavery in the Atlantic world. A more recent and very influential hypothesis, that slave resistance (sometimes described in broad terms, ranging from deliberate acts of violence to infectious diseases) was at the center of the struggle against the contraband slave trade, has been defended by a number of historians. The Malê revolt of 1835, the 1838 uprising in Vassouras, the so-called Conspiracy of 1848 in the Paraíba Valley, the outbreak of yellow fever in 1849–1850, and the crisis involving free Africans also during 1849–1850 all combined to contribute, according to this view, to the emergence of growing public opinion against the contraband slave trade and the subsequent actions taken against the traffic by Brazilian statesmen.[113]

Jeffrey Needell criticized most of these ideas in a recent study. He contends that many of these studies of slave resistance are based on a problematic use of sources. Some discussions of yellow fever, for example, are based on speeches given later by members of the parliamentary opposition but presented as if they expressed the earlier intentions of the government. Other historians track allusions to the dangers of slave revolts in court records, later writing exaggerated accounts of these events. Needell contrasts these accounts with a serious analysis of the administrative correspondence of the statesmen responsible for suppressing mutinies and investigating rumors. Finally, he notes that the contraband slave trade not only grew during much of the Malê revolt but also actually grew at a faster rate in the following years. He concludes by noting the "obvious lack of significance" of the revolt and, by extension, of other cases of slave resistance.[114]

Needell's methodological analysis seems largely correct, but it is problematic in a few areas. Ignoring some important parliamentary debates about slavery, Needell did not note the significant impact of the Malê revolt on the public sphere, instead conflating it with the less influential slave actions that followed. While it is true that the Malê revolt did not influence the official decisions of 1850, the same can't be said about events in the 1830s. As we have seen, the revolt generated discussions that favored the Regressistas, with their calls for the reopening of the slave trade against the growing number of antislavery proposals and texts published after 1835. Moreover, the historian rejected all interpretations acknowledging the influence of slave revolts, not considering that the slave conspiracy of 1848 differed from the others. It occurred in close proximity to the court precisely when the Paula Sousa cabinet came into power. Needell offers a vague explanation of the new cabinet's decision to discuss the end of the slave trade, associating it with the Aberdeen Act.[115]

Historian Robert Slenes has offered one of the most significant interpretations of the 1848 slave conspiracy. A few months after slavery was abolished in the French Empire, authorities in Vassouras, Rio de Janeiro, discovered plans for a slave revolt involving the entire Paraíba Valley region. This secret society of slaves—organized into groups of fifty slaves each and ranked using symbols from the Kingdom of Kongo in central Africa—planned to poison masters and overseers and then crown an African leader. Slenes hypothesizes that a "slave identity" emerged in the Brazilian Southeast during the nineteenth century based on secret societies with a Kongo background, whose religious rituals could easily transform into political protests. According to the author, the slave conspiracy of 1848 was an expression of this form of cultural organization. Particularly important to our argument, however, are the connections he sees between slave actions and the passage of anti–slave trade measures by the government. Slenes argues that the events in the Paraíba Valley not only "galvanized" opponents but also "created an opinion" against the slave trade. Without this new consensus against the traffic, the attacks by the British navy would have been completely ineffective.[116]

Two main aspects of Slenes's argument must be discussed here. First, he transcribes a speech by Eusébio de Queirós of 1852 mentioning the slave conspiracy in order to explain all the decisions of the Brazilian government since 1848—and he does so based on indirect citations, indicating that he did not consult the congressional records. Had the author analyzed the political context of the 1852 speech with the same rigor that he applied to his studies of slave culture in southeastern Brazil, he would certainly have uncovered some of the problems in Eusébio's speech. Second, Slenes treats the administrative history of the Brazilian Empire from 1848 to 1850 as a single coherent unit, because the 1848 slave conspiracy supposedly led to a reconsideration of the 1837 anti–slave trade bill (in 1848) and its passage in 1850. The argument for a new anti–slave trade consensus is, in fact, not new, having already appeared in an article by Francisco Iglésias in *História Geral da Civilização Brasileira*, edited by Sérgio Buarque de Holanda. According to him, after 1848, the government did not dare to "defend the traffic because it was unsustainable, besides the fact that it was largely based on foreign financial interests, most notably Portuguese." The argument was later repeated by Alencastro and, in more restrained fashion, Needell.[117]

Considering the chronological proximity of events in the Paraíba Valley, and given that region's geographical proximity to Rio de Janeiro, it seems likely that they influenced the decisions of liberal ministers in 1848. When the minister of the empire, José Pedro Dias de Carvalho, listed in the Senate the economic and social reasons that had led him to reconsider the 1837 proposal, he argued that "most of our planters, aiming to increase their establishments, incurred debts that, instead of putting them in a more advantageous position, left them in the worst circumstances." He then added: "I believe that Brazil has not benefited from the introduction of this species of population [Africans], that the utmost care and effort of the government must be [given] to introduce white colonists in order to remove this heterogeneous population that . . . continues to inspire some fears. Some facts in this country have demonstrated that these fears are not completely unfounded."

This is probably the only congressional reference in 1848 that confirms the existence of a slave conspiracy. While it reinforces the links between the conspiracy and the reconsideration of Barbacena's proposal, as Leslie Bethell and Robert Slenes argue, it is not an indisputable indicator of the existence of such a relation. The correspondence of the Brazilian ambassador in London reveals that the main concern of the cabinet was proving to England that the Aberdeen Act could not be effectively used against Brazil. Dias de Carvalho's speech also does not help toward an understanding of the administrative decisions of the following years, after the cabinet returned to Saquarema hands.[118]

The last article of the 1837 proposal recommended the revocation of the 1831 anti–slave trade law. Since liberal leaders had never developed a coherent pro–slave trade policy, deputies were deeply divided about the bill. Many of them truly opposed the arrival of more Africans and associated the revocation of the law with the desire of planters and slave traders to reopen the business later. (The Penal Law of 1845 in Cuba—protecting the property of slaves who had been illegally introduced onto the island and allowing the reopening of the traffic later—indicates that these Brazilian deputies were probably right.) After long debates, pressure from the ministers, and two secret sessions, the majority of deputies voted against the revocation of the 1831 law (32 to 29), forcing the cabinet to resign.[119]

The Chamber of Deputies was then dissolved, and the Saquaremas again ascended to power. José da Costa Carvalho became the minister of the empire, Rodrigues Torres the minister of finance, Eusébio de Queirós the minister of justice, Manuel Vieira Tosta the minister of the navy, Manuel Felizardo the minister of war, and the Viscount of Olinda the minister of foreign affairs (until late 1849, when he was replaced by Paulino Soares). On September 29, 1848, two days before the ascension of this conservative cabinet, Bernardo Pereira de Vasconcelos suggested that the Saquaremas were not willing to continue the efforts of the liberal cabinet to pass a new anti–slave trade law:

This [liberal] government appear in the Chambers and says—No traffic—: well said, the laws have, for good or for evil, decided so, it is a right of the country—no traffic.—Time is spent debating a *law that was born eleven years ago, that should be debated*; time is spent with this law, great tumults take place, *the official press has insulted everyone who has felt repugnance toward this debate*, even some proclamations appeared: *I was part of the ones mistreated by these proclamations*; and, after a longer debate, of secret sessions, the conclusion was reached that this project should be indefinitely postponed! Well, on such a serious measure, to decide for the postponement is incomprehensible, gentlemen. But even more incomprehensible is that at the same time that the doors to the traffic are closed, also closed are the doors to colonization. What is the intention of such a system?[120]

In that same year, Vasconcelos also denied the rumors that the slave conspiracy in the Paraíba Valley had influenced Dias de Carvalho: "I should start by declaring... I don't know how to explain, that I do not believe in any of these insurrections, and because of this I do not fear the arrival of African arms."[121] The following year, the Viscount of Olinda instructed the Brazilian ambassador in London to resume negotiations for a proposal to transport Africans as free colonists to Brazil. Then, in the early 1850s, after a series of seizures of Brazilian ships by the Royal Navy and tensions between the British and Brazilian authorities at the Paranaguá fort, Paulino Soares considered investigating France's position on the slave trade to Brazil. It is clear from all this that the Saquarema proposal in 1849 was neither negrophobic nor urgently opposed to the slave trade.[122]

There were a number of turbulent discussions regarding the suppression of the transatlantic slave trade in Great Britain during 1849. While a special commission nominated by the House of Commons submitted a motion denouncing the expensive and inefficient anti–slave trade activities of the Royal Navy, one of the most conservative British newspapers, the *Times*, suggested on August 28 that London should consider the possibility of tolerating the transatlantic slave trade with new legal regulations. In October, the article was translated and published in *Jornal do Comércio*, certainly influencing the decision making of Brazilian statesmen.[123] During the great diplomatic crisis of 1850, which was caused by British incursions into Brazilian ports and inlets, Paulino Soares confessed that the British motion of 1849 had influenced the Brazilian government (although he had been ardently maintaining that the conservative cabinet came into power in 1848 having decided to suppress the slave trade). He even admitted in an apologetic tone that his group took some time to decide: "The Viscount of Olinda also had prepared some work about this point [the suppression of the traffic]; but either because the difficulties of the position were serious or *because he judged it convenient to wait for the timely moment*, [his] *counterproposals were never presented*." On the issue of his own silence in 1849, he was evasive: "I also had to examine other serious pending issues."[124]

Despite the hopes of the Saquaremas, the major obstacles to the slave trade remained strong. After the end of hostilities with Argentina under the government of Juan Manuel de Rosas, British vessels were redirected from La Plata to Brazil. By mid-1849, they had already seized five suspected slavers and partially blocked the port of Santos. It was only after these events that the conservative cabinet ordered the seizure of the first slave ships, in late 1849, thus challenging Needell's argument that "before the English had fired a shot, the Saquaremas had already determined to repress the traffic." Needell also cites references favoring the suppression of the traffic in the report of the minister of justice and in articles published in the conservative newspaper *O Brasil*—all of them from January 1850—to prove that the Saquaremas had by then already decided to pass the new anti–slave trade legislation as quickly as possible in order to avoid war. Even here, however, the issue is not so clear.[125]

Only in a dispatch of February 12, 1850, one month after the most violent British attacks, did Paulino mention to the Brazilian representative in London the possibility that a new anti–slave trade law would be passed in Parliament, instructing him to use this news to convince the Foreign Office to cease hostilities.[126] But the imperial government again decided to wait. On March 19, 1850, member of Parliament William Hutt submitted a motion to deactivate the British squadron operating off the coast of Africa, but the proposal was defeated by a 232 to 154 vote. A Brazilian representative in London argued that "deactivation would basically imply a virtual revocation of Lord Aberdeen's bill: perhaps it would lead Parliament to make its revocation legal." It seems likely that *O Brasil*, which had been publishing anti–slave trade articles in January 1850, preferred to wait during the following months for the outcome of the debate in England.[127]

Evidence of this was the meeting between the Viscount of Olinda and the Spanish representative in Rio de Janeiro, who was very interested in the tensions between Brazil and Britain because of their similarities with the situation in Cuba. Shortly before Hutt's defeat, Olinda confessed that the imperial government was still unsure of what to do. Planters from his province, Pernambuco, had established a sharecropping system with freedmen, providing land, seeds, animals, and part of the harvest in exchange for labor. These planters, however, suffered great losses, which convinced them of the necessity for the contraband slave trade. On the other hand, Olinda lamented, "there were no signs that the English cabinet would stop persecuting the commerce in African slaves." In sum, Brazilian authorities found themselves in a very delicate situation, having to choose between avoiding a virtual war and maintaining a rapidly growing economy.[128]

Transcripts of a debate in the Senate also confirm this desire to wait for the outcome of discussions in Britain. On May 13, perhaps in response to news of Hutt's defeat, Holanda Cavalcanti—a liberal senator from a conservative family who was very close to the Saquaremas—presented an unorthodox solution to the problem. According to him, the Brazilian Empire should officially reopen the slave trade for a specific period of time before ending it definitively. The idea had been inspired by proposals published in the *Times*, in the book *The Slave Trade Regulated* by Robert Stokes (1850), and in the pamphlet *The Brazilian Slave Trade and Its Remedy, Showing the Futility of Repressive Force Measures* of Thomas Richard Heywood Thomson (1850). Cavalcanti made three main points. First, abolitionist sentiment was similar to new currents of European social thought such as communism, which opposed private property. Second, Brazilians had the right to revoke national laws such as the law of November 7, 1831. Finally, in no other place in the world could an African slave have the same prospects for social mobility that he enjoyed in the Brazilian Empire.[129] This last point was a reference to the extension of citizenship rights to freedmen, which had been used in defense of the slave trade during critical moments such as the parliamentary debates of 1827 (Cunha Matos), the alliance to reopen the slave trade in the 1830s (Carneiro da Silva's *Memória sobre o comércio de escravos*), and the crisis generated by the Aberdeen Act (Pereira da Silva's *Inglaterra e Brasil: Tráfego de escravos*). In Cavalcanti's words:

The slave in Brazil is happier than the slave in Africa: I don't say it based on theories; I spent years in Africa, visited all Portuguese possessions, found myself in circumstances of having a great knowledge about this. It did not come to my knowledge, while in Africa, that an individual manumitted a negro; and do you want to see which blacks in Brazil have been manumitted? Go to the fish, poultry, and the fruit and vegetable markets and you will see that most [people] in these markets are negroes still carrying the marks of their nation; I go there every day; I cannot only take any noble senator, but also any English[man] that wants to go with me and I will tell them that these Africans that were imported as slaves to Brazil are happier than most of their fellow citizens. Do you want to see how slaves are treated in Brazil? Go to these registries where there are wills and you will see the amount of generosity that is practiced with them; go to the baptismal fonts and you will see there how many are freed; go to our farms, to our plantations, where you will find men who were freed in compensation for the good services rendered to their masters; and it is not necessary to check the third generation: slaves coming from Africa in great numbers have been freed, and if the Constitution does not give them the name of Brazilians, it gives it to their children when they are free. In what nation, in what part of the world, does the mixed race enjoy the prerogatives that they enjoy in Brazil? And the English are the ones that come teach us philanthropy![130]

At that moment, two senators took the chance to present alternative proposals. Paula Souza called for the elimination of all legal avenues to freedom based on the 1831 law, while Candido Batista de Oliveira, based on the outbreak of yellow fever in the country, offered a real anti–slave trade proposal that sought to reinforce that same law. The Senate then nominated a special commission—formed by Holanda Cavalcanti (elected with twenty votes), Batista de Oliveira (nineteen votes), the Viscount of Abrantes (eighteen votes), Paula Souza (eighteen votes), and Limpo de Abreu (sixteen votes)—to review the proposals. During the meetings, the committee received a memorial from João Clemente Vieira Souto calling for the reopening of the slave trade and the establishment of heavy taxes on it, which could then be applied toward the immigration of free colonists.[131] After over a month of discussions, the commission released a short report, leading a member of the House to exclaim: "And what has the commission been doing? Wasn't it created one month ago? It is sleeping . . . now, Mr. President, when we find ourselves blockaded, when Rio de Janeiro is blockaded because of the traffic."[132]

It was precisely between May, when the proposals were presented, and July, when the commission released the report, that the conservative cabinet—after watching the defeat of Hutt's motion and the continuation of British hostilities—started the debate leading to the law of September 4, 1850, which finally suppressed the transatlantic slave trade to Brazil. In a letter from April 26 about Hutt's defeat, the Brazilian representative in London warned that the Brazilian government should consider not the possibility of a defeat of anti–slave trade politics in the British Parliament but an eventual alliance between Britain, France, and the United States against Brazil—an alliance that had been alluded to by Prime Minister John Russell. "It is remarkable that Lord John Russell included the American Union in this alliance," the Brazilian official wrote, "at a moment when the latter provides to the civilized world the sad spectacle of a dispute that threatens the stability of its institutions and that is totally connected to the issue of slavery itself." He then lamented: "Unfortunately, this particularity does not exclude the possibility of such a fact."[133] Moreover, on June 20, 1850, the British representative told Paulino that the Foreign Office had accepted the recent military aggression as a precedent for new attacks—one year later the Brazilian minister still remembered the fateful orders of June.[134]

Only after these events did the Senate commission finally decide (on July 1) to endorse "the idea of means that tend to repress the traffic, according to the letter and spirit of the law of November 7, 1831." By that time, the Saquaremas had already concluded that revoking the law would threaten the defense of the empire and open space for more debate in the public sphere about the Africans who had already been illegally introduced into the country. Thus, their strategy consisted of suppressing the traffic and any reference to its past history along with it. This strategy was similar to the one the Cubans had adopted in 1844, when, although critical of the Reglamento, they had decided to suspend the traffic to avoid complaints from the British and local opponents of the contraband slave trade.

In the context of British seizures of Brazilian vessels and their firefight with Brazilian authorities at Paranaguá fort, Brazilian ministers (in possession of the report) called for a meeting of the Council of State to discuss new measures on July 11. Paulino, the author of the survey submitted to members of the council, was very clear about the fact that Brazil was in a state of virtual war with Great Britain. According to him, Britain had been "visiting, seizing, and judging our embarkations, entering our ports, burning our ships, and destroying all resistance to her. The facts prove it. The position of Brazil is very dangerous." Thus, the survey began by asking if Brazil should fight back, and then proceeded to consider the alternatives. Should the country establish direct negotiations with Britain? Should it seek the intermediation of a third power? Should it prepare an official protest? Was there any other way to resolve the situation?[135]

The Viscount of Olinda argued that the treaty of 1826 went against Brazilian interests and should ideally be revoked. "If this could not be achieved, then [Brazil] should accept and faithfully fulfill the treaty; other than this, only by waging a war." Brazil, however, was a small nation, and "justice [was] the only weapon that it could rely on." This assessment was followed by others: if the situation eventually called for a war, declaring war was out of question. Other members of the council argued that other nations would refuse to intermediate in the issue, except for the United States, whose help would nonetheless arrive too late. Some noted that a protest would have no effect, recalling the frustrated attempt to gain international diplomatic support with the Protest of the Imperial Government Against the Aberdeen Act of 1845. Finally, they concluded that the only way to remedy the situation was to suppress, once and for all, the contraband slave trade. In possession of the report from the Council of State, Eusébio de Queirós discussed in a secret session the following day at the Chamber of Deputies the nature of a future anti–slave trade law.[136]

With the support of the Council of State, Paulino Soares gave a one-hour speech to convince the Chamber of Deputies of the necessity of ending the contraband slave trade. The speech did not make reference to national ethnic homogeneity, indebted planters, or the danger of slave revolts—arguments that had been used by Dias de Carvalho in 1848 and could have been reiterated here. His words echoed the warning from the Brazilian representative in London about Brazil's international isolation after the defeat of Hutt's motion:

> I will ask those who feel that the continuation of the traffic is convenient if it is possible that it can continue at least for a long time. When a powerful nation such as Great Britain continued with tireless tenacity for over forty years in the effort to end the traffic with a perseverance that was never contradicted; when she decides to spend 650,000 pounds per year only to keep ships to repress the traffic; when she obtains acceptance from all European and American maritime nations; when the traffic is reduced to Brazil and Cuba, can we resist this torrent that impels us, since we are placed in this world? Moreover, gentlemen, if the traffic does not end by these means, it should end one day.[137]

The risk of going to war with Great Britain seemed so great that in June 1850 the government budget included additional amendments to prevent military attacks, while Paulino instructed the Brazilian representative in Washington to ask for US support in case of an eventual British occupation of Brazilian waters. Finally, it is important to note a key difference between the parliamentary debates of 1848 and 1850: while the liberal cabinet used parts of two secret sessions to try to (unsuccessfully) convince the Chamber of Deputies of the necessity to revoke the 1831 law, the conservative cabinet, in a state of virtual war, convinced their deputation to revoke the same law with the same amount of debating time.[138]

Considering the discussion above, it is not clear, as Needell has argued, that the actions of the executive during 1849 and early 1850, such as the seizures of slavers, the publication of anti–slave trade articles in *O Brasil*, the reference to suppressive measures in the minister of justice's report, and the direct negotiations with slave traders and planters in the Paraíba Valley, were expressions of anti–slave trade politics.[139] These actions more likely had the objective of alleviating tensions with Britain until the end of the crisis. In fact, it was only after mid-1850 that the Spanish consul in Rio de Janeiro noted an abrupt change, writing that, if on the one hand, the cabinet adopted a "new policy" to save "this country from great complications that would lead to a rupture with this power [Great Britain]," on the other, the "transition was too violent not to leave a mark on national dignity in this process."[140] Brazilian statesmen extended the pro–slave trade orientation of Brazilian politics for as long as they possibly could. Because of their ideological convictions and political expectations, they understood that the end of the illegal traffic would directly affect the interests of social groups with whom they had established strong alliances.

The analysis of the Triennium of 1848–1850 as a homogeneous whole, as argued by Slenes, is also problematic. Assuming that the slave conspiracy of 1848 may have contributed to the reconsideration of Barbacena's proposal in Parliament, all the decisions of Brazilian statesmen in the following years were taken according to parliamentary debates in Britain and the actions of the Royal Navy in Brazilian waters. Eusébio de Queirós famously delivered the only parliamentary speech (on July 16, 1852) that alluded to the 1848 slave conspiracy, a point used by Slenes to support his hypothesis. The Saquarema leader had three main objectives: to refute the interpretation put forward by James Hudson, the British representative in Rio de Janeiro, in his letters; to prove that the Saquarema cabinet had already decided to suppress the traffic before British aggression had taken place; and to clarify the reasons behind the suppression of the slave trade.

The speech given by Queirós can only be fully understood within its immediate context. Since the end of the contraband slave trade, an obstinate liberal opposition had been working to refute Saquarema narratives regarding the events of 1850. Important members of the liberal party such as José Pedro Dias de Carvalho, Joaquim Antão Fernandes Leão, and Manuel de Melo Franco (all three from Minas Gerais), as well as the former conservatives Bernardo de Souza Franco (from Pará) and Joaquim José Pacheco (from São Paulo), blamed the conservative cabinet for the virtual war between Britain and Brazil. According to them, the hostilities could have been avoided if the Saquaremas had continued the anti–slave trade efforts of their liberal predecessors after coming into power in 1848.[141] Their insistence led Eusébio de Queirós do call for the immediate end of accusations: "I wish that all noble deputies who know the sensitivity of certain issues not start debates about them." If "the minister, either by ignorance or thoughtlessness, did not defend his position well, it would not be the country, nor the opposition, nor the government that would be benefited by this; it would be the foreigner." It was not long before new accusations came from liberals, leading to new protests from Eusébio: "I will need to repeat that it [the conduct of the opposition] is very contrary to the interests of the country." Every deputy "should forget that he belongs to the opposition and only remember that he is Brazilian."[142]

His words were once again ignored. In the following session of 1852, liberal deputies accused the Saquarema administration of only acting after hearing "the sounds of British cannons" and refusing to arrest the great figures behind the illegal traffic. Souza Franco emphasized the past connections of the Conservative Party with slave traders: "After the relations of the noble ministers, in the position they found themselves along with most of those with whom they were forced to combat the traffic, shouldn't this procedure with their friends have perhaps been painful, this violence that some could even consider disloyal?" In the heat of the debate, another deputy went even further: "Mr. Hudson [the British official] pulled Mr. Paulino by his hair and took him wherever he wanted to."[143] It was in this context of repeated debate over the issue that Eusébio de Queirós delivered a speech, on July 16, 1852, in which he made a reference to the slave conspiracy of 1848 for the first time.

The speech is plausible in many of its details, but it nonetheless contains inconsistencies such as the argument that the Saquarema had ascended to power in 1848 with the objective of suppressing the slave trade once and for all. Neither the Brazilian parliamentary documents nor the Brazilian and Spanish diplomatic correspondence support this argument. Eusébio also tried to attribute the reopening of the slave trade in the 1830s exclusively to the necessities of agriculture, ignoring the active role of his own party in the process.[144] Newspapers, parliamentary speeches, and memorials from provincial and municipal assemblies of the 1830s easily contradict this interpretation. Equally problematic is his comment about the alleged impact of the 1848 slave conspiracy on Brazilian slaveholding classes and statesmen:

> Some events, or actually, symptoms of a grave nature that appeared in Campos, in Espírito Santos, and in a few other places such as the important municipalities of Valença and Vassouras, produced a terror that I considered healthy, because it led to the development of a strong opinion against the traffic. All the people who were at the time in Rio de Janeiro and had spent some time with the matter recognized that at the time the same planters who until then had defended the necessity of the traffic were the first to contest that the moment to repress it had arrived.[145]

The actions of the government, in his view, were typical of representative systems: when society manifests its public opinion, the party fulfills its desires with the help of the state. Thus, Brazilian public opinion had been the driving force behind the emergence of the contraband slave trade (because of economic reasons) and its definitive end (because of general indebtedness and the fear of slave revolts). This approach explains all government decisions based on national factors, leaving Great Britain without any influence over the political sovereignty of the Brazilian Empire.

Such a discourse reinforces the legitimacy of the representative government while completely justifying the actions of the Conservative Party, none of them condemnable. Evidence that Paraíba Valley planters turned against the slave trade, however, is scarce. In 1849 alone (thus after the 1848 conspiracy), they purchased more than forty-five thousand enslaved Africans, thirty thousand more than three years earlier. How can the "terror" mentioned by Eusébio be reconciled with the great number of slaves disembarked in the region? Where is this fear if the only memorial against the contraband slave trade from civil society between 1848 and 1850 came not from the Paraíba Valley or Espírito Santo, centers of the conspiracy, but from the distant province of Bahia?[146] The Brazilian slaveholding classes never expressed the desire to suppress the traffic because of an alleged fear of slave revolts, as their Cuban counterparts had repeatedly done after the Escalera Conspiracy.

Having established the main force behind the suppression of the traffic in 1850, we must pose another crucial question. Why did Great Britain employ its military force against the Brazilian Empire but not against Havana, the second-greatest slave port of the Atlantic? There seem to be three main reasons for the different treatment. The most obvious one is of a legal nature. The Anglo-Spanish Treaty of 1835 prevented the signatories from resorting to tactics other than those explicitly allowed by the treaty itself—for instance, the polemical tactics that were loosely permitted by the "law of nations,"[147] which had been the basis of the Palmerston Act against Portugal in 1839 and the Aberdeen Act against Brazil in 1845. Moreover, the Cuban Penal Law of 1845 coincided with the decrease of the contraband traffic to Cuba. The dramatic drop in the numbers of slaves imported to the Caribbean was accompanied by the growth of the trade in Brazil. And here lies the second reason. Estimates are that around 265,000 enslaved Africans were introduced in Brazil against 15,000 in Cuba from 1846 to 1850. In April 1850, precisely when Palmerston recognized the legitimacy of British incursions into Brazilian waters, Prime Minister John Russell assured him that Spain had gone a long way toward suppressing the traffic and "that but little further action is required to put an entire stop to the trade."[148]

Despite the importance of these two factors, the most decisive was certainly the third one: the real danger of an eventual annexation of Cuba to the United States. The calls for annexation in Cuba, which had been growing during the great crisis between the actions of Turnbull in 1841 and the Escalera Conspiracy of 1844, decreased after the bloody repression of the conspiracy, the legal security of slave property provided by the Penal Law of 1845, and, especially, the new political practices of the Second Spanish Empire. This fragile balance, however, came to an end with events that were beyond the control of Spanish authorities and Cuban slaveholding classes. The US impulse toward Texas, New Mexico, and California led to a successful war against Mexico in 1846, providing a concrete example of the power of US military force and the political dynamics involving the incorporation of new territories. The event immediately revived the hopes of annexationists in Cuba and the United States. In this context, the 30 percent drop in sugar prices between 1846 and 1848 further stimulated the calls for change in the political regime of the colony.[149]

News of secessionist activities in Havana (the Havana Club) and Trinidad—inspired by the Texan pattern of independence followed by annexation—had already appeared at the beginning of the Mexican-American War in 1846. At the same time, the Consejo Cubano in New York—formed by exiled planters such as Gaspar Betancourt Cisneros and José Aniceto Iznaga—published the annexationist newspaper *La Verdad*. Two episodes related to the proclamation of the Second Republic in France in 1848 reinforced the sedition movement in Cuba. First, the alleged support of the British consul in Spain for the Spanish opposition, during a time marked by republican mutinies in the country inspired by the events in Paris, led the Spanish government to cut diplomatic relations with Britain for two years. The fear of an eventual British invasion soon spread among Cubans, especially after member of Parliament George Bentick stated that purchasing the Spanish island would be less expensive than trying to stop the slave trade with naval action. Second, news of emancipation in the British Caribbean had an immediate impact on Cuban planters: if republicans ascended to power in Madrid, so they thought, the same would be imposed on Cuba.[150]

Also in 1848, the Democratic government of the United States tried to negotiate the purchase of the island from Spain in order to avoid a war that could lead to the end of slavery. After the failure of negotiations, the annexationist movement—formed by North Americans and exiled Cubans in New Orleans and New York as well as by the Havana Club—attracted generals with experience in the war against Mexico (such as William Jenkins Worth and John Quitman, governor of Mississippi at the time). Although both refused to be personally involved, they provided moral and ideological support for the crusade, which was led by Narciso López. López, who had been governor of Trinidad and president of the Permanent Military and Executive Commission in Cuba when Gerónimo Valdés was the captain general, tried to take over the Spanish island five times from 1848 to 1851. He was twice expelled from the island by colonial authorities and twice stopped by the US government itself (during Whig administrations, which were less inclined toward annexation). In his fifth attempt at a takeover, López got carried away by news that an uprising organized by the Sociedad Libertadora de Puerto Príncipe (founded in 1849) had been crushed by the captain general. Immediately after disembarking in the province of Pinar del Río on the western side of the island, López's men were defeated and killed. López and fifty North Americans were sentenced to death in Havana. Britain was witnessing the rebirth of the annexationist movement precisely when most of its military force was engaged in the Crimean War.[151]

The British government became much more cautious in Cuba than it had been in Brazil. As the governor of Bahamas warned, if the United States annexed Cuba, they would have total control over the Caribbean in case of war, since Florida and the northern coast of the Gulf of Mexico had already become part of the country. "Havana would be to America," he said, "what Gibraltar is for England."[152] Another British representative warned the Spanish consul in Rio de Janeiro that if "the North Americans fulfilled their desire in relation to the island of Cuba, the English Antilles and Canada should be considered lost for his country."[153] These assessments, coming from the periphery of the British Empire, reflected the concerns of London. For this reason, successive chiefs of the Foreign Office—especially Palmerston and the Earl of Malmesbury—tried without success to negotiate a multilateral convention involving Great Britain, France, and the United States to prohibit intervention in Cuba.

This backdrop explains the contrasting British actions against the slave trade in Cuba and in Brazil. While the British ships that had been redirected from Río de la Plata to Rio de Janeiro joined the anti–slave trade squadron and participated in a series of seizures and conflicts with Brazilian authorities, the ones sent to the Caribbean were only instructed to prevent attacks by North American filibustering annexationist expeditions against Cuba. Lord Stanley explained to Malmesbury in 1852 the reasons behind these differences: "The alternative of giving, in the case of Cuba, orders similar to those that have been given by Palmerston and recalled by us in that of Brazil, is one approaching so nearly to the declaration of War," which would inevitably be followed by the annexation of the island by the United States. His argument shows how, in the geopolitical game of the North Atlantic, Cuba became a great obstacle to ending the contraband slave trade: "The difficulty is how to do this without exciting the jealousy, or encouraging the aggression, of the US. If you remove the few vessels that occasionally touch at

Havana, you make known your difference to the Americans, and they are thus encouraged in their designs. If on the other hand, you establish a blockade or anything approaching to one, you excite in America a cry of 'British interference,' and instantly it is believed you are going to seize upon Cuba."[154]

Brazilian politicians recognized these differences in treatment. In the turbulent year of 1850, the Brazilian representative in Madrid told the minister of foreign affairs, Paulino Soares, that the interruption of diplomatic relations between Spain and Britain in 1848 had been overcome because of, among other reasons, the "interest of England in making a common cause with this country [Spain], to repel the dangers that threaten the island of Cuba because of the United States." During the 1850s, Brazilian deputies and senators, annoyed by the British refusal to suspend the Aberdeen Act, noted that London was punishing a country that had suppressed the slave traffic while ignoring the one that continued to engage in it. In a speech praised by former enthusiasts of the contraband slave trade such as Honório Hermeto Carneiro Leão and Rodrigo Torres, the Viscount of Jequitinhonha asked the following questions about Britain's behavior: "Does she exert in Spain the same authority that she is presently representing in Brazil? Isn't it public and notorious the traffic carried on in Cuba? No doubt at all. Has she by any chance made her oppressive system prevail there with the same force and violence? Has she ever insulted Spanish authorities?"

The difference, he believed, had a reason other than the extinction of the slave trade. The deputy Luís Pedreira do Couto Ferraz also denounced London's behavior: "Could England through a convention obtain from Brazil more than she has obtained until today in relation to this point? What is the use of the treaties she celebrated with Spain? Don't we see the traffic in slaves taking place in Cuba? Don't we see even their own employees intervening in this traffic?"[155] While one deputy said that US intentions about the eventual annexation of Cuba were notorious, Senator Cândido Borges argued that if there were tolerable and intolerable procedures, then it was clear that the Aberdeen Act violated international law:

The English press has recently denounced that the traffic in slaves was carried on in a large scale on the island of Cuba, and then not only in the same press but also in the English Parliament appeared the idea of employing, in relation to Spanish possessions, the measure that had been employed in relation to Brazil, i.e., to extend to the island of Cuba the coercive measures of the Aberdeen Act, an idea that the first lord of admiralship declared would be useful, but it was not possible to adopt without the consent of the Spanish government. So that, the honorable member notes, to exert the right of sovereignty over Spanish territory, the English government understands that it is indispensable the consent of Spain; but when it is about Brazil, then it can go against its will and despite its successive complaints, persist in the execution of iniquitous measures that harm its sovereignty and independence.[156]

The revival of the contraband slave trade in the 1850s reveals the genesis of the events that led to its end in Cuba and in Brazil. With very few enslaved Africans arriving in Cuba during the second half of the 1840s, the experience of terror and repression of the Escalera Conspiracy was gradually forgotten. The absence of external factors—such as an abolitionist movement in the metropolis or a belligerent state—prevented the transformation of the effects of the conspiracy of 1844 into a definitive political agenda. In Brazil, on the other hand, despite a few attempts in the 1850s, the state of "suspended war" restrained the possibilities of an effective reopening of the illegal business.

This is reflected, for example, in the events following the landing of slaves in Bracuí in 1853.[157] Slaves traders were arrested, police forces entered the plantations, some of the violators, including a few great planters, were indicted, and heated debates took place in Parliament. The minister of justice at the time explained that the searches did not have the objective of questioning the legality of properties acquired between 1831 and 1850 but only to "inspire fear in planters, who will not want to be harmed; and as long as it is not easy to receive the African *boçais* in the plantations, the undertakers will be discouraged." Although the action had the goal of normalizing the future (by openly ignoring the crimes committed in the previous twenty years), it is important to note that a similar action would have been impossible in Cuba, where the Penal Law of 1845 had excluded such a possibility because of the great social fears generated by the actions of Turnbull and the Escalera Conspiracy. In Cuba, the contraband slave trade could not be treated this way, leading a Brazilian senator to note that some slave traders "came to Brazil, but fearing the new measures taken by the government, and know[ing] what had happened in Bracuí, they went to the island of Cuba, where they started an extremely advantageous business, because the Senate knows the encouragement that the traffic in Africans has received on that island."[158]

In order to preserve its political sovereignty, the Brazilian Empire had to completely suppress the contraband slave trade. The government paid secret informants, deported slave traders, passed supplemental laws, and denied titles to planters who continued to purchase African boçais. The persistence of the contraband slave trade in Cuba in turn can be attributed to the same reason—respecting the political status quo. Spain and Britain knew that suppressing the traffic would encourage the annexation of the island to the United States. The different destinies of the slave trade in Brazil and Cuba, however, did not mean that the two countries followed independent trajectories. The abolition of the Brazilian slave trade in 1850 led many slave traders to relocate (along with their capital) from Rio de Janeiro to Portugal, Cuba, and the United States, contributing to the growth of the traffic in the Spanish colony. In a sense, despite these transformations, Cuba and Brazil continued to share a common history in the following decades.

Brazil and Cuba in the Third Atlantic

————————

THE 1975 PUBLICATION of David Brion Davis's pioneering study of the problem of slavery in the Age of Revolution generated a number of debates on the comparative trajectories of slave societies in the Americas during the crisis of early European colonialism. Despite his focus on Anglo-Saxon societies, Davis tried to incorporate events and processes from the French and, to a smaller degree, Iberian worlds.[1] In the following decade, the book led to a fruitful—albeit sometimes harsh—discussion about the relationship between capitalism, slavery, and antislavery in the Age of Revolution. The terms of this debate continue to inspire the primary competing approaches to the study of the last century of black slavery in the Americas. In these final remarks, we discuss how this debate has enlarged Davis's original focus in order to include more systematic comparisons of slavery in the North and South Atlantic during the revolutionary era that marked the turn of the nineteenth century.

One of the main perspectives that emerged from this debate came from Seymour Drescher. Reaching the conclusion that the British assault on black slavery was in direct contradiction to the economic expansion of the institution in the British Caribbean, Drescher argued that a minor social group of antislavery and abolitionist activists were the principal actors behind the destruction of this ancient and powerful institution. Such an unlikely outcome can be best understood, in his view, by looking at the political sphere instead of its economic counterpart. The success of the first antislavery militants was a direct result of the strength of the British public sphere, which was capable of mobilizing and influencing government policies.

It was this political success in Great Britain that paved the way for the ensuing emancipation processes in the rest of the Americas. Drescher's model—and it is possible to call it a model if we consider the coherence of his premises and conclusions—places Great Britain at the center of the global social forces that attacked slave systems in the New World throughout the nineteenth century. This approach carries important methodological implications for historical comparisons. In his book *Abolition: A History of Slavery and Antislavery*, Drescher basically juxtaposes the local trajectories of nineteenth-century slavery, describing them as isolated reactions to abolitionist pressures instead of considering them as part of a process of mutual conditionings. Brazil and Cuba remain as passive secondary agents of an irresistible historical process that is imposed on them. This single historical time slowly—albeit inexorably—carries the Western world from slavery to freedom, always within the orbit of the Anglo-Saxon cultural world.[2]

What Drescher considers the "age of emancipation," however, can be differently defined as the age of mass slavery. In an essay published more than twenty years ago (which has been a major influence on the present book), Dale Tomich developed the concept of "Second Slavery" to help explicate the new elements of Atlantic slavery in the nineteenth century (in opposition to a "first slavery" marked by the predominance of mercantilist policies). According to Tomich, the transformations generated by the emergence of an industrial world economy in the nineteenth century forced slaveholders in the Americas to constantly improve the productivity of their slaves in order to remain competitive in the world market. These dynamics led, on the one hand, to the collapse of the old producing regions in the British and French Caribbean, which not only had been under the pressure of antislavery movements based on their metropolises but had also reached the limit of their productive capacity. On the other hand, they generated new opportunities to regions that had been on the periphery of slave societies in the New World. During that process, Cuba, Brazil, and United States became intimately connected: their respective specialized productions of sugar, coffee, and cotton remodeled their economies in a history defined by mutual and interlocking influences.[3]

One of the arguments of our book is that the "first slavery" was marked by the existence of two different temporalities, one connected to the Iberian Atlantic system and another to its northwestern European counterpart (temporality here meaning the contradictory relationship between the material world and the political sphere in the longue durée). Thus, the category of "second slavery" can be interpreted as belonging to a third temporality of the

Atlantic world, a temporality born from the crisis of the two systems that had preceded it. Generally, the chronological boundaries of this new historical time can be divided as follows: first, a period of formation between 1790 and the 1820s, marked by the Saint-Domingue Revolution, the emancipation of most Spanish colonies in the Americas, and the development of political configurations that institutionally protected slavery in Brazil, Cuba, and the United States; second, a period of expansion between the 1830s and the 1860s, which was accompanied by the final crisis of slavery in the Atlantic system of northwestern Europe and the economic crisis that followed emancipation in the British Caribbean; and finally, a period of crisis that started with the US Civil War and continued with the chain of events leading to free womb laws in Cuba (the Moret Law of 1870) and Brazil (the Rio Branco Law of 1871), and finally the abolition of slavery in 1886 and 1888.

The idea that the "second slavery" can actually be understood as a third phase of Atlantic slavery was also suggested by Robin Blackburn in his book *The American Crucible*. After agreeing with Tomich on the new characteristics of nineteenth-century slavery in Brazil, Cuba, and the United States, Blackburn stresses the discontinuities between what he calls baroque and modern slavery (both of them as part of the Old Regime).[4] As we have seen in chapter 1, our own concepts of the Iberian and northwestern European Atlantic systems were largely inspired by the work of Blackburn. Despite some important differences, we employed his framework to understand the crisis of colonial slavery and its renewal in the nineteenth century as part of a broader process of national state formation during the Age of Revolution. Blackburn emphasizes the role of actors such as landholders, free persons, and slaves in the institutional construction of slavery on the local and Atlantic levels, a polycentric perspective that organically integrates the different political units of the Americas. Instead of analyzing slave societies as separate units that were external to each other, Blackburn, like Dale Tomich, places them within a unified process of mutual conditionings. The approaches to history of both authors consider class conflicts and the different economic conjunctures as mediators of the long and short durées of social dynamics.

In this book, we have tried to carefully explore the multiple dimensions of the new temporality of nineteenth-century slavery in the specific contexts of the Spanish Empire and the Brazilian monarchy. A brief synthesis of the main characteristics of this new temporality can be outlined based on the

same points used to discuss the Iberian and northwestern European Atlantic
systems, starting with the new dynamics of the transatlantic slave trade. The
expansion of the slave frontier in Brazil and Cuba during the nineteenth
century led to the development of new mechanisms—conditioned by the
operational and institutional dynamics of the illegal slave trade—for the
reproduction of slave labor. The growing concentration of ownership of slave
ventures made the contraband slave trade an easy prey for national anti-
slave trade policies. For this reason, its operations depended on the collabo-
ration of political agents in multiple spheres, from local politics to the central
power. During critical periods for the traffic such as the years between 1831
and 1835 in Brazil or those between 1843 and 1848 in Cuba, the illegal slave
trade operations could be moved to other regions. The continuation of the
slave trade and the stability of these slave societies in the New World also
depended on an articulated strategy to circumvent British diplomatic pressure in the international arena.

The contraband slave trade, in other words, was attuned to the shifting
dynamics of national and international politics, allowing its main carriers to
quickly respond to the rising demand for enslaved Africans in Brazil and
Cuba. The scale of human suffering generated by the business was unprecedented: between 1831 and 1850, Brazil and Cuba received approximately
10 percent of the total number of enslaved Africans carried to the New World
during four centuries. In the twenty years after 1831, the annual rate of slaves
shipped to Brazil and Cuba was five times higher than to all other American
regions between 1500 and 1830.

The combination of the continuous flows of enslaved Africans and similar
dynamics of manumission in Brazil and Cuba generated almost identical
demographic structures in the two countries, with populations composed of
balanced numbers of free white people, free people of color, and slaves. However, the uneven impact of the Haitian Revolution and British emancipation
led to distinct Brazilian and Cuban perceptions of their own societies. These
perceptions shaped not only the social practices and mechanisms of social
control but also the institutional configurations of the Spanish and Brazilian
Empires. The gradual hardening of racial barriers, in the first case, led to the
political exclusion of castas in Cádiz, the suspension of the Constitution
overseas and the subsequent expulsion of Cuban deputies from the Cortes of
1836–1837, the elimination of any debate related to slavery in the public

sphere, and finally the bloody repression of the Escalera Conspiracy. Cuban planters bitterly remembered for many years the submission of an antislavery project to the Cádiz Cortes, while the publication of a review critical of the contraband slave trade by José Antonio Saco led to his exile. A simple antislavery article, such as the one published in *El Corresponsal* in 1840, could easily lead to a hysterical reaction from colonial corporations.

In the case of Brazil, the proslavery strategy inscribed in the Constitution of 1824, which had granted political and civil rights to former slaves, was never questioned by any of the groups participating in the imperial public sphere, not even by the greatest supporters of the demands of pardos and mulattoes. Moreover, except for a few occasions, spaces for debate about slavery in Parliament and the press were not affected by fears of slave revolts. Antislavery proposals in the 1830s may have been encouraged by events such as the Malê revolt, but they did not stimulate uprisings involving slaves and free people of color. These proposals were easily suppressed without the need to censor the press or dissolve Parliament. In sum, Brazil and Cuba protected themselves in different ways from a repetition of the revolutionary events that had taken place in the Atlantic system of northwestern Europe.

These social configurations were accompanied by ideological justifications of slavery, which were by then common in the discursive field of liberal thought. Brazil and Cuba again followed distinct trajectories within a common history. The creation of forms of political representation in a nonrepresentative system in the Hispanic world—such as the coexistence of the facultades omnímodas of captains general in Cuba with the government's consultations with Cuban planters on slavery-related issues—led to the emergence of justifications of slavery based on racial arguments. Assessments of the racial demographics of the island conditioned the application of the basic notions of liberalism at the Spanish Cortes such as private property, political rights, self-government, and a representative state. According to Cuban proslavery defenders, the preservation of the social structure of the colonies depended on the strict subordination of blacks and mulattoes—whether they were free or slaves—to whites. Thus, formal liberal institutions were restricted to the metropolis, where, however, they depended on the systematic exploitation of slaves in the colonial world to become consolidated.

In the Empire of Brazil, the dynamics of liberalism and slavery were different. The definition of citizenship in the Constitution of 1824 supported slavery not only because it brought internal stability to the system by dividing Africans from both blacks and mulattoes born in the national territory, but also because it provided arguments in defense of the expansion of the transatlantic slave trade. Although based on the slave trade, the Constitution offered a nonracial defense of slavery. After arriving in Brazil, the African, barbarous in his continent of origin, would contribute with his physical strength to the material and intellectual progress of the new nation, where he would learn the values of labor and eventually become manumitted. In this process of integration, slaves' children would become, based on their own efforts, Brazilian citizens. This ideological construct was completely based on liberal precepts. The trade in human beings served, among other things, to produce more freedom and inevitably more inequality.

A full analysis of this new historical structure of the Third Atlantic, a new historical *time*, must integrate the United States. The country was the main market for Cuban sugar and Brazilian coffee. It was also the greatest international bulwark against British antislavery pressure, not only because of its diplomatic activities but also for its participation in the transatlantic slave trade. Cuban planters quickly realized the economic and political potential of their northern neighbor, turning annexationism into a permanent feature of the politics of slavery in Cuba, from Juan Bernardo O'Gavan to the annexationist groups of the 1850s. Brazilian slaveholders and statesmen (as well as Cuban planters in the aftermath of the Escalera Conspiracy, for that matter) were in turn inspired by the stability of the US slave system and its basis on the natural reproduction of captives. Saquarema politicians more than once also cited the slaveholding liberalism of the United States as an institutional example for the Empire of Brazil. Not surprisingly, the crisis of the historical structure of nineteenth-century slavery began in the United States after the end of the Civil War.

The chain of events started by abolition in the United States sealed the destiny of slavery in Cuba and Brazil, a story that will have to be told elsewhere. This story must be written from a truly global and totalizing perspective, a perspective that is capable not only of dialectically articulating material and mental spheres but also of integrating the multiple relations between slavery in the Americas and the other forms of labor—coercive or not—that were constantly mobilized as new commodity frontiers were incorporated by the capitalist world-economy.

NOTES

Abbreviations

ACD	*Anais da Câmara dos Deputados do Império do Brasil*
AGMAE	Archivo General del Ministerio de Asuntos Exteriores
AHI	Arquivo Histórico do Itamaraty
AHN	Archivo Histórico Nacional
AS	*Anais do Senado do Império do Brasil*
BNRJ	Biblioteca Nacional do Rio de Janeiro
BPR	Biblioteca del Palacio Real
DAG	*Diário da Assembléia Geral Constituinte e Legislativa do Império do Brasil*
DCG	*Diário das Cortes Gerais e Extraordinárias da Nação Portuguesa*
DSCC	*Diário de Sessiones de las Cortes Constituyentes*
DSC-Cádiz	*Diário de Sesiones de las Cortes de Cádiz*
DSC-Madrid	*Diário de Sesiones de las Cortes de Madrid*

Introduction

1. Barros, "Memória sobre o café," 10. The newspaper was included in the CD-ROM collection edited by Lorelai Kury, *Iluminismo e império no Brasil*. On the Real Consulado de La Habana, see Álvarez Cuartero, *Memorias de la ilustración*, 49–72; and González-Ripoll Navarro, *Cuba, la isla de los ensayos*, 182–92.

2. Ofício reservado, "Al Ministro Residente de S. M. en Rio de Janeiro, Madrid," April 19, 1849, Archivo Histórico Nacional, Legajo 8044/13, no. 10. On the conjuncture of 1848–1849, see Guerra y Sanchéz, *Manual de historia de Cuba*, 454–75.

3. The absence of comparative studies of the social structures of the two spaces was noted in a pioneering article by Röhrig Assunção and Zeuske, "'Race,' Ethnicity and Social Structure," 376–77, and in an unpublished dissertation by Lamonier, "Between Slavery and Free Labour," 4. For recent publications, see Schmidt-Nowara, *Slavery, Freedom, and Abolition*; Cowling, *Conceiving Freedom*; Barcia, *West African Warfare in Bahia and Cuba*; and Graden, *Disease, Resistance, and Lies*.

4. The categories space of experience and horizon of expectation come from Koselleck, *Futures Past*.

5. Temperley, *British Antislavery*, 191–220.

6. On Atlantic history, see the comments by Dale Tomich in "O Atlântico como espaço histórico," 221–40. A recent example of a formal comparison that ignores structural connections between Cuba and Brazil is Bergad, *Comparative Histories of Slavery*. For a critical review of the problems and possibilities of comparisons between Cuba and Brazil, see Zeuske, "Comparing or Interlinking?," 174–82.

7. McMichael, "Incorporating Comparison Within a World-Historical Perspective," 385–97.

Chapter 1

1. Plantation slavery and the transatlantic slave trade—through a triangular commerce that connected them to the metropolitan market—had a fundamental role in the capital accumulation necessary for the Industrial Revolution (thesis 1). The success of the latter in turn led to pressure to end monopolies within the slave trade and, ultimately, to end slavery as a necessary step to expand capitalism (thesis 2). On the political and historiographical context of *Capitalism and Slavery*, see Sheridan, "Eric Williams and *Capitalism and Slavery*," 326; and Patterson, "Slavery," 427.

2. A good overview of the work of Tannenbaum and the debates it generated can be found in de la Fuente, "Slave Law and Claims-Making in Cuba."

3. Tannenbaum, "A Note on the Economic Interpretation of History," 247–53.

4. Marquese, "Estrutura e agência na historiografia da escravidão," 70. The influence of Williams can be clearly seen in Novais, *Portugal e Brasil*.

5. See, respectively, Knight, *Slave Society in Cuba*; and Klein, *Slavery in the Americas*.

6. David Armitage, for example, describes Williams and Tannenbaum as pioneers in the field; Armitage, "Three Concepts of Atlantic History." Bernard Bailyn, on the other hand, completely excludes both from his extremely biased "genealogy" of Atlantic history; Bailyn, *Atlantic History*. For a critique of Bailyn, see Steele, "Bernard Bailyn's American Atlantic," 48–58.

7. Williams, *From Columbus to Castro*. On Williams's conception of linear time, see Tomich, *Through the Prism of Slavery*, 99–101.

8. Besides Bailyn, *Atlantic History*, other overviews of Atlantic history can be found in Horst Pietschmann's introduction to his edited volume, *Atlantic History: History of the Atlantic System*; and Greene and Morgan, *Atlantic History: A Critical Appraisal*. For debates on British antislavery, see Bender, *Antislavery Debate*. Even Robin Blackburn, who treats the New World slave colonies as a whole, does not effectively integrate the cases of Brazil and Cuba in his first analysis of the Atlantic antislavery movement. See chapter 10, "Cuba and Brazil: The Abolitionist Impasse," in Blackburn, *The Overthrow of Colonial Slavery*. In his latest book, however, Blackburn provides a much more encompassing analysis of both spaces; see Blackburn, *The American Crucible*, 251–327, 445–88.

9. On the leyenda negra, see Keen, "The Black Legend Revisited," 703–19. On "Prescott's paradigm," see Kagan, "Prescott's Paradigm," 423–46; and Cañizares-Esguerra, *Puritan Conquistadors*.

10. On the leyenda blanca of Spanish colonialism in the nineteenth century (which is based on the same principles as the twentieth century's luso-tropicalism), see Schmidt-Nowara, *The Conquest of History*, 28–43.

11. Davis, *The Problem of Slavery in Western Culture*, 263. The strongest critiques to Tannenbaum's approach came from Marvin Harris; see Harris, *Patterns of Race in the Americas*. An overview of the debate can be found in de la Fuente, "Slave Law and Claims-Making in Cuba," and, for the specific case of Brazil, in Lara, *Campos da violência*, 97–113.

12. Mintz, "Slavery and Emergent Capitalisms," 27–37. Mintz reviews Elkins, *Slavery: A Problem in American Institutional and Intellectual Life*.

13. Elliott, *Empires of the Atlantic World*.

14. Alejandro de la Fuente has stressed the central role of slave manumissions in the Iberian world. Beside his aforementioned article, see de la Fuente, "Slaves and the Creation of Legal Rights in Cuba," 659–92. For the Brazilian case, see Marquese, "A dinâmica da escravidão no Brasil," 107–23. For a general overview, see Cottrol, *The Long, Lingering Shadow*.

15. Tomich, "O Atlântico como espaço histórico," 221–40.

16. Tomich, *Through the Prism of Slavery*, 56–71.

17. Meinig, *The Shaping of America*, 6–16.

18. Ibid., 51.

19. Mattoso, "1096–1325: Dois séculos de vicissitudes políticas"; and Bernand and Gruzinski, *História do novo mundo*, 68–98.

20. Mattoso, "Antecedentes medievais da expansão portuguesa"; and Magalhães, "Articulações inter-regionais e economias-mundo," 18–9, 308–9.

21. Miskimin, *A Economia do renascimento europeu*, 70–73.

22. Riley, "A apropriação do espaço: Ilhas atlânticas e costa Africana," 137–62; and Bernand and Gruzinski, *História do novo mundo*, 96.

23. See Crosby, *Ecological Imperialism*, esp. chapter 4, "The Fortunate Isles."

24. Alencastro, "A economia política dos descobrimentos," 193-94.

25. Saunders, *História social dos escravos e libertos negros*, 25-62.

26. Spanish merchants only became large-scale slave traders after 1807, as discussed in chapter 2.

27. J. Miller, "O Atlântico escravista," 17. See also Galloway, *The Sugar Cane Industry*, 19-61; and Schwartz, *Segredos internos*, 21-30.

28. On the initial exploitation period of the Caribbean, see Watts, *Las Indias occidentales*, 118-74; on the transatlantic slave trade, see Bowser, *El esclavo africano*, 50-52.

29. On the captaincies and the general government of Brazil, see Holanda, "A instituição do governo geral," 108; on the sugar crisis in Santo Domingo and Puerto Rico, see Moya Pons, *Historia del Caribe*, 49-52.

30. An excellent description of the structural weakness of Iberian metropolitan economies can be found in Stein and Stein, *Silver, Trade, and War*, 3-39.

31. In Arrighi's words, "the central aspect of this pattern is the alternation of epochs of material expansion (MC phases of capital accumulation) with phases of financial rebirth and expansion (CM phases). In phases of material expansion, money capital 'sets in motion' an increasing mass of commodities (including commoditized labor-power and gifts of nature); and in phases of financial expansion, an increasing mass of money capital 'sets itself free' from its commodity form, and accumulation proceeds through financial deals (as in Marx's abridged formula MM). Together, the two epochs or phases constitute a full systemic cycle of accumulation (MCM)." Arrighi, *The Long Twentieth Century*, 6.

32. Ibid., 84.

33. "Territorialist rulers identify power with the extent and populousness of their domains, and conceive of wealth/capital as a means or a by-product of the pursuit of territorial expansion. Capitalist rulers, in contrast, identify power with the extent of their command over scarce resources and consider territorial acquisitions as a means and a by-product of the accumulation of capital." Ibid., 33.

34. According to Arrighi, "the network of commercial and financial intermediation controlled by the Genoese merchant elite *occupied* places, but was not *defined* by the places it occupied. Marketplaces like Antwerp, Seville, and the mobile Bisenzone fairs were all as critical as Genoa itself to the organization of the space-of-flows through which the Genoese diaspora community of merchant bankers controlled the European system of interstatal payments. But none of these places—Genoa included—in itself defined the Genoese system of accumulation. Rather, the system was defined by the flows of precious metals, bills of exchange, contracts with the Imperial government of Spain, and monetary surpluses which linked these places to one another." Ibid., 82-83.

35. On African slavery in Spanish America, see Klein and Vinson, *La esclavitud Africana*, 29-60; Delgado Ribas, "The Slave Trade in the Spanish Empire,"

13–42; and Menard and Schwartz, "Por que a Escravidão Africana?," 11–16. On Portuguese involvement in the slave trade to Spanish America and the Iberian Union, see Alencastro, *O trato dos viventes*, 77–116; on the numbers of the transatlantic slave trade, see the *Slave Voyages* database (www.slavevoyages. org), which provides all the estimates used in this book.

36. Sanchez-Albornoz, "A população da América espanhola colonial," 47–55.

37. Pioneering analyses of this shift can be found in Boxer, *Salvador de Sá*, 262–305; Verger, *Fluxo e refluxo do tráfico de escravos*, 19–52; and, more recently, Alencastro, *O trato dos viventes*, 188–246.

38. On this issue, see the updated manual of Klein and Vinson, *La esclavitud Africana*, 223–31.

39. Ibid., 37–54.

40. For a good synthesis of the vast literature on the subject, see Lockhart and Schwartz, *A América latina na época colonial*, 162–65. See also the excellent essay by Josep M. Fradera, "A cultura de 'castas,'" 77–108.

41. For an overview of the subject, see Russell-Wood, *Escravos e libertos no Brasil colonial*, 191–231. The absence of casta categories in Portuguese America may have been a consequence of the treaties of the fifteenth century, which turned Africa into an exclusive Portuguese zone of expansion. Thus, the descendants of manumitted Africans in the New World were not considered strangers during the process of Portuguese colonization.

42. Our argument here is based on Zeron, *Linha de Fé*.

43. Hanke, *Aristotle and the American Indians*, 14; Pagden, *The Fall of Natural Man*, 27.

44. By reducing slavery to these four characteristics, authors of the so-called Second Scholastic ignored the justification of the African slave trade based on the conversion of pagans. In this sense, they revised and limited the papal bulls of the fifteenth century that only authorized Portuguese subjects to conquer pagan peoples overseas with the objective of converting them. Charles Boxer did not consider the post-tridentine context when he stated that the papal bulls were the "magna carta" of Iberian expansion. See Boxer, *O império marítimo português*, 42–43. In any case, the need to convert pagan peoples continued to be used as a justification for expansion by Iberian powers.

45. H. B. Mattos, "A escravidão moderna nos quadros do império português," 149. On the *gracias al sacar*, see Elliott, *Empires of the Atlantic World*, 171–72.

46. A description of the episode can be found in Andrés-Gallego, *La esclavitud en la América española*, 42–52.

47. On the commercial community of the English Channel, see Meinig, *The Shaping of America*, 46–48. On the English and French attempts during the sixteenth century see, respectively, Pluchon, *Histoire de la colonisation française*, vol. 1; and Appleby, "War, Politics, and Colonization."

48. Braudel, *Civilização material, economia e capitalismo*, vol. 3, 126–36, 189–92.

49. In the words of Immanuel Wallerstein, "the story of the 'second' sixteenth century is the story of how Amsterdam picked up the threads of the dissolving Hapsburg Empire, creating a framework of smooth operation for the world-economy that would enable England and France to begin to emerge as strong states, eventually to have strong 'national economies.'" Wallerstein, *The Modern World-System*, vol. 1, 199.

50. On English and French actions, see, respectively, Pluchon, *Histoire de la colonisation française*, vol. 1; and Appleby, "War, Politics, and Colonization." A good overview of Dutch activities can be found in Boxer, *O império marítimo português*, 115–34.

51. Batie, "Why Sugar?"; Dunn, *Sugar and Slaves*, 3–45; Devèze, *Antilles, Guyanes, la Mer des Caraïbes*, 140–48, 176–78; and Butel, "Le temps des fondations," 53–78.

52. Batie, "Why Sugar?"; Dunn, *Sugar and Slaves*, 49–57; Sheridan, *Sugar and Slavery*, 262–63, 37–40; and Schnakenbourg, "Note sur les origines de l'industrie sucrière," 267–315. See also Butel, "Un nouvel age colonial," 79–80; and Wallerstein, *The Modern World-System*, vol. 2, 75–80.

53. Arrighi, *The Long Twentieth Century*, 127–39.

54. In Arrighi's words: "All variants of mercantilism had one thing in common: they were more or less conscious attempts on the part of territorialist rulers to *imitate* the Dutch, to become themselves capitalist in orientation as the most effective way of attaining their own power objectives. . . . The creation of world-embracing commercial empires, the rerouting of commodity and money flows to entrepôts within one's own control and jurisdiction, the systematic accumulation of pecuniary surpluses in the balance of payments with other domains, were all expressions of this imitative predisposition of territorialist organizations." Arrighi, *The Long Twentieth Century*, 140–41.

55. We tend to agree with Robin Blackburn's argument about the unprecedented nature of Caribbean plantations, a view also shared by Joseph Miller. See Blackburn, *The Making of New World Slavery*, 309, 332–44; and J. Miller, "O Atlântico escravista," 31–36. For a different view, see Schwartz, Review of *The Making of New World Slavery*, 440–41.

56. Klein, *The Atlantic Slave Trade*, 97.

57. Among the vast literature on the asientos established with the French and British after the end of the Iberian Union, see Palmer, *Human Cargoes*. See also Delgado Ribas, "The Slave Trade in the Spanish Empire," 26–30.

58. According to Chouki El Hamel, "historical attitudes toward slavery and its practice were exchanged throughout the Mediterranean basin—one country's practice of slavery was influenced by another's." El Hamel, "'Race,' Slavery and Islam," 49.

59. This point is reinforced by Ira Berlin's discussion about "Atlantic creoles" who were part of the first generations responsible for the colonization of British North America. Berlin, *Generations of Captivity*, 23–49.

60. Sala-Molins, *Le code noir*. See also Ghachem, *The Old Regime and the Haitian Revolution*, 29-76.

61. Joseph Miller has emphasized this point. See, among his publications, "Stratégies de marginalité"; "A Theme in Variations," 169-94; and *The Problem of Slavery as History*.

62. On the autonomy of English colonists in the creation of colonial legislation and the centrality of this for the consolidation of the Caribbean slave system, see Craton, "Property and Propriety," 497-529; and Bush, "The British Constitution." On the specific case of slave laws, see Goveia, "The West Indian Slave Laws," 346-62; and Rugemer, "The Development of Mastery and Race," 429-58.

63. Berlin, *Many Thousands Gone*, 109-17; Blackburn, *The Making of New World Slavery*, 256-58; Jordan, *White over Black*, 71-82; and Hurwitz and Hurwitz, "A Token of Freedom," 423-31.

64. On this distinction, see Breña, *El primer liberalismo español*, 192-95. See also the broader work of Richard Tuck in *Natural Rights Theories*.

65. According to James Farr, the theory of just war was especially used by Locke to attack the supporters of Stuart absolutism. Farr, "So Vile and Miserable an Estate," 263-89.

66. On Montesquieu's climate theory, see Estéve, "La theórie des climats," 62; and Estéve, *Montesquieu, Rousseau, Diderot*, 23-86. On the history of the word "race" from the fifteenth century until its conceptual transformations in the eighteenth and nineteenth centuries, see Conze, "Rasse," 135-61; and Boulle, "La construction du concept de race," 155-75.

67. On the political culture of Atlantic republicanism in British America, see E. Morgan, *American Slavery, American Freedom*, 369-87; on imperial identities, see Greene, "Empire and Identity"; and Greene, "Liberty, Slavery, and the Transformation of British Identity," 1-31.

68. Pagden, "The Struggle for Legitimacy"; and Armitage, *The Ideological Origins of the British Empire*, 61-99.

69. Davis, *The Problem of Slavery in Western Culture*, 215-16; Jordan, *White over Black*, 180-210; Jenergan, "Slavery and Conversion," 504-27; and Klein, "Anglicanism, Catholicism, and the Negro Slave," 295-327.

70. On French imperial ideologies in the seventeenth century, see Pagden, *Señores de todo el mundo*, 193-96. On the Code Noir, see Marquese, *Feitores do corpo, missionários da mente*, 34-35.

71. Cited in Peabody, "A Dangerous Zeal," 80.

72. Blackburn, *The Making of New World Slavery*, 311, 368n94; Emmer, "The Dutch and the Making of the Second Atlantic System," 78.

73. Koselleck, *Futures Past*, 266. Our argument is similar to that made by Richard Morse on other topics. See Morse, *O espelho de Próspero*.

74. Heckscher, *Mercantilism*, 344.

75. On the Spanish arbitristas, see John Elliott's chapter "Self-Perception and

Decline in Early Seventeenth-Century Spain" in Elliott, *Spain and Its World*; on their Portuguese counterparts, see José Luís Cardoso's chapter "Trajetórias do mercantilismo em Portugal: O pensamento econômico na época da Restauração" in Cardoso, *Pensar a economia em Portugal*; and Novais, *Portugal e Brasil*, 129–31, 200–206.

76. Koselleck, *Futures Past*, 28.

77. Stein and Stein, *Silver, Trade, and War*, 20–30; Novais, *Portugal e Brasil*, 133.

78. According to Evaldo Cabral de Mello, "the problem experienced by Portugal during the war against Spain can be summed up in the question: how to preserve independence if national wealth depended on the safety of communication with the South Atlantic? Incapable of ensuring this, the country had to enter into an alliance with one of the great maritime powers." Mello, *O negócio do Brasil*, 178.

79. Excellent discussions of these relations of subordination can be found in Stein and Stein, *Silver, Trade, and War*, 57–94; and in Maxwell, "Hegemonies Old and New," 81. In the words of Fernando Novais, "gradually, and, especially, as ascending powers (Holland, France, England) also competed with each other, the system that emerged in the aftermath of the War of the Spanish Succession (1713) became more evident: Portugal is increasingly attached to the English alliance while Spain depends on French protection, which was guaranteed by the ascension of the Bourbon dynasty to the Spanish throne. This system of alliances allows Portugal and Spain to maintain their respective overseas dominions, symbols of the old hegemony during the entire eighteenth century: the Iberian colonial empires survived based on the support of the two greatest powers, with their permanent rivalry and conflicts." Novais, *Portugal e Brasil*, 18–19.

80. Bethell, *The Cambridge History of Latin America*, vol. 2, 47.

81. The literature on the subject is extensive. For an overview, see the still useful Boxer, *A idade de ouro do Brasil*. For innovative works about the regional impact of mining, see Borrego, *A teia mercantil*; and Carrara, *Minas e currais*.

82. V. N. Pinto, *O ouro brasileiro*, 255–315; José V. Serrão, "O quadro econômico," 74–77, 94–99; and Maxwell, *A devassa da devassa*, 21–28.

83. The recovery of mining in the Andes took place only after the 1740s. See Bakewell, "A mineração na América espanhola colonial," 136–40. On the growing importance of a peripheral region, Venezuela, in the first half of the eighteenth century (based on cocoa production), see Piñero, "The Cacao Economy," 75–100. A good overview of economic growth during this period in Spanish America as a whole can be found in Elliott, *Empires of the Atlantic World*, 255–62.

84. According to Kenneth Maxwell, "there were on average over the decades between 1724–78 about sixty major French commercial houses established in Cádiz. Of the declared value of the Cádiz merchants, moreover, the French merchants accounted for 43 percent and the Spanish merchants only 18 percent.

Until 1789, the French remained the largest foreign colony in Cádiz, always sensitive, like the British factory in Lisbon, to any infringement of their treaty rights." Maxwell, "Hegemonies Old and New," 81–82. For Spanish relations with the powers from northwestern Europe between the Peace of Westphalia and the treaties of Utrecht, see Stein and Stein, *Silver, Trade, and War*, 57–144.

85. Sorhegui D'Mares and de la Fuente, "El surgimiento de la sociedad criolla de Cuba"; Sorhegui D'Mares and de la Fuente, "La organización de la sociedad criolla"; and Moreno Fraginals, *Cuba/España, España/Cuba*, 34–104.

86. Moreno Fraginals, *O engenho*, 1:7–11; Portuondo Zúñiga, "La consolidación de la sociedad criolla," 196–201; and M. García Rodríguez, *La aventura de fundar ingenious*, 29. According to estimates from *Slave Voyages* (www.slavevoyages. org), Spanish America received approximately fifty-five thousand enslaved Africans during this period (over one thousand captives per year for the entire continent). The estimates of the database, as John Elliott notes, are only for the traffic from Africa to the Americas. They do not include the numbers of the active contraband slave trade from the British and French Caribbean to Spanish colonies. In any case, all estimates indicate that the traffic to Spanish America in the first half of the eighteenth century was significantly smaller than the slave trade to Brazil and British and French possessions in the New World. Elliott, *Empires of the Atlantic World*, 459n32.

87. All these transformations are analyzed soundly in Blackburn, *The Making of New World Slavery*, 373–456. On demographics in the Caribbean, see Watts, *Las Indias occidentales*, 359–70; on the first Maroon war in Jamaica, see Craton, *Testing the Chains*, 67–92.

88. On the economies of New England and the Middle Colonies, see McCusker and Menard, *The Economy of British America*, 91–116, 189–208. On North American trade in the Caribbean, see Sheridan, "The Formation of Caribbean Plantation Society," 406–9.

89. Shy, "The American Colonies in War and Revolution," 300–310.

90. On the neo-Roman concept of liberty, see Skinner, *Liberdade antes do liberalismo*, 26–81. Two fascinating and contrasting studies of two British slaveholding families (one resident in England and the other in Virginia) during the American Revolution are S. D. Smith, *Slavery, Family and Gentry Capitalism*; and Isaac, *Landon Carter's Uneasy Kingdom*.

91. Our argument here is based on the interpretation of Jack Greene and, therefore, in contrast to the classic argument of Bernard Bailyn. Greene, *"Empire and Identity"*; and Bailyn, *The Ideological Origins of the American Revolution*. On the centrality of African slavery in the discourses against Britain by patriot slaveholders, see Furstenberg, "Beyond Freedom and Slavery," 1295–330.

92. O'Shaughnessy, *An Empire Divided*.

93. On sugar production and the broader economic development of Saint-Domingue, see Devèze, *Antilles, Guyanes, la Mer des Caraïbes*, 267–75;

Blackburn, *The Making of New World Slavery*, 431–51; and Cauna, *Au temps des isles à sucre*, 13–14. On coffee production, see Trouillot, "Motion in the System," 331–88; Trouillot, "Coffee Planters and Coffee Slaves"; and Debien, *Études antillaises*, 1–137.

94. These two paragraphs are based on the innovative work of John Garrigus, in his *Before Haiti: Race and Citizenship in French Saint-Domingue*. See also Dubois, *Avengers of the New World*, 60–90.

95. Brown, *Moral Capital*, 33–55.

96. Ibid., 106–53. In another work, Brown argues that, for Caribbean slaveholders, "the imperial state emerged after the American Revolution as an almost constant antagonist rather than a reliable ally." Brown, "The Politics of Slavery," 229. See also O'Shaughnessy, *An Empire Divided*, 238–48.

97. Brown, *Moral Capital*, 259–368. See also Davis, *The Problem of Slavery in the Age of Revolution*, 33–34; Drescher, *Capitalism and Antislavery*, 59–67; and Blackburn, *The Overthrow of Colonial Slavery*, 137–46.

98. Brown, *Moral Capital*, 393–450.

99. Davis, *The Problem of Slavery in the Age of Revolution*, 213.

100. Brown, *Moral Capital*, 137–39. See also Fehrenbacher, *The Slaveholding Republic*, 16–18.

101. K. Morgan, "Slavery and the Debate over Ratification," 40.

102. The number of seats allotted to each state in the House of Representatives was determined based on the size of a state's population; in slaveholding states, each slave would be counted as three-fifths of a free person.

103. On the debates about slavery during the Constitutional Convention, see Fehrenbacher, *The Slaveholding Republic*, 28–37; Maltz, "The Idea of the Proslavery Constitution," 37–59; Kaplanoff, "The Federal Convention and the Constitution," 474–75, 478–79; Waldstreicher, *Slavery's Constitution*; and Van Cleve, *A Slaveholder's Union*.

104. K. Morgan, "Slavery and the Debate over Ratification," 59–60; Fehrenbacher, *The Slaveholding Republic*, 38–47; and Maltz, "The Idea of the Proslavery Constitution," 37–38, 57–58.

105. On the impact of the fall of Havana on Spain, see Brading, "A espanha dos Bourbons e seu império americano," 402; on the threats to Rio de Janeiro during the Seven Years' War and the impact of the fall of Havana on Portuguese authorities, see Bicalho, *A cidade e o império*, 60–77. According to Bicalho, the French had already shown how unprotected Rio de Janeiro was half a century earlier.

106. Koselleck, *Futures Past*, 317. On Campomanes, see Campomanes, *Reflexiones sobre el comercio español a Indias*. On the broader context of the imperial thought of Bourbon reformers, see Pagden, *Señores de todo el mundo*, 162–64; Pagden, "Escuchar a Heraclides," 430–35; G. Paquette, *Enlightenment, Governance, and Reform*, 38–45, 106–7, 117–21; G. Paquette, *Enlightened Reform in*

Southern Europe; and Kuethe and Andrien, *The Spanish Atlantic World in the Eighteenth Century*, 231–304.

107. Tornero Tinajero, *Crecimiento económico y transformaciones sociales*, 34–44, 346–57.

108. Campomanes, *Reflexiones sobre el comercio español a Indias*, 207; and Crame, *Discurso político sobre la necesidad de fomentar la Isla de Cuba*, 240. See also Prieto, "Crónica anunciada de una Cuba azucarera," 55–66.

109. Kuethe, *Cuba, 1753–1815*, 68–69. See also Gonzáles-Ripoll Navarro, *Cuba, la isla de los ensayos*.

110. Kuethe, *Cuba, 1753–1815*, 24–77.

111. On all these themes, see Novais, *Portugal e Brasil*, 47–48; Novais, "O reformismo ilustrado luso-brasileiro"; Maxwell, *A devassa da devassa*, 54–56; Adelman, *Sovereignty and Revolution in the Iberian Atlantic*, 13–15, 25–31; and Ana Rosa Cloclet da Silva, *Inventando a nação*, 42–48.

112. Mansuy-Diniz Silva, "Portugal e Brasil," 488–98; and Maxwell, *A devassa da devassa*, 21–53.

113. Mansuy-Diniz Silva, "Portugal e Brasil"; Maxwell, *A devassa da devassa*, 21–53; J. Ribeiro, *Colonização e monopólio no nordeste brasileiro*; and Palacios, *Cultivadores libres*, 112–20.

114. On economic measures in the 1760s in Brazil and Africa, see, respectively, Maxwell, *Marquês de Pombal*, 132–33; and J. Miller, "A economia política do tráfico angolano de escravos," 28–35. On the broader debates about slavery in the Portuguese Empire between 1750 and 1777, see Parron, "A *Nova e Curiosa Relação* (1764)," 92–107. For an example of how abolitionist measures in the metropolis reverberated in Portuguese America without questioning the local slave order, see Luiz Geraldo Silva, "Esperança de liberdade," 107–49.

115. On Cuba, see Kuethe, *Cuba, 1753–1815*, 41–42. On Portuguese America, see Russell-Wood, *Escravos e libertos no Brasil colonial*, 133, 138–39; and Luiz Geraldo Silva, "Negros patriotas," 499–501.

116. Lara, *Fragmentos setecentistas*, 266–69, 279, 284.

117. Sheila de Castro Faria has noted this point. See Faria, "A riqueza dos libertos," 21. Two other criticisms of Lara's interpretation can be found in Guedes, *Egressos do Cativeiro*, 19–27; and M. de S. Soares, *A remissão do cativeiro*, conclusion.

118. Our interpretation here is based on Silveira, "Soberania e luta social," 36; and Silveira, "Acumulando forças," 131–56.

119. Geggus, "The Effects of the American Revolution," 526–27; Wallerstein, *The Modern World-System*, vol. 3, 81–84; and Vovelle, *Breve história da revolução francesa*, 12–13.

120. Debbash, "Au coeur du 'gouvernement des esclaves,'" 43–44; Debien, *Les Esclaves aux Antilles Françaises*, 485–86; Dubois, *Avengers of the New World*, 31; Marquese, *Feitores do corpo, missionários da mente*, 121; Ghachem, *The Old Regime and the Haitian Revolution*, 150–66.

121. On French legislation during the revolutionary period and its connection to events in the Caribbean, see Geggus, "Racial Equality, Slavery, and Colonial Secession," 290–308; Blackburn, *The Overthrow of Colonial Slavery*, 161–264; Dubois, *Avengers of the New World*, 60–90; and Garrigus, *Before Haiti*, 227–63. On the Society of the Friends of the Blacks and its dispute with the Massiac Club, see Dorigny and Gainot, *La Société des Amis des Noirs*; Debien, *Les colons de Saint-Domingue*; and Dubois, *A Colony of Citizens*, 62–73, 98. Finally, on the organization of the slave rebellion itself, see Fick, *The Making of Haiti*, 91–117.

122. A good overview of this process can be found in Dubois, *Avengers of the New World*, 97–170. See also Popkin, *You Are All Free*.

123. Dubois, *A Colony of Citizens*, 279.

124. Ibid., 100–101, 171–78, 277–88; and Spieler, "The Structure of Colonial Rule," 365–408.

125. Dubois, *Avengers of the New World*, 209–79; and Gainot, "Métropole/colonies."

126. The articles by Davis, "Impact of the French and Haitian Revolutions," Drescher, "The Limits of Example," and Blackburn, "The Force of Example," are all found in Geggus, *The Impact of the Haitian Revolution in the Atlantic World*, 4, 11, 17–18 (quotations). The three authors have expanded their arguments in their more recent books: Davis, *The Problem of Slavery in the Age of Emancipation*, 45–81; Drescher, *Abolition: A History of Slavery and Antislavery*, 146–80; and Blackburn, *The American Crucible*, 171–273. Their debate has been restated in Drescher and Emmer, *Who Abolished Slavery?* For a general overview of the impacts of the Haitian Revolution in the longue durée, see Gómez, *Le spectre de la révolution noir*; see also Geggus and Fiering, *The World of the Haitian Revolution*. Finally, for a well-balanced historiographical essay, see Covo, "La révolution haïtienne," 259–88.

127. The interpretation presented by Robin Blackburn in the volume edited by Geggus was further explored in his essay "Haiti, Slavery, and the Age of the Democratic Revolution," 643–74.

128. Blackburn, *The Overthrow of Colonial Slavery*, 300–310; and Duffy, "The French Revolution and British Attitudes," 81–93.

129. For a detailed study of the new dynamics in Demerara's case, see the magisterial book by Emília Viotti da Costa, *Crowns of Glory, Tears of Blood*. For an overview of the connections between the metropolitan abolitionist movement and these revolts, see Matthew, *Caribbean Slave Revolts*.

Chapter 2

1. On the specific historiography about the relationship between slavery and independence, see the first part of Venegas Delgado, "El fantasma de la Revolución Haitiana," 26–29. On the historiography of the periods before and after the

Cuban Revolution, see R. Smith, "Twentieth-Century Cuban Historiography," 44–73; Zanetti Lecuona, "Cuba 1899–1922," 43–52; and Pérez, "In the Service of the Revolution," 79–89.

2. Moreno Fraginals, "Nación o Plantación," 250.

3. Ortiz, *Contrapunteo cubano*; and Pérez de la Riva, "Una isla con dos historias," 189–206. On the common background of these two interpretations, see Schmidt-Nowara, *The Conquest of History*, 100–103.

4. Piqueras, "Leales en época de insurrección," 185–86. See also Opatrný, "El estado-nación o la 'cubanidad,'" 323–26.

5. Maxwell, "A geração de 1790 e a idéia do império luso-brasileiro," 157–207.

6. Dias, *A interiorização da metrópole e outros estudos*, 23.

7. Focusing on the province of Bahia, João José Reis expanded the perspectives of Maxwell and Dias with his pioneering argument about the role of the "black party" in the process of independence. See his essay "O jogo duro do Dois de Julho: O 'Partido Negro' na independência da Bahia." His study has inspired studies about other Brazilian provinces such as Maranhão, Minas Gerais, and Pernambuco. See Röhrig Assunção, "Miguel Bruce e os 'horrores da anarquia' no Maranhão"; Ana Rosa Cloclet da Silva, "Identidades políticas"; and M. J. M. de Carvalho, "Os negros armados pelos brancos e suas independências no Nordeste"; all included in Jancsó, *Independência: História e historiografia*. It is important to note that, in his discussion of Brazilian independence, Robin Blackburn frequently cites the classic works of Maxwell and Dias. See Blackburn, *The Overthrow of Colonial Slavery*, chapter 10. For an overview of the reverberation of news on the Haitian Revolution in Brazil, see Gomes, "Experiências transatlânticas e significados locais," 209–46; and Reis and Gomes, "Repercussions of the Haitian Revolution in Brazil," 284–313.

8. A number of isolated studies about the problem of slavery in Iberian constitutional experiences have been extremely useful for the present investigation. See King, "The Colored Castes and American Representation," 33–64; Fradera, *Gobernar colonias*, 51–69; Chust, *La cuestión nacional americana*, 79–114; J. P. Marques, *Os sons do silêncio*, 157–91; Jaime Rodrigues, *O infame comércio*, 52–55; Jaime Rodrigues, "Liberdade, humanidade e propriedade," 159–67; Grinberg, *O fiador dos brasileiros*, 109–15; Schultz, "La independencia de Brasil"; and Slemian, "Seriam todos cidadãos?" See also Sartorius, *Ever Faithful*, 21–51; and Schmidt-Nowara, "Wilberforce Spanished," 158–75.

9. Galloway, "Agricultural Reform and the Enlightenment," 763–79; and Marquese, *Feitores do corpo, missionários da mente*, 173–92.

10. In the words of Oliveira Mendes, "from the summary of this mercantile and private quasi-history of the Gold Coast, it is possible to see the state of the referred commerce, and the state of misery, in which slavery finds itself, which ordered by itself, and disposed by the invisible Hand of the Omnipotent, who rules everything, seems to be asking that this kind of Commerce with the

purchase and subjection of our equals is forever banished from the surface of the Earth. . . . All observations are in favor that it [i.e., the "negotiation of slaves"] is forever ended, terminated, and proscribed until it is forgotten by the memory of men. All setbacks experienced in the two different epochs, [seem] to have been preludes, that refining it, prognosticating, and asking for its extension in this last state of ruin." Oliveira Mendes, "Discurso preliminar, histórico, introdutivo," 131, 141.

11. Azeredo Coutinho, "Memória sobre o preço do açúcar," 273–80.

12. Oliveira Mendes, "Discurso acadêmico ao programa" (1983), 364–420. Robert Slenes discovered the existence of two versions of Oliveira Mendes's memoir. See Slenes, "African Abrahams, Lucretias and Men of Sorrows," 157–59.

13. Azeredo Coutinho, *Analyse sur le justice du commerce*, "Avertissement de l'éditeur." on the refusal of the academy to publish the piece, see Neves, "Guardar mais silêncio do que falar," 19. For Azeredo Coutinho's proslavery ideology, see Schultz, "Slavery, Empire and Civilization," 98–117.

14. J. P. Marques, *Os sons do silêncio*, 57–64.

15. Lara, *Campos da violência*, 35; and Vallim, "Da sedição dos mulatos à conjuração baiana de 1798," 31.

16. "Carta de Martinho de Mello e Castro," 449–52.

17. Coutinho, "Memória sobre o melhoramento dos domínios de Sua Majestade na América," 47–66. Besides Kenneth Maxwell in his article "A geração de 1790 e a idéia do império luso-brasileiro," other historians have interpreted the "Memória" of dom Rodrigo within the broader context of a crisis of European colonial relations. See Novais, *Portugal e Brasil*, chapter 3; and Lyra, *A utopia do poderoso império*, chapters 1, 2.

18. On the publishing activities of Velloso, who received Coutinho's support, see Curto, *A casa literária do Arco do Cego*.

19. A transcription of the document can be found in Verger, *Fluxo e refluxo do tráfico de escravos*, 113–15.

20. Maxwell, "The Impact of the American Revolution," 538.

21. Jancsó, "Bahia 1798: A hipótese de auxílio francês," 372. See also Jancsó, *Na Bahia, contra o império*, esp. chapter 4.

22. Röhrig Assunção and Zeuske, "'Race,' Ethnicity and Social Structure," 440. Ada Ferrer has studied in depth the impact of the Saint-Domingue Revolution on Cuba. See, among others, her "Cuba en la sombra de Haití," 179–231; and *Freedom's Mirror*.

23. The literature about Arango is extensive. See, especially, Pierson, "Francisco de Arango y Parreño," 451–78; González-Ripoll Navarro, *Cuba, la isla de los ensayos*, 123–94; G. García Rodríguez, "Tradición y modernidad en Arango y Parreño," 1–56; and Piqueras, "Los amigos de Arango en la Corte de Carlos IV" (2009), 151–66.

24. Arango y Parreño, "Primer papel sobre el comercio de negros," in Arango y Parreño, *Obras*, 1:117. All references to Arango's texts cited here come from this edition.

25. Arango y Parreño, "Representación manifestando las ventajas de una absoluta libertad en la introducción de negros, y solicitando se amplie a ocho la prorroga concedida por dos años," 1:131–35; "Papel número 2 que se cita en la representación antecedente," 1:136–37; and "Ofício acompañando copia de la representación sobre la introducción de negros, y corroborándola con razones muy sólidas," 1:138–39. These three documents are from 1791. On the role of political economy in Arango's discourses, see Tomich, "The Wealth of Empire," 4–28.

26. Gomariz, "Francisco de Arango y Parreño," 48.

27. Zeuske, "Comparando el Caribe," 386.

28. Arango y Parreño, "Representación hecha a su majestad con motivo de la sublevación de esclavos en los domínios franceses de la isla de Santo Domingo," 1:141–42. On the Haitian Revolution as a "nonevent," see Trouillot, *Silencing the Past*, 70–107.

29. Arango y Parreño, "Discurso sobre la agricultura de La Habana y medios de fomentarla," 1:152–59.

30. Ibid., 1:165.

31. Arango y Parreño, "Informe que se presentó en 9 de junio de 1796 a la Junta de Gobierno del Real Consulado de Agricultura y Comercio de esta ciudad e isla por los señores don José Manuel de Torrontegui, Sindico Procurador General del Común, y don Francisco de Arango y Parreño, Oidor Honorario de la Audiencia del Distrito y Síndico de dicho Real Consulado, cuando examino la mencionada Real Junta el Reglamento y Arancel de capturas de esclavos cimarrones, y propuso al Rey su reforma," 1:269–71.

32. Halperin Donghi, *Reforma y disolución*, 78–92; and Adelman, *Sovereignty and Revolution in the Iberian Atlantic*, 105.

33. Arango y Parreño, "Comercio de extranjeros amigos y neutrales," 1:294–99.

34. Arango y Parreño, "Comisión de Arango en Santo Domingo," 1:355–61.

35. R. Paquette, "Revolutionary Saint-Domingue," 204–25.

36. In this sense, the Haitian Revolution became a "thinkable event" for Arango in the early 1800s, challenging Michel-Rolph Trouillot's generalizations about contemporary political thought. Trouillot, *Silencing the Past*, 70–107.

37. Zermeño Padilla, "História, Experiência e Modernidade," 7.

38. Davis, *The Problem of Slavery in the Age of Revolution*, 285–342; and Blackburn, *The Overthrow of Colonial Slavery*, chapter 8.

39. Nearly every historian who has studied the Cádiz Cortes has analyzed the problems related to the occupation of Spain by Napoleonic troops and the difficulties generated by the war. For an example from that vast literature, see the classic work by Miguel Artola, *Espanha de Fernando VII*.

40. Arango y Parreño, "Documentos de que hasta ahora se compone el expediente que principiaron las Cortes extraordinarias sobre el tráfico y esclavitud de los negros," 2:85–86.

41. Davis, *The Problem of Slavery in the Age of Revolution*, 23–31; and Blackburn, *The Overthrow of Colonial Slavery*, 117–26.

42. *Diário de Sesiones de las Cortes de Cádiz* (henceforth DSC-Cádiz), April 1, 1811.

43. DSC-Cádiz, April 2, 1811; reproduced in Arango y Parreño, "Documentos de que hasta ahora se compone el expediente," 2:87.

44. Chust, *La cuestión nacional americana*, 79–114.

45. Arango y Parreño, "Documentos de que hasta ahora se compone el expediente," 2:88–89.

46. Ibid., 2:90–91.

47. Rieu-Millan, *Los diputados americanos*, 171. Someruelos's letter is reproduced in Saco, *Historia de la esclavitud*, 5:63; and also in Arango y Parreño, "Documentos de que hasta ahora se compone el expediente," 2:92–93. On the links between the actions of Jáuregui in Cádiz and the letter of Someruelos, see Piqueras, "Leales en época de insurrección," 194–95. On the Cuban deputation in Cádiz, see Piqueras, "La política de los intereses en Cuba," 465–83.

48. In order to demonstrate his knowledge about the Atlantic configuration, Arango attached a number of texts about these experiences to his memorial, such as a document prohibiting the importation of slaves into the United States; Article 7 of the constitution of the state of Kentucky; a report from the British Majesty's commissioners on trade and foreign colonies; and Article 10 of the 1810 Treaty of Friendship and Alliance between Great Britain and Portugal. See Arango y Parreño, "Documentos de que hasta ahora se compone el expediente," 2:53–59.

49. Arango y Parreño, "Representación de la Ciudad de La Habana a las Cortes Españolas," 2:48.

50. For a more detailed analysis of the actions of Jáuregui during these sessions, see Piqueras, "Leales en época de insurrección," 192–98. The relations between Arango and Jáuregui seem to have included more than the common proslavery nature of their proposals. According to Manuel Moreno Fraginals, Jáuregui frequently worked as a business agent for Arango. See Moreno Fraginals, *O engenho*, 1:132.

51. "Article 22: Spaniards whose family origins are connected to Africa shall not normally be citizens but may accede to citizenship through special merit, talent, or virtuous conduct in the service of the *Patria*. The *Cortes* will grant a letter of citizenship to such persons on condition that they be legitimate sons of freeborn parents and married to freeborn women, residing in Spanish dominions and exercising a useful profession or occupation with sufficient capital of their own. . . . Title 3: On the Cortes. Chapter 1: On the Composition of the Cortes. Article 27: The *Cortes* is the gathering of all representatives of the

Nation, chosen by the citizens of Spanish dominions in the manner specified below. Article 28: The basis of national representation is the same in both hemispheres. Article 29: Representation will be calculated on the basis of the native-born population whose descent and origin lies solely in Spanish dominions, with the addition of those who hold letters of citizenship granted by the *Cortes* and the children of foreigners as described in Article 21." "Cádiz Constitution of 1812," 100–101.

52. The problems of this first American inclusion are discussed in François-Xavier Guerra's chapter "Dos anos cruciales (1808–1809)," in Guerra, *Modernidad e independencias*, 115–48.

53. Anna, "A Independência do México e da América central"; and Bushnell, "A Independência da América do Sul Espanhola."

54. The manifesto can be found in Chust, *La cuestión nacional americana*, 87.

55. DSC-Cádiz, September 4–14, 1811.

56. Chust, "Nación y federación." See also Herzog, "Communities Becoming a Nation," 156–63.

57. Chust, "Nación y federación."

58. DSC-Cádiz, September 25, 1811.

59. These numbers come from Instituto de Historia de Cuba, *Historia de Cuba*, 466.

60. Kuethe, *Cuba, 1753–1815*, 123–26.

61. Arango y Parreño, "Discurso sobre la agricultura de La Habana y medios de fomentarla," 1:171.

62. On this issue, see the excellent book by Matt D. Childs, *The 1812 Aponte Rebellion in Cuba and the Struggle against Atlantic Slavery*, 17, 61, 68–69, 72, 89–91. See also Kuethe, *Cuba, 1753–1815*, 166–67; and Röhrig Assunção and Zeuske, "'Race,' Ethnicity and Social Structure," 395.

63. See Lasso, "A Republican Myth of Racial Harmony," 43–63; and Lasso, "Race War and Nation in Caribbean Gran Colombia," 336–61.

64. Childs, *The 1812 Aponte Rebellion*, 147.

65. These positions can be found, respectively, in DSC-Cádiz, June 13, 1812, and DSC-Cádiz, September 9, 1812.

66. Alexandre, *Os sentidos do império*, part 3.

67. "Tratado de 19 de fevereiro de 1810." See "Legislação sobre escravos africanos na América portuguesa."

68. J. P. Marques, *Os sons do silêncio*, 57.

69. "In Great Britain," Coutinho argued, "the majority of the British Parliament had to fight for more than twenty years before obtaining from the opposition the abolition of the slave trade. Now, even though an exuberant population fills the territory (small) of the islands (West Indies), it chooses to insist that His Royal Highness of Portugal must suddenly abolish a trade which alone can provide the needed hands for the mines and the fields of Brazil. It is obvious

that, even with a half-century, His Royal Highness could not end this sad but necessary trade in Brazil, as he would very much wish, if it were compatible with the public good and the existence of these peoples. Such a result may only be obtained slowly and progressively, and not at all by force, a procedure which the British government seems to wish to adopt, which irritates without bringing about any good. The unjust capture of Portuguese vessels makes His Royal Highness fear that the Portuguese people and merchants have reached a point of irritation such that it would become difficult for His Royal Highness to suppress manifestations without there resulting some reprisals against English properties in Brazil, which would cause great sorrow to His Royal Highness. All this could in this way ruin in an instant the constant efforts of His Royal Highness to lay the permanent foundation for perpetual alliance and Friendship between the two Nations. The consequences from this would be the most harmful for the success of the battle waged against the common enemy." Arquivo do Estado da Bahia, códice 112, fólio 522; cited in Verger, *Trade Relations Between the Bight of Benin and Bahia*, 258.

70. On *Idade d'Ouro do Brasil*, see the article of November 1812 published in issue 48 and transcribed in Maria Beatriz Nizza da Silva, *A primeira gazeta da Bahia*, 72–73; on proslavery articles in *O Investigador Português em Inglaterra* in 1813, see Alexandre, "O império luso-brasileiro," 401–2; on the clean version of Oliveira Mendes, see Oliveira Mendes, "Discurso acadêmico ao programa," 7–50; and on "Alvará com força de lei de 24 de novembro de 1813," see its reproduction in "Legislação sobre escravos africanos na América portuguesa," 403–8.

71. On the policies implemented by the Duke of Palmela, António de Saldanha da Gama, and Joaquim Lobo da Silveira in the name of Portugal during the Congress of Vienna, see Alexandre, *Os sentidos do império*, part 3, chapters 3, 4; and J. P. Marques, *Os sons do silêncio*, 95–112.

72. Bethell, *A abolição do comércio brasileiro de escravos*, 34; and Alexandre, *Os sentidos do império*, 318. On the slave trade in the South Atlantic at the turn of the nineteenth century, see Florentino, *Em costas negras*.

73. Murray, *Odious Commerce*, 54–56.

74. Our analysis here is based on Santos, "A convenção de 1817."

75. Ofícios reservados, London to Rio de Janeiro, October 8, 1817, Arquivo Histórico do Itamaraty (henceforth AHI), códice 198/03/01.

76. This was the immediate context of the publication in book form of "Documentos de que hasta ahora se compone el expediente que principiaron las Cortes extraordinarias sobre el tráfico y esclavitud de los negros." See Corwin, *Spain and the Abolition of Slavery in Cuba*, 25; and Murray, *Odious Commerce*, 34. On the connections between the Cuban slaveholding elite and the restoration of Fernando VII, see Saco, *Historia de la esclavitud*, 5:78–79; Moreno Fraginals, *Cuba/España, España/Cuba*, 162; and Guerra y Sanchéz, *Manual de historia de Cuba*, 244.

77. On the decree regarding Cuban forests, see Moreno Fraginals, *O engenho*, 1:199–208; and Funes Monzote, *De bosque a sabana*, 201–12. On the other decrees, see Guerra y Sanchéz, *Manual de historia de Cuba*, 251–52; Navarro, *De los domínios del rey*, 153–90; and Moreno Fraginals, *Cuba/España, España/Cuba*, 209 (quotation).

78. On imperial finances, see Fradera, *Colonias para después de un imperio*, 25–54. See also Marichal, *Bankruptcy of Empire*, 249–55.

79. Murray, *Odious Commerce*, 56–69.

80. Arango y Parreño, "Voto particular de varios Consejeros de Indias sobre la abolición del tráfico de esclavos," February 15, 1816, 2:126–32.

81. Arango y Parreño, "Ideas sobre los medios de estabelecer el libre comercio de Cuba y de realizar un emprestimo de veinte millones de pesos," August 25, 1816, 2:143–55.

82. "Representación del consulado de La Habana de 21 de octubre de 1818," 131–38.

83. Murray, *Odious Commerce*, 85.

84. See the letters from Madrid to Rio de Janeiro of January 25, February 5, and December 19, 1817, AHI, códice 338/2/11.

85. Pimenta, *Brasil y las independencias de Hispanoamérica*, 13–29.

86. Blanchard, *Under the Flags of Freedom*; and Piqueras, "El mundo reducido a una isla," 319–42.

87. Manuel Moreno Fraginals sums up the issue: "with Riego's Revolution (1820), the new martyrdom of the plantocracy began." Moreno Fraginals, *Cuba/España, España/Cuba*, 209.

88. Guatemala sent six deputies from 1813 to 1814, two in 1820, and six in 1821; Lima sent, respectively, twenty, five, and five; Venezuela, three, two, and four; Cuba, four, two, and four; Buenos Aires, five, three, and three; the Philippines, none, two, and two; Santa Fé de Bogotá, none, two, and two; Chile, one, two, and two; Santo Domingo, one, one, and one; Puerto Rico, one, one, and one; Nicarágua, one, none, and one; and Panamá, four, none, and one. See Medina Plana, *Soberania, monarquia y representación*, 76.

89. Frasquet, *Las caras del águila*. The author analyzes the autonomist proposals presented by representatives from New Spain and the influence of these proposals on the formation of the Mexican national state.

90. *Diário de Sesiones de las Cortes de Madrid, 1820–1823* (henceforth DSC-Madrid), July 5, 1820.

91. DSC-Madrid, November 3, 1820.

92. DSC-Madrid, February 1, 1821.

93. DSC-Madrid, March 23, 1821, 640.

94. Wellesley's pressure on Toreno is described in Murray, *Odious Commerce*, 82–83. See also Corwin, *Spain and the Abolition of Slavery in Cuba*, 36, and Torres-Cuevas, "De la ilustración reformista," 335–42.

95. See "Capítulo séptimo de las instrucciones de la diputación provincial de La Habana," 146–47, related to the slave trade.

96. O'Gavan, *Observaciones sobre la suerte de los negros del Africa*, 4. A transcription of this document can also be found in Torres-Cuevas and Reyes, *Esclavitud y sociedad*, 139–46.

97. O'Gavan, *Observaciones sobre la suerte de los negros del Africa*, 4.

98. Ibid., 9. In these comparisons, O'Gavan used proslavery arguments similar to those developed by English, French, and Portuguese authors at the turn of the nineteenth century. See, for example, Edwards, *The History, Civil and Commercial, of the British Colonies*; Moreau de Saint-Méry, *Description topographique, physique, civile, politique et historique*; and José Joaquim da Cunha de Azeredo Coutinho's memoir, especially the extended version of 1808: "Análise sobre a justiça do comércio do resgate dos escravos da costa da África."

99. O'Gavan, *Observaciones sobre la suerte de los negros del Africa*, 11–12.

100. On annexationist proposals, see Guerra y Sanchéz, *Manual de historia de Cuba*, 205–33. See also Torres-Cuevas, "De la ilustración reformista," 332; and Murray, "The Slave Trade, Slavery and Cuban Independence," 114–18.

101. Murray, *Odious Commerce*, 83, explores the episode based on the British diplomatic records; the best analysis of the entire episode can be found in the introduction written by José Antonio Piqueras for the edited volume *Félix Varela y la prosperidad de la pátria criolla*; see Piqueras, "De español americano a patriota cubano," 48–50.

102. On the political process in Cuba between 1820 and 1823, see Guerra y Sanchéz, *Manual de historia de Cuba*, 258–90; Torres-Cuevas, "De la ilustración reformista" 335–40; Moreno Fraginals, *Cuba/España, España/Cuba*, 209–12, Murray, "The Slave Trade, Slavery and Cuban Independence," 115–16; Fradera, *Colonias para después de un imperio*, 130–32; Venegas Delgado, "El fantasma de la Revolución Haitiana"; Piqueras, "El mundo reducido a una isla"; Hernández González, "El liberalismo criollo cubano en el Trienio Liberal," 219–22; and Piqueras, "De español americano a patriota cubano," 43–45.

103. Varela's proposal is reproduced in Saco, *Historia de la esclavitud*, 5:158–75; see also de la Torre, "Posiciones y actitudes en torno a la esclavitud," 80–81.

104. Piqueras, "De español americano a patriota cubano," 46.

105. Arango y Parreño, "Reflexiones de un habanero sobre la independencia de esta isla," 2:184–208.

106. Alexandre, *Os sentidos do império*, part 5, chapter 1; and Berbel, *A nação como artefato*, chapter 1.

107. The *Bases da constituição política da monarquia portuguesa* was passed on March 9, 1821. This short text is divided into two sections: the first a declaration of rights and the second a list of general definitions of the political and constitutional foundations of the state. Article 16 of Section 2 defined "the Portuguese nation" as "the union of all Portuguese from both hemispheres," without

making reference to citizenship. A single reference to the electoral process can be found in Article 21: "Only the Nation can make its Constitution or fundamental law, through its legitimately elected representatives. This fundamental law will for now be mandatory only for the Portuguese resident in the Kingdoms of Portugal and the Algarves, which are legally represented in the present Cortes. It will be extended to those residing in the other three parts of the world as soon as their legitimate representatives declare that this is their will." See Joel Serrão, *Liberalismo, socialismo, republicanismo.*

108. The governor of Minas Gerais, Manuel de Portugal e Castro, noted the dangers of applying the Cádiz Constitution in Portuguese America after learning about the electoral terms of the Lisbon Cortes. If the articles of the 1812 Constitution were, in fact, applied in the provinces of Brazil, "it would be necessary to understand that *pardos* or *crioulos* of Portuguese and African descent would not be part of the National representation." This could threaten "public safety with dangerous disturbances," since it would affect the level of economic, social, and political integration of the pardo population in Brazil. This was an argument similar to that used by Brazilian deputies in Lisbon and Rio de Janeiro to defend the extension of citizenship rights to former slaves. The comments of Portugal e Castro are analyzed in Ana Rosa Cloclet da Silva, "Identidades políticas," 548–49.

109. *Diário das Cortes Gerais e Extraordinárias da Nação Portuguesa de 1821 e 1822* (henceforth DCG), August 2, 1821. A copy can be found at the Biblioteca Nacional de Lisboa and online at http://debates.parlamento.pt.

110. Andrada e Silva, *Escritos políticos*, 18.

111. On this defense and its impact, see Berbel, *A nação como artefato*, 127–67.

112. According to Antônio Carlos, "Brazil cannot fear the competition of other nations in the production of sugar and other crops. . . . Although humanity cries, the labor of slaves is cheap because of their small consumption." DCG, April 27, 1822. With this statement, he turned Adam Smith's argument (that the only interest of the slave was to eat as much and to labor as little as possible) upside down. On the importance of Adam Smith to the antislavery ideas of José Bonifácio, see A. P. Rocha, "Idéias antiescravistas da ilustração européia." Antônio Carlos also dismissed an eventual international competition based on free labor: "And the same can be said of Spain and English America. Could the sugar from Havana eventually rival ours . . . ? There is nothing to fear despite their cheap prices, their inferiority is sufficient to calm us down. . . . Although this labor is performed by slaves in Havana, the price of their labor is so high, and so small is the price of their freedom, that they can not compete with us." The clear reference here is to the bilateral slave trade between Africa and Brazil, which made Brazilian production more competitive than its Cuban counterpart.

113. The initial proposal of the Paulistas for the defense of the Kingdom of Brazil

did not mention the autonomy of provinces, while Bahian deputies feared the concentration of power in Rio de Janeiro. The Paulistas incorporated this request in their program, proposing the establishment of two administrative centers for the kingdom and the convocation of a constituent assembly to address the demands from the inhabitants of America.

114. DCG, March 18, 1822.

115. Ibid.

116. J. P. Marques, *Os sons do silêncio*, 160. On the issue of slavery in other writings of Borges de Barros, see Alcides, "O lado B do neoclassicismo luso-brasileiro," 128–33.

117. DCG, April 17, 1822.

118. A similar argument was presented by Custodio Gonçalves Ledo from Rio de Janeiro: "There are many freedmen in Brazil who are of great interest to society today, and are extremely diligent, and many have families; for this reason it would be a great injustice to deprive these citizens from voting, and I dare to say that it would increase the evils of slavery." DCG, April 17, 1822.

119. Ibid.

120. DCG, July 22, 1822.

121. Ibid.

122. On this specificity of Portuguese constitutions, see Ana Cristina Nogueira da Silva, "A cidadania nos trópicos."

123. DCG, August 13, 1822.

124. Ibid.

125. Ibid.

126. Ibid.

127. Ibid.

128. H. B. Mattos, *Escravidão e cidadania*, 32–33.

129. "Projeto de constituição para o império do Brasil," 206.

130. *Diário da Assembléia Geral Constituinte e Legislativa do Império do Brasil, 1823* (henceforth DAG), September 23, 1823, 3:90.

131. DAG, September 23, 1823, 91.

132. DAG, September 24, 1823, 105.

133. The speech of the Bahian representative Francisco Carneiro de Campos is significant in this respect: "The slaves and the foreigners will also be able to consider themselves members in the sense of this Chapter? Most certainly not; they enter the society of men, but not the society of men who enjoy the rights of the city according to the Constitution. Our intention is only to determine who are the Brazilian Citizens, and having understood who they are, the others could be simply called Brazilians, to be born in this country, such as slaves, *crioulos*, Indians, etc., but the Constitution does not consider them, because they are not part of the social pact: they live in civil society, but are rigorously not part of it." DAG, September 24, 1823, 106.

134. Jancsó and Pimenta, "Peças de um mosaico"; and G. S. Ribeiro, *A liberdade em construção.*
135. DAG, September 27, 1823, 130.
136. Ibid., 133.
137. Ibid.
138. Andrada e Silva, *Escritos políticos*, 18 (text of the *Instruções*); and Andrada e Silva, "Representação à Assembléia Geral Constituinte e Legislativa." On the antislavery ideas of Bonifácio, see, among a vast literature, Ana Rosa Cloclet da Silva, *Construção da nação e escravidão*; and A. P. Rocha, "Idéias antiescravistas da ilustração européia."
139. Bethell, *A abolição do comércio brasileiro de escravos*, 66–69.
140. "Projeto de constituição para o império do Brasil," 235.
141. DAG, September 30, 1823, 134–35. The rhetorical use of the Saint-Domingue example by defenders of the gradual emancipation of slaves was very common in the British abolitionist movement from the mid-1790s to 1823; in this sense, Silva Lisboa seems to have been directly inspired by this tendency of Atlantic abolitionism. See A. P. Rocha, *A economia política na sociedade escravista.*
142. In the words of Maciel da Costa, "Let's not be more philanthropic than the Americans of the North are to Africans: they try, as we know, to end slavery, but do not want anything from them to the affairs of American society, instead they want to get rid of them and this is their objective. And in this case their repugnance reaches a level that they do not grant political rights, nor jobs to the free men of color, and in this they are unreasonable while we have an advantage." DAG, September 30, 1823, 136–37.
143. Ibid., 138.
144. On the proslavery thought of Maciel da Costa, see Marquese, "Escravismo e independência," 809–27.
145. On these two episodes, see the still useful José Honório Rodrigues, *Brasil e África*, 1:133–45.
146. Waddell, "International Politics and Latin American Independence," 217.
147. On the support of French diplomacy in Verona (by the well-known writer François-René de Chateaubriand) toward the Spanish contraband slave trade, see W. P. Costa, "Entre Viena e Verona."
148. Alencastro, "La traite négrière," 395–419. See also Santos, "No calidoscópio da diplomacia."
149. *Inventário analítico do arquivo da Assembléia Geral*, 96.
150. References to the secret session of 1823 were made by José Clemente Pereira, José Custódio Dias, and Francisco de Paula Souza e Melo on July 4, 1827, but none of them revealed the deadline established by the constituent assembly. *Anais da Câmara dos Deputados do Império do Brasil* (henceforth ACD), July 4, 1827, 1:43, 49. In the 1840s, Manuel Joaquim Carneiro da Cunha also referred to the secret session of 1823, declaring that he had requested it and that he voted

against the delegation of negotiating powers to the executive. ACD, February 8, 1843, 1:590. The four-year deadline is mentioned in a letter from the consul general in Rio de Janeiro, Henry Chamberlain, to George Canning in October 1823. See Bethell, *A abolição do comércio brasileiro de escravos*, 69. Fears of the opposition to the end of the slave traffic were part of the unsuccessful negotiations for the convention of 1825.

151. Alencastro, "Vida privada e ordem privada," 17.
152. Bethell, *A abolição do comércio brasileiro de escravos*, 72; and José Honório Rodrigues, *Brasil e África*, 1:147.
153. Pimenta, "O Brasil e a América espanhola."
154. Tomich, *Through the Prism of Slavery*, 56–71, 75–94.
155. An explanation of this divergence can be found in Röhrig Assunção and Zeuske, "'Race,' Ethnicity and Social Structure," 397.
156. Finley, "Slavery," 13:307–13.
157. Mintz, *O poder amargo do açúcar*, 89–116.
158. Ferrer, "Speaking of Haiti," 229.
159. On the political demands of these groups, see Silveira, "Soberania e luta social," 36; and Silveira, "Acumulando forças," 131–56. On 1798, see Jancsó, "Bahia 1798: A hipótese de auxílio francês"; and Jancsó, *Na Bahia, contra o império*. On the dynamics of manumission, see Rafael de Bivar Marquese, "A dinâmica da escravidão no Brasil," 107–23. The geographic reasons behind the different impact of the Haitian Revolution on Cuba and Brazil show the distinction made by Reinhart Koselleck between "metahistorical spatial conditions and historical spaces of human organization." Koselleck, *Los estratos del tiempo*, 101.
160. The exception to this blockade was the intense circulation of people between the northern frontier of Portuguese America and French Guiana—although the latter was a somewhat unimportant colony within the French Empire, relatively distant from the events in Saint-Domingue. On Grão Pará, see Gomes, "Experiências transatlânticas e significados locais," 216–21. On the notices of Haiti in the Joanine Court at Rio de Janeiro, see Schultz, *Versalhes tropical*, 192–93.
161. See Reis and Gomes, "Repercussions of the Haitian Revolution in Brazil," 291.
162. This is the argument, for example, that has been made by Luiz Geraldo Silva, "Negros y pardos en la era de las independencias," 19. We would like to thank the author for generously sharing his work with us.
163. DAG, September 23, 1823, 93.
164. Our interpretation, therefore, is different from the one offered by Silvia Hunold Lara. In her words: "That the independence process passed over all these tensions [related to the 'structuring presence of slavery and the disorganizing emergence of freed blacks and mulattoes'] perhaps indicates how delicate the issue was. Preferring accommodation and compromise with the metropolis, local elites many times reinforced the ties to the royal court, choosing to ignore

important social and political questions—from the continuity of slavery to the social insertion of *pardos* and free blacks and freedmen." Lara, *Fragmentos Setecentistas*, 284–85.

Chapter 3

1. Data for world production of coffee can be found in Clarence-Smith and Topik, *The Global Coffee Economy*, 428–37. For sugar production, see Moreno Fraginals, *O engenho*, 3:347. Also see Marquese and Tomich, "O Vale do Paraíba escravista," 339–87.

2. Bethell, *A abolição do comércio brasileiro de escravos*, 38–70; for the Spanish case, see Murray, *Odious Commerce*, 86. For a recent comparison, see Graden, *Disease, Resistance, and Lies*. On the slave trade and national unity, see Luiz Felipe de Alencastro, "La traite négrière," 395–419.

3. Bill of Clemente Pereira, ACD, May 19, 1826, 85; and the report from the commission, ACD, June 8 and 15, 1826, 79, 149. These documents can be found at www.camara.gov.br/publicações. For the whole debate, see Parron, *A política da escravidão no império do Brasil*, 64–80; and Scanavini, "Embates e embustes," 167–209.

4. See the introduction to the treaty written by the Marquis of Queluz in ACD, May 22, 1827, 124. One day earlier, on May 21, Queluz had participated in a ninety-minute secret session with the chamber, probably to discuss the treaty and its publication in newspapers the following day. The Viscount of Cairu confirmed in the Senate that the secret session was related to the treaty. See *Anais do Senado do Império do Brasil* (henceforth AS), July 27, 1827, 71; see also ACD, May 19 and 21, 1827, 137, 142.

5. ACD, July 2, 1827, 10–11.

6. ACD, August 10, 1826, 103. On the life of Cunha Matos, see G. Soares, *Cunha Matos*; and José Honório Rodrigues, "Nota preliminar," 7–21. References to Cunha Matos's works can be found in Blake, *Diccionario bibliographico brazileiro*, 5:112–14; see also Cunha Matos, "Memória história sobre a população," 102–11; and Cunha Matos, "Relatório apresentado ao conselho administrativo," 344–64. Besides *Compêndio histórico*, Cunha Matos's *Corografia história da província de Minas Gerais* (1837) has also been recently edited.

7. ACD, July 2, 1827, 11–18.

8. ACD, July 3, 1827, 21, 26, 28. Otávio Tarquínio de Souza wrote a biography of Vasconcelos, *História dos fundadores do Império do Brasil: Bernardo Pereira de Vasconcelos*.

9. *Sustentação dos votos dos deputados Raimundo José da Cunha Matos e Luiz Augusto May*. In a letter to Cunha Matos, May revealed that "an issue of such immediate and lively interest, or with so serious consequences, has never

been treated in Brazil until today." The separate publication of his speeches showed to Brazil and to his constituents in Minas Gerais that he attempted "with all [his] strength and with all . . . resources to eliminate from Brazil the evils of political impatience," which were caused by charlatans. Pedro Plancher-Seignot, Pedro I's publisher, added that the opinions in favor of the traffic were "absurd and dangerous."

10. ACD, June 4, 1827, 50.

11. ACD, July 29, 1826, 366.

12. ACD, August 27, 1827, 241.

13. See Vergueiro's speech in ACD, August 20, 1827, 165; and that of Lino Coutinho in ACD, May 13, 1828, 62–63.

14. ACD, May 8, 1830, 89.

15. Prado, *História econômica do Brasil*, 157; E. V. da Costa, *Da monarquia à república*, 282; J. M. de Carvalho, *A construção da ordem*, 294; Moura, *Dicionário da escravidão negra*, 240–41, s.v. "lei para inglês ver"; and Needell, *The Party of Order*, 120.

16. See the full treaty in A. P. Pinto, *Apontamentos para o direito internacional*, 1:344; the 1831 law can be found in Moura, *Dicionário da escravidão negra*, 18–19.

17. AS, June 16, 1831, 378, 379; see also the session of June 21, 1831, 409. Considering the interval between September 1830 and June 1831, it seems likely that the real number of enslaved Africans introduced into the country had reached approximately twenty thousand. See the estimates at Voyages: The Trans-Atlantic Slave Trade Database. On the seasonality of the slave trade, see Florentino, *Em costas negras*, 60.

18. AS, June 16, 1831, 377–78, and June 21, 1831, 410. See also Mamigonian, "To Be a Liberated African in Brazil," 24; and Chalhoub, *A força da escravidão*.

19. ACD, June 4, 1832, 71–72; ACD, May 10, 1833, 116; AS, June 25, 1834, 316; and *Jornal do Comércio*, February 29, 1832, cited in El Youssef, *O problema da escravidão em periódicos brasileiros*, 19. See also the citations of ministerial reports in Conrad, *Tumbeiros*, 93–103. For the broader context of the public debate on the press, see El Youssef, "Imprensa e escravidão."

20. *Declaração de Diogo Antônio Feijó em nome do imperador dirigida ao presidente da Província da Bahia que não se processe mais o tráfico de pretos africanos, para que não se realize a compra de tais escravos e outras questões relativas à proibição*, Rio de Janeiro, April 17, 1832. Cited in Conrad, *Tumbeiros*, 101.

21. Aureliano de Souza e Oliveira Coutinho to the Justice of the Peace of the town of Vassouras, December 5, 1833. Cited in Mamigonian, "To Be a Liberated African," 71; part of the letter is also reproduced in Gerson, *A escravidão no império*, 50.

22. Andrade, "Rebelião escrava na comarca do Rio das Mortes," 45–82; and Reis, *Rebelião escrava no Brasil*, 19–43, 125–57, 421–50.

23. Cited in Andrade, "Rebelião escrava na comarca do Rio das Mortes," 79.

24. ACD, June 11, 1833, 241; August 27, 1833, 193; September 3, 1833, 218–19; and September 16, 1833, 256.

25. For an analysis of newspaper articles related to the Malê revolt, see El Youssef, *O problema da escravidão em periódicos brasileiros*, 29–35. See also "Propostas da Câmara da vila de Itaparica à Assembléia Legislativa Provincial," February 28, 1835, cited in Reis, *Rebelião escrava no Brasil*, 529; part of the petition from Bahia can be found in Moura, *Dicionário da escravidão negra*, 20, s.v. "Africanos libertos, Expulsão dos."

26. In 1834, the judge João Antônio Rodrigues de Carvalho managed to pass two bills in the Senate, which were then sent to the Chamber of Deputies. One aimed at regulating the sales of slaves in order to prevent the introduction of slaves after 1831; the other permitted the destruction of vessels employed in the traffic. See ACD, May 6 and 7, 1834, 20–25; July 20, 1834, 91–92; July 23, 1834, 105; and July 24, 1834, 109. The proposals of Ferreira França can be found in ACD, June 6, 1835, 154, 156; and May 7, 1836, 24; Cordeiro's proposal can be found in ACD, June 27, 1835, 216; and the ambitious plan of Silva Manso can be found in ACD, August 29, 1835, 218–25. Finally, the plans of Henriques de Rezende and Ribeiro de Andrada can be found, respectively, in ACD, July 9, 1836, 55; and ACD, July 26, 1836, 115.

27. Diogo Antônio Feijó, "Do tráfico dos pretos africanos," *O Justiceiro*, no. 8 (December 25, 1834). The article can also be found in Feijó, *Diogo Antônio Feijó*, 151–54.

28. Montezuma's measures were debated in the Chamber of Deputies. See ACD, May 30, 1838, 248. See also the "Artigos Adicionais" in A. P. Pinto, *Apontamentos para o direito internacional*, 394–98. On the decisions of the government, see Fenelon, "Levantamento e sistematização da legislação," 587.

29. Burlamaqui, "Memória analítica acerca do comércio de escravos," 101–22; and Torres Homem, "Consideraçoens economicas sobre a escravatura," 35–82.

30. ACD, May 15, 1843, 130–31; see also El Youssef, "Imprensa e escravidão," 22–29.

31. AS, May 24, 1844, 559–60.

32. Piqueras, "El mundo reducido a una isla," 324–26. On the Liberal Triennium in Cuba, see Guerra y Sánchez, *Manual de historia de Cuba*, 269–99; and Hernández González, "El liberalismo exaltado en el Triênio Liberal cubano," 67–79. According to Piqueras, the best study on this period is still Jacobo de la Pezuela, *Historia de la isla de Cuba*, vol. 4. Among the signers of the Havana petition were: the county of O'Reilly, whose presence was an indication of the polarization between the Ayuntamiento (dominated by the piñeristas) and the Deputación (dominated by the supporters of O'Reilly); Andrés de Zayas, who had called for the censorship of the Alexander von Humboldt's "Ensayo político sobre la isla de Cuba" in 1827 (which had been recently translated into Spanish); and the Count of Mopox y Jaruco, an admiral and captain general of the Indies who

was, according to Manuel Moreno Fraginals, a key figure in Spanish politics at the turn of the nineteenth century. See Moreno Fraginals, *Cuba/España, España/Cuba*, 204; on Andrés de Zayas, see Zeuske, "Humboldt, Historismus und Humboldteanisierung."

33. Piqueras, "El mundo reducido a una isla," 330.

34. Venegas Delgado, "El fantasma de la Revolución Haitiana," 25–54; Eduardo Torres-Cuevas, "De la ilustración reformista," 335–42; and Guerra y Sánchez, *Manual de historia de Cuba*, 269–99. On Varela, see Piqueras, *Félix Varela y la prosperidad de la patria criolla*, 78–89. See the articles in *El Habanero*, "Paralelo entre la revolución que puede formarse en la isla de Cuba por sus mismos habitantes y la que se formara por la invasión de tropas extranjeras" (1824) and "Es necesario, para un cambio político en la isla de Cuba, esperar las tropas de Colombia o México?" (1825), in Varela y Morales, *Obras*, 2:197–201, 249.

35. The text of the royal order can be found in Cabrera, *Cuba y sus jueces*, 235; see also Fradera, *Gobernar colonias*, 71–93; and Alonso Romero, *Cuba en la España liberal*, 20–26.

36. Piqueras, *Sociedad civil y poder en Cuba*, 102–11. It is not surprising, therefore, that colonial opposition to the facultades omnímodas only emerged in the 1830s. In his articles published in *El Habanero*, for example, Varela only criticized the military commissions without mentioning the royal order that had established the state of siege in Cuba. In the 1830s, however, José Antonio Saco put forward the interpretation of the facultades omnímodas as an antiliberal, centralizing, and oppressive system. See, respectively, "Comisión militar en La Habana" (1825), in Varela y Morales, *Obras*, 2:233–36; and "Paralelo entre las islas de Cuba y algunas colonias inglesas" (1837), in Varela y Morales, *Obras*, 3:130–56.

37. Murray, *Odious Commerce*, 88–91, 96, 108; and Cayuela Fernández, "Los capitanes generales," 415–53.

38. Cited in García, "Vertebrando la resistencia," 297–98.

39. Barcia Paz, "La rebelión de esclavos de 1825"; and García, "Vertebrando la resistencia," 295–98. For the broader context, see Yacou, *La longue guerre des nègres marrons*.

40. Ayllón, *Reglamento de esclavos*, 1–12.

41. Marquese, *Feitores do corpo, missionários da mente*, 307–20. On the slave quarters, see "El barracón de ingenio en la época esclavista," in Pérez de la Riva, *El barracón*, 13–40; on Ayllón's fears regarding alliances between slaves and free people of color, see García, "Vertebrando la resistencia," 296–97.

42. Arango y Parreño, "Consulta sobre los riesgos que amenazan a Cuba al terminarse el año 1825," 2:399–403.

43. Arango y Parreño, "Consulta sobre los riesgos que amenazan a Cuba al terminarse el año 1825," 2:401, 402, 403. On the issue of slavery in Venezuela, see Lombardi, *The Decline and Abolition of Negro Slavery*.

44. On Varela's parliamentary experience and his connections while in exile in the United States, see Piqueras, *Félix Varela y la prosperidad de la patria criolla*, 46–61, 78–89. See also the *El Habanero* articles "Consideraciones sobre el estado actual de la isla de Cuba" (1824), "Tranquilidad de la isla de Cuba" (1824), "Sociedades secretas en la isla de Cuba" (1825), and "Que debera hacerse en caso de uma invasión" (1825). Varela y Morales, *Obras*, 2:152–55, 159–66, 169–77, 197–201, 250–51.

45. Varela attempted to show that the United States was not in principle opposed to Cuban independence, except in the context of socioeconomic disturbances. See Varela y Morales, *Obras*, 2:275. The official US position on the issue, however, was one of the reasons why Varela closed down *El Habanero* and opened *El Mensajero Semanal*, whose editorial line was not proindependence. Torres-Cuevas, "De la ilustración reformista," 342.

46. Saiz Pastor, "El colonialismo español en el Caribe," 212–20; Saiz Pastor, "Império de ultramar y fiscalidad colonial," 77–93; Zanetti Lecuona, "Las relaciones comerciales hispano-cubanas," 95–117; and Barcia Paz, "El conde de Villanueva," 289–300.

47. Arango y Parreño, "Informe del Real Consulado de La Habana, en el expediente para formar las instrucciones y proponer a la persona que se encargue de la comisión de pasar a Jamaica a examinar el estado de adelanto en que se halla esa isla con respecto al cultivo y elaboración de los frutos coloniales," 2:411–31.

48. Sagra, *Cuba en 1860*, 264–68. In the 1840s, import taxes generated 5,439,993 pesos fuertes for the public treasury while export taxes generated only 1,435,696 pesos fuertes. The burden of taxes fell on Cuban consumers instead of the great exporters, as planned by Arango. The Empire of Brazil had a similar fiscal system—import taxes generated three times the revenue of export taxes. See Carreira, *História financeira e orçamentária*. We would like to thank Wilma Peres Costa for providing data on the Brazilian tax system.

49. Marquese and Tomich, "O Vale do Paraíba escravista." See also Pérez, *Winds of Change*.

50. Guerra y Sánchez, *Manual de historia de Cuba*, 332–39; Torres-Cuevas, "De la ilustración reformista," 324–53; and Opatrný, "El estado-nación o la 'cubanidad,'" 362–71.

51. Arango y Parreño, "Carta al Secretario del Supremo Consejo de Indias en que el autor avisa estar traduciendo uma 'Memoria sobre la Abolición de la Esclavitud en las Colonias Europeas,'" August 24, 1831, 2:527–28; and Arango y Parreño, "Representación ao Rey sobre la extinción del tráfico de negros y medios de mejorar la suerte de los esclavos coloniales," May 28, 1832, 2:529–36.

52. "Análisis por D. José Antonio Saco de una obra sobre el Brasil, intitulada: *Notices of Brazil in 1828 and 1829, by Rev. R. Walsh, author of a journey from Constantinople*, etc. (Noticias del Brasil en 1828 y 1829 por el presbítero R. Walsh, autor de un viaje a Constantinopla, etc.)." Saco, *Obras*, 2:57–66.

53. Saco, *Obras*, 2:73–75.

54. Arango y Parreño, "Carta a D. Juan Gualberto Gonzáles sobre la efectiva abolición del tráfico de negros, con motivo de un artículo publicado en la 'Revista Bimestre Cubana,'" 2:616–17.

55. Trouillot, *Silencing the Past*, 70–107. See also James Stephen's *The Crisis of the Sugar Colonies: Or, An Enquiry into the Objects and Probable Effects of the French Expedition to the West Indies*, as cited in Drescher, *The Mighty Experiment*, 101.

56. Tocqueville, *Writings on Empire and Slavery*, 199. See also Porter, "Trusteeship, Anti-Slavery, and Humanitarianism," 198–221; Blackburn, *The Overthrow of Colonial Slavery*, 421–71; Davis, *Slavery and Human Progress*, 210–15; and Temperley, *British Antislavery*, 9–18.

57. Drescher, *The Mighty Experiment*, 144. See also Ofício ostensivo da legação brasileira em Londres, Eustáquio Adolfo de Mello Mattos to Bento da Silva Lisboa (Minister of Foreign Affairs), July 5, 1833, AHI, códice 216/1/14.

58. Murray, *Odious Commerce*, 97; and Bethell, *A abolição do comércio brasileiro de escravos*, 118.

59. *Tratado entre su Magestad la Reina de España y su Magestad el Rey del Reino Unido*. The Spanish government took ten years to finally pass an anti–slave trade law. At the time of its publication, the Brazilian agent in Madrid described the political debates leading to the treaty and its article establishing the necessity of a Spanish law against the traffic. Ofício ostensivo da legação brasileira em Madrid, José Francisco de Paula Cavalcanti e Albuquerque to Ernesto Ferreira França, March 3, 1845, AHI, códice 220/01/05.

60. The Artigos Adicionais are reproduced in A. P. Pinto, *Apontamentos para o direito internacional*, 1:394–98. In October 1828, the Council of State decided to finance the campaign in Mexico with the support of Cuban resources. Moreno Fraginals, *Cuba/España, España/Cuba*, 216. The following year, the same Council of State defended the slave trade with the same arguments that had been used by Cubans earlier in that decade. Murray, *Odious Commerce*, 94–95.

61. Ofício ostensivo, Eustáquio Adolfo de Mello Mattos to Bento da Silva Lisboa, December 4, 1833, AHI, códice 216/1/14; see also Ofício reservado, M. Lisboa to Manoel Alves Branco, September 2, 1835, AHI, códice 217/03/03. There is a booming field of research on the impact of slavery abolition in the British Caribbean on US national politics. See, for example, Davis, *Inhuman Bondage*, 280–84; Mitton, "The Free World Confronted"; Rugemer, *The Problem of Emancipation*; and Karp, "This Vast Southern Empire."

62. On the regency, see Pereira da Silva, *História do Brasil*; and P. P. de Castro, "A experiência 'republicana,'" 9–67.

63. See the analysis of the reforms put forward by the Regresso in J. M. de Carvalho, *A construção da ordem*, 144–68. See also the detailed study of the social composition and political ideology of the Regresso in Needell, *The Party of Order*.

64. ACD, July 24, 1835, 109.
65. *O Sete de Abril,* August 1, 1835, cited in El Youssef, *O problema da escravidão em periódicos brasileiros,* 43.
66. ACD, June 25, 1836, 224.
67. ACD, July 11, 1836, 61.
68. *O Sete de Abril,* July 13, 1836. See El Youssef, *O problema da escravidão em periódicos brasileiros,* 52.
69. *O Sete de Abril,* July 27, 1836. We would like to thank Alain El Youssef for mentioning this issue of *O Sete de Abril.*
70. Ibid.
71. AS, May 28, 1839, 279–80.
72. ACD, June 17, 1837, 272.
73. ACD, August 18, 1837, 330.
74. ACD, July 11, 1836, 61; July 12, 1837, 97; May 5, 1838, 47; May 10, 1838, 69; May 23, 1838, 190; May 28, 1838, 220–21; May 8, 1839; and August 16, 1839, 642.
75. "Representação da Assembléia Legislativa Provincial de Minas Gerais, Março de 1839," Arquivo da Câmara dos Deputados, 1839, lata 126, maço 11, pasta 4; and "Representação de cidadãos da província da Bahia solicitando a derrogação da Lei de 7 de Novembro de 1831, que proíbe a introdução de africanos no Brasil," Arquivo da Câmara dos Deputados, 1841, lata 126, maço 7, pasta 7.3. The text from Bahia was published in *Jornal do Comércio,* generating some controversy at the Chamber of Deputies. See *Jornal do Comércio,* August 16, 1839, 642, 659, 660, 695. The Foreign Antislavery Society later had access to the text and published it in the *Second Annual Report of the British and Foreign Anti-Slavery Society* (London, 1841), 113; see Conrad, *Tumbeiros,* 23.
76. AS, June 30, 1837, 175–81; AS, July 7, 1837, 204; and ACD, September 2, 1837, 453–54.
77. See the complaints by Montezuma in ACD, May 30, 1838, 248; July 3, 1838, 26; and July 4, 1838, 32–33. Vasconcelo's response came on July 3, 1838, 33; the seizure of thirty vessels is mentioned in Conrad, *Tumbeiros,* 106–7.
78. ACD, July 7, 1840, 106–7; see Montezuma's questions in ACD, June 22, 1840, 839; July 22, 1840, 842; and July 23, 1840, 384. Leslie Bethell and Luiz Felipe de Alencastro argue that the small number of Brazilian ships in the struggle against the traffic was due to the beginning of the Farroupilha revolt in 1835, but the argument ignores the active role of the Brazilian state in deciding not to police the coast. Furthermore, how can the absence of Brazilian warships after 1845 be explained, the last year of the rebellion in Rio Grande do Sul? See Bethell, *A abolição do comércio brasileiro de escravos,* 84; and Alencastro, "Le commerce des vivants," 3:485.
79. ACD, July 17, 1839, 336–37. Martim Francisco's accusations were made during the same session; see ACD, July 17, 1839, 332–33. The gag rule was passed in 1836 to prevent the submission of antislavery petitions to the House of Representatives.

The rule would only be repealed in 1844 as a result of protests from northern representatives. See W. L. Miller, *Arguing About Slavery*, 210. See also Pamplona, *Revoltas, república e cidadania*.

80. See [José Carneiro da Silva], *Memória sobre o comércio dos escravos*. This work is analyzed in Marquese and Parron, "Azeredo Coutinho, Visconde de Araruama," 99–126; and Taunay, *Manual do agricultor brasileiro*. The conservatives also sponsored the publication of another pro–slave trade writing; see Barreto, *Memória sobre a abolição do comércio da escravatura*.

81. See Gomes, *Histórias de quilombolas*, 179–321, which mentions the article by Vasconcelos (*O Sete de Abril*, November 30, 1838) on page 270.

82. ACD, May 23, 1840, 445–46.

83. Carta de Martim Francisco Ribeiro de Andrada e Silva, April 6, 1841, seção de manuscritos, Biblioteca Nacional, doc. I-3, 24, 39; cited in Grinberg, *O fiador dos brasileiros*, 175, 190. On the eleições do cacete, see Flory, *Judge and Jury in Imperial Brazil*, 169–70.

84. Flory, *Judge and Jury in Imperial Brazil*, 28–121; Dohlnikoff, *O pacto imperial*, 81–124; and Slemian, *Sob o império da lei* (2009), 229–304.

85. As Miriam Dohlnikoff argues, moderate liberals attempted to create (without success) the position of mayor during the debates over the Additional Act. Some provincial assemblies then used their new powers to establish the position of mayor themselves. See Dohlnikoff, *O pacto imperial*, 118–25.

86. Flory, *Judge and Jury in Imperial Brazil*, 129–99; J. M. de Carvalho, *A construção da ordem*, 145–68; and I. R. Mattos, *O tempo saquarema*, 142–204. The seminal, albeit understudied, work of Justiniano José da Rocha, *Acção, reacção e transacção* (1855), not only established the terms used to describe the reforms and the parties of the period but also demonstrated that the Regressistas continued to influence state affairs, even when not in power (an argument that anticipated the idea of a Saquarema hegemony). See J. J. da Rocha, *Acção, reacção e transacção*.

87. ACD, June 25, 1836, 224; and ACD, September 2, 1837, 453.

88. Some historians mention the submission of Barbacena's proposal in 1837 but do not analyze its surreptitious function while shelved in the assembly. See Bethell, *A abolição do comércio brasileiro de escravos*, 88–94; and Jaime Rodrigues, *O infame comércio*, 110–19.

89. See Voyages: The Trans-Atlantic Slave Trade Database.

90. *Notícia histórica, política, civil e natural*, 21. Cited in Jeanne Berrance de Castro's dissertation, "O povo em armas," 187. Castro's dissertation was published as *A milícia cidadã: A Guarda Nacional de 1831 a 1850*; see J. B. de Castro, *A milícia cidadã*. On the *exaltados* at the beginning of the regency, see Basile, *Ezequiel Corrêa dos Santos*.

91. Cited in J. B. de Castro, "O povo em armas," 187–88. For different interpretations of the "mulatto press," see H. B. Mattos, *Escravidão e cidadania*; and

Flory, "Race and Social Control," 199–224. For the efforts of moderate liberals to establish racial equality in Brazil, see Flory, *Judge and Jury in Imperial Brazil*, 22–27. See also Ferretti, "Entre profecias e prognósticos," 1–22.

92. With regard to political rights, the Brazilian Constitution followed the criteria established by the French revolutionaries in distinguishing between passive citizens, enjoying only civil rights, and active citizens, who would directly participate in the electoral process because they fulfilled certain minimum income requirements. The Constitution of 1824 established that, in two-tier indirect elections, Brazilian citizens (excluding males under twenty-five years of age, offspring living with their parents, and house servants) who had "a yearly net income above a hundred thousand réis derived from real estate property, industry, trade, or employment" could vote in the parochial assemblies, which chose the provincial electors. In the second stage, freed slaves and all those with a yearly net income below two hundred thousand réis would be excluded from voting.

93. Cited in J. B. de Castro, *A milícia cidadã*, 136; for an analysis of Rebouças's speeches criticizing the exclusion of freedmen from officer ranks, see Grinberg, *O fiador dos brasileiros*, 101–32.

94. Tomás Villanueva, *El sistema político del Estatuto Real*, 591.

95. Fradera, *Colonias para después de un imperio*, 143.

96. Serapio de Mojarrieta did not take an oath, while Echevarría y O'Gaban's term was canceled by the *estamento de próceres*.

97. In Pérez de la Riva, *Correspondência reservada*, 171–72, esp. the document of June 30, 1835.

98. On the electoral process in Cuba, see Guerra y Sanchéz, *Manual de história de Cuba*, 363–65; Opatrný, "El estado-nación o la 'cubanidad'"; Pérez de la Riva, *Correspondência reservada*; and Piqueras, *Sociedad civil y poder en Cuba*, 59–95.

99. Disconnected from sugar production and the slaveholding interests of the western part of the island, planters from the East wanted to contest the power of the captain general and the support of the Havana Ayuntamiento. See Opatrný, "El estado-nación o la 'cubanidad.'"

100. Ibid.

101. Piqueras, *Sociedad Civil y poder en Cuba*.

102. Guerra y Sanchéz, *Manual de historia de Cuba*, 371, mentions a "petition submitted by Tacón and signed by more than four thousand representatives of a great part of the wealth of Cuba, which asked that no changes in the present system be introduced." The petition was allegedly presented at the Cortes in the session of March 25, 1837, in response to a request (made on March 11) that deputies should have access to documents related to the electoral process in Cuba. We have found the request of March 11 in the documentation, but not the references to this discussion of March 25. Moreover, we have also not found

references to the petition signed by four thousand Cubans in the reports of the
sessions. In any case, Josef Opatrný argues that "Intendente Pinillos participated in an action organized by the wealthy proprietors of the island, who
signed a manifesto against the participation of Cuban deputies in the assembly
and the implementation of the Constitution on the island." Opatrný, "El
estado-nación o la 'cubanidad,'" 393.

103. Opatrný, "El estado-nación o la 'cubanidad.'"

104. The Congress of Deputies did not publish these secret sessions, but the deputies
who participated in them described some of the discussions in subsequent public sessions.

105. "Ditame de las comissiones reunidas de Ultramar y Constituicion," *Diário de
Sessiones de las Cortes Constituyentes, 1836–1837* (henceforth DSCC), December 2,
1837.

106. Fradera, "L'esclavage et la logique constitutionnelle," 533–60.

107. Fradera, *Colonias para después de un imperio*, 155–57.

108. The Cortes voted for the exclusion of American deputies and the promulgation
of special laws. The decision to exclude the deputies won by a vote of 90 to 65,
while the special laws were passed by a vote of 150 to 65. DSCC, April 16, 1837.

109. DSCC, February 27, 1837, 1810.

110. On the centralizing policies of the Cádiz and their relation to autonomism in
America, see Artola et al., *Las Cortes de Cádiz*; García Godoy, *Las Cortes de
Cádiz y América*; García Laguardia, *Centroamerica en las Cortes de Cádiz*;
Martínez, *La union con España*; and Rieu-Millan, *Los diputados americanos*.
On the same issues discussed at the Triennium Cortes, see Frasquet, *Las caras
del águila*.

111. On ideas of heterogeneity and the construction of new inequalities in the
metropolis-colony relationship, see Fradera, *Colonias para después de un
imperio*, 61–140.

112. DSCC, February 12, 1837, 1492.

113. Ibid.

114. Ibid.

115. DSCC, March 10, 1837, 2049.

116. DSCC, April 8, 1837, 2697.

117. DSCC, March 10, 1837, 2050.

118. DSCC, April 12, 1837, 2696.

119. Ibid.

120. The argument here is different from the one offered by Josep Fradera: "Still, at
the moment these questions were debated in Cádiz, the idea of race that
emerges is none other than the traditional one, inherited from the old political
culture of the Empire." Fradera, *Gobernar colonias*, 65. In our view, the idea of
casta was characteristic of the old political culture, but not the idea of race (not
even with an alleged archaic content). For this reason we use two different

notions, one based on the idea of casta and characteristic of the Old Regime, and another based on the idea of race and generally adopted in the Atlantic system of northwestern Europe in the second half of the eighteenth century.

121. DSCC, March 9, 1837, 2021.

122. Ibid.

123. DSCC, April 5, 1837, 2505. Montesquieu's climate theory influenced both anti-slavery and proslavery ideas (such as those offered by Juan Bernardo O'Gavan in 1821).

124. DSCC, April 5, 1837, 2512.

125. Ibid.

126. DSCC, March 9, 1837, 2021.

127. DSCC, March 10, 1837.

128. DSCC, March 25, 1837, 2310.

129. DSCC, April 5, 1837, 2507.

130. Saco, *Examen analíctico del informe de la comisión especial*, 17.

131. The arguments of the Galician Ramón de la Sagra (in response to Saco) were published in 1837. See Sagra, *Apuntes destinados a ilustrar la discusión*, 31. This same document is analyzed in Fradera, *Colonias para después de un imperio*, 163.

132. On the changes in constitutional texts and colonial policies in the nineteenth century, see Aja and Sole Tura, *Constituciones y periodos constituyentes*; Alonso Romero, *Cuba en la España liberal*; and Fradera, *Gobernar colonias*.

133. Schmidt-Nowara, *Empire and Antislavery*, 3–6. Nowara uses the term in opposition to the framework employed in studies such as R. Paquette, *Sugar Is Made with Blood*, 114–15; and Martínez-Fernández, *Torn Between Empires*, 5. For a similar critique of Paquette's study, see Dale Tomich's review of his book in Tomich, Review of *Sugar Is Made with Blood*, 657–60.

Chapter 4

1. On Cuba, see Blackburn, *The Overthrow of Colonial Slavery*, 397–98; and Saiz Pastor, "El colonialismo español en el Caribe," 212–20. On Brazil, see *Estatísticas históricas do Brasil*, 601–16; and J. M. de Carvalho, *A construção da ordem*, 276–77, graphs 2, 3.

2. Temperley, *British Antislavery*, 42–92 (quotation on 94); Drescher, *The Mighty Experiment*, 151–52, 166–67; Huzzey, *Freedom Burning*; and Mulligan and Bric, *A Global History of Anti-Slavery*.

3. See the anti–slave trade treaties in A. P. Pinto, *Apontamentos para o direito internacional*, 441–42. Also see Eltis, *Economic Growth and the Ending of the Transatlantic Slave Trade*, 87–89. According to Eltis, France did not ratify the treaty of 1841.

4. Temperley, *British Antislavery*, 280-320. On the annexation of Texas, see Freeh-ling, *The Road to Disunion*, 1:355-452; and Roeckell, "Bonds over Bondage," 257-78.

5. ACD, April 30, 1840, 193; and [Andrada e Silva], *Representação à Assembléia Geral e Constituinte*.

6. See, respectively, Alexandre, "O liberalismo português," 319-40; Capela, *As burguesias portuguesas*, 45-46; and J. P. Marques, *Os sons do silêncio*, 193-214.

7. Cited in *Documentos officiaes relativos a negociação*, 31, 32. The text can also be found in one of the strongest proslavery books produced in the Portuguese world; see Brasahemeco, *Rights of Portugal*, 2:172-73.

8. On the Portuguese case, see J. P. Marques, *Os sons do silêncio*, 192-265. For the reinterpretation of the treaty of 1826, see Bethell, *A abolição do comércio brasileiro de escravos*, 166-90. On how the anti-slave trade policy of the For-eign Office impacted the entrepreneurial and political strategies of slave dealers in Brazil and Cuba, see L. Marques, "The United States and the Transatlantic Slave Trade."

9. On Madden, see Murray, *Odious Commerce*, 121-32.

10. "Interrogatorio de Mr. R. R. Madden," 367-74. On del Monte, see R. Paquette, *Sugar Is Made with Blood*, 100-102; see also Piqueras, *Sociedad civil y poder en Cuba*, 27-31. On the emigration from Santo Domingo, see Esteban Deive, *Las emigraciones dominicas a Cuba*.

11. Turnbull, *Travels in the West*, 340-50.

12. Cited in R. Paquette. *Sugar Is Made with Blood*, 136. On Turnbull, see also Mur-ray, *Odious Commerce*, 133-58; and Yacou, *Essor des plantations*, 421-82.

13. Murray, *Odious Commerce*, 133-58; and R. Paquette, *Sugar Is Made with Blood*, 131-57. On the Espartero administration, see Gómez Urdáñez, "Progresismo y poder político," 623-71; and Fontana, *Historia de España*, 6:185-218. On Sagra's slavery critique, see Sánchez Cobos, "A propósito de la abolición de la esclavi-tud," 259-99.

14. "Exposición del Ilustre Ayuntamiento de La Habana," 5:236-41. This text can also be found in González del Valle y Ramírez, *La Habana en 1841*, 403-8. The content of these reports have been analyzed from a different perspective than ours in Corwin, *Spain and the Abolition of Slavery in Cuba*, 70; Tardieu, "*Morir o dominar*," 76-84; and Yacou, *Essor des plantations*, 421-82.

15. On the Ayuntamiento, see Tardieu, "*Morir o dominar*," 76-77.

16. "El Tribunal de Comercio de esta Plaza de La Habana," 5:242-52. The text was partially transcribed and commented on by María Dolores Pérez Murillo. See Pérez Murillo, "El pensamiento esclavista," 407-13. A copy of the document can be found in AHN, Madrid, sessão Ultramar, Cuba Gobierno, Esclavitud, legajo 3547, maço 9.

17. "Exposición de la Junta de Fomento de la isla de Cuba," 5:185-92. On Salvador

Samá and the Marquis of Real de la Proclamación, see Bahamonde and
Cayuela, *Hacer las Américas*, 21, 25, 39, 40. The Count of Barreto descended
from families who had not only been living in Cuba since the eighteenth century but had been ennobled as a result of their participation in the Seven Years'
War. See Pezuela, *Diccionario geográfico*, 1:344.

18. "Acuerdo de la Junta de Fomento," 5:200.

19. On the Peñalver family, see Bahamonde and Cayuela, *Hacer las Américas*, 175,
203.

20. "Informe de la Junta de Fomento," 5:211–31 (quotations on 211, 223, 225). The
authors explicitly transformed the Haitian Revolution into a historical nonevent, and in a sense this strategy was very close to the argument put forward
by Michel-Rolph Trouillot in *Silencing the Past*, 70–107.

21. "Informe de la Junta de Fomento," 5:211–31 (quotations on 230–31).

22. "Informe reservado del Real Consulado," 5:211–31 (quotation on 225).

23. "Informe del censor de la Real Sociedad Patriótica," 5:201–10; and "Informe del
Ldo. D. Bernardo M. Navarro," 5:253–65.

24. Murray, *Odious Commerce*, 149–50.

25. See Merlin, *Los esclavos en las colonias españolas*, 2, 19, 22, 35–38, 63, 78–79. On
the countess, see Flouret, "Ilustración y esclavitud en Cuba," 265–71.

26. Torrente, *Cuestión importante sobre la esclavitud*, 8–9, 46–50, 60. For a different analysis of the writings from the 1840s, see Fradera, *Colonias para después
de un imperio*, 267.

27. Tardieu, *"Morir o dominar,"* 84.

28. Valdés to the minister of foreign affairs, November 3, 1841, Arquivo Histórico
Nacional, estado, leg. 8038; cited in R. Paquette, *Sugar Is Made with Blood*,
148.

29. On Valdés's anti–slave trade activities, see Guerra y Sánchez, *Manual de historia de Cuba*, 391, 197–398; and R. Paquette, *Sugar Is Made with Blood*, 145–46.
On British perceptions, see Murray, *Odious Commerce*, 183–86. After Valdés
prohibited the purchase of foreign ships, many sellers of US-built vessels (sold
annually in Cuba to be used in the contraband slave trade) returned to the
United States without completing their transactions.

30. The questions and answers can be found in Tardieu, *"Morir o dominar,"*
206–63.

31. *Tratado entre su Magestad la Reina de España y su Magestad el Rey del Reino
Unido*, 60–61.

32. R. Paquette, *Sugar Is Made with Blood*, 131–57, 177; Murray, *Odious Commerce*,
133–58.

33. In his letters to London, Crawford said that white delegates had asked him if
Great Britain would support independence and the abolition of slavery in
Cuba, since other whites had established an alliance with the United States to
preserve slavery. See R. Paquette, *Sugar Is Made with Blood*, 158–81.

34. García, "Vertebrando la resistencia," 311–16; for an analysis of the broader context, see Barcia, *Seeds of Insurrection*; and Barcia, *West African Warfare in Bahia and Cuba*.

35. García, "Vertebrando la resistencia," 309; see also R. Paquette, *Sugar Is Made with Blood*, 51–80; and Guerra y Sánchez, *Manual de historia de Cuba*, 395–96, 414.

36. Tardieu, *"Dominar o morir,"* 126–30.

37. Pérez, "Cuba and the United States," 57–82.

38. For the first approach, see Genovese, *A economia política da escravidão*, 203–30; McCardell, *The Idea of a Southern Nation*, 227–36; and Foner, *A History of Cuba*. For the second approach, see May, "Young American Males and Filibustering," 857–86; and Chaffin, "Sons of Washington," 79–108.

39. Guerra y Sánchez, *Manual histórico de Cuba*, 377–88; and R. Paquette, *Sugar Is Made with Blood*, 183–205 (quotation on 194).

40. See, respectively, Cepero Bonilla, *Azúcar y abolición*, 49; Carmen Barcia and Torres-Cuevas, "El debilitamiento de las relaciones sociales esclavistas," 338–40; and Moreno Fraginals, *Cuba/España, España/Cuba*, 249–56. On Cuban historiography, see Cruz-Taura, "Annexation and National Identity," 90–109.

41. See the list in R. Paquette, *Sugar Is Made with Blood*, 172.

42. A complete transcript of the report from the Marquis of Arcos, dated May 19, 1842, can be found in Tardieu, *"Dominar o morir,"* 211–16.

43. Report from the Marquis of Arcos, May 19, 1842, in Tardieu, *"Dominar o morir,"* 213, 214, 216.

44. See the report by Ramón de la Sagra on Wenceslao de Villa Urrutia in Sagra, *Cuba en 1860*, 82–84; see also Marquese, *Feitores do corpo, missionários da mente*, 320–21.

45. Tardieu, *"Dominar o morir,"* 249–57.

46. Ibid., 257.

47. For a comparative analysis of reglamentos in Cuba and Puerto Rico, see Lucena Salmoral, *Los códigos negros*, 151–59. On the differences between the 1842 Reglamento and the proposal of García Oña, see Tardieu, *"Dominar o morir,"* 126–30 (García Oña's proposal is discussed on pages 202–6); on the specific innovations of this reglamento in comparison with previous ones, see Marquese, *Feitores do corpo, missionários da mente*, 316–19. Valdés's text was reproduced in Ortiz, *Los esclavos negros*, 308–14, and in Lucena Salmoral, *Los códigos negros*, 295–300. On Articles 34 and 35, see de la Fuente, "Slaves and the Creation of Legal Rights in Cuba," 659–92.

48. Pérez-Cisneros, *La abolición de la esclavitud en Cuba*, 19; Lucena Salmoral, *Los códigos negros*, 140–59; and Tardieu, *"Dominar o morir,"* 178–83.

49. Martínez García, "La sublevación de la Alcancía," 41–48; and García, "Vertebrando la resistencia," 395–96. For the broader context of these revolts, see Finch, "Insurgency at the Cross Roads," 26–289.

50. García, "Vertebrando la resistencia," 317; and R. Paquette, *Sugar Is Made with Blood*, 209–11.

51. "Importante exposición de los hacendados de Matanzas," 5:279–82; and "Exposición al Excelentísimo Sr. Gobernador General de la isla de Cuba," 5:283–85. A transcript of the document can also be found in Torres-Cuevas and Reyes, *Esclavitud y sociedad*, 206–8. See also *Resumen del censo de población de la Isla de Cuba*. The objective of the Niger expedition was to dismantle the slave trade between the river and the Bight of Benin, one of the great centers of Cuban and Bahian slave trade operations. The expedition was a failure, with most of its members contracting malaria. See Drescher, *The Mighty Experiment*, 166–68; and Temperley, *White Dreams, Black Africa*, 161–62.

52. The interviewed slaves were from the Santísima Trinidad and Jesús María estates, owned by María Josefa de Oviero; the Santa Rosa and Santo Domingo estates, owned by Domingo Aldama; the Majagua estate, owned by Gonzalo Alfonso; and La Trinidad, owned by Francisco Hernández Morejón. See García, "Vertebrando la resistencia," 317–18; and "Exposición al Excelentísimo Sr. Gobernador General de la isla de Cuba," 5:283–85.

53. See Carmen Barcia and Torres-Cuevas, "El debilitamiento de las relacionoes sociales esclavistas," 436–37; and García, "Vertebrando la resistencia," 317–18.

54. R. Paquette, *Sugar Is Made with Blood*, 233–66 (quotation on 245); Carmen Barcia and Torres-Cuevas, "El debilitamiento de las relacionoes sociales esclavistas," 436–37; Helg, "Race and Black Mobilization," 53–74; and Reid-Vazquez, *The Year of the Lash*, 117–72.

55. See "Parecer de la Real Junta sobre el reglamento de esclavos," in Tardieu, *"Morir o dominar,"* 264–71 (quotation on 266).

56. "It is impossible to either nullify or reform it, 1st because any of these two measures would have to receive this prejudicial publicity, so that they could be effective; 2nd because the slaves would be alarmed against their masters, believing that the derogation or reform of the *reglamento* had been decided by them and a superior authority; 3rd because any of these two innovations could be transcendental to the external relations of the supreme government." See "Parecer de la Real Junta sobre el reglamento de esclavos," in Tardieu, *"Morir o dominar,"* 268.

57. Despite the arguments of scholars such as Fernando Ortiz, the Reglamento was used by *síndicos procuradores* of slaves a few years after the Escalera Conspiracy. See de la Fuente, "Slaves and the Creation of Legal Rights in Cuba," 659–92.

58. "Primera circular para las autoridades locales," "Segunda circular para los dueños de fincas rurales, sus administradores y mayorales," "Instrucción del 24 de septiembre de 1844," and "Circular del 8 de febrero de 1845," all written by O'Donnell, appear in Tardieu, *"Morir o dominar,"* 272–78.

59. Ofício ostensivo de José Francisco de Paula Cavalcanti e Albuquerque para Ernesto Ferreira França, March 3, 1845, AHI, códice 220/01/05.

60. Murray, *Odious Commerce*, 182.

61. "Informe sobre la promulgación de una ley penal," 5:286–87.

62. The most extensive study of these reports is Moreno García, "Actitudes de los nacionalistas cubanos," 478–98. The reports submitted by Aldama, the *Socie-dad Patriótica*, and the *Junta de Fomento* are reproduced in Saco, *Historia de la esclavitud*, 5:289–326. The texts from Pizarro, Villa Urrutia, the *Superintenden-cia General Delegada de la Hacienda*, the *Junta de Fomento*, the *Tribunal de Comercio*, and the Real Sociedad Patriótica can be found in AHN, Madrid, Legajo 3547, maço n. 12, Ultramar, Cuba Gobierno, Esclavitud. Part of the report from the *Superintendencia* was based on a previous report from Vicente Vázquez Queipo; see Vázquez Queipo, *Cuba, se ressources, son administration, sa population*, 342–50.

63. See "Informe de Villa Urrutia," June 20, 1844; and "Informe de D. José Pizarro y Gardin," February 21, 1844, at Arquivo Histórico Nacional (henceforth AHN), Madrid, Legajo 3547, maço n. 12, Ultramar, Cuba Gobierno, Esclavitud. Aldama's report can be found in Saco, *Historia de la esclavitud*, 5:289–96; Her-rera's report is summarized in Moreno García, "Actitudes de los nacionalistas cubanos," 486–87.

64. See the reports from the *Cancellería* and the *Tribunal* of Puerto Príncipe in Moreno García, "Actitudes de los nacionalistas cubanos," 481–82. "Informe del Tribunal de Comercio sobre la esclavitud," May 29, 1844; "Informe de la Super-intendencia General Delegada de Hacienda, Havana," April 20, 1844; "Informe de la Sociedad Económica de amigos del país," May 30, 1844; and "Informe de la Real Junta de Fomento," April 29, 1844 can be found in AHN, Madrid, Legajo 3547, maço n. 12, Ultramar, Cuba Gobierno, Esclavitud. The last two can also be found in Saco, *Historia de la esclavitud*, 5:297–326.

65. The Penal Law of 1845 is reproduced in Torres-Cuevas and Reyes, *Esclavitud y sociedad*, 210–13; also see *Tratado entre su Magestad la Reina de España y su Magestad el Rey del Reino Unido*, 4–5.

66. *Diario de sesiones de Cortes, Senado*, December 23, 1844 (presentation of the matter at the Senate); December 30, 1844 (presentation of the bill prepared by a committee of the Senate); and January 4, 7, and 8, 1845 (discussion of the arti-cles of the bill). The quotation is from a session on January 4, 1845, 279.

67. Ibid., January 7–8, 1845, 296–97, 321.

68. "Ofício do Ministro de Marina y Gobierno de Ultramar, para o capitão gen-eral," February 25, 1845, AHN, Madrid, Legajo 3547, maço n. 12, Ultramar, Cuba Gobierno, Esclavitud.

69. Bergad, Iglesias García, and Carmen Barcia, *The Cuban Slave Market*, 31.

70. See the estimates at Voyages: The Trans-Atlantic Slave Trade Database; on the internal movement of slaves from coffee plantations to sugar mills, see Moreno

Fraginals, *O engenho*, 1:360–61; on Asian contract immigration, see Juan Pérez de la Riva's articles "Aspectos económicos del tráfico de cúlies: Chinos a Cuba (1853–1874)" and "La situación legal del cúli en Cuba," in Pérez de la Riva, *El barracón*, 89–140. see also Corbitt, "Immigration in Cuba," 280–308.

71. The following paragraphs are based on Parron, *A política da escravidão no império do Brasil*, 193–230.

72. J. A. L. G., "Reflexões sobre a escravatura."

73. Ibid.

74. *Falla dirigida á Assembléa Legislativa Provincial de Minas-Gerais*, 62. See also E. V. da Costa, *Da senzala à colônia*, 212.

75. ACD, June 10, 1843, 592–94. In 1843, Rodrigues Torres submitted the bill to the Chamber of Deputies, which passed it on September 19.

76. Motta, *Nas fronteiras do poder*; J. M. de Carvalho, *A construção da ordem*, 329–54; I. R. Mattos, *O tempo saquarema*, 251–52; and Lima, *Pequena história territorial do Brasil*.

77. Martins, *O cativeiro da terra*; for a different perspective, see Lígia Osório Silva, *Terras devolutas e latifúndio*.

78. AS, April 27, 1843, 393.

79. See, respectively, Oliveira Lima, "O império brasileiro," 422; Souza, *História dos fundadores do império do Brasil*, 5:247, 260; J. M. de Carvalho, *Bernardo Pereira de Vasconcelos*, 19; I. R. Mattos, *O tempo saquarema*, 139; and Alencastro, "Le commerce des vivants," 3:516.

80. AS, April 26, 1843, 353.

81. Ibid., 327–53.

82. Ibid., 351.

83. AS, April 27, 1843, 404–6.

84. AS, July 7, 1845, 253. Vasconcelos frequently repeated this argument. See AS, April 27, 1843, 404–6; AS, July 24, 1846, 344; AS, August 30, 1847, 440–43, 460–61; AS, April 27, 1847, 377; and AS, August 9, 1848, 428–29.

85. AS, August 21, 1848, 396–97; see a similar statement in AS, August 27, 1847, 442–43. In August 1845, Vasconcelos repeated the argument as shared by the conservatives as a whole: "The Saquaremas, based on the experience of other peoples, also understand that men from cold European countries were not able to bear the sun of the tropics; they wanted a more apt population. In sum, they had taken many providences." AS, August 9, 1845, 428–29.

86. Lígia Osório Silva (*Terras devolutas e latifúndio*, 108) considers this passage to be an explicit celebration of the slave trade. It is important to note that in 1842, before the Land Law bill was submitted to Parliament, Honório Hermeto Carneiro Leão and Vasconcelos told the British ambassador that Brazil would not sign any anti-slave trade treaty until Britain had formally agreed to allow the immigration of African colonists to Brazil. See Bethell, *A abolição do comércio brasileiro de escravos*, 226n1.

87. AS, August 21, 1848, 398–99. See also AS, April 27, 1843, 391–410; AS, May 6, 1843, 9–10, 25; and AS, August 27, 1845, 518–19.
88. Bethell, *A abolição do comércio brasileiro de escravos*, 226n1.
89. "Instructions to US Ministers," series IV, J. C. Calhoun to Henry Wise, May 20, 1844, DINA, cited in Wright, *Desafio americano à preponderância britânica no Brasil*, 239–41. See also "Ofícios da missão especial em Londres, 1843, de José de Araújo Ribeiro a Paulino José Soares de Souza," November 23 and December 28, 1943, AHI, códice 271/4/6.
90. On the alternatives to slavery, based more often on coerced rather than free labor, see Mamigonian, "To Be a Liberated African in Brazil," 80–133. See also Asiegbu, *Slavery and the Politics of Liberation*, 48–60; Northrup, *Indentured Labor in the Age of Imperialism*; and Drescher, *The Mighty Experiment*, 155, 156, 173, 187.
91. See *Falla dirigida á Assembléa Legislativa Provincial de Minas-Gerais*, 62.
92. See the brief reference to the Brazilian requests for permission to carry Africans as free colonists to the country in Bethell, *A abolição do comércio brasileiro de escravos*, 254.
93. The protest was published in the February 7 and 8, 1846, issues of *La Gaceta*. See "Ofício ostensivo de José Francisco de Paula Cavalcanti e Albuquerque para Ernesto Ferreira França," February 8, 1846, AHI, códice 220/01/05. The protest would later be frequently praised in the Chamber of Deputies as an exemplary response from the Brazilian government. See, for example, ACD, July 13 and 17, 1855, 161, 194–95.
94. Antônio Paulino Limpo de Abreu, "Protesto do Governo Imperial contra o Bill Aberdeen (22 de outubro de 1845)." Reproduced in A. P. Pinto, *Apontamentos para o direito internacional*, 426–45; the document is also reproduced in Bonavides and Amaral, *Textos políticos da história do Brasil*, 139–48.
95. Bethell, *A abolição do comércio brasileiro de escravos*, 257n2; and Blake, *Diccionario bibliographico brazileiro*, 5:269–71, s.v. "Justiniano José da Rocha"; and 3:479–82, s.v. "J. M. Pereira da Silva."
96. Innocencio Francisco da Silva, *Diccionario bibliographico portuguez*, 10:302–4; 11:298. In the twentieth century, Tancredo Barros de Paiva also had no doubt that Pereira da Silva was the sole author. See Paiva, *Achegas a um diccionario de pseudonymos*, 48.
97. Innocencio Francisco da Silva, *Diccionario bibliographico portuguez*, 10:302–3; Blake, *Diccionario bibliographico brazileiro*, 3:479; and Candido, *Formação da literatura brasileira*, 2:11–13, 326–28, 382–83.
98. See [Pereira da Silva], *Inglaterra e Brasil*, 3–4. The US minister to Brazil, Henry A. Wise, also connected the activities of Brazilian politicians to the continuation of the contraband slave trade: "The Ministers & Councillors of State & Senators and Delegates in the Chambers are, undoubtedly, engaged in this bold as well as horrid traffic." Letter to James Buchanan, Rio de Janeiro, December 9, 1846. Cited in Conrad, *The Destruction of Brazilian Slavery*, 22.

99. [Pereira da Silva], *Inglaterra e Brasil*, 213–14.

100. Ibid., 223–24.

101. Ibid., 226, 257–58.

102. Ibid., 230–31, 262–63.

103. Ibid., 71–72.

104. Ibid., 7.

105. Ibid., 237–41.

106. Ibid., 67–69. This argument was almost reproduced verbatim by the curator of liberated Africans, Luiz de Assis Mascarenhas, in his response to British accusations that the Brazilian government had not been taking care of the liberated slaves. "Many laborers in Europe would consider themselves happy if they had the same chance the liberated Africans had in Brazil," he argued. "I do not know of any liberated African who begged for his living in the streets of such a big city [Rio de Janeiro]," while in Europe "disgraced people did not find food indispensable for life." Luiz de Assis Mascarenhas para Paulino Limpo de Abreu, November 18, 1845, AN, IJ6 523; cited in Mamigonian, "To Be a Liberated African in Brazil," 155–56.

107. [Pereira da Silva], *Inglaterra e Brasil*, 253, 251.

108. On the tariffs on sugar and coffee, see Bethell, *A abolição do comércio brasileiro de escravos*, 222–31; and Alencastro, "Le commerce des vivants," 2:490. On Ruviroza y Urzellas, see Ferreira, "*Dos sertões ao Atlântico*," 122.

109. Oliveira Lima, "O império brasileiro," 469. On suppression efforts in Luanda, see Ferreira, "Brasil e Angola no tráfico ilegal," 150–60. The argument in the following pages is based on Tâmis Parron, *A política da escravidão no império do Brasil*, 230–52.

110. ACD, May 28, 1847, 178, 187. See also ACD, May 29, 1847, 201; and ACD, July 15, 1847, 145–46.

111. Silva, *Francisco Félix de Souza*, 145.

112. See the request for information on the seizure of vessels by the Brazilian navy in ACD, June 6, 1848, 181. On African colonists, see "Ofício reservado de José Marques Lisboa para Bernardo de Souza Franco," November 3, 1848, AHI, 217/3/6. Discussions of the Senate's old bill (no. 133) began on September 1. See ACD, September 1, 1848, 324–31. It is important to remember that the proposal of 1837 aimed not only at increasing the scope of possible evidence against suspected slavers (with the equipment clause) but also at protecting the slaves who had been illegally introduced into the country (with an eventual revocation of the 1831 law).

113. Some of the primary studies of slave resistance in the first half of the nineteenth century are Reis, *Rebelião escrava no Brasil*; Gomes, *Histórias de quilombolas*; and Karasch, *A vida dos escravos*. On the conspiracy of 1848, see Slenes, "Malungo, Ngoma vem"; see also Slenes, "A árvore de *Nsanda* transplantada," 273–314. On free Africans, see Mamigonian, "To Be a Liberated African in

Brazil," 181–90. On yellow fever, see Chalhoub, *Cidade febril*, 60–96; and Graden, "An Act 'Even of Public Security,'" 249–82. On the effects of accumulated fears of slaves, see Jaime Rodrigues, *O infame comércio*, 31–62, 97–119.

114. Needell, *The Party of Order*, 138–55, n73, n78; 376–79.

115. Ibid., 140.

116. See Slenes, "Malungo, Ngoma vem"; and Slenes, "A árvore de *Nsanda* transplantada."

117. Iglésias, "Vida política," 43; Alencastro, "La traite négrière," 411–13; and Needell, *The Party of Order*, 151–55.

118. AS, August 21, 1848, 396–99. See also the letter to Bernardo de Souza Franco (who was no longer the minister of foreign affairs) dated November 3, 1848, AHI, 217/3/6.

119. On September 22, a secret session of Parliament discussed the 1831 law. On November 1, Nunes Machado already made clear that he did not accept the revocation of the law or the legalization of the property of slaves illegally introduced into the country after 1831. "For Brazil, considering things in relation to the external, there are no slaves. If, therefore, there are no slaves in the sense of the Minister's argument . . . the evil is so great that, in order to deal with the means to remedy it, there can be no freedom of thought, nor freedom of discussion: the thought of the orator is another one, he does not know how to express himself without offending the accepted rules of behavior." On the votes, see the letter from the British ambassador cited by Paulino Soares in ACD, June 6, 1851, 405; and Bethell, *A abolição do comércio brasileiro de escravos*, 279.

120. AS, September 27, 1848, 384.

121. AS, August 21, 1848, 396–97.

122. "Ofício reservado de José Marques Lisboa ao Visconde de Olinda," May 4, 1849, AHI, 217/3/6; and "Ofício reservado de Joaquim Thomaz do Amaral a Paulino José Soares de Souza," March 4, 1850, AHI, 217/3/6.

123. Alencastro, "Le commerce des vivants," 2:510. From London, the Brazilian ambassador referred to Thomas Miller Gibson—a free trader who criticized British anti–slave trade policies—as a "useful individual" and sent newspaper articles with underlined passages mentioning the motion to cease the operations of the anti–slave trade naval squadron. After the motion was defeated, he wrote that the result "will not eliminate the moral effects that the hard truths thrown at the face of this government [Britain] by Mr. Gibson and his friends will produce in our favor." According to the Brazilian representative, the view that British slave trade policies not only did not help end the traffic but also were unfair to Brazil was gaining ground in the House of Commons, the House of Lords, and the press. See the lengthy letters from José Marques Lisboa to the Viscount of Olinda, February 5 and May 4, 1849, AHI, 217/3/6.

124. ACD, July 15, 1850, 197. The speech is reproduced in Uruguai, *Visconde de Uruguai*, 537–72, esp. 546, 569.

125. Needell, *The Party of Order*, 152, 155n82, 379; on British seizures in mid-1849, see Bethell, *A abolição do comércio brasileiro de escravos*, 293.

126. "Ofícios reservados de Joaquim Thomaz do Amaral a Paulino José Soares de Souza," April 26, 1850, and March 30, 1850, AHI, 217/3/6.

127. "Ofício reservado de Joaquim Thomaz do Amaral a Paulino José Soares de Souza," April 26, 1850, AHI, 217/3/6. See also Needell, *The Party of Order*, 379n82; on the defeat of Hutt's motion, see Bethell, *A abolição do comércio brasileiro de escravos*, 303–7.

128. See "Ofício Reservado no. 1682," April 20, 1850, from Rio de Janeiro to Madrid, AGMAE, Madrid, legajo H 1413.

129. AS, May 13, 1850, 14. *The Slave Trade Regulated* and *The Brazilian Slave Trade and Its Remedy* are included in the bibliography in Bethell, *A abolição do comércio brasileiro de escravos*, 383. It is important to note that the subheading of the second publication—*The blockade has only injured legitimate trade; the remedy is regulated African emigration to Brazil and the abolition of slavery*—posits the immigration of free Africans as the solution to the end of slavery, in clear contrast to Cavalcanti's speech.

130. AS, May 27, 1850, 127–30.

131. AS, June 8, 1850, 109. With the title "Ways to Abolish Slavery in Brazil," the memorial surprised some senators. Paula Souza rejected it outright. In his view, its acceptance could lead people to think that the special committee had the intention of abolishing slavery, "and this has some impact on the public Peace of a nation where at least one-third of the population is slave." The first secretary had to explain that the document actually called for the reopening of the slave trade. See ACD, June 8, 1850, 110.

132. AS, July 1, 1850, 45–53; see the oppositional speeches of Costa Ferreira in AS, June 27, 1850, 433, 438.

133. "Ofício reservado de Joaquim Thomaz do Amaral a Paulino José Soares de Souza," April 26, 1850, AHI, 217/3/6.

134. See Paulino mentioning the orders of June 1850 in AS, June 24, 1851, 317.

135. J. H. Rodrigues, *Atas do Conselho de Estado*, 3:248.

136. Ibid., 3:247–67. See also ACD, July 12, 1850, 176.

137. ACD, July 15, 1850, 208; see also Uruguai, *Visconde de Uruguai*, 570. This passage is also cited in Needell, *The Party of Order*, 153.

138. ACD, September 22, 26, 1848, 415; ACD, July 13, 1850, 176.

139. Alencastro, "Le commerce des vivants," 528–29, 558n174a.

140. See "Ofício 1699," August 2, 1850, AGMAE, legajo H 1413.

141. ACD, June 2, 1851, 319–20, 334–35; ACD, June 3, 1851, 343; ACD, June 4, 1851, 365–66; ACD, June 5, 1851, 385; ACD, June 7, 1851, 413; and ACD, June 28, 1851, 648–50.

142. See the opposition speeches in ACD, July 26, 1851, 319–20, 328; ACD, July 30, 1851, 383–84; and August 9, 1851, 525. See also Eusébio de Queirós's responses in ACD, July 26, 1851, 323; ACD, August 1, 1851, 409–10; and ACD, August 9, 1851, 527–28.

143. ACD, June 2, 1852, 142; ACD, June 3, 1852, 160; ACD, June 4, 1852, 186; ACD, June 7, 1852, 206; ACD, July 12, 1852, 177–78; and ACD, July 15, 1852, 225.

144. ACD, July 16, 1852, 247–48.

145. Ibid., 249; see also Slenes, "A árvore de Nsanda transplantada," 308.

146. See "Representação da câmara municipal da cidade da Bahia contra o tráfico de africanos," AS, August 7, 1850, 109. The text can be found at the Centro de Documentação e Informação, Coordenação de Arquivo, Mapoteca, Arquivo da Câmara dos Deputados, Brasília.

147. The Law of Nations, a work of political philosophy by Emer de Vattel published in 1758, became a loose basis for the practice of international diplomacy during the ensuing century, modernizing the theory and practice of international law.

148. Russell to Palmerston, in Murray, Odious Commerce, 215.

149. See Guerra y Sanchéz, Manual de historia de Cuba, 430–38.

150. Murray, Odious Commerce, 208–40; Cruz-Taura, "Annexation and National Identity," 90–109; and Paz Sánchez, "'El Lugareño' contra la esclavocracia," 617–39.

151. Guerra y Sanchéz, Manual de historia de Cuba, 444–59; and May, "Young American Males and Filibustering," 879. See also Henderson, "Southern Designs on Cuba," 371–85.

152. Cited in Murray, Odious Commerce, 224.

153. "Ofício Reservado n. 1815," February 8, 1852, from Rio de Janeiro to Madrid, AGMAE, legajo H 1413.

154. Cited in Murray, Odious Commerce, 230–31.

155. See, respectively, "Ofício ostensivo de José Francisco de Paula Cavalcanti e Albuquerque a Paulino José Soares de Souza," April 2, 1850, and June 19, 1850, AHI, 222/1/6; AS, June 2, 1850, 30; ACD, July 1, 1853, 7–8; and ACD, June 14, 1854, 153.

156. AS, July 10, 1857, 245–46.

157. On this episode, see Abreu, "O caso do Bracuhy."

158. See, respectively, AS, September 20, 1853, 289; and ACD, May 18, 1853, 237. See also AS, May 18, 1853, 100–101; AS, June 6, 1853, 279; ACD, May 17, 1853, 219; ACD, May 18, 232–51; ACD, June 9, 1853, 130–32; ACD, June 28, 1853, 331; ACD, July 13, 1853, 193–95; ACD, July 14, 1853, 211; and ACD, July 15, 1853, 230.

Epilogue

1. Davis, The Problem of Slavery in the Age of Revolution. His more recent book also focuses almost exclusively on the British and French worlds. See Davis, The Problem of Slavery in the Age of Emancipation.

2. Drescher, Abolition: A History of Slavery and Antislavery.

3. Tomich, Through the Prism of Slavery, 56–71.

4. Blackburn, The American Crucible, 289.

BIBLIOGRAPHY

Primary

Parliamentary Records

Anais da Câmara dos Deputados do Império do Brasil, 1826–1850. Available at www.camara.gov.br/publicações.

Anais do Senado do Império do Brasil, 1826–1850. Available at www.senado.gov.br.

Diário da Assembléia Geral Constituinte e Legislativa do Império do Brasil, 1823. 3 vols. Brasília: Centro Gráfico do Senado Federal, 1973.

Diário das Cortes Gerais e Extraordinárias da Nação Portuguesade 1821 e 1822. Available at http://debates.parlamento.pt.

Diário de Sesiones de las Cortes de Cádiz, 1810–1814. CD ROM. Congreso de los Diputados, Historical Series.

Diário de Sesiones de las Cortes de Madrid, 1820–1823. CD ROM. Congreso de los Diputados, Historical Series.

Diario de las Sesiones de Cortes: Estamento de procuradores, legislatura de 1834 a 1835. CD ROM, Congreso de los Diputados, Historical Series.

Diário de Sesiones de las Cortes Constituyentes, 1836–1837. CD ROM. Congreso de los Diputados, Historical Series.

Diários de Sesiones de Cortes, Senado, 1844–1845. Available at www.senado.es.

Manuscript Sources

ARQUIVO DA CÂMARA DOS DEPUTADOS, BRASÍLIA

"Representação da Assembléia Legislativa Provincial de Minas Gerais, Março de 1839," 1839, lata 126, maço 11, pasta 4.

"Representação de cidadãos da província da Bahia solicitando a derrogação da Lei de 7 de Novembro de 1831, que proíbe a introdução de africanos no Brasil," 1841, lata 126, maço 7, pasta 7.3.

ARCHIVO GENERAL DEL MINISTERIO
DE ASUNTOS EXTERIORES, MADRID

Legajo H 1413, Correspondence from Rio de Janeiro to Madrid, 1848–1852.

ARQUIVO HISTÓRICO DO ITAMARATY, RIO DE JANEIRO

Códice 217/3/3, Correspondence from London to Rio de Janeiro.
Códice 198/3/1, Correspondence from London to Rio de Janeiro, 1817.
Códice 338/2/11, Correspondence from Madrid to Rio de Janeiro, 1817.
Códice 216/1/14, Correspondence from London to Rio de Janeiro, 1833.
Códice 271/4/6, Correspondence from the Brazilian special mission in London, 1843.
Códice 220/2/5, Correspondence from Madrid to Rio de Janeiro, 1845.
Códice 220/1/5, Correspondence from Madrid to Rio de Janeiro, 1846.
Códice 217/3/6, Ofícios reservados from London to Rio de Janeiro, 1848–1850.
Códice 222/1/6, Ofícios ostensivos from Madrid to Rio de Janeiro, 1850.

ARCHIVO HISTÓRICO NACIONAL, MADRID

Legajo 3547, Ultramar, Cuba, Gobierno, Esclavitud.

BIBLIOTECA DEL PALACIO REAL, MADRID

Crame, Agustín. *Discurso político sobre la necesidad de fomentar la Isla de Cuba* (1768), ii–2827.

BIBLIOTECA NACIONAL DO RIO DE JANEIRO,
SESSÃO DE MANUSCRITOS, RIO DE JANEIRO

J. A. L. G. "Reflexões sobre a escravatura." *O Despertador,* July 24, 1841. In *Elemento servil: Recorte de jornais brasileiros e franceses sobre a escravidão,* ii–32, 10, 4, n13.

Published Primary Sources

"Acuerdo de la Junta de Fomento sobre manumisión de los negros introducidos desde el año 1820." In José Antonio Saco, *Historia de la esclavitud de la raza africana en el nuevo mundo y en especial en los paises americo-hispanos,* 5:200. Havana: Editorial Alfa, 1944.

Andrada e Silva, José Bonifácio de. *Escritos políticos*. São Paulo: Editora Obelisco, 1964.

———. "Representação à Assembléia Geral Constituinte e Legislativa do Império do Brasil sobre a escravatura." 1823. In *Memórias sobre a escravidão*, edited by Graça Salgado. Rio de Janeiro: Arquivo Nacional, 1988.

[Andrada e Silva,] José Bonifácio [de]. *Representação à Assembléia Geral e Constituinte do império do Brasil sobre a escravatura*. Rio de Janeiro: J. E. S. Cabral, 1840.

Arango y Parreño, Francisco de. *Obras*. 2 vols. Edited by Gloria García Rodríguez. Havana: Ediciones Imagen Contemporánea, Casa de Altos Estudios Don Fernando Ortiz, 2004.

Ayllón, Cecílio. *Reglamento de esclavos*. Matanzas: Imprenta del Gobierno de Matanzas, 1825.

Azeredo Coutinho, José Joaquim da Cunha de. "Análise sobre a justiça do comércio do resgate dos escravos da costa da África." 1st ed., 1808. In *Obras Econômicas*. Edited by Sérgio Buarque de Holanda. São Paulo: Companhia Editora Nacional, 1966.

———. *Analyse sur le justice du commerce du rachat des esclaves de le côte d'Afrique*. London: Baylis, 1798.

———. "Memória sobre o preço do açúcar" (1791). In *Memórias econômicas da Academia Real das Ciências de Lisboa, para o adiantamento da agricultura, das artes, e da indústria em Portugal, e suas conquistas (1789–1815)*, vol. 3, edited by José Luís Cardoso, 273–80. Lisbon: Banco de Portugal, 1993.

Barreto, Domingos Alves Branco Moniz. *Memória sobre a abolição do comércio da escravatura*. Rio de Janeiro: Typographia Imparcial de F. P. Brito, 1837.

Barros, Domingos Borges de. "Memória sobre o café, sua história, cultura e amanhos," part 3. *O Patriota*, no. 8, August 1813.

Blake, Augusto Victorino Alves Sacramento. *Diccionario bibliographico brazileiro*. Vols. 3, 5. Rio de Janeiro: Imprensa Nacional, 1889.

Bonavides, Paulo, and Roberto Amaral. *Textos políticos da história do Brasil*. Vol. 9. Brasília: Senado Federal, 2002.

Brasahemeco, Ananias Dortano [António Barão de Mascarenhas]. *Rights of Portugal in Reference to Great Britain and the Question of the Slave Trade; or, The Manifesto and Protest of the Weak Against the Ingratitude, Opression, and Violence of the Strong*. 2 vols. Bristol: n.p., 1840.

Burlamaqui, Frederico Leopoldo César. "Memória analítica acerca do comércio de escravos e da escravidão doméstica." 1837. In *Memórias sobre a escravidão*, edited by Graça Salgado. Rio de Janeiro: Arquivo Nacional; Brasília: Fundação Petrônio Portela, 1988.

"The Cádiz Constitution of 1812." In *Latin American Independence: An Anthology of Sources*, edited by Sarah C. Chambers and John Charles Chasteen, 100–101. Indianapolis, IN: Hackett, 2010.

Campomanes, Pedro Rodríguez de. *Reflexiones sobre el comercio español a Indias*. 1st ed., 1762. Edited by Vicente Llombart Rosa. Madrid: Instituto de Estudios Fiscales, 1988.

"Capítulo séptimo de las instrucciones de la diputación provincial de La Habana." In *Esclavitud y sociedad: Notas y documentos para la historia de la esclavitud negra en Cuba*, edited by Eduardo Torres-Cuevas and Eusebio Reyes. Havana: Editorial de Ciencias Sociales, 1986.

"Carta de Martinho de Mello e Castro [para Bernardo José de Lorena, Governador da Capitania de São Paulo] sobre a expedição para a descoberta de La Perouse, 21 de fevereiro de 1792." In *Documentos interessantes para a história e costumes de São Paulo*, vol. 45 (1924).

Constituição de Hespanha. Lisbon: Impressão Régia, 1820.

Coutinho, Rodrigo de Sousa. "Memória sobre o melhoramento dos domínios de Sua Majestade na América." In *Textos Políticos, Económicos e Financeiros (1783–1811)*, vol. 2, edited by Andrée Mansuy Diniz Silva, 47–66. Lisbon: Banco de Portugal, 1993.

———. *Textos Políticos, Económicos e Financeiros (1783–1811)*. 2 vols. Edited by Andrée Mansuy Diniz Silva. Lisbon: Banco de Portugal, 1993.

Cunha Matos, Raimundo José da. *Compêndio histórico das possessões de Portugal na África*. Rio de Janeiro: Arquivo Nacional, 1963.

———. *Corografia história da província de Minas Gerais*. 2 vols. 1st ed., 1837. São Paulo: Editora da Universidade de São Paulo; Belo Horizonte: Itatiaia, 1981.

———. "Memória história sobre a população, emigração e colonização que convém ao império do Brasil." *O Auxiliador da Indústria Nacional* (Rio de Janeiro) 5, no. 4 (1837): 102–11.

———. "Relatório apresentado ao conselho administrativo da Sociedade Auxiliadora da Indústria Nacional a respeito do prospecto do estabelecimento da companhia inglesa de agricultura e do açúcar da Índia oriental." *O Auxiliador da Indústria Nacional* (Rio de Janeiro) 5, no. 4 (1837): 344–64.

Documentos officiaes relativos a negociação do tractado entre Portugal e a Gram Bretanha para a supressão do trafico da escravatura, mandados imprimir por ordem da Camara dos Senadores. Lisbon: Imprensa Nacional, 1839.

Edwards, Bryan. *The History, Civil and Commercial, of the British Colonies in the West Indies*. 2 vols. London: John Stockdale, 1793.

"El Tribunal de Comercio de esta Plaza de La Habana representa a la regencia del reino contra la emancipación de los esclavos de esta ilsa, fecha 30 de marzo de 1841, extendida por el Sr. Indendente Don Wenceslao de Villa-Urrutia." In José Antonio Saco, *Historia de la esclavitud de la raza africana en el nuevo mundo y en especial en los paises americo-hispanos*, 5:242–52. Havana: Editorial Alfa, 1944.

"Encuesta sobre la reforma del sistema higiênico, moral y alimentar de los siervos, con respuestas de Jacinto González Larrinaga, marqués de Arcos, Joaquín

Muñoz Izaguirre, Rafael O'Farril, Sebastián I. de Lasa, Joaquín Gómez, José Manuel Carrillo, Ignacio de Herrera, El conde de Fernandina, Domingo de Aldama, Wenceslao de Villa Urrutia, Juan Montalvo, 1842." In Jean-Pierre Tardieu, *"Morir o dominar": En torno al reglamento de esclavos de Cuba (1841–1866)*, 206–63. Frankfurt: Iberoamericana Vervuert, 2003.

Estatísticas históricas do Brasil: Séries econômicas, demográficas e sociais de 1550 a 1988. Rio de Janeiro: Instituto Brasileiro de Geografia e Estatística, 1990.

"Exposición al Excelentísimo Sr. Gobernador General de la isla de Cuba." In José Antonio Saco, *Historia de la esclavitud de la raza africana en el nuevo mundo y en especial en los paises americo-hispanos*, 5:283–85. Havana: Editorial Alfa, 1944.

"Exposición de la Junta de Fomento de la isla de Cuba a la regencia provisional del reino, pidiendo entre otras cosas la cesación de la trata y la colonización blanca." In José Antonio Saco, *Historia de la esclavitud de la raza africana en el nuevo mundo y en especial en los paises americo-hispanos*, 5:185–92. Havana: Editorial Alfa, 1944.

"Exposición del Ilustre Ayuntamiento de La Habana." In José Antonio Saco, *Historia de la esclavitud de la raza africana en el nuevo mundo y en especial en los paises americo-hispanos*, 5:236–41. Havana: Editorial Alfa, 1944.

Falla dirigida á Assembléa Legislativa Provincial de Minas-Gerais na abertura da sessão ordinaria do anno de 1843 pelo presidente da provincia, Francisco José de Souza Soares d'Andrea. Ouro Preto, Brazil: Typographia do Correio de Minas, 1843.

Feijó, Diogo Antônio. *Diogo Antônio Feijó.* Edited by Jorge Caldeira. São Paulo: Editora 34, 1999.

Fenelon, Dea Ribeiro. "Levantamento e sistematização da legislação relativa aos escravos no Brasil." In *Nuevas aportaciones a la historia juridica de Iberoamerica*, edited by Silvia Hunold Lara. CD-ROM. Madrid: Fundación Histórica Tavera; Digibis; Fundación Hernando de Laramendi, 2000.

González del Valle y Ramírez, Francisco. *La Habana en 1841.* Edited by Raquel Catala. Havana: Oficina del Historiador de la Ciudad de La Habana, 1952.

"Importante exposición de los hacendados de Matanzas ao Gobernador Capitán General, pidiendo la supresión de la trata" In José Antonio Saco, *Historia de la esclavitud de la raza africana en el nuevo mundo y en especial en los paises americo-hispanos*, 5:279–82. Havana: Editorial Alfa, 1944.

"Informe de la Junta de Fomento." In José Antonio Saco, *Historia de la esclavitud de la raza africana en el nuevo mundo y en especial en los paises americo-hispanos*, 5:211–31. Havana: Editorial Alfa, 1944.

"Informe del censor de la Real Sociedad Patriótica, don Manuel Martínez Serrano, sobre el convenio propuesto por el gobierno de S. M. B. para la abolición del tráfico de esclavos." In José Antonio Saco, *Historia de la esclavitud de la raza africana en el nuevo mundo y en especial en los paises americo-hispanos*, 5:201–10. Havana: Editorial Alfa, 1944.

"Informe del Ldo. D. Bernardo M. Navarro, residente en Matanzas, acerca del proyecto de convenio sobre emancipación propuesto por la Inglaterra." In José Antonio Saco, *Historia de la esclavitud de la raza africana en el nuevo mundo y en especial en los paises americo-hispanos*, 5:253–65. Havana: Editorial Alfa, 1944.

"Informe reservado del Real Consulado, emitido por la misma comisión que redactó la anterior exposición." In José Antonio Saco, *Historia de la esclavitud de la raza africana en el nuevo mundo y en especial en los paises americo-hispanos*, 5:211–31. Havana: Editorial Alfa, 1944.

"Informe sobre la promulgación de una ley penal contra los traficantes de esclavos africanos." In José Antonio Saco, *Historia de la esclavitud de la raza africana en el nuevo mundo y en especial en los paises americo-hispanos*, 5:286–87. Havana: Editorial Alfa, 1944.

"Interrogatorio de Mr. R. R. Madden, absuelto por mim en 17 de septiembre de 1839, por Domingo del Monte." In José Antonio Saco, *Historia de la esclavitud de la raza africana en el nuevo mundo y en especial en los paises americo-hispanos*, 5:367–74. Havana: Editorial Alfa, 1944.

Inventário analítico do arquivo da Assembléia Geral Constituinte e Legislativa do Império do Brasil, 1823. Brasília: Câmara dos Deputados, Coordenação de Publicações, 1987.

"Legislação sobre escravos africanos na América portuguesa." In *Nuevas aportaciones a la historia juridica de Iberoamerica*, edited by Silvia Hunold Lara. CD-ROM. Madrid: Fundación Histórica Tavera; Digibis; Fundación Hernando de Laramendi, 2000.

Merlin, Condesa de. *Los esclavos en las colonias españolas*. Madrid: Imprenta de Alegría y Charlain, 1841.

Moreau de Saint-Méry, Médéric Louis Élie. *Description topographique, physique, civile, politique et historique de la partie française de l'isle de Saint-Domingue*. 3 vols. 1st ed., 1797. Paris: Société Française d'Histoire d'Outre-Mer, 1984.

Notícia histórica, política, civil e natural do império do Brasil em 1833. Rio de Janeiro: Imperial Typographia de Pedro Plancher-Seignot, 1833.

O'Gavan, Juan Bernardo. *Observaciones sobre la suerte de los negros del Africa, considerados en su propia patria, y transplantados a las Antillas españolas: Y reclamacion contra el tratado celebrado con los ingleses el año de 1817*. Madrid: Imprenta del Universal, 1821.

Oliveira Mendes, Luis Antonio de. "Discurso acadêmico ao programa: Determinar com todos os seus sintomas as doenças agudas, e crônicas, que mais freqüentemente acometem os pretos recém-tirados da África." In *As companhias Pombalinas de grão-pará e Maranhão e Pernambuco e Paraíba*, edited by Antonio Carreira. Lisbon: Editorial Presença, 1983.

———. "Discurso acadêmico ao programa: Determinar com todos os seus sintomas as doenças agudas, e crônicas, que mais freqüentemente acometem os pretos recém-tirados da África." In *Memórias econômicas da Academia Real das Ciências de Lisboa, para o adiantamento da agricultura, das artes, e da indústria em Portugal, e suas conquistas (1789–1815)*, vol. 4, edited by José Luís Cardoso. 1st ed., 1812. Lisbon: Banco de Portugal, 1993.

———. "Discurso preliminar, histórico, introdutivo com natureza de descrição econômica da comarca, e Cidade do Salvador" (1790). In *Aspectos da economia colonial*, edited by Pinto de Aguiar. Salvador: Livraria Progresso Editora, 1957.

"Parecer de la Real Junta sobre el Reglamento de Esclavos, 1845." In Jean-Pierre Tardieu, *"Morir o dominar": En torno al reglamento de esclavos de Cuba (1841–1866)*, 264–71. Frankfurt: Iberoamericana Vervuert, 2003.

[Pereira da Silva, João Manoel]. *Inglaterra e Brasil: Tráfego de escravos*. Rio de Janeiro: Typographia Brasil, 1845.

Peréz de la Riva, Juan, ed. *Correspondência reservada del Capitan General Don Miguel Tacón (1834–1836)*. Havana: Biblioteca Nacional José Martí, 1963.

"Projeto de constituição para o império do Brasil." 1823. In *O constitucionalismo liberal luso-brasileiro*, edited by Jorge Miranda. Lisbon: Comissão Nacional para as Comemorações dos Descobrimentos Portugueses, 2001.

"Proyecto de reglamento de policia rural, Antonio García Oña, 1841." In Jean-Pierre Tardieu, *"Morir o dominar": En torno al reglamento de esclavos de Cuba (1841–1866)*, 201–6. Frankfurt: Iberoamericana Vervuert, 2003.

"Representación del consulado de La Habana de 21 de octubre de 1818." In *Esclavitud y sociedad: Notas y documentos para la historia de la esclavitud negra en Cuba*, edited by Eduardo Torres-Cuevas and Eusebio Reyes. Havana: Editorial de Ciencias Sociales, 1986.

Resumen del censo de población de la Isla de Cuba a fin del año de 1841. Havana: Imprenta del Gobierno, 1842.

Rocha, Justiniano José da. *Acção, reacção e transacção: Duas palavras acerca da actualidade política do Brasil*. Rio de Janeiro: Typographia Imperial e Constitucional de Villeneuve, 1855.

Rodrigues, José Honório, ed. *Atas do Conselho de Estado*. Vol. 3. Brasília: Senado Federal, 1978.

Saco, José Antonio. *Examen analíctico del informe de la comisión especial*. Madrid: Imprenta de Tomás Jordan, 1837.

———. *Obras*. 5 vols. Facsimile reproduction. In *Biblioteca digital de clásicos cubanos: Orígenes del pensamento cubano I*, edited by Eduardo Torres-Cuevas and Luis Miguel García Mora. CD-ROM. Madrid: Casa de Altos Estudios Don Fernando Ortiz; Fundación Mapfre Tavera, 2002.

Sagra, Ramón de la. *Apuntes destinados a ilustrar la discusión del artículo adicional del proyeto de Constitución que dice "las provincias de Ultramar serán gobernadas por leyes especiales."* Paris: Imprenta de Maulde et Renon, 1837.

[Silva, José Carneiro da]. *Memória sobre o comércio dos escravos, em que se pretende mostra que este tráfico é, para eles, antes um bem do que um mal. Escrita por*

———, *natural dos Campos dos Goytacazes*. Rio de Janeiro: Typographia Imperial e Constitucional de Villeneuve, 1838.

Sustentação dos votos dos deputados Raimundo José da Cunha Matos e Luiz Augusto May, sobre a convenção para a final extincção do commercio de escravos. Rio de Janeiro: Imperial Typographia de Pedro Plancher-Seignot, 1827.

Taunay, Carlos Augusto. *Manual do agricultor brasileiro.* 1839. Edited by Rafael Bivar de Marquese. São Paulo: Companhia das Letras, 2001.

Tocqueville, Alexis de. *Writings on Empire and Slavery.* 1839. Edited by Jennifer Pitts. Baltimore, MD: Johns Hopkins University Press, 2001.

Torrente, Mariano. *Cuestión importante sobre la esclavitud.* Madrid: Imprenta de la Viuda de Jordán e Hijos, 1841.

Torres Homem, Francisco de Sales. "Consideraçoens economicas sobre a escravatura." *Nitheroy: Revista Brasiliense* (Paris) (1836).

Tratado entre su Magestad la Reina de España y su Magestad el Rey del Reino Unido, de la Gran Bretaña é Irlanda, para la abolición del tráfico de esclavos, concluido y firmado en Madrid en 28 de Junio de 1835. Madrid: Prenta Real, 1835.

Uruguai, Visconde de. *Visconde de Uruguai.* Edited by José Murilo de Carvalho. São Paulo: Editora 34, 1999.

Varela y Morales, Félix. *Obras.* 3 vols. Facsimile reproduction. In *Biblioteca digital de clásicos cubanos: Orígenes del pensamiento cubano I,* edited by Eduardo Torres-Cuevas and Luis Miguel García Mora. CD-ROM. Madrid: Casa de Altos Estudios Don Fernando Ortiz; Fundación Mapfre Tavera, 2002.

Vázquez Queipo, Vicente. *Cuba, se ressources, son administration, sa population, au point de vue de la colonisation européenne et de l'émancipation progressive des esclaves.* Paris: Imprimerie Nationale, 1851.

Secondary

Reference Works

Paiva, Tancredo Barros de. *Achegas a um diccionario de pseudonymos: Iniciais, abreviaturas e obras anonymas de auctores brasileiros e de estrangeiros, sobre o Brasil ou no mesmo impressas.* Rio de Janeiro: Editores J. Leite e Companhia, 1929.

Pezuela, Jacobo de la. *Diccionario geográfico: Estadístico e histórico de la isla de Cuba.* 4 vols. Madrid: Imprenta del Establecimiento de Mellado, 1863.

Pinto, Antônio Pereira. *Apontamentos para o direito internacional ou collecção completa dos tratados celebrados pelo Brasil com differentes nações, acompanhada de uma notícia histórica e documentada sobre as convenções mais importantes.* 4 vols. Rio de Janeiro: F. L. Pinto, 1864.

Sagra, Ramón de la. *Cuba en 1860 o sea cuadro de sus adelantos en la población, la agricultura, el comercio e las rentas públicas: Suplemento a la primera parte de la historia política y natural de la isla de Cuba.* Paris: Hachette, 1862.

Silva, Innocencio Francisco da. *Diccionario bibliographico portuguez.* 22 vols. Lisbon: Imprensa Nacional, 1883 (vol. 10), 1884 (vol. 11).

Voyages: The Trans-Atlantic Slave Trade Database. Available at www.slavevoyages.org.

Books and Articles

Abreu, Martha. "O caso do Bracuhy." In *Resgate: Uma janela para o oitocentos*, edited by Hebe Maria Mattos de Castro and Eduardo Schnoor. Rio de Janeiro: Topbooks, 1995.

Adelman, Jeremy. *Sovereignty and Revolution in the Iberian Atlantic.* Princeton, NJ: Princeton University Press, 2006.

Aja, Eliseo, and Jordi Sole Tura. *Constituciones y periodos constituyentes en España (1808–1936).* Madrid: Siglo XXI, 1977.

Alcides, Sérgio. "O lado B do neoclassicismo luso-brasileiro: Patriotismo e poesia no 'poderoso império.'" In *Iluminismo e império no Brasil: O Patriota (1813–1814)*, edited by Lorelai Kury. Rio de Janeiro: Editora Fiocruz; Fundação Biblioteca Nacional, 2007.

Alencastro, Luiz Felipe de. "Le commerce des vivants: Traite d'esclaves et 'pax lusitana' dans l'Atlantique sud." 3 vols. PhD dissertation, Université Paris X Nanterre, 1986.

———. "A economia política dos descobrimentos." In *A descoberta do homem e do mundo*, edited by Adauto Novaes. São Paulo: Companhia das Letras, 1998.

———. "La traite négrière et l'unité national brésilienne." *Revue Française d'Histoire d'Outre-Mer* 66, no. 244–45 (1979): 395–419.

———. *O trato dos viventes: Formação do Brasil no Atlântico sul, séculos XVI e XVII.* São Paulo: Companhia das Letras, 2000.

———. "Vida privada e ordem privada no império." In *História da vida privada no Brasil.* Vol. 2, *Império: A corte e a modernidade nacional*, edited by Luiz Felipe de Alencastro. São Paulo: Companhia das Letras, 1997.

Alexandre, Valentim. "O império luso-brasileiro em face do abolicionismo inglês (1807–1820)." In *Brasil: Colonização e escravidão*, edited by Maria Beatriz Nizza da Silva. Rio de Janeiro: Nova Fronteira, 2000.

———. "O liberalismo português e as colónias de África, 1820–1839." *Análise Social* 26, no. 111 (1980): 319–40.

———. *Os sentidos do império: Questão nacional e questão colonial na crise do antigo regime português.* Porto: Afrontamento, 1993.

Alonso Romero, Maria Paz. *Cuba en la España liberal (1837–1898).* Madrid: Centro de Estudios Políticos y Constitucionales, 2002.

Álvarez Cuartero, Izaskun. *Memorias de la ilustración: Las sociedades económicas de amigos del país en Cuba (1783–1832).* Madrid: Real Sociedad Bascongada de los Amigos del País., 2000.

Andrade, Marcos Ferreira de. "Rebelião escrava na comarca do Rio das Mortes, Minas Gerais: O caso Carrancas." *Afro-Ásia*, no. 21–22 (1998–1999): 45–82.

Andrés-Gallego, José. *La esclavitud en la América española*. Madrid: Ediciones Encuentro; Madrid: Fundación Ignacio Larramendi, 2005.

Anna, Timothy. "A independência do México e da América central." In *História da América latina*. Vol. 3, *Da independência até 1870*, edited by Leslie Bethell. São Paulo: Editora da Universidade de São Paulo; Brasília: Fundação Alexandre de Gusmão, 2001.

Appleby, John C. "War, Politics, and Colonization, 1558–1625." In *The Oxford History of the British Empire*. Vol. 1, *The Origins of the Empire: British Overseas Enterprise to the Close of the Seventeenth Century*, edited by Nicholas Canny. New York: Oxford University Press, 1998.

Armitage, David. *The Ideological Origins of the British Empire*. Cambridge: Cambridge University Press, 2000.

———. "Three Concepts of Atlantic History." In *The British Atlantic World, 1500–1800*, edited by David Armitage and Michael J. Braddick. New York: Palgrave Macmillan, 2002.

Arrighi, Giovanni. *The Long Twentieth Century: Money, Power, and the Origins of Our Times*. London: Verso, 1994.

Artola, Miguel. *Espanha de Fernando VII*. Madrid: Espasa, 1999.

Artola, Miguel, et al. *Las Cortes de Cádiz*. Madrid: Marcial Pons, 1991.

Asiegbu, Johnson U. J. *Slavery and the Politics of Liberation, 1787–1861: A Study of Liberated African Emigration and British Antislavery Policy*. New York: Africana Publishing Corporation, 1969.

Bahamonde, Angel, and José Cayuela. *Hacer las Américas: Las elites coloniais españolas en el siglo XIX*. Madrid: Alianza Editorial, 1992.

Bailyn, Bernard. *Atlantic History: Concept and Contours*. Cambridge, MA: Harvard University Press, 2005.

———. *The Ideological Origins of the American Revolution*. Cambridge, MA: Belknap Press of Harvard University Press, 1992.

Bakewell, Peter. "A mineração na América espanhola colonial." In *História da América Latina*. Vol. 2, *América Latina Colonial*, edited by Leslie Bethell. São Paulo: Editora da Universidade de São Paulo; Brasília: Fundação Alexandre de Gusmão, 1999.

Barcia Paz, Manuel. "El conde de Villanueva y la alternativa de la Cuba Grande: Una aproximación a la labor de Claudio Martínez de Pinillos al frente de a Intendencia de Hacienda de la isla de Cuba, 1825–1851." In *Francisco Arango y la invención de la Cuba azucarera*, edited by María Dolores González-Ripoll and Izaskun Álvarez Cuartero, 289–300. Salamanca: Ediciones Universidad de Salamanca, 2009.

———. "La rebelión de esclavos de 1825 en Guamacaro." Master's thesis, Universidade de Habana, 2000.

——— [Manuel Barcia]. *Seeds of Insurrection: Domination and Resistence in Western Cuban Plantations, 1808–1848*. Baton Rouge: Louisiana State University Press, 2008.

——— [Manuel Barcia]. *West African Warfare in Bahia and Cuba: Soldier Slaves in the Atlantic World, 1807–1844*. Oxford: Oxford University Press, 2014.

Basile, Marcello Otávio. *Ezequiel Corrêa dos Santos: Um jacobino na corte imperial*. Rio de Janeiro: Editora da Fundação Gétulio Vargas, 2001.

Batie, Robert C. "Why Sugar? Economic Cycles and the Changing of Staples in the English and French Antilles, 1624–1654." In *Caribbean Slave Society and Economy: A Student Reader*, edited by Hilary Beckles and Verene Shepherd. Kingston: Ian Randle; London: James Currey, 1991.

Bender, Thomas, ed. *The Antislavery Debate: Capitalism and Abolitionism as a Problem in Historical Interpretation*. Berkeley: University of California Press, 1992.

Berbel, Márcia Regina. *A nação como artefato: Deputados do Brasil nas Cortes Portuguesas (1821–1822)*. São Paulo: Editora Hucitec, 1999.

Bergad, Laird W. *The Comparative Histories of Slavery in Brazil, Cuba, and the United States*. Cambridge: Cambridge University Press, 2007.

Bergad, Laird W., Fe Iglesias García, and María del Carmen Barcia. *The Cuban Slave Market, 1790–1880*. Cambridge: Cambridge University Press, 1995.

Berlin, Ira. *Generations of Captivity: A History of African-American Slaves*. Cambridge, MA: Belknap Press of Harvard University Press, 2003.

———. *Many Thousands Gone: The First Two Centuries of Slavery in North America*. Cambridge, MA: Belknap Press of Harvard University Press, 1998.

Bernand, Carmen, and Serge Gruzinski. *História do novo mundo: Da descoberta à conquista, uma experiência européia (1492–1550)*. São Paulo: Editora da Universidade de São Paulo, 2001.

Bethell, Leslie. *A abolição do comércio brasileiro de escravos: A Grã-Bretanha, o Brasil e a questão do comércio de escravos, 1807–1869*. 1st ed., 1969. Brasília: Senado Federal, 2002.

———, ed. *The Cambridge History of Latin America*. Vol. 2, *Colonial Latin America*. Cambridge: Cambridge University Press, 1984.

Bethencourt, Francisco, and Kirti Chaudhuri, Kirti, eds. *História da expansão portuguesa*. Vol. 1, *A formação do império (1415–1570)*. Lisbon: Temas e Debates, 1998.

Bicalho, Maria Fernanda. *A cidade e o império: O Rio de Janeiro no século XVIII*. Rio de Janeiro: Civilização Brasileira, 2003.

Blackburn, Robin. *The American Crucible: Slavery, Emancipation and Human Rights*. London: Verso, 2011.

———. "The Force of Example." In *The Impact of the Haitian Revolution in the Atlantic World*, edited by David P. Geggus. Columbia: University of South Carolina Press, 2001.

———. "Haiti, Slavery, and the Age of the Democratic Revolution." *William and Mary Quarterly*, 3rd ser., 63, no. 4 (October 2006): 643–74.

————. *The Making of New World Slavery: From the Baroque to the Modern, 1492–1800*. London: Verso, 1997.

————. *The Overthrow of Colonial Slavery: 1776–1848*. London: Verso, 1988.

Blanchard, Peter. *Under the Flags of Freedom: Slave Soldiers and the Wars of Independence in Spanish South America*. Pittsburgh, PA: University of Pittsburgh Press, 2008.

Borrego, Maria Aparecida de Menezes. *A teia mercantil: Negócios e poderes em São Paulo colonial (1711–1765)*. São Paulo: Alameda, 2010.

Boulle, Pierre H. "La construction du concept de race dans la France d'Ancien Régime." *Revue Française d'Histoire d'Outre-Mer* 89, no. 336–37 (2002): 155–75.

Bowser, Frederick P. *El esclavo africano en el Perú colonial, 1524–1650*. Mexico City: Siglo XXI, 1977.

Boxer, Charles R. *A idade de ouro do Brasil: Dores de crescimento de uma sociedade colonial*. 1st ed., 1962. Rio de Janeiro: Nova Fronteira, 2000.

————. *O império marítimo português (1415–1825)*. Lisbon: Edições 70, 2001.

————. *Salvador de Sá e a luta pelo Brasil e Angola, 1602–1686*. 1st ed., 1952. São Paulo: Companhia Editora Nacional; Editora da Universidade de São Paulo, 1973.

Brading, David A. "A Espanha dos Bourbons e seu império americano." In *História da América latina*. Vol. 1, *América latina colonial*, edited by Leslie Bethell. São Paulo: Editora da Universidade de São Paulo; Brasília: Fundação Alexandre de Gusmão, 1997.

Braudel, Fernand. *Civilização material, economia e capitalismo, séculos XV–XVIII*. Vol. 3, *O tempo do mundo*. São Paulo: Martins Fontes, 1996.

Breña, Roberto. *El primer liberalismo español y los procesos de emancipación de América, 1808–1824: Una revisión historiográfica del liberalismo hispânico*. Mexico City: El Colégio de México, Centro de Estudios Internacionales, 2006.

Brown, Christopher Leslie. *Moral Capital: Foundations of British Abolitionism*. Chapel Hill: University of North Carolina Press, 2005.

————. "The Politics of Slavery." In *The British Atlantic World, 1500–1800*, edited by David Armitage and Michael J. Braddick. New York: Palgrave Macmillan, 2002.

Bush, Jonathan. "The British Constitution and the Creation of American Slavery." In *Slavery and the Law*, edited by Paul Finkelman. Madison, WI: Madison House, 1997.

Bushnell, David. "A independência da América do Sul Espanhola." In *História da América latina*. Vol. 3, *Da independência até 1870*, edited by Leslie Bethell. São Paulo: Editora da Universidade de São Paulo; Brasília: Fundação Alexandre de Gusmão, 2001.

Butel, Paul. "Un nouvel age colonial: Les Antilles sous Louis XIV." In *Histoire des Antilles et de la Guyane*, edited by Pierre Pluchon. Paris: Privat, 1982.

————."Le temps des fondations: Les Antilles avant Colbert." In *Histoire des Antilles et de la Guyane*, edited by Pierre Pluchon. Paris: Privat, 1982.

Cabrera, Raimundo. *Cuba y sus jueces (rectificaciones oportunas)*. Philadelphia, PA: Levytype, 1891.

Candido, Antonio. *Formação da literatura brasileira (momentos decisivos)*. 2 vols. 2nd ed. São Paulo: Livraria Martins Editora, 1962.

Cañizares-Esguerra, Jorge. *Puritan Conquistadors: Iberianizing the Atlantic, 1550–1700*. Stanford, CA: Stanford University Press, 2006.

Capela, José. *As burguesias portuguesas e a abolição do tráfico da escravatura*. Porto: Afrontamento, 1979.

Cardoso, José Luís. *Pensar a economia em Portugal: Digressões históricas*. Lisbon: Difel, 1997.

Carmen Barcia, María del, and Eduardo Torres-Cuevas. "El debilitamiento de las relaciones sociales esclavistas: Del reformismo liberal a la revolución independentista." In *Historia de Cuba: La colonia; Evolución socioeconómico y formación nacional*, edited by Instituto de Historia de Cuba. Havana: Editora Política, 1994.

Carrara, Angelo Alves. *Minas e currais: Produção rural e mercado interno de Minas Gerais, 1674–1807*. Juiz de Fora, Brazil: Editora Universidade Federal de Juiz de Fora, 2007.

Carreira, Liberato de Castro. *História financeira e orçamentária do império do Brasil*. Brasília: Senado Federal; Rio de Janeiro: Fundação Casa Rui Barbosa/MEC, 1980.

Carvalho, José Murilo de. *Bernardo Pereira de Vasconcelos*. Coleção Formadores do Brasil. São Paulo: Editora 34, 1999.

———. *A construção da ordem: Teatro de sombras*. Rio de Janeiro: Civilização Brasileira, 2003.

Carvalho, Marcus J. M. de. "Os negros armados pelos brancos e suas independências no Nordeste (1817–1848)." In *Independência: História e historiografia*, edited by István Jancsó. São Paulo: Editora Hucitec; Fundação de Amparo à Pesquisa do Estado de São Paulo, 2005.

Castro, Jeanne Berrance de. *A milícia cidadã: A Guarda Nacional de 1831 a 1850*. São Paulo: Companhia Editora Nacional, 1977.

———. "O povo em armas: Guarda Nacional, 1831–1850." PhD dissertation, Universidade de São Paulo, 1968.

Castro, Paulo Pereira de. "A experiência 'republicana,' 1831–1840." In *História geral da civilização brasileira*. Vol. 2, *O Brasil monárquico: Dispersão e unidade*, edited by Sérgio Buarque de Holanda. São Paulo: Difel, 1985.

Cauna, Jacques. *Au temps des isles à sucre: Histoire d'une plantation de Saint-Domingue au XVIIIe siècle*. Paris: Karthala, 1987.

Cayuela Fernández, José G. "Los capitanes generales ante la cuestión de la abolición (1854–1862)." In *Esclavitud y derechos humanos: La lucha por la libertad del negro en el siglo XIX*, edited by Francisco de Solano Agustín Guimerá. Madrid: Editorial Consejo Superior de Investigaciones Científicas, 1990.

Cepero Bonilla, Raúl. *Azúcar y abolición*. 1st ed., 1948. Barcelona: Editorial Crítica, 1976.

Chaffin, Tom. "Sons of Washington: Narciso López, Filibustering, and U.S. Nationalism, 1848–1851." *Journal of the Early Republic* 15, no. 1 (Spring 1995): 79–108.

Chalhoub, Sidney. *Cidade febril: Cortiços e epidemias na Corte imperial*. São Paulo: Companhia das Letras, 1996.

———. *A força da escravidão: Ilegalidade e costume no Brasil oitocentista*. São Paulo: Companhia das Letras, 2012.

Childs, Matt D. *The 1812 Aponte Rebellion in Cuba and the Struggle against Atlantic Slavery*. Chapel Hill: University of North Carolina Press, 2006.

Chust, Manuel. *La cuestión nacional americana en las Cortes de Cádiz*. Valencia: Fundación Instituto de Historia Social; Mexico City: Instituto de Investigaciones Históricas, Universidad Nacional Autónoma de México, 1999.

———. "Nación y federación: Cuestiones del doceañismo hispano." In *Federalismo y cuestion federal en España*, edited by Manuel Chust. Castellón de la Plana, Spain: Universitat Jaume I, 2004.

Clarence-Smith, William Gervase, and Steven Topik. *The Global Coffee Economy in Africa, Asia, and Latin America, 1500–1989*. Cambridge: Cambridge University Press, 2003.

Conrad, Robert. *The Destruction of Brazilian Slavery, 1850–1888*. Berkeley: University of California Press, 1972.

———. *Tumbeiros: O tráfico de escravos para o Brasil*. São Paulo: Editora Brasiliense, 1985.

Conze, Werner. "Rasse." In *Geschichtliche Grundbegriffe: Historisches Lexikon zur politisch-sozialen Sprache in Deustchland*, edited by Otto Brunner, Werner Conze, and Reinhart Koselleck. Stuttgart: Klett-Cotta, 1984.

Corbitt, Duvon C. "Immigration in Cuba." *Hispanic American Historical Review* 22, no. 2 (May 1942): 280–308.

Corwin, Arthur F. *Spain and the Abolition of Slavery in Cuba, 1817–1886*. Austin: University of Texas Press, 1967.

Costa, Emília Viotti da. *Crowns of Glory, Tears of Blood: The Demerara Slave Rebellion of 1823*. Oxford: Oxford University Press, 1994.

———. *Da monarquia à república: Momentos decisivos*. São Paulo: Editora UNESP, 1999.

———. *Da senzala à colônia*. 1st ed., 1966. São Paulo: Editora UNESP, 1998.

Costa, Wilma Peres. "Entre Viena e Verona: Olhares do velho mundo sobre o surgimento das nações da América (1815–1822)." Paper presented at the International Seminar Brasil: De um Império a outro (1750–1850), Departamento de História, Universidade de São Paulo, September 2005.

Cottrol, Robert J. *The Long, Lingering Shadow: Slavery, Race, and Law in the American Hemisphere*. Athens: University of Georgia Press, 2013.

Covo, Manuel. "La révolution haïtienne entre etudes révolutionnaires et *Atlantic History*." In *L'atlantique révolutionnaire: Une perspective ibéro-américaine*, edited by Clément Thibaud, Gabriel Entin, Alejandro Gómez, and Federica Morelli, 259–88. Bécherel, France: Éditions Les Perséides, 2013.

Cowling, Camillia. *Conceiving Freedom: Women of Color, Gender, and the Abolition of Slavery in Havana and Rio de Janeiro*. Chapel Hill: University of North Carolina Press, 2013.

Craton, Michael. "Property and Propriety: Land Tenure and Slave Property in the Creation of a British West Indian Plantocracy, 1612–1740." In *Early Modern Conceptions of Property*, edited by John Brewer and Susan Staves. London: Routledge, 1996.

———. *Testing the Chains: Resistance to Slavery in the British West Indies*. Ithaca, NY: Cornell University Press, 1982.

Crosby, Alfred W. *Ecological Imperialism: The Biological Expansion of Europe, 900–1900*. Cambridge: Cambridge University Press, 1986.

Cruz-Taura, Graciella. "Annexation and National Identity: Cuba's Mid-Nineteenth-Century Debate." *Cuban Studies* 27 (1997): 90–109.

Curto, Diogo Ramada, et al., eds. *A casa literária do Arco do Cego (1799–1801): Bicentenário*. Lisbon: Biblioteca Nacional–Imprensa Nacional–Casa da Moeda, 1999.

Davis, David Brion. "Impact of the French and Haitian Revolutions." In *The Impact of the Haitian Revolution in the Atlantic World*, edited by David P. Geggus. Columbia: University of South Carolina Press, 2001.

———. *Inhuman Bondage: The Rise and Fall of Slavery in the New World*. Oxford: Oxford University Press, 2006.

———. *The Problem of Slavery in the Age of Emancipation*. New York: Alfred A. Knopf, 2014.

———. *The Problem of Slavery in the Age of Revolution, 1770–1823*. 1st ed., 1975. Oxford: Oxford University Press, 1999.

———. *The Problem of Slavery in Western Culture*. 1st ed., 1966. New York: Oxford University Press, 1988.

———. *Slavery and Human Progress*. Oxford: Oxford University Press, 1984.

Debbash, Yvan. "Au coeur du 'gouvernement des esclaves': La souveraineté domestique aux Antilles françaises (XVIIe-XVIIIe siècles)." *Revue Française d'Histoire d'Outre-Mer* 72, no. 266 (1985): 31–54.

Debien, Gabriel. *Les colons de Saint-Domingue et la revolution: Essai sur le Club Massiac*. Paris: Armand Colin, 1953.

———. *Les esclaves aux Antilles françaises (XVIIe–XVIIIe siècles)*. Basse-Terre: Société d'Historie de la Guadeloupe; Fort-de-France: Société d'Historie de la Martinique, 1974.

———. *Études antillaises: XVIIIe siècle*. Paris: Armand Colin, 1956.

De la Fuente, Alejandro. "Slave Law and Claims-Making in Cuba: The Tannenbaum Debate Revisited." *Law and History Review* 22, no. 2 (Summer 2004).

———. "Slaves and the Creation of Legal Rights in Cuba: *Coartación* and *Papel*." *Hispanic American Historical Review* 87, no. 4 (November 2007): 659–92.

De la Torre, Miltred. "Posiciones y actitudes en torno a la esclavitud en Cuba, 1790–1830." In *Temas acerca de la esclavitud*, edited by various authors. Havana: Editorial de Ciencias Sociales, 1988.

Delgado Ribas, Josep M. "The Slave Trade in the Spanish Empire (1501–1808): The Shift from Periphery to Center." In *Slavery and Antislavery in Spain's Atlantic Empire*, edited by Josep M. Fradera and Christopher Schmidt-Nowara, 13–42. New York: Berghahn Books, 2013.

Devèze, Michel. *Antilles, Guyanes, la Mer des Caraïbes de 1492 à 1789*. Paris: Société d'Études pour le Développement Économique et Social, 1977.

Dias, Maria Odila Leite da Silva. *A interiorização da metrópole e outros estudos*. São Paulo: Alameda, 2005.

Dohlnikoff, Miriam. *O pacto imperial: Origens do federalismo no Brasil*. São Paulo: Editora Globo, 2005.

Dorigny, Marcel, and Bernard Gainot. *La Société des Amis des Noirs, 1788–1799: Contribution à l'histoire de l'abolition de l'esclavage*. Paris: UNESCO-UNICEF, 1998.

Drescher, Seymour. *Abolition: A History of Slavery and Antislavery*. Cambridge: Cambridge University Press, 2009.

———. *Capitalism and Antislavery: British Mobilization in Comparative Perspective*. New York: Oxford University Press, 1987.

———. "The Limits of Example." In *The Impact of the Haitian Revolution in the Atlantic World*, edited by David P. Geggus. Columbia: University of South Carolina Press, 2001.

———. *The Mighty Experiment: Free Labor Versus Slavery in British Emancipation*. Oxford: Oxford University Press, 2002.

Drescher, Seymour, and Pieter C. Emmer. *Who Abolished Slavery? Slave Revolts and Abolitionism: A Debate with João Pedro Marques*. New York: Berghahn Books, 2010.

Dubois, Laurent. *Avengers of the New World: The Story of the Haitian Revolution*. Cambridge, MA: Belknap Press of Harvard University Press, 2004.

———. *A Colony of Citizens: Revolution and Slave Emancipation in the French Caribbean, 1787–1804*. Chapel Hill: University of North Carolina Press, 2004.

Duffy, Michael. "The French Revolution and British Attitudes to the West Indian Colonies." In *A Turbulent Time: The French Revolution and the Greater Caribbean*, edited by David P. Geggus and David B. Gaspar. Bloomington: Indiana University Press, 1997.

Dunn, Richard S. *Sugar and Slaves: The Rise of the Planter Class in the English West Indies, 1624–1713*. New York: W. W. Norton, 1973.

El Hamel, Chouki. "'Race,' Slavery and Islam in Maghribi Mediterranean Thought: The Question of the *Haratin* in Morocco." *Journal of North African Studies* 7, no. 3 (Autumn 2002): 29–52.

Elkins, Stanley. *Slavery: A Problem in American Institutional and Intellectual Life*. Chicago, IL: University of Chicago Press, 1959.

Elliott, John H. *Empires of the Atlantic World: Britain and Spain in America, 1492–1830*. New Haven, CT: Yale University Press, 2006.

———. *Spain and Its World, 1500–1700*. New Haven, CT: Yale University Press, 1989.

Eltis, David. *Economic Growth and the Ending of the Transatlantic Slave Trade*. New York: Oxford University Press, 1987.

El Youssef, Alain. "Imprensa e escravidão: Política e tráfico negreiro no império do Brasil, Rio de Janeiro, 1822–1850." Master's thesis, Universidade de São Paulo, 2010.

———. *O problema da escravidão em periódicos brasileiros da década de 1830:* Jornal do Comércio, Diário da Bahia, O Justiceiro, O Sete de Abril e O Catão. São Paulo: Fundação de Amparo à Pesquisa do Estado de São Paulo, 2006.

Emmer, Pieter C. "The Dutch and the Making of the Second Atlantic System." In *Slavery and the Rise of the Atlantic System*, edited by Barbara L. Solow. Cambridge: Cambridge University Press, 1991.

Esteban Deive, Carlos. *Las emigraciones dominicas a Cuba (1795–1808)*. Santo Domingo: Fundación Cultural Dominicana, 1989.

Estève, Laurent. *Montesquieu, Rousseau, Diderot: Du genre humaine au bois d'ébène; Les silences du droit naturel*. Paris: UNESCO, 2002.

———. "La theórie des climats ou l'encodage d'une servitude naturelle." In *Déraison, esclavage et droit: Les fondements idéologiques et juridiques de la traite négrière et de l'esclavage*, edited by Isabel Castro Henriques and Louis Sala-Molins. Paris: UNESCO, 2002.

Faria, Sheila de Castro. "A riqueza dos libertos: Os alforriados no Brasil escravista." In *Território, conflito e identidade*, edited by Cláudia Maria das Graças Chaves and Marco Antonio Silveira. Belo Horizonte: Argvmentvm, 2007.

Farr, James. "'So Vile and Miserable an Estate': The Problem of Slavery in Locke's Political Thought." *Political Theory* 14, no. 2 (May 1986): 263–89.

Fehrenbacher, Don E. *The Slaveholding Republic: An Account of the United States Government's Relations to Slavery*. Completed and edited by Ward M. McAfee. Oxford: Oxford University Press, 2001.

Ferreira, Roquinaldo Amaral. "Brasil e Angola no tráfico ilegal de escravos, 1830–1860." In *Angola e Brasil: Nas rotas do Atlântico sul*, edited by Selma Pantoja and José Flávio Sombra Saraiva. Rio de Janeiro: Bertrand, 1999.

———. "Dos sertões ao Atlântico: Tráfico ilegal de escravos e comércio lícito em Angola, 1830–1860." Master's thesis, Universidade Federal do Rio de Janeiro, 1996.

Ferrer, Ada. "Cuba en la sombra de Haití: Noticias, sociedad y esclavitud." In *El Rumor de Haití en Cuba: Temor, raza y rebeldía, 1789–1844*, edited by María Dolores González-Ripoll, Consuelo Naranjo, Ada Ferrer, Gloria García, and Josef Opatrný. Madrid: Editorial Consejo Superior de Investigaciones Científicas, 2004.

———. *Freedom's Mirror: Cuba and Haiti in the Age of Revolution*. Cambridge: Cambridge University Press, 2014.

——. "Speaking of Haiti: Slavery, Revolution, and Freedom in Cuba Slave Testimony." In *The World of the Haitian Revolution*, edited by David P. Geggus and Norman Fiering. Bloominton: Indiana University Press, 2009.

Ferretti, Danilo José Zioni. "Entre profecias e prognósticos: Januário da Cunha Barbosa, a escravidão e o futuro da nação (1830–1836)." *Tempo* 20 (2014): 1–22.

Fick, Carolyn E. *The Making of Haiti: The Saint-Domingue Revolution from Below.* Knoxville: University of Tennessee Press, 1990.

Finch, Aisha. "Insurgency at the Cross Roads: Cuban Slaves and the Conspiracy of La Escalera, 1841–1844." PhD dissertation, New York University, 2007.

Finley, Moses I. "Slavery." In *International Encyclopedia of the Social Sciences*, edited by David L. Sills and Robert K. Merton, 13:307–13. New York: Macmillan, 1968.

Florentino, Manolo Garcia. *Em costas negras: Uma história do tráfico atlântico de escravos entre a África e o Rio de Janeiro (séculos XVIII e XIX).* Rio de Janeiro: Arquivo Nacional, 1995.

Flory, Thomas. *Judge and Jury in Imperial Brazil, 1808–1871: Social Control and Political Stability in the New State.* Austin: University of Texas Press, 1981.

——. "Race and Social Control in Independent Brazil." *Journal of Latin American Studies* 9, no. 2 (November 1977): 199–224.

Flouret, Michèle. "Ilustración y esclavitud en Cuba: El testimonio de la condesa de Merlin sobre la esclavitud en Cuba a mediados del siglo XIX." In *Homenaje a Noël Salomon: Ilustración española e independencia de América.* Barcelona: Universidad Autónoma de Barcelona, 1979.

Foner, Philip S. *A History of Cuba and Its Relations with the United States, 1845–1895.* New York: International Publishers, 1963.

Fontana, Josep. *Historia de España.* Vol. 6, *La época del liberalismo.* Barcelona: Editorial Crítica/Editorial Pons, 2007.

Fradera, Josep M. *Colonias para después de un imperio.* Barcelona: Edicions Bellaterra, 2005.

——. "A cultura de 'castas' e a formação do cidadão moderno (Um ensaio sobre a particularidade do Império Espanhol)." In *A experiência constitucional de Cádis: Espanha, Portugal e Brasil*, edited by Márcia Berbel and Cecília Helena de Salles Oliveira, 77–108. São Paulo: Alameda, 2012.

——. "L'esclavage et la logique constitutionnelle des empires." *Annales: Histoire, Sciences Sociales* 63, no. 3 (May–June 2008): 533–60.

——. *Gobernar colonias.* Barcelona: Península, 1999.

Frasquet, Ivana. *Las caras del águila: Del liberalismo gaditano a la república federal mexicana (1820–1824).* Castellón de la Plana, Spain: Universitat Jaume I, 2008.

Freehling, William W. *The Road to Disunion.* 2 vols. New York: Oxford University Press, 1990.

Funes Monzote, Reinaldo. *De bosque a sabana: Azúcar, deforestación y médio ambiente en Cuba, 1492–1926.* Mexico City: Siglo XXI, 2004.

Furstenberg, François. "Beyond Freedom and Slavery: Autonomy, Virtue, and Resistance in Early American Political Discourse." *Journal of American History* 89, no. 4 (March 2003): 1295–330.

Gainot, Bernard. "Métropole/colonies: Projets constitutionnels et rapports de forces, 1798–1802." *Rétablissement de l'esclavage dans les colonies françaises, 1802,* edited by Yves Benot and Marcel Dorigny. Paris: Maisonneuve et Larose, 2003.

Galloway, J. H. "Agricultural Reform and the Enlightenment in Late Colonial Brazil." *Agricultural History* 53, no. 4 (October 1979): 763–79.

———. *The Sugar Cane Industry: An Historical Geography from Its Origins to 1914.* Cambridge: Cambridge University Press, 1989.

García, Gloria. "Vertebrando la resistencia: La lucha de los negros contra el sistema esclavista, 1790–1845." In *El rumor de Haití en Cuba: Temor, raza y rebeldía, 1789–1844,* edited by María Dolores González-Ripoll, Consuelo Naranjo, Ada Ferrer, Gloria García, and Josef Opatrný. Madrid: Editorial Consejo Superior de Investigaciones Científicas, 2004.

García Godoy, María Teresa. *Las Cortes de Cádiz y América: El primero vocabulario liberal y mejicano (1810–1814).* Seville: Diputación Provincial de Sevilla, 1998.

García Laguardia, Jorge Mario. *Centroamerica en las Cortes de Cádiz.* Mexico City: Fondo de Cultura Económica, 1994.

García Rodríguez, Gloria. "Tradición y modernidad en Arango y Parreño." In *Francisco de Arango y Parreño, Obras,* edited by Gloria García Rodríguez, 1:1–56. Havana: Ediciones Imagen Contemporánea, Casa de Altos Estudios Don Fernando Ortiz, 2004.

García Rodríguez, Mercedes. *La aventura de fundar ingenios: La refacción azucarera en La Habana del siglo XVIII.* Havana: Editorial de Ciencias Sociales, 2004.

Garrigus, John D. *Before Haiti: Race and Citizenship in French Saint-Domingue.* New York: Palgrave Macmillan, 2006.

Geggus, David P. "The Effects of the American Revolution on France and Its Empire." In *A Companion to the American Revolution,* edited by Jack P. Greene and J. R. Pole. Malden, MA: Blackwell, 2004.

———, ed. *The Impact of the Haitian Revolution in the Atlantic World.* Columbia: University of South Carolina Press, 2001.

———. "Racial Equality, Slavery, and Colonial Secession During the Constituent Assembly." *American Historical Review* 94, no. 5 (December 1989): 1290–308.

Geggus, David P., and Norman Fiering. *The World of the Haitian Revolution.* Bloomington: Indiana University Press, 2009.

Genovese, Eugene. *A economia política da escravidão.* 1st ed., 1965. Rio de Janeiro: Pallas Editora, 1976.

Gerson, Brasil. *A escravidão no império.* Rio de Janeiro: Pallas Editora, 1975.

Ghachem, Malick W. *The Old Regime and the Haitian Revolution.* Cambridge: Cambridge University Press, 2012.

Gomariz, José. "Francisco de Arango y Parreño: El discurso esclavista de la ilus-
     tración cubana." *Cuban Studies* 35 (2004): 45–61.
Gomes, Flávio [dos Santos]. "Experiências transatlânticas e significados locais: Idé-
     ias, temores e narrativas em torno do Haiti no Brasil Escravista." *Tempo* 13
     (2002): 209–46.
———. *Histórias de quilombolas: Mocambos e comunidades de senzalas no Rio de
     Janeiro, século XIX*. Rio de Janeiro: Arquivo Nacional, 1995.
Gómez, Alejandro E. *Le spectre de la révolution noir: L'impact de la révolution haïti-
     enne dans le monde atlantique, 1790–1886*. Rennes: Presses Universitaires de
     Rennes, 2013.
Gómez Urdáñez, Gracia. "Progresismo y poder político en la España isabelina: El
     gobierno de Olózaga a finales de 1843." *Hispania: Revista Española de Historia*
     60, no. 2 (May–August 2000): 623–71.
González-Ripoll Navarro, María Dolores. *Cuba, la isla de los ensayos: Cultura y socie-
     dad (1790–1815)*. Madrid: Editorial Consejo Superior de Investigaciones Científi-
     cas, 1999.
Goveia, Elsa. "The West Indian Slave Laws of the Eighteenth Century." In *Caribbean
     Slave Society and Economy: A Student Reader*, edited by Hilary Beckles and
     Verene Shepherd. Kingston: Ian Randle; London: James Currey, 1991.
Graden, Dale T. "An Act 'Even of Public Security': Slave Resistance, Social Tensions,
     and the End of the International Slave Trade to Brazil, 1835–1856." *Hispanic
     American Historical Review* 76, no. 2 (May 1996): 249–82.
———. *Disease, Resistance, and Lies: The Demise of the Transatlantic Slave Trade to
     Brazil and Cuba*. Baton Rouge: Louisiana State University Press, 2014.
Greene, Jack P. "Empire and Identity from the Glorious Revolution to the American
     Revolution." In *The Oxford History of the British Empire*. Vol. 2, *The Eighteenth
     Century*, edited by P. J. Marshall. New York: Oxford University Press, 1998.
———. "Liberty, Slavery, and the Transformation of British Identity in the Eighteenth-
     Century West Indies." *Slavery and Abolition* 21, no. 1 (April 2000): 1–31.
Greene, Jack P., and Philip D. Morgan. *Atlantic History: A Critical Appraisal*. Oxford:
     Oxford University Press, 2009.
Grinberg, Keila. *O fiador dos brasileiros: Cidadania, escravidão e direito civil no
     tempo de Antônio Pereira Rebouças*. Rio de Janeiro: Civilização Brasileira, 2002.
Guedes, Roberto. *Egressos do cativeiro: Trabalho, família, aliança e mobilidade social
     (Porto Feliz, São Paulo, c. 1798–1850)*. Rio de Janeiro: Mauad X–Faperj, 2008.
Guerra, François-Xavier. *Modernidad e independencias*. Mexico City: Fondo de Cul-
     tura Económica, 1997.
Guerra y Sanchéz, Ramiro. *Manual de historia de Cuba*. 1st ed., 1938. Havana: Edito-
     rial de Ciencias Sociales, 1971.
Halperin Donghi, Tulio. *Reforma y disolución de los impérios ibéricos*. Madrid:
     Alianza Editorial, 1985.
Hanke, Lewis. *Aristotle and the American Indians*. London: Hollis and Carter, 1959.

Harris, Marvin. *Patterns of Race in the Americas*. New York: Greenwood Press, 1964.

Heckscher, Eli F. *Mercantilism*. London: Routledge, 1994.

Helg, Aline. "Race and Black Mobilization in Colonial and Early Independent Cuba: A Comparative Perspective." *Ethnohistory* 44, no. 1 (Winter 1997): 53–74.

Henderson, Gavin B. "Southern Designs on Cuba, 1854–1857, and Some European Opinions." *Journal of Southern History* 5, no. 3 (August 1939): 371–85.

Hernández González, Manuel. "El liberalismo criollo cubano en el Trienio Liberal: *El Americano Libre*." In *La excepción americana: Cuba en el ocaso del imperio americano*, edited by Imilcy Balboa and José A. Piqueras. Valencia: Centro Francisco Tomás y Valiente; Fundación Instituto Historia Social, 2006.

———. "El liberalismo exaltado en el Triênio Liberal cubano." In *Cuba: Algunos problemas de su historia*, edited by Josef Opatrný. Prague: Charles University in Prague, 1995.

Herzog, Tamar. "Communities Becoming a Nation: Spain and Spanish America in the Wake of Modernity (and Thereafter)." *Citizenship Studies* 11, no. 2 (May 2007): 151–72.

Holanda, Sérgio Buarque de. "A instituição do governo geral." In *História geral da civilização Brasileira*. Vol. 1, *A época colonial: Do descobrimento à expansão territorial*, edited by Sérgio Buarque de Holanda. 1st ed., 1960. São Paulo: Bertrand, 2001.

Hurwitz, Samuel J., and Edith F. Hurwitz. "A Token of Freedom: Private Bill Legislation for Free Negroes in Eighteenth-Century Jamaica." *William and Mary Quarterly*, 3rd ser., 24, no. 3 (July 1967): 423–31.

Huzzey, Richard. *Freedom Burning: Anti-Slavery and Empire in Victorian Britain*. Ithaca, NY: Cornell University Press, 2012.

Iglésias, Francisco. "Vida política, 1848–1868." In *História geral da civilização brasileira*. Vol. 2, *O Brasil monárquico: Dispersão e unidade*, edited by Sérgio Buarque de Holanda. 1st ed., 1967. Rio de Janeiro: Bertrand, 2004.

Instituto de Historia de Cuba, ed. *Historia de Cuba: La colonia; Evolución socioeconómico y formación nacional*. Havana: Editora Política, 1994.

Isaac, Rhys. *Landon Carter's Uneasy Kingdom: Revolution and Rebellion on a Virginia Plantation*. Oxford: Oxford University Press, 2004.

Jancsó, István. "Bahia 1798: A hipótese de auxílio francês ou a cor dos gatos." In *Diálogos oceânicos: Minas Gerais e as novas abordagens para uma história do império ultramarino português*, edited by Júnia Ferreira Furtado. Belo Horizonte: Editora da Universidade Federal de Minas Gerais, 2001.

———, ed. *Independência: História e historiografia*. São Paulo: Editora Hucitec; Fundação de Amparo à Pesquisa do Estado de São Paulo, 2005.

———. *Na Bahia, contra o império: História do ensaio de sedição de 1798*. São Paulo: Editora Hucitec; Editora da Universidade Federal da Bahia, 1996.

Jancsó, István, and João Paulo Pimenta. "Peças de um mosaico (ou apontamentos para o estudo da emergência da identidade nacional brasileira)." In *Viagem incompleta: A experiência brasileira 1500–2000*, edited by Carlos G. Mota. São Paulo: Editora Senac, 2000.

Jenergan, Marcus W. "Slavery and Conversion in the American Colonies." *American Historical Review* 21, no. 3 (April 1916): 504–27.

Jordan, Winthrop. *White over Black: American Attitudes Toward the Negro, 1550–1812*. Chapel Hill: University of North Carolina Press, 1968.

Kagan, Robert L. "Prescott's Paradigm: American Historical Scholarship and the Decline of Spain." *American Historical Review* 101, no. 2 (April 1996): 423–46.

Kaplanoff, Mark D. "The Federal Convention and the Constitution." In *A Companion to the American Revolution*, edited by Jack P. Greene and J. R. Pole. Malden, MA: Blackwell, 2004.

Karasch, Mary C. *A vida dos escravos no Rio de Janeiro, 1808–1850*. São Paulo: Companhia das Letras, 2000.

Karp, Matthew Jason. "'This Vast Southern Empire': The South and the Foreign Policy of Slavery, 1833–1861." PhD dissertation, University of Pennsylvania, 2011.

Keen, Benjanim. "The Black Legend Revisited: Assumptions and Realities." *Hispanic American Historical Review* 49, no. 4 (November 1969): 703–19.

King, James F. "The Colored Castes and American Representation in the Cortes of Cadiz." *Hispanic American Historical Review* 33, no. 1 (February 1953): 33–64.

Klein, Herbert S. "Anglicanism, Catholicism, and the Negro Slave." *Comparative Studies in Society and History* 8, no. 3 (April 1966): 295–327.

———. *The Atlantic Slave Trade*. Cambridge: Cambridge University Press, 2010.

———. *Slavery in the Americas: A Comparative Study of Cuba and Virginia*. Chicago, IL: University of Chicago Press, 1967.

Klein, Herbert S., and Ben Vinson III. *La esclavitud africana en América latina y el Caribe*. 2nd ed. Lima: Instituto de Estudios Peruanos, 2008.

Knight, Franklin W. *Slave Society in Cuba During the Nineteenth Century*. Madison: University of Wisconsin Press, 1970.

Koselleck, Reinhart. *Los estratos del tiempo: Estudios sobre la historia*. Barcelona: Ediciones Paidós, 2001.

———. *Futures Past: On the Semantics of Historical Time*. Translated by Keith Tribe. Cambridge, MA: MIT Press, 1985.

Kuethe, Allan J. *Cuba, 1753–1815: Crown, Military, and Society*. Knoxville: University of Tennessee Press, 1986.

Kuethe, Allan J., and Kenneth J. Andrien. *The Spanish Atlantic World in the Eighteenth Century: War and the Bourbon Reforms, 1713–1796*. Cambridge: Cambridge University Press, 2014.

Kury, Lorelai, ed. *Iluminismo e império no Brasil: O Patriota (1813–1814)*. Rio de Janeiro: Editora Fiocruz; Fundação Biblioteca Nacional, 2007.

Lamonier, Maria Lucia. "Between Slavery and Free Labour: Experiments with Free Labour and Patterns of Slave Emancipation in Brazil and Cuba, 1830–1888." PhD dissertation, London School of Economics and Political Science, 1993.

Lara, Silvia Hunold. *Campos da violência: Escravos e senhores na capitania do Rio de Janeiro, 1750–1808.* Rio de Janeiro: Paz e Terra, 1988.

———. *Fragmentos setecentistas: Escravidão, cultura e poder na América portuguesa.* São Paulo: Companhia das Letras, 2007.

Lasso, Marixa. "Race War and Nation in Caribbean Gran Colombia, Cartagena, 1810–1832." *American Historical Review* 111, no. 2 (April 2006): 336–61.

———. "A Republican Myth of Racial Harmony: Race and Patriotism in Colombia, 1810–1812." *Historical Reflections / Reflexions Historiques* 29, no. 1 (Spring 2003): 43–63.

Lima, Ruy Cirne. *Pequena história territorial do Brasil: Sesmarias e terras devolutas.* 1st ed., 1954. São Paulo: Secretaria do Estado da Cultura, 1990.

Lockhart, James, and Stuart B. Schwartz. *A América latina na época colonial.* Rio de Janeiro: Civilização Brasileira, 2002.

Lombardi, John. *The Decline and Abolition of Negro Slavery in Venezuela, 1820–1854.* Westport, CT: Greenwood Press, 1971.

Lucena Salmoral, Manuel. *Los códigos negros de la América española.* Alcalá de Henares, Spain: Ediciones UNESCO/Universidad de Alcalá, 1996.

Lyra, Maria de Lourdes Viana. *A utopia do poderoso império: Portugal e Brasil; Bastidores da política, 1798–1822.* Rio de Janeiro: Sette Letras, 1994.

Magalhães, Joaquim Romero. "Articulações inter-regionais e economias-mundo." In *História da expansão portuguesa.* Vol. 1, *A formação do império (1415–1570),* edited by Francisco Bethencourt and Kirti Chaudhuri. Lisbon: Temas e Debates, 1998.

Maltz, Earl M. "The Idea of the Proslavery Constitution." *Journal of the Early Republic* 17, no. 1 (Spring 1997): 37–59.

Mamigonian, Beatriz Galloti. "To Be a Liberated African in Brazil: Labour and Citizenship in the Nineteenth Century." PhD dissertation, University of Waterloo, Ontario, 2002.

Mansuy-Diniz Silva, Andrée. "Portugal e Brasil: A reorganização do Império, 1750–1808." In *História da América latina.* Vol. 1, *América latina colonial,* edited by Leslie Bethell. São Paulo: Editora da Universidade de São Paulo; Brasília: Fundação Alexandre de Gusmão, 1997.

Marcílio, Maria Luiza. "A população do Brasil colonial." In *História da América latina.* Vol. 2, *América latina colonial,* edited by Leslie Bethell. São Paulo: Editora da Universidade de São Paulo; Brasília: Fundação Alexandre de Gusmão, 1999.

Marichal, Carlos. *Bankruptcy of Empire: Mexican Silver and the Wars Between Spain, Britain, and France, 1760–1810.* Cambridge: Cambridge University Press, 2007.

Marques, João Pedro. *Os sons do silêncio: O Portugal de oitocentos e a abolição do tráfico de escravos.* Lisbon: Imprensa de Ciências Sociais, 1999.

Marques, Leonardo. "The United States and the Transatlantic Slave Trade to the Americas, 1776–1867." PhD dissertation, Emory University, 2013.

Marquese, Rafael de Bivar. "A dinâmica da escravidão no Brasil: Resistência, tráfico negreiro e alforrias, séculos XVII a XIX." *Novos Estudos CEBRAP* 74 (March 2006): 107–23.

———. "Escravismo e independência: A ideologia da escravidão no Brasil, em Cuba e nos Estados Unidos nas décadas de 1810 e 1820." In *Independência: História e historiografia*, edited by István Jancsó. São Paulo: Editora Hucitec; Fundação de Amparo à Pesquisa do Estado de São Paulo, 2005.

———. "Estrutura e agência na historiografia da escravidão: A obra de Emília Viotti da Costa." In *O historiador e seu tempo*, edited by Antonio Celso Ferreira, Holien Gonçalves Bezerra, and Tânia Regina de Luca. São Paulo: Editora UNESP, 2008.

———. *Feitores do corpo, missionários da mente: Senhores, letrados e o controle dos escravos nas Américas, 1660–1860*. São Paulo: Companhia das Letras, 2004.

Marquese, Rafael de Bivar, and Tâmis Peixoto Parron. "Azeredo Coutinho, Visconde de Araruama e a *Memória sobre o comércio de escravos* de 1838." *Revista de História* 152 (2005): 99–126.

Marquese, Rafael, and Dale Tomich. "O Vale do Paraíba escravista e a formação do mercado mundial do café no século XIX." In *O Brasil Império*, vol. 2, *1808–1889*, edited by Keila Grinberg and Ricardo Salles. Rio de Janeiro: Civilização Brasileira, forthcoming.

Martínez, Pascual. *La unión con España: Exigência de los diputados americanos en las Cortes de Cádiz*. Madrid: Editorial Castalia, 2001.

Martínez-Fernández, Luis. *Torn Between Empires: Economy, Society, and Patterns of Political Thought in the Hispanic Caribbean, 1848–1878*. Athens: University of Georgia Press, 1994.

Martínez García, Daniel. "La sublevación de la Alcancía: Su rehabilitación histórica en el proceso conspirativo que concluye en La Escalera (1844)." *Rábida* 19 (2000): 41–48.

Martins, José de Souza. *O cativeiro da terra*. 1st ed., 1986. São Paulo: Editora Hucitec, 1996.

Matthew, Gelien. *Caribbean Slave Revolts and the British Abolitionist Movement*. Baton Rouge: Louisiana State University Press, 2006.

Mattos, Hebe Maria. *Escravidão e cidadania no Brasil monárquico*. Rio de Janeiro: Jorge Zahar, 2000.

———. "A escravidão moderna nos quadros do império português: O antigo regime em perspectiva atlântica." In *Antigo regime nos trópicos: A dinâmica imperial portuguesa (séc. XVI–XVIII)*, edited by João Luís Ribeiro Fragoso, Maria Fernanda Bicalho, and Maria de Fátima Gouvêa. Rio de Janeiro: Civilização Brasileira, 2001.

Mattos, Ilmar Rohloff de. *O tempo saquarema: A formação do estado imperial*. 1st ed., 1986. São Paulo: Editora Hucitec, 2004.

Mattoso, José. "1096–1325: Dois séculos de vicissitudes políticas." In *História de Portugal*. Vol. 2, *A monarquia feudal (1096–1480)*, edited by José Mattoso. Lisbon: Estampa, 1993.

———. "Antecedentes medievais da expansão portuguesa." In *História de Portugal*. Vol. 1, *Antes de Portugal*, edited by José Mattoso. Lisbon: Estampa, 1993.

Maxwell, Kenneth. *Chocolates, piratas e outros malandros: Ensaios tropicais*. São Paulo: Paz e Terra, 1999.

———. *A devassa da devassa: A inconfidência mineira; Brasil e Portugal, 1750–1808*. Rio de Janeiro: Paz e Terra, 1978.

———. "A geração de 1790 e a idéia do império luso-brasileiro." In *Chocolates, piratas e outros malandros: Ensaios tropicais*, 157–207. São Paulo: Paz e Terra, 1999.

———. "Hegemonies Old and New: The Ibero-Atlantic in the Long Eighteenth Century." In *Colonial Legacies: The Problem of Persistence in Latin American History*, edited by Jeremy Adelman. New York: Routledge, 1999.

———. "The Impact of the American Revolution on Spain and Portugal and Their Empires." In *A Companion to the American Revolution*, edited by Jack P. Greene and J. R. Pole. Malden, MA: Blackwell, 2004.

———. *Marquês de Pombal: Paradoxo do iluminismo*. Rio de Janeiro: Paz e Terra, 1996.

May, Robert E. "Young American Males and Filibustering in the Age of Manifest Destiny: The United States Army as a Cultural Mirror." *Journal of American History* 78, no. 3 (December 1991): 857–86.

McCardell, John. *The Idea of a Southern Nation: Southern Nationalistas and Southern Nationalism*. New York: W. W. Norton, 1979.

McCusker, John J., and Russell R. Menard. *The Economy of British America, 1607–1789*. Chapel Hill: University of North Carolina Press, 1985.

McMichael, Philip. "Incorporating Comparison Within a World-Historical Perspective: An Alternative Comparative Method." *American Sociological Review* 55, no. 3 (June 1990): 385–97.

Medina Plana, Raquel. *Soberania, monarquia y representación en las Cortes del Trienio*. Madrid: Fundación Universitaria Española, 2005.

Meinig, David W. *The Shaping of America: A Geographical Perspective on 500 Years of History*. Vol. 1, *Atlantic America, 1492–1800*. New Haven, CT: Yale University Press, 1986.

Mello, Evaldo Cabral de. *O negócio do Brasil: Portugal, os países baixos e o nordeste, 1641–1669*. Rio de Janeiro: Topbooks, 1998.

Menard, Russell R., and Stuart B. Schwartz. "Por que a escravidão Africana? A transição da força de trabalho no Brasil, no México e na Carolina do Sul." In *História econômica do período colonial*, edited by Tamás Szmrecsányi. São Paulo: Editora Hucitec, 1996.

Miller, Joseph C. "O Atlântico escravista: Açúcar, escravos e engenhos." *Afro-Ásia*, no. 19–20 (1997): 9–36.

——. "A economia política do tráfico angolano de escravos no século XVIII." In *Angola e Brasil nas rotas do Atlântico sul*, edited by Selma Pantoja and José Flávio Sombra Saraiva. Rio de Janeiro: Bertrand, 1999.

——. *The Problem of Slavery as History: A Global Approach.* New Haven, CT: Yale University Press, 2012.

——. "Stratégies de marginalité: Une approche historique de l'utilisation des êtres humains et des ideologies de l'esclavage; Progéniture, piété, protection personele et prestige; Produit et profits des propriétaires." In *Déraison, esclavage et droit: Lês fondements idéologiques et juridiques de la traite négrière et de l'esclavage*, edited by Isabel Castro Henriques and Louis Sala-Molins. Paris: UNESCO, 2002.

——. "A Theme in Variations: A Historical Schema of Slaving in the Atlantic and Indian Ocean Regions." *Slavery and Abolition* 25, no. 2 (August 2004): 169–94.

Miller, William Lee. *Arguing About Slavery: The Great Battle in the United States Congress.* New York: Alfred A. Knopf, 1996.

Mintz, Sidney W. *O poder amargo do açúcar: Produtores escravizados, consumidores proletarizados.* Recife: Editora Universidade Federal de Pernambuco, 2003.

——. "Slavery and Emergent Capitalisms." In *Slavery in the New World: A Reader in Comparative Perspective*, edited by Laura Foner and Eugene Genovese. Englewood Cliffs, NJ: Prentice Hall, 1969.

Miskimin, Harry A. *A economia do renascimento europeu, 1300–1600.* Lisbon: Estampa, 1984.

Mitton, Steven Heath. "The Free World Confronted: The Problem of Slavery and Progress in American Foreign Relations, 1833–1844." PhD dissertation, Louisiana State University, 2005.

Moreno Fraginals, Manuel. *Cuba/España, España/Cuba: Historia común.* Barcelona: Editorial Crítica, 1995.

——. *O engenho: Complexo sócio-econômico açucareiro cubano.* 2 vols. São Paulo: Editora Hucitec; Editora UNESP, 1987.

——. "Nación o plantación (el dilema político cubano visto a través de José Antonio Saco)." In *Homenaje a Silvio Zavala.* Mexico City: El Colégio de México, Estudios Históricos Americanos, 1953.

Moreno García, Julia. "Actitudes de los nacionalistas cubanos ante la ley penal de abolición y represión del tráfico de esclavos (1845)." In *Esclavitud y derechos humanos: La lucha por la libertad del negro en el siglo XIX*, edited by Francisco de Solano and Agustín Guimerá. Madrid: Editorial Consejo Superior de Investigaciones Científicas, 1990.

Morgan, Edmund. *American Slavery, American Freedom: The Ordeal of Colonial Virginia.* New York: W. W. Norton, 1975.

Morgan, Kenneth. "Slavery and the Debate over Ratification of the United States Constitution." *Slavery and Abolition* 22, no. 3 (December 2001): 40–65.

Morse, Richard. *O espelho de Próspero: Cultura e idéias nas Américas*. São Paulo: Companhia das Letras, 1988.

Motta, Márcia Maria Menendes. *Nas fronteiras do poder: Conflitos de terra e direito agrário no Brasil de meados do século XIX*. Rio de Janeiro: Vício de Leitura; Arquivo Público do Estado do Rio de Janeiro, 1998.

Moura, Clóvis. *Dicionário da escravidão negra no Brasil*. São Paulo: Editora da Universidade de São Paulo, 2004.

Moya Pons, Frank. *Historia del Caribe: Azúcar y plantaciones en el mundo atlântico*. Santo Domingo: Editora Búho, 2008.

Mulligan, William, and Maurice Bric, eds. *A Global History of Anti-Slavery in the Nineteenth Century*. Basingstoke, England: Palgrave Macmillan, 2013.

Murray, David. *Odious Commerce: Britain, Spain and the Abolition of the Cuban Slave Trade*. Cambridge: Cambridge University Press, 1980.

———. "The Slave Trade, Slavery and Cuban Independence." *Slavery and Abolition* 20, no. 3 (December 1999): 106–269.

Navarro, Imilcy Balboa. *De los domínios del rey al imperio de la propiedad privada: Estructura y tenencia de la tierra en Cuba (siglos XVI–XIX)*. Madrid: Editorial Consejo Superior de Investigaciones Científicas, 2013.

Needell, Jeffrey. *The Party of Order: The Conservatives, the State, and Slavery in the Brazilian Monarchy, 1831–1871*. Stanford, CA: Stanford University Press, 2006.

Neves, Guilherme Pereira das. "Guardar mais silêncio do que falar: Azeredo Coutinho, Ribeiro dos Santos e a escravidão." In *A economia política e os dilemas do império luso-brasileiro (1790–1822)*, edited by José Luís Cardoso. Lisbon: Comissão Nacional para as Comemorações dos Descobrimentos Portugueses, 2001.

Northrup, David. *Indentured Labor in the Age of Imperialism, 1834–1922*. Cambridge: Cambridge University Press, 1995.

Novais, Fernando A. *Aproximações: Estudos de história e historiografia*. São Paulo: Cosac Naify, 2005.

———. *Portugal e Brasil na crise do antigo sistema colonial (1777–1808)*. São Paulo: Editora Hucitec, 1979.

———. "O reformismo ilustrado luso-brasileiro: alguns aspectos." In *Aproximações: Estudos de História e Historiografia*. São Paulo: Cosac Naify, 2005.

Oliveira Lima, Manoel de. "O império brasileiro." In *O movimento da independência: O império brasileiro*. São Paulo: Editora Melhoramentos, 1958.

Opatrný, Josef. "El estado-nación o la 'cubanidad': Los dilemas de los portavoces de los criollos cubanos de la época antes de La Escalera." In *El Rumor de Haití en Cuba: Temor, raza y rebeldía, 1789–1844*, edited by María Dolores González-Ripoll, Consuelo Naranjo, Ada Ferrer, Gloria García, and Josef Opatrný. Madrid: Editorial Consejo Superior de Investigaciones Científicas, 2004.

Ortiz, Fernando. *Contrapunteo cubano del tabaco y el azúcar*. 1st ed., 1940. Caracas: Biblioteca Ayacucho, 1987.

———. *Los esclavos negros.* 1st ed., 1916. Havana: Editorial de Ciencias Sociales, 1996.

O'Shaughnessy, Andrew J. *An Empire Divided: The American Revolution and the British Caribbean.* Philadelphia: University of Pennsylvania Press, 2000.

Pagden, Anthony. "Escuchar a Heraclides: El malestar en el imperio, 1619–1812." In *España, Europa y el mundo atlántico: Homenaje a John H. Elliott,* edited by Richard Kagan and Geoffrey Parker. Madrid: Marcial Pons, 2001.

———. *The Fall of Natural Man: The American Indian and the Origins of Comparative Ethnology.* Cambridge: Cambridge University Press, 1982.

———. *Señores de todo el mundo: Ideologías del imperio en España, Inglaterra y Francia (en los siglos XVI, XVII y XVIII).* Barcelona: Península, 1997.

———. "The Struggle for Legitimacy and the Image of Empire in the Atlantic to c. 1700." In *The Oxford History of the British Empire.* Vol. 1, *The Origins of the Empire: British Overseas Enterprise to the Close of the Seventeenth Century,* edited by Nicholas Canny. New York: Oxford University Press, 1998.

Palacios, Guillermo. *Cultivadores libres: Estado y crisis de la eclavitud en Brasil en la época de la revolución industrial.* Mexico City: Fondo de Cultura Económica, 1998.

Palmer, Colin. *Human Cargoes: The British Slave Trade to Spanish America, 1700–1739.* Urbana: University of Illinois Press, 1981.

Pamplona, Marco. *Revoltas, república e cidadania: Nova York e Rio de Janeiro na consolidação da ordem republicana.* Rio de Janeiro: Grupo Editorial Record, 2003.

Paquette, Gabriel B., ed. *Enlightened Reform in Southern Europe and Its Atlantic Colonies, c. 1750–1830.* New York: Palgrave Macmillan, 2008.

———. *Enlightenment, Governance, and Reform in Spain and Its Empire, 1759–1808.* New York: Palgrave Macmillan, 2008.

Paquette, Robert L. "Revolutionary Saint-Domingue in the Making of Territorial Louisiana." In *A Turbulent Time: The French Revolution and the Greater Caribbean,* edited by David P. Geggus and David B. Gaspar. Bloomington: Indiana University Press, 1997.

———. *Sugar Is Made with Blood: The Conspiracy of La Escalera and the Conflict Between Empires over Slavery in Cuba.* Middletown, CT: Wesleyan University Press, 1988.

Parron, Tâmis. "A *Nova e Curiosa Relação* (1764): Escravidão e ilustração em Portugal durante as reformas pombalinas." *Almanack Braziliense,* no. 8 (November 2008): 92–107.

———. *A política da escravidão no império do Brasil, 1826–1865.* Rio de Janeiro: Civilização Brasileira, 2011.

Patterson, Orlando. "Slavery." *Annual Review of Sociology* 3 (1977): 407–49.

Paz Sánchez, Manuel de. "'El Lugareño' contra la esclavocracia: Las cartas de Gaspar Betancourt y Cisneros (1803–1866)." *Revista de Indias* 58, no. 214 (1998): 617–39.

Peabody, Sue. "'A Dangerous Zeal': Catholic Missions to Slaves in the French Antilles, 1635–1800." *French Historical Studies* 25, no. 1 (Winter 2002): 53–90.

Pereira da Silva, João Manoel. *História do Brasil durante a menoridade de D. Pedro II (1831–1840)*. Rio de Janeiro: Garnier, 1878.

Pérez, Louis A., Jr. "Cuba and the United States: Origins and Antecedents of Relations, 1760s–1860s." *Cuban Studies* 21 (1997): 57–82.

————. "In the Service of the Revolution: Two Decades of Cuban Historiography, 1959–1979." *Hispanic American Historical Review* 60, no. 1 (February 1980): 79–89.

————. *Winds of Change: Hurricanes and the Transformation of Nineteenth-Century Cuba*. Chapel Hill: University of North Carolina Press, 2001.

Pérez-Cisneros, Enrique. *La abolición de la esclavitud en Cuba*. San José, Costa Rica: Litografía e Imprenta Lil, 1987.

Pérez de la Riva, Juan. *El barracón: Esclavitud y capitalismo en Cuba*. Barcelona: Editorial Crítica, 1978.

————. "Una isla con dos historias." In *La conquista del espacio cubano*. 1st ed., 1968. Havana: Fundación Fernando Ortiz, 2004.

Pérez Murillo, María Dolores. "El pensamiento esclavista del Tribunal de Comercio de La Habana (año de 1841)." In *Esclavitud y derechos humanos: La lucha por la libertad del negro en el siglo XIX*, edited by Francisco de Solano and Agustín Guimerá. Madrid: Editorial Consejo Superior de Investigaciones Científicas, 1990.

Pezuela, Jacobo de la. *Historia de la isla de Cuba*. 4 vols. Madrid: Bailly-Baillière, 1878.

Pierson, William Whatley. "Francisco de Arango y Parreño." *Hispanic American Historical Review* 16, no. 4 (November 1936): 451–78.

Pietschmann, Horst, ed. *Atlantic History: History of the Atlantic System, 1580–1830*. Göttingen, Germany: Vandenhoeck and Ruprecht, 2002.

Pimenta, João Paulo Garrido. "O Brasil e a América espanhola (1808–1822)." PhD dissertation, Universidade de São Paulo, 2004.

————. *Brasil y las independencias de Hispanoamérica*. Castellón de la Plana, Spain: Universitat Jaume I, 2007.

Piñero, Eugenio. "The Cacao Economy of the Eighteenth-Century Province of Caracas and the Spanish Cacao Market." *Hispanic American Historical Review* 68, no. 1 (February 1988): 75–100.

Pinto, Virgílio Noya. *O ouro brasileiro e o comércio anglo-português*. São Paulo: Companhia Editora Nacional, 1979.

Piqueras, José Antonio. "Los amigos de Arango en la Corte de Carlos IV." Paper presented at the international conference Francisco Arango y la Invención de la Cuba Azucarera, Madrid, Consejo Superior de Investigaciones Científicas, June 2008.

————. "Los amigos de Arango en la Corte de Carlos IV." In *Francisco Arango y la invención de la Cuba azucarera*, edited by María Dolores González-Ripoll and Izaskun Álvarez Cuartero. Salamanca: Ediciones Universidad de Salamanca, 2009.

———. "De español americano a patriota cubano: El itinerario político e ideológico de Félix Varela." In *Félix Varela y la prosperidad de la pátria criolla*. Madrid: Fundación Mapfre Tavera; Ediciones Doce Calles, 2007.

———. *Félix Varela y la prosperidad de la pátria criolla*. Madrid: Fundación Mapfre Tavera; Ediciones Doce Calles, 2007.

———. "Leales en época de insurrección: La élite criolla cubana entre 1810 y 1814." In *Visiones y revisiones de la independencia americana*, edited by Izaskun Álvarez Cuartero and Julio Sánchez Gómez. Salamanca: Ediciones Universidad de Salamanca, 2003.

———. "El mundo reducido a una isla: La unión cubana a la metrópoli en tiempos de tribulaciones." In *Las Antillas en la era de las luces y la revolución*, edited by José Antonio Piqueras. Madrid: Siglo XXI, 2005.

———. "La política de los intereses en Cuba y la revolución (1810–1814)." In *Las guerras de independencia en la América española*, edited by José Antonio Serrano Ortega and Marta Terán. Zamora: Instituto Nacional de Antropología e Historia; Zamora: El Colégio de Michoacán; Morelia: Universidad Michoacana de San Nicolás de Hidalgo, 2002.

———. *Sociedad civil y poder en Cuba: Colonia y poscolonia*. Madrid: Siglo XXI, 2005.

Pluchon, Pierre. *Histoire de la colonisation française*. Vol. 1, *Le premier empire colonial: Des origines à la restauration*. Paris: Fayard, 1991.

———, ed. *Histoire des Antilles et de la Guyane*. Paris: Privat, 1982.

Popkin, Jeremy D. *You Are All Free: The Haitian Revolution and the Abolition of Slavery*. Cambridge: Cambridge University Press, 2010.

Porter, Andrew. "Trusteeship, Anti-Slavery, and Humanitarianism." In *The Oxford History of the British Empire*. Vol. 3, *The Nineteenth Century*, edited by Andrew Porter. Oxford: Oxford University Press, 1999.

Portuondo Zúñiga, Olga. "La consolidación de la sociedad criolla (1700–1765)." In *Historia de Cuba: La Colonia; Evolución socioeconómico y formación nacional*, edited by Instituto de Historia de Cuba. Havana: Editora Política, 1994.

Prado, Caio, Jr. *História econômica do Brasil*. São Paulo: Editora Brasiliense, 1945.

Prieto, Leida Fernández. "Crónica anunciada de una Cuba azucarera." In *Francisco Arango y la invención de la Cuba azucarera*, edited by María Dolores González-Ripoll and Izaskun Álvarez Cuartero, 55–66. Salamanca: Ediciones Universidad de Salamanca, 2009.

Reid-Vazquez, Michele. *The Year of the Lash: Free People of Color in Cuba and the Nineteenth Century Atlantic World*. Athens: University of Georgia Press, 2011.

Reis, João José. "O jogo duro do Dois de Julho: O 'Partido Negro' na independência da Bahia." In *Negociação e conflito: A resistência negra no Brasil escravista*, edited by João José Reis and Eduardo Silva. São Paulo: Companhia das Letras, 1989.

———. *Rebelião escrava no Brasil: A história do levante dos Malês em 1835*. Revised and expanded ed. São Paulo: Companhia das Letras, 2003.

Reis, João José, and Flávio dos Santos Gomes. "Repercussions of the Haitian Revolution in Brazil, 1791–1850." In *The World of the Haitian Revolution*, edited by David P. Geggus and Norman Fiering, 284–313. Bloomington: Indiana University Press, 2009.

Reis, João José, and Eduardo Silva. *Negociação e conflito: A resistência negra no Brasil escravista*. São Paulo: Companhia das Letras, 1989.

Ribeiro, Gladys Sabina. *A liberdade em construção: Identidade nacional e conflitos antilusitanos no primeiro reinado*. Rio de Janeiro: Relume Dumará, 2002.

Ribeiro, José, Jr. *Colonização e monopólio no nordeste brasileiro: A Companhia Geral de Pernambuco e Paraíba (1759–1780)*. São Paulo: Editora Hucitec, 1976.

Rieu-Millan, Marie Laure. *Los diputados americanos em las Cortes de Cádiz*. Madrid: Editorial Consejo Superior de Investigaciones Científicas, 1990.

Riley, Carlos. "A apropriação do espaço: Ilhas atlânticas e costa Africana." In *História da expansão portuguesa*. Vol. 1, *A formação do império (1415–1570)*, edited by Francisco Bethencourt and Kirti Chaudhuri, 137–62. Lisbon: Temas e Debates, 1998.

Rocha, Antonio Penalves. *A economia política na sociedade escravista (um estudo dos textos econômicos de Cairu)*. São Paulo: Editora Hucitec; Programa de Pós-Graduação em História Econômica, Universidade de São Paulo, 1996.

———. "Idéias antiescravistas da ilustração européia na sociedade escravista brasileira." *Revista Brasileira de História* 20, no. 39 (2000): 37–68.

Rodrigues, Jaime. *O infame comércio: Propostas e experiências no final do tráfico de africanos para o Brasil (1800–1850)*. Campinas, Brazil: Editora da Unicamp, 2000.

———. "Liberdade, humanidade e propriedade: Os escravos e a Assembléia Constituinte de 1823." *Revista do Instituto de Estudos Brasileiros* 39 (1995): 159–67.

Rodrigues, José Honório. *Brasil e África: Outro horizonte*. 2 vols. 2nd ed. Rio de Janeiro: Civilização Brasileira, 1964.

———. "Nota preliminar." In *Compêndio histórico das possessões de Portugal na África*, edited by Raimundo José da Cunha Matos, 7–21. Rio de Janeiro: Arquivo Nacional, 1963.

Roeckell, Lelia M. "Bonds over Bondage: British Opposition to the Annexation of Texas." *Journal of the Early Republic* 19, no. 2 (Summer 1999): 257–78.

Röhrig Assunção, Matthias. "Miguel Bruce e os 'horrores da anarquia' no Maranhão, 1822–1827." In *Independência: História e historiografia*, edited by István Jancsó. São Paulo: Editora Hucitec; Fundação de Amparo à Pesquisa do Estado de São Paulo, 2005.

Röhrig Assunção, Matthias, and Michael Zeuske. "'Race,' Ethnicity and Social Structure in 19th Century Brazil and Cuba." *Ibero-Amerikanisches Archiv* 24, no. 3/4 (1998): 375–443.

Rugemer, Edward B. "The Development of Mastery and Race in the Comprehensive Slave Codes of the Greater Caribbean During the Seventeenth Century." *William and Mary Quarterly* 70, no. 3 (July 2013): 429–58.

———. *The Problem of Emancipation: The Caribbean Roots of the American Civil War.* Baton Rouge: Louisiana State University Press, 2008.

Russell-Wood, A. J. R. *Escravos e libertos no Brasil Colonial.* Rio de Janeiro: Civilização Brasileira, 2005.

Saco, José Antonio. *Historia de la esclavitud desde los tiempos mas remotos hasta nuestros dias.* 6 vols. 2nd ed. Havana: Editoral Alfa, 1944.

Saiz Pastor, Candelaria. "El colonialismo español en el Caribe durante el siglo XIX: El caso cubano, 1833–1868." In *Cuba, la perla de las Antillas: Actas de las I Jornadas sobre "Cuba y su Historia,"* edited by Consuelo O. Naranjo and Tomás Mallo Gutiérrez. Madrid: Ediciones Doce Calles; Editorial Consejo Superior de Investigaciones Científicas, 1994.

———. "Império de ultramar y fiscalidad colonial." In *La ilusión de un império: Las relaciones económicas hispano-cubanas en el ultimo siglo de dominación colonial,* edited by Candelaria Saiz Pastor and Salvador Palazón Ferrando. Alicante, Spain: Universidad de Alicante, 1998.

Sala-Molins, Louis. *Le code noir ou le calvaire de Canaan.* Paris: Presses Universitaires de France, 1987.

Sanchez-Albornoz, Nicolás. "A população da América espanhola colonial." In *História da América latina.* Vol. 2, *América latina colonial,* edited by Leslie Bethell. São Paulo: Editora da Universidade de São Paulo; Brasília: Fundação Alexandre de Gusmão, 1999.

Sánchez Cobos, Amparo. "A propósito de la abolición de la esclavitud." In *La reinvención colonial de Cuba,* edited by Imilcy Balboa Navarro, 259–99. Santa Cruz de Tenerife: Ediciones Idea, 2012.

Santos, Guilherme de Paula Costa. "A convenção de 1817: Debate político e diplomático sobre o tráfico de escravos durante o governo de D. João no Rio de Janeiro." Master's thesis, Universidade de São Paulo, 2007.

———. "No calidoscópio da diplomacia: Formação da monarquia constitucional e reconhecimento da independência e do império do Brasil, 1822–1827." PhD dissertation, Universidade de São Paulo, 2014.

Sartorius, David. *Ever Faithful: Race, Loyalty, and the Ends of Empire in Spanish Cuba.* Durham, NC: Duke University Press, 2014.

Saunders, A. C. de C. M. *História social dos escravos e libertos negros em Portugal, 1441–1555.* Lisbon: Imprensa Nacional–Casa da Moeda, 1994.

Scanavini, João Eduardo Finardi Álvares. "Embates e embustes: A teia do tráfico na Câmara do Império (1826–1827)." In *Monarquia, liberalismo e negócios no Brasil: 1780–1860,* edited by Izabel Andrade Marson and Cecília H. L. de Salles Oliveira, 167–209. São Paulo: Editora da Universidade de São Paulo, 2013.

Schmidt-Nowara, Christopher. *The Conquest of History: Spanish Colonialism and National Histories in the Nineteenth Century.* Pittsburgh, PA: University of Pittsburgh Press, 2006.

——. *Empire and Antislavery: Spain, Cuba, and Puerto Rico, 1833–1874*. Pittsburgh, PA: University of Pittsburgh Press, 1999.

——. *Slavery, Freedom, and Abolition in Latin America and the Atlantic World*. Albuquerque: University of New Mexico Press, 2011.

——. "Wilberforce Spanished: Joseph Blanco White and Spanish Antislavery, 1808–1814." In *Slavery and Antislavery in Spain's Atlantic Empire*, edited by Josep M. Fradera and Christopher Schmidt-Nowara, 158–75. New York: Berghahn Books, 2013.

Schnakenbourg, Christian. "Note sur les origines de l'industrie sucrière en Guadeloupe au XVIIe siècle (1640–1670)." *Revue Française d'Histoire d'Outre-Mer* 55, no. 200 (1968).

Schultz, Kirsten. "La independencia de Brasil, la ciudadanía y el problema de la esclavitud: A Assembléia Constituinte de 1823." In *Revolución, independencia y las nuevas naciones de América*, edited by Jaime E. Rodríguez O. Madrid: Fundación Mapfre Tavera, 2005.

——. "Slavery, Empire and Civilization: A Luso-Brazilian Defense of the Slave Trade in the Age of Revolutions." *Slavery and Abolition* 34, no. 1 (March 2013): 98–117.

——. *Versalhes tropical: Império, monarquia e a corte real portuguesa no Rio de Janeiro, 1808–1821*. Rio de Janeiro: Civilização Brasileira, 2008.

Schwartz, Stuart B. Review of *The Making of New World Slavery: From the Baroque to the Modern, 1492–1800*, by Robin Blackburn. *William and Mary Quarterly*, 3rd ser., 55, no. 3 (July 1998): 440–41.

——. *Segredos internos: Engenhos e escravos na sociedade colonial, 1550–1835*. São Paulo: Companhia das Letras, 1988.

Serrão, Joel, ed. *Liberalismo, socialismo, republicanismo: Antologia de pensamento político português*. 2nd ed. Lisbon: Livros Horizonte, 1979.

Serrão, José Vicente. "O quadro econômico." In *História de Portugal*. Vol. 4, *O antigo regime*, edited by José Mattoso (series editor) and António Manuel Hespanha (volume editor). Lisbon: Estampa, 1993.

Sheridan, Richard B. "Eric Williams and *Capitalism and Slavery*: A Biographical and Historiographical Essay." In *British Capitalism and Caribbean Slavery: The Legacy of Eric Williams*, edited by Barbara L. Solow and Stanley L. Engerman. Cambridge: Cambridge University Press, 1987.

——. "The Formation of Caribbean Plantation Society, 1689–1748." In *The Oxford History of the British Empire*. Vol. 2, *The Eighteenth Century*, edited by P. J. Marshall. New York: Oxford University Press, 1998.

——. *Sugar and Slavery: An Economic History of the British West Indies, 1623–1775*. 1st ed., 1974. Kingston: Canoe Press, 1994.

Shy, John. "The American Colonies in War and Revolution, 1748–1783." In *The Oxford History of the British Empire*. Vol. 2, *The Eighteenth Century*, edited by P. J. Marshall. New York: Oxford University Press, 1998.

Silva, Alberto da Costa e. *Francisco Félix de Souza: Mercador de escravos*. Rio de
Janeiro: Editora Nova Fronteira; Editora da Universidade do Estado do Rio de
Janeiro, 2004.

Silva, Ana Cristina Nogueira da. "A cidadania nos trópicos: O ultramar no constitucionalismo monárquico português (1820–1880)." PhD dissertation, Universidade Nova de Lisboa, 2004.

Silva, Ana Rosa Cloclet da. *Construção da nação e escravidão no pensamento de José
Bonifácio, 1783–1823*. Campinas, Brazil: Editora da Centro de Memória, Unicamp, 1999.

———. "Identidades políticas e a emergência do novo estado nacional: O caso min-
eiro." In *Independência: História e historiografia*, edited by István Jancsó. São
Paulo: Editora Hucitec; Fundação de Amparo à Pesquisa do Estado de São
Paulo, 2005.

———. *Inventando a nação: Intelectuais ilustrados e estadistas luso-brasileiros na crise
do antigo regime português (1750–1822)*. São Paulo: Editora Hucitec, 2006.

Silva, Lígia Osório. *Terras devolutas e latifúndio: Efeitos da lei de 1850*. Campinas:
Editora da Centro de Memória, Unicamp, 1996.

Silva, Luiz Geraldo. "Esperança de liberdade: Interpretações populares da abolição
ilustrada (1773–1774)." *Revista de História* 144 (2001): 107–49.

———. "Negros patriotas: Raça e identidade social na formação do estado nação (Pernambuco, 1770–1830)." In *Brasil: Formação do estado e da nação*, edited by István Jancsó. São Paulo: Editora Hucitec; São Paulo: Fundação de Amparo à
Pesquisa do Estado de São Paulo; Ijuí, Brazil: Editora Unijuí, 2003.

———. "Negros y pardos en la era de las independencias latinoamericanas: Militari-
zación, ciudadanía y política (1780–1830)." Paper presented at the seminar
Bicentenarios de Independencias: Nuevas Miradas, Cartagena, Colombia,
October 2008.

Silva, Maria Beatriz Nizza da. *A primeira gazeta da Bahia: Idade d'Ouro do Brasil*.
São Paulo: Cultrix/MEC, 1978.

Silveira, Marco Antonio. "Acumulando forças: Luta pela alforria e demandas políticas
na capitania de Minas Gerais (1750–1808)." *Revista de História* 158 (2008): 131–56.

———. "Soberania e luta social: Negros e mestiços libertos na Capitania de Minas
Gerais (1709–1763)." In *Território, conflito e identidade*, edited by Cláudia Maria
das Graças Chaves and Marco Antonio Silveira. Belo Horizonte: Argvmentvm,
2007.

Sio, Arnold A. "Interpretations of Slavery: The Slave Status in the Americas." *Comparative Studies in Society and History* 7, no. 3 (April 1965): 289–308.

Skinner, Quentin. *Liberdade antes do liberalismo*. São Paulo: Editora UNESP, 1999.

Slemian, Andréa. "Seriam todos cidadãos? Os impasses na construção da cidadania
nos primórdios do constitucionalismo no Brasil (1823–1824)." In *Independência:
História e historiografia*, edited by István Jancsó. São Paulo: Editora Hucitec;
Fundação de Amparo à Pesquisa do Estado de São Paulo, 2005.

———. "Sob o império da lei: Constituição e unidade nacional na formação do Brasil (1822–1834)." PhD dissertation, Universidade de São Paulo, 2006.

———. *Sob o império da lei: Constituição e unidade nacional na formação do Brasil (1822–1834)*. São Paulo: Editora Hucitec, 2009.

Slenes, Robert. "African Abrahams, Lucretias and Men of Sorrows: Allegory and Allusion in the Brazilian Anti-slavery Lithographs (1827–1835) of Johann Moritz Rugendas." *Slavery and Abolition* 23, no. 2 (2002): 147–68.

———. "A árvore de *Nsanda* transplantada: Cultos *kongo* de aflição e identidade escrava no sudeste brasileiro (século XIX)." In *Trabalho livre, trabalho escravo: Brasil e Europa, séculos XVIII e XIX*, edited by Douglas Cole Libby and Júnia Ferreira Furtado. São Paulo: Annablume Editora, 2007.

———. "'Malungo, Ngoma vem': África coberta e descoberta no Brasil." In *Mostra do redescobrimento: Negro de corpo e alma; Black in Body and Soul*, edited by Nelson Aguilar. São Paulo: Associação Brasil 500 Anos de Artes Visuais, 2000.

Smith, Robert Freeman. "Twentieth-Century Cuban Historiography." *Hispanic American Historical Review* 44, no. 1 (February 1964): 44–73.

Smith, S. D. *Slavery, Family and Gentry Capitalism in the British Atlantic: The World of the Lascelles, 1648–1834*. Cambridge: Cambridge University Press, 2006.

Soares, Gerusa. *Cunha Matos, 1776–1839: Fundador do Instituto Histórico Geográfico Brasileiro*. Rio de Janeiro: Paulo, Pongetti e Companhia, 1931.

Soares, Márcio de Sousa. *A remissão do cativeiro: A dádiva da alforria e o governo dos escravos nos Campos dos Goitacases, c. 1750–c. 1830*. Rio de Janeiro: Apicuri, 2009.

Sorhegui D'Mares, Arturo, and Alejandro de la Fuente. "La organización de la sociedad criolla (1608–1699)." In *Historia de Cuba: La Colonia; evolución socioeconómico y formación nacional*, edited by Instituto de Historia de Cuba. Havana: Editora Política, 1994.

———. "El surgimiento de la sociedad criolla de Cuba (1553–1608)." In *Historia de Cuba: La Colonia; evolución socioeconómico y formación nacional*, edited by Instituto de Historia de Cuba. Havana: Editora Política, 1994.

Souza, Otávio Tarquínio de. *História dos fundadores do império do Brasil: Bernardo Pereira de Vasconcelos*. 10 vols. Rio de Janeiro: Livraria José Olympio Editora, 1957.

Spieler, Miranda. "The Structure of Colonial Rule During the French Revolution." *William and Mary Quarterly* 66, no. 2 (April 2009): 365–408.

Steele, Ian K. "Bernard Bailyn's American Atlantic." *History and Theory* 46, no. 1 (February 2007): 48–58.

Stein, Stanley J., and Barbara H. Stein. *Silver, Trade, and War: Spain and America in the Making of Early Modern Europe*. Baltimore, MD: John Hopkins University Press, 2000.

Tannenbaum, Frank. "A Note on the Economic Interpretation of History." *Political Science Quarterly* 61, no. 2 (June 1946): 247–53.

——. *Slave and Citizen: The Negro in the Americas*. New York: Vintage Books, 1946.

Tardieu, Jean-Pierre. *"Morir o dominar": En torno al reglamento de esclavos de Cuba (1841–1866)*. Frankfurt: Iberoamericana Vervuert, 2003.

Temperley, Howard. *British Antislavery, 1833–1870*. London: Longman, 1972.

——. *White Dreams, Black Africa: The Antislavery Expedition to the River Niger, 1841–1842*. New Haven, CT: Yale University Press, 1991.

Tomás Villanueva, Joaquim. *El sistema político del Estatuto Real (1834–1836)*. Madrid: Instituto de Estudios Políticos, 1958.

Tomich, Dale. "O Atlântico como espaço histórico." *Estudos Afro-Asiáticos* 26, no. 2 (March–August 2004): 221–40.

——. Review of *Sugar Is Made with Blood: The Conspiracy of La Escalera and the Conflict Between Empires over Slavery in Cuba*, by Robert L. Paquette. *Journal of Social History* 23, no. 3 (Spring 1990): 657–60.

——. *Through the Prism of Slavery: Labor, Capital, and World Economy*. Lanham, MD: Rowman and Littlefield, 2004.

——. "The Wealth of Empire: Francisco Arango y Parreño, Political Economy, and the Second Slavery in Cuba." *Comparative Studies in Society and History* 45, no. 1 (2003): 4–28.

Tornero Tinajero, Pablo. *Crecimiento económico y transformaciones sociales: Esclavos, hacendados y comerciantes en la Cuba colonial (1760–1840)*. Madrid: Ministerio de Trabajo y Seguridad Social, 1996.

Torres-Cuevas, Eduardo. "De la ilustración reformista al reformismo liberal." In *Historia de Cuba: La colonia; Evolución socioeconómico y formación nacional*, edited by Instituto de Historia de Cuba. Havana: Editora Política, 1994.

Torres-Cuevas, Eduardo, and Eusebio Reyes, eds. *Esclavitud y sociedad: Notas y documentos para la historia de la esclavitud negra en Cuba*. Havana: Editorial de Ciencias Sociales, 1986.

Trouillot, Michel-Rolph. "Coffee Planters and Coffee Slaves in the Antilles: The Impact of a Secondary Crop." In *Cultivation and Culture: Labor and the Shaping of Slave Life in the Americas*, edited by Ira Berlin and Philip D. Morgan. Charlottesville: University of Virginia Press, 1993.

——. "Motion in the System: Coffee, Color, and Slavery in Eighteenth-Century Saint-Domingue." *Review: A Journal of the Fernand Braudel Center* 5, no. 3 (Winter 1982): 331–88.

——. *Silencing the Past: Power and the Production of History*. Boston, MA: Beacon Press, 1995.

Tuck, Richard. *Natural Rights Theories: Their Origin and Development*. 1st ed., 1979. Cambridge: Cambridge University Press, 2002.

Turnbull, David. *Travels in the West: Cuba; With Notices of Porto Rico, and the Slave Trade*. London: Longman, Orme, Brown, Green, and Longmans, 1840.

Vallim, Patrícia. "Da sedição dos mulatos à conjuração baiana de 1798: A construção de uma memória histórica." Master's thesis, Universidade de São Paulo, 2007.

Van Cleve, George William. *A Slaveholder's Union: Slavery, Politics, and the Constitution in the Early American Republic.* Chicago, IL: University of Chicago Press, 2010.

Venegas Delgado, Hernán. "El fantasma de la revolución haitiana y la independencia de Cuba." *Projeto História* 31 (December 2005): 25–54.

Verger, Pierre. *Fluxo e refluxo do tráfico de escravos entre o Golfo de Benin e a Bahia de Todos os Santos, dos séculos XVII a XIX.* 1st ed., 1968. São Paulo: Corrupio, 1987.

———. *Trade Relations Between the Bight of Benin and Bahia from the 17th to 19th Century.* Ibadan, Nigeria: Ibadan University Press, 1976.

Vovelle, Michel. *Breve história da revolução francesa.* Lisbon: Editorial Presença, 1986.

Waddell, D. A. G. "International Politics and Latin American Independence." In *The Cambridge History of Latin America*, vol. 3, edited by Leslie Bethell. Cambridge: Cambridge University Press, 1985.

Waldstreicher, David. *Slavery's Constitution: From Revolution to Ratification.* New York: Hill and Wang, 2009.

Wallerstein, Immanuel. *The Modern World-System.* Vol. 1, *Capitalist Agriculture and the Origins of the European World-Economy in the Sixteenth Century.* New York: Academic Press, 1974.

———. *The Modern World-System.* Vol. 2, *Mercantilism and the Consolidation of the European World-Economy, 1600–1750.* New York: Academic Press, 1980.

———. *The Modern World-System.* Vol. 3, *The Second Era of Great Expansion of the Capitalist World-Economy, 1730–1840s.* New York: Academic Press, 1989.

Watts, David. *Las Indias occidentales: Modalidades de desarrollo, cultura y cambio medioambiental desde 1492.* Madrid: Alianza Editorial, 1992.

Williams, Eric. *Capitalism and Slavery.* Chapel Hill: University of North Carolina Press, 1944.

———. *From Colombus to Castro: The History of Caribbean.* 1st ed., 1970. New York: Vintage Books, 1984.

Wright, Antonia F. P. de Almeida. *Desafio americano à preponderância britânica no Brasil, 1808–1850.* São Paulo: Companhia Editora Nacional; Brasília: Instituto Nacional do Livre, 1978.

Yacou, Alain. *Essor des plantations et subversion antiesclavagiste à Cuba (1791–1845).* Paris: Karthala, 2010.

———. *La longue guerre des nègres marrons de Cuba (1796–1852).* Paris: Karthala; Centre d'Études et de Recherches Comparatistes, 2009.

Zanetti Lecuona, Oscar. "Cuba 1899–1922: Iniciación republicana y discurso histórico nacional." In *Cuba: de colonia a república*, edited by Martín Rodrigo y Alharilla. Madrid: Editorial Biblioteca Nueva, 2006.

———. "Las relaciones comerciales hispano-cubanas en el siglo XIX." In *La ilusión de un império: Las relaciones económicas hispano-cubanas en el ultimo siglo de dominación colonial*, edited by Candelaria Saiz Pastor and Salvador Palazón Ferrando. Alicante, Spain: Universidad de Alicante, 1998.

Zermeño Padilla, Guillermo. "História, Experiência e Modernidade na América Ibérica, 1750–1850." *Almanack Braziliense*, no. 7 (May 2008): 5–26.

Zeron, Carlos Alberto de Moura Ribeiro. *Linha de Fé: A companhia de Jesus e a escravidão no processo de formação da sociedade colonial (Brasil, séculos XVI e XVII)*. São Paulo: Editora da Universidade de São Paulo, 2011.

Zeuske, Michael. "Comparando el Caribe: Alexander Humboldt, Saint-Domingue y los comienzos de la comparación de la esclavitud en las Américas." *Estudos Afro-Asiáticos* 26, no. 2 (May-August 2004): 381–416.

———. "Comparing or Interlinking? Economic Comparisons of Early Nineteenth-Century Slave Systems in the Americas in Historical Perspective." In *Slave Systems: Ancient and Modern*, edited by Enrico dal Lago and Constantina Katsari. Cambridge: Cambridge University Press, 2008.

———. "Humboldt, Historismus und Humboldteanisierung: Der 'Geschichtsschreiber von Amerika,' die Massensklaverei und die Globalisierung der Welt." *HiN: Internationale Zeitschrift für Humboldt-Studien* 3, no. 4 (2002). Available at www.uni-potsdam.de/u/romanistik/humboldt/hin/hin4/inhalt.htm.

INDEX